ANTHOLOGY OF TURKISH SCIENCE FICTION STORIES

POSTHUMANISM SERIES: 6

Anthology of Turkish Science Fiction Stories

Edited by Sümeyra Buran & Veli Uğur

Copyeditor and Proofreader: Conrad Scott

Copyright © 2023 Transnational Press London

All rights reserved. This book or any portion thereof may not be reproduced or used in any manner whatsoever without the express written permission of the publisher except for the use of brief quotations in a book review or scholarly journal.

First published in 2023 by Transnational Press London in the United Kingdom, 13 Stamford Place, Sale, M33 3BT, UK.
www.tplondon.com

Transnational Press London® and the logo and its affiliated brands are registered trademarks.

Requests for permission to reproduce material from this work should be sent to: sales@tplondon.com

Paperback
ISBN: 978-1-80135-128-7
Hardcover
ISBN: 978-1-80135-245-1
Digital
ISBN: 978-1-80135-129-4

Cover Photo Drawing and Design: Sezai Özden

Transnational Press London Ltd. is a company registered in England and Wales No. 8771684.

ANTHOLOGY
OF TURKISH SCIENCE FICTION STORIES

Edited by
Sümeyra Buran & Veli Uğur

Copyedited and proofread by Conrad Scott

TRANSNATIONAL PRESS LONDON
2023

CONTENTS

A HUNDRED YEARS OF TURKISH SCIENCE FICTION 21

KILLING X 41
    Algan Coşkun

DEA EX MACHINA 49
    Arda Tipi

TERROR OF EMPATHY 57
    Belma Fırat

PROXIMUS 65
    Bora Keskin

A NEW LIFE 75
    Buğra Mert Alkayalar

TROJAN-137 81
    Burak Cem Coşkun

ART TIME 87
    Burak Katipoğlu

THE PASSAGE 97
    Cem Sinan Altun

CROSSING THE OCEAN 107
    Deniz Ezgi Avci Vile

THE HIERARCHY OF COGNITIVE FALLINGS 113
    Deniz K. Üstündağ

A PROPHET OF ALL 117
    Duran Emre Kanacı

A REBIRTH OF SPIRIT 127
    Edip Sönmez

DON'T AVOID EMOTIONS 135
    Ekin Açıkgöz

GERMAKOCHI 145
    Eren Kasapoğlu

MOTHER BABEL 155
    Erol Çelik

A KIND OF BLACK 165
    Ezo Evrim Harsa

BETTER YOU 173
    Fatmagül Bolat

TWIN HOPES 179
    Gizem Çetin

THE SPLITTING 189
    İsmail Yiğit

DEPERSONALIZATION 197
    Mehmet Ali Kaynak

ALTERATION 205
    Melda Uytun

CONSIDERATION 213
    Melike Kuyumcu

THE SMART DOOR 223
    Müfit Özdeş

THE MIND RENTAL BUREAU 231
    Neptune E. Kosi

THE CURTAIN 239
    Nur İpek Önder Mert

THE UNKNOWN RATIO 247
    Özgür Hünel

THE REASONABLE MAN 255
    Özlem Kurdoğlu

YELLOW WRISTBAND 263
    Pelin Cansu Sarıyıldız

THE PHOTOGRAPHER OF THE OTHER REALM 271
    Sadık Yemni

THE ROOT 279
    Serpil Ülger

BUG FIELDS 287
    Sezai Özden

COGITO 319
    Tevfik Uyar

THE JUNKMAN 327
    Uğur Aydın

DEARTH FETE 335
    Ümit Yaşar Özkan

A GREAT TIME TRAVEL 343
    Türkhan Bozkurt

ACKNOWLEDGEMENTS

We would like to extend our heartfelt gratitude to Dr. Conrad Scott for his meticulous proofreading of this anthology. His dedicated approach and attention to detail have immensely contributed to the refinement and coherence of this book, ensuring that the text is free of errors and flows seamlessly. We deeply appreciate his commitment and hard work in enhancing the readability and integrity of the manuscript.

Additionally, we would like to express our sincere thanks to one of the authors who contributed to our anthology, Sezai Özden, also for his remarkable drawing that graces the cover of this book. His artistic talent and creative vision have resulted in a captivating illustration that perfectly encapsulates the essence of this work, adding a visual appeal and enriching the overall reader experience. His contribution has brought a unique aesthetic dimension to the book, making it a visual delight.

We feel immensely fortunate to have worked with such talented authors, and we are truly grateful for their time, effort, and dedication in helping bring this book to fruition. Their respective skills and contributions have played a pivotal role in shaping and enriching this work, and for that, we are profoundly thankful.

Lastly, Türkhan Bozkurt, one of the young Turkish science fiction authors who we lost in the devastating 2023-February Turkey earthquake and the author of the novel titled *Yörünge 3185* (*Orbit 3185*, Edebiyatist 2019), sent us a short story titled "A Great Time Travel." In the wake of the heartbreaking and devastating earthquake that claimed Türkhan Bozkurt's life, we have included her short story, "A Great Time Travel," in this anthology exactly as she first submitted it to us, in its untouched and original draft, bereft of any opportunity for the editorial process. We extend our sincere thanks to Türkhan Bozkurt for her valuable contributions to our book and appreciate her support and dedication. By presenting her work in its authentic form in this pioneering anthology, we aspire to pay tribute to her memory and the fervent enthusiasm she held for this venture.

CONTRIBUTORS

EDITORS

Sümeyra Buran

Dr Buran is an Associate Professor of English at Istanbul Medeniyet University and a Visiting Associate Professor in the Department of English at the University of Florida. She is the founding and managing editor of the *Journal of Posthumanism*, the editor of Transnational Press London's *Posthumanism Series*, the editor of *Edebiyatta Posthümanizm* (*Posthumanism in Literature* 2020), the editor of *Çokludisiplinlerde Posthumanizm* (*Posthumanism in Multidisciplinary Studies* 2022), the co-editor (with Sherryl Vint) of *Technologies of Feminist Speculative Fiction: Gender, Artificial Life, and Politics of Reproduction* (Palgrave 2022), the co-editor of the first *Anthology of Turkish Science Fiction* (Transnational Press London 2022), the co-editor (with Jim Clarke) of *Religious Futurisms* (Manchester University Press 2022), and the co-editor (with Jire Gözen) of *Beyond the Occident: Perspectives on Past, Present and Speculative Future in Fiction, Art, Media and Film* (Routledge 2022). Also, she is a country focal point representative of the European Observatory on Femicide (EOF), a committee member of BIPOC at IAFA, and a country representative (Turkey) at SFRA. Buran is currently writing her monograph on *Su-fi: Sufi Science Fiction*.

Veli Uğur

Dr Uğur graduated from Boğaziçi University's Department of Turkish Language and Literature, then continued his academic studies in the field of new Turkish literature before completing his doctoral thesis, *Popular Novels in Turkish Literature After 1980*, at Istanbul University (later published as a book by Koç University Press in 2013). He lectured on Turkish Literature and Language at Koç University between 1998-2013 and is currently working as an Associate Professor teaching Contemporary Turkish Literature and Popular Fiction in the Department of Turkish Language and Literature at Muğla Sıtkı Koçman University. Dr. Uğur's most recent monograph, *Turkish Science Fiction Literature and Archetypes* (2019) is the first contribution to Turkish Science Fiction literary studies as an outcome of the national project he managed by TUBITAK (The Scientific and Technological Research Council of Türkiye).

Conrad Scott

Conrad Scott holds a PhD from the University of Alberta (English and Film Studies) and an MA from the University of Victoria (English). The first SSHRC Postdoctoral Fellow with Athabasca University, he is also an

Assistant Lecturer with the University of Alberta and an Individualized Study Tutor for the University of Athabasca's new "The Ecological Imagination" course. He is honoured to serve as the current Co-President for the Association for Literature, Environment, and Culture in Canada (ALECC) and is the Science Fiction Research Association's (SFRA) Country Rep for Canada. Conrad researches contemporary sf and environmental literature, with current projects focused on plant and animal futures, as well as the spatial turn, building on previous work about the interconnection between place, culture, and society in contemporary North American fiction that focuses on environment and dystopia/utopia. His academic writing has appeared in *Transmotion*, *Extrapolation*, *Paradoxa*, *The Anthropocene and the Undead*, *Environmental Philosophy*, *The Goose*, *UnderCurrents*, *Science Fiction Studies*, *The SFRA Review*, *The Routledge Encyclopedia of Modernism*, and *Canadian Literature*, with forthcoming chapters in *The Routledge Handbook of CoFuturisms* (2023) and *Animals and SF* (Palgrave, 2023). He is also a co-editor for the forthcoming *Utopian and Dystopian Explorations of Pandemics and Ecological Breakdown: Entangled Futurities* (Routledge Environmental Humanities Book Series 2024), the proofreader for the forthcoming English-translated *Anthology of Turkish Science Fiction Stories (*Transnational Press London 2023), and the author of the poetry collection *Waterline Immersion* (Frontenac House 2019).

AUTHORS

Algan Coşkun

Coşkun was born in İzmir. He has a bachelor's degree in the field of International Relations and a minor degree in Philosophy from METU (Middle East Technical University). He spent one year studying European Studies at The Hague University of Applied Sciences and three years at Ankara University for European Union & International Economic Relations. In 2018, he started working as a freelancer editor/content creator for websites and publishers in İzmir. He has been interested in tabletop role-playing games since early 2010 and fantasy and science-fiction literature since high school. He has been writing fantasy and science fiction stories since 2010 and building new worlds for hobbies and games. His other hobbies are cycling and cooking.

Arda Tipi

Tipi got acquainted with science fiction at an early age through comics, movies, and science fiction classics. His enthusiasm compelled him to create his own illustrated stories as a teenager. In later years, he attended college to study Fine Arts, graduating from Ankara University's Department of Classical Philology, from which he holds a master's degree in Systematic Philosophy and Logic. During these years, he wrote poems, essays, and short movie scripts– "Yaş" ("Teardrop" 2007), "Oyunbozan" ("Spoilsport" 2008), and "Bit Yiğitte" ("Lice on the Valiant" 2009)–which were ranked in several competitions. Most recently, he has contributed to the *YBKY Bilimkurgu Öykü Seçkisi* (*Indigenous Science Fiction Rising Platform*) collection *Anthology of Science Fiction Stories* (2018, 2019, 2020, 2022), with his stories "Bir Hayaletin Güncesi" ("Diary of a Spectre," Paradigma 2018), "Ateşin Çocukları" ("Children of Fire," Paradigma 2019), "Dea Ex Machina" (Liman 2020), and "Derin Mavi" ("Fathomless Blue," Liman 2022). He currently administrates and creates content for the science fiction e-magazine *Yerli Bilimkurgu Yükseliyor* (*Indigenous Science Fiction Rising Platform*) (yerlibilimkurguyukseliyor.com).

Belma Fırat

Fırat is a graduate of Middle East Technical University (METU), earning both her Bachelor's and Master's Degrees in Economics. She has taken a second Master's Degree in Philosophy at Bosphorus University (BU) and attended PhD courses in Philosophy at Mimar Sinan Fine Arts University (MSGSÜ). Her stories, articles, and essays on literature have been published in literary magazines and anthologies. Two of her stories were given awards as part of Kaos GL's 2012 and 2014 Women to Women Story Contests, respectively. Her published story stories are "Alışın Buradayız" ("We're Here, Get Used to It," NotaBene 2014), "Kuyuda" ("In a Well," NotaBene 2016) and "Bugün Anne Gibi Değilim" ("I'm not Like a Mother Today," NotaBene 2018), respectively. "Kuyuda" ("In a Well") won the Muratpaşa Best Short Fiction Award in 2016 at Antalya Literature Days organized by Muratpaşa Municipality. Her first novel, *Sözleşme* (*Contract,* NotaBene 2021), is a philosophical science fiction.

Bora Keskin

Keskin has been writing since his elementary school days. Participating in many literature competitions, he has found a place for his stories and poems in local anthologies. He received a writer's certificate from İLESAM's (The Professional Association of Turkish Literary And Scientific Works) literature workshops and founded the blog of Asiller Topluluğu Özgün Edebiyat Bloğu (Noble Society Unique Literature) with other authors.

Buğra Mert Alkayalar

Alkayalar completed his Bachelor's Degree in Cinema and Television at the Faculty of Communication Sciences at Anadolu University in 2020 and is currently doing his Master's Degree in Cinema and Television there. He has taken part in many national and international festivals, such as The Golden Boll Film Festival, the Fabisad GIO Awards, and the H.P. Lovecraft Film Festival. He works as a Research Assistant at Istanbul Kültür University while continuing his film work, developing voice-over, story, and cinema writing. His first short story collection *Birtakım Rivayetler* (*Some Hearsays*), was published in June 2023 by Porsuk Kültür Publishing.

Burak Cem Coşkun

Coşkun received a Bachelor's Degree in Physics Engineering from Istanbul Technical University (İTÜ) in 2017 and worked in the field of neutron stars both at İTÜ and at the KTH Royal Institute of Technology (as an exchange student) in 2016-2017. While he was doing his Master's Degree in theoretical astrophysics at Friedrich Wilhelm University of Bonn in Germany, he decided to continue his higher education at Sabancı University and work on magnetars. He writes popular science, history, and philosophy of science articles for the journal *Herkese Bilim ve Teknoloji* (*Science and Technology For All*) in addition to his personal blog "Don't you have time to think?" (burakcemcoskun.blogspot.com). He also writes poems, hosts a podcast called *Demokritos'un Çocukları* (*Children of Democritus*), translates comics (*Feynman*, Alfa Yayınları 2021), and is the author of the science-fiction novels *Kusur* (*The Defect*, KDY 2020) and *Işık Getiren* (*Light Bringer,* KDY 2021), as well as the poetry book *Bilim ve Şiir* (*Science and Poetry,* KDY 2022).

Burak Katipoğlu

Katipoğlu is a science fiction enthusiast working as a Wind Engineer in Istanbul. He has a Bachelor's Degree in Astronautical Engineering from Istanbul Technical University (İTÜ) and a Master's Degree in Energy Conversion from the Swiss Federal Institute of Technology, Zürich (ETH-Z). He was a member of a student club publishing the Istanbul Technical University Sci-Fi Fanzine. His stories "Uzun Gün" ("Long Day," Paradigma Kültür 2018) and "Gelişme Hedefleri" ("Improvement Goals," Lora 2021) have been published in local anthologies. A strong believer in criticism, feedback, and its place in quality fiction, he also launched a site aimed at collecting fast, quantifiable feedback for sci-fi short stories using glyphs and symbols (www.kozmikatolye.com). He is currently living in Istanbul with his lovely wife Zeynep and two-year-old son Mete.

Cem Sinan Altun

Altun is a manager in the private sector. After undergraduate studies in Labor Economics and then Tourism Management, Altun continues his graduate education in Radio-TV-Cinema at Ankara University. Altun started writing in the late 90s with stories in various genres, from drama to sci-fi and humor to mystery, some of which were published in journals such as *Dedektif* and *Lacivert Edebiyat*. Some of his stories received awards, such as with the NBeyin Magazine Science Fiction Short Story Contest and the Dedektif Dergi Zehirli Kalem Polisiye Öykü Yarışması (Detektif Magazine Zehirli Kalem Detective Short Story Contest). His short story "Derin Derin" ("Deeper Derin" 2015) was made into a short movie directed by Aytekin Çakmakç in the same year. Another short movie (1 minute-long) written and directed by Altun is "Daymare" (2018), listed in the Just Before Midnight Film Fest, the African Smartphone International Film Festival, the "One Shot" Film Festival, and the 60 Second Intl. Film Festival. Altun leans more toward sci-fi and mystery, including with their screenplays. The writer presently works on the screenplay of his long detective story entitled "Kod" ("The Code," 2021) and other tales of science fiction entitled "Tic Toc" and "Elçi" ("Ambassador") (both in progress). Altun wishes to produce more works of literature and cinema in the detective genre.

Deniz Ezgi Avcı Vile

Avci Vile is a fiction writer/lecturer. She received her Master's in Applied Linguistics from the University of Nottingham in 2017. She is based in Toronto and is currently working as a lecturer. Her literary work and photography have been published or are upcoming in journals such as *Yolk*, *Qwerty*, *Sözcükler*, *Altzine*, *Trendeki Yabanci*, *Hece Öykü*, *Lacivert Poem and Short*

Story, *Prolog*, *Hisht Hisht*, *Ecinniler*, *Olasi Olmayan*, and *Mahal*. Her short story "Termodinamiğin İkinci Yasası" ("Second Law of Thermodynamics") was awarded third place in a short story contest organized by the journal Şahsiyet in 2021.

Deniz K. Üstündağ

Üstündağ graduated from the Department of Chemistry at Karadeniz Technical University. She has been working as a chemist and is currently a student of Sociology at Eskişehir Anadolu University. She published her short story "Veda ya da Bir Şişe Kayısı Şarabı" in the 2019 collection *Yerli Bilimkurgu Yükseliyor Öykü Seçkisi* (*2019 Indigenous Science Fiction Rising*). Her short story, "The Hierarchy of the Cognitive Fallings," was also published as a comic in the special issue of "Science Fiction" in the journal *Yabani* (2020). She continues publishing short stories on different platforms and is currently working on her collection.

Duran Emre Kanacı

Kanacı graduated from Istanbul University as a geneticist and, in 2016, completed his postgraduate studies at Boğaziçi University. He trained young geneticists at Bahçeşehir University until 2020. Currently, he is researching the molecular basis of learning and memory in neuroscience at the University of Cologne. His first short fiction book, *Yapı ve Yasa* (*Formation and Law*, Epona Publications 2021), was shortlisted for the 2022 Vedat Türkali Literature Awards. He is the short fiction editor of the literary magazine *Prolog Dergi*, and his short stories and poems have been included in several anthologies. He is working on his novella in Turkish and his first film screenplay in English. His stories in Turkish and English have been published in various literary magazines and platforms, such as *Kitap-lık*, *Sözcükler*, and *Story*. One, along with his interviews and writings about his book, can also be accessed via demrekanaci.wordpress.com

Edip Sönmez

Sönmez holds a BA in English Language and Literature from Istanbul University and an MA in Literary and Cultural Studies from the University of Regensburg, Germany. His master thesis is titled *Dangerous Toys: Abuse of Technology and its Socio-psychological Implications – Technophobia and Ethics in Dystopian Fiction: A Case Study of Black Mirror* (UR 2019). After working as a journalist, copywriter, and English teacher, he is currently employed as an editor, localisation specialist, and translator. He has translated nearly forty books from English and German into Turkish, including *Political Sociology in a Global Era* (*Küresel Çağda Siyasal Sosyoloji,* Bilgi Üniversitesi Yayınları 2014), *A Wrinkle in Time* (*Zamanda Kıvrılma,* Beyaz Balina Yayınevi 2016), *Economic*

History of the Modern Era (*Wirtschaftsgeschichte der Neuzeit*, Runik Kitap 2020), *The Shy Child* (*Çekingen Çocuk*, Philip Zimbardo, Pegasus Yayınları 2023) and *Fox* (*Tilki*, Dubravka Ugrešić, Everest Yayınları 2023).

Ekin Açıkgöz

Açıkgöz has a Bachelor of Science degree in Statistics from Middle East Technical University (METU) and a Bachelor of Arts in Turkish Language and Literature from Anadolu University. She's an MBA student at Istanbul Technical University (ITU). Her novel *Her İşte Bir Hayır Vardır* (*Everything Happens for a Reason*, Ayizi Kitap 2015) was her first publication. Her short stories have since been published in numerous anthologies, such as her short story "Bozulmamış Kırmızı Gül" ("The Unspoiled Red Rose") in *Tüm Panayırların Heyulası* (*The Bogy of All Fairs*, Kayıp Rıhtım Anthology Series, İthaki 2022). She writes articles in her column "Polisiyelerin Ölümsüz Silahları" ("Immortal Weapons of Mystery") and "At, Edebiyat ve Silah" ("Horses, Literature and Weapons") for *221B-Magazine*. She's a voluntary author/contributor at www.cinairoman.com – the one and only Turkish digital mystery/suspense archive. She's both a Member and a Director of the Türkiye Polisiye Yazarları Birliği (POYABİR, Association of Mystery Writers of Turkey) and is a continuing juror for the "Kristal Kelepçe" Mystery Novel Award (at POYABİR) and the Türkiye Bilişim Derneği Bilimkurgu Öykü Yarışması (Turkish Informatics Association Science Fiction Short Story Contest). She lives in Istanbul with her husband and two kids.

Eren Kasapoğlu

Kasapoğlu graduated from the Department of Statistics at Mimar Sinan University. He has been interested in cartoons, comics, horror, fantasy, and science fiction literature since his childhood. Instead of settling in his later years, this curiosity increased, and he took a comics course in order to realize the comic book project he had designed in his mind for a while. He was honored in several short story competitions and selections he participated in, such as *Ölümsüz Öyküler* (*Immortal Stories*) and a few times in *Yerli Bilimkurgu Yükseliyor* (*YBKY, Indigenous Science Fiction Rising Platform*). Some of his awarded and published stories are "Yeniçeri" (Janissary) in *Ölümsüz Öyküler II* in 2015, "Değişkin" ("Transformed") in the *Bilimkurgu Öykü Seçkisi* (*Science Fiction Short Story Collection*) in 2019, "Kamos" ("Kamos") in *YBKY Magazine* in 2022, "Değişmeyen Tek Şey" ("The Only Thing Unchanged") in the *Bilimkurgu Öykü Seçkisi* (*Science Fiction Short Story Collection*) in 2022. He shares some of his stories and essays on https://oykusehir.blog.

Erol Çelik

Çelik is a writer and film director. His published novels are *Heyula*

(*Phantasm*, Avrupa Yakası 2007*)*, *Satranç ve Şövalye* (*Chess and the Knight*, Avrupa Yakası 2009*)*, *19 Numaralı Koltuk* (*Seat Number 19*, Avrupa Yakası 2011), *Ağlatan* (*Lacrymary*, Avrupa Yakası 2013*)*, and *Cellatlar Kahvesi* (*Headsmen Coffeehouse*, Cadı Yayınları 2019). His six films and documentaries as a writer and director were screened and given awards at festivals. Five of his cinematic works were given awards at domestic festivals, such as with five awards including the best movie and the best director for *Cennete Açılan Çiçekler* (*Bloom to Heaven* 2014) at the Sinema ve Televizyon Eseri Sahipleri Meslek Birliği-SETEM (Association of Film Directors, Writers, and Composers) Academy Awards, and four films given awards at thirteen international festivals like the Ukrainian Dream Film Festival Honor Award with the documentary called *Sanatın Kadınları (Women of Art* 2022). He continues to produce works in the horror-thriller and dystopian science fiction fields, as well as work on his current, ongoing trilogy series, "*Söz Ustası*" ("Wordsmith"), which consists of dystopian stories. He has worked for one of Turkey's largest television channels, NTV Channel, for more than two decades, and now he is producing social media posts for his YouTube channel. He is married and has one child.

Ezo Evrim Harsa

Harsa studied Business Administration and holds an undergraduate and a postgraduate degree from Galatasaray University. She immigrated to Canada in late 2017 with her family and lives in Toronto. She studied traditional arts (Tezhip and Kaati) at Mim Sanat Academy between 2010 and 2017 and continues to practice as an independent artist. She is the author of a fantasy trilogy, *Kökler Diyarı* (*Realm of Roots*, Bu 2020), a fantasy novella *Gecebakan* (*Nightgazer*, Mantis 2021), and a short story published in an anthology "Gündüzdüşü" ("Daydream," *Dark İstanbul* 2021). Her other published science fiction short stories include "Sincap Zulası" ("Squirrel Stash," Bilimkurgu Kulübü 2018), "Pepto Bismol" ("Pepto Bismol," Bilimkurgu Kulübü 2019), "Çocuk" ("Kid," Bilimkurgu Kulübü 2021), and "Frekans" ("Frequency," *Lagari Bilimkurgu Fanzin* 2021).

Fatmagül Bolat

Bolat holds Bachelor's and Master's degrees in landscape architecture from Çukurova University and a Doctoral degree in landscape architecture from Istanbul University-Cerrahpaşa. While her primary focus is landscape ecology, she possesses a keen interest in examining the links between ecology and science fiction. She is currently working as a full-time adjunct in the Forestry Vocational School at Istanbul University-Cerrahpaşa and taking part in various environmental studies in Turkish and French academic institutions. She lives in Istanbul.

Gizem Çetin

Çetin is an electrical electronics engineer and an author. She graduated from the TOBB ETÜ Electrical and Electronics Engineering program in 2020. At the age of 15, she started to write a science fiction novel called *İsyancı* (*The Rebel*), which was her first completed work. Later, she published it online under the name of *Üç Kentin İsyancısı* (*Rebel of Three Cities,* Wattpad 2017). Her second published novel was *Papatya Tarlasında Rönesans* (*Renaissance in the Daisy Field,* Başlangıç Publishing House 2018*)* and, in 2017, she started writing *Yedi Mum* (*Seven Candles*), a science fiction series with seven books. The first three books of the Seven Candles Series, *Yedinci Mum* (*The Seventh Candle,* 2021), *Altıncı Mum* (*The Sixth Candle,* 2021), and *Beşinci Mum* (*The Fifth Candle,* 2023), were published by Nar Ağacı Publishing House. She has a website https://gizemcetin.com and a YouTube channel @acimatriyarka, and she regularly publishes stories there.

İsmail Yiğit

Yiğit graduated from the Department of Electrical and Electronics Engineering at Bilkent University in 2005. He works as the chief expert in network systems and security at the Banking Regulation and Supervision Agency. He holds an MS degree in the Science, Technology, and Society program and started his PhD in the Art History Department at Istanbul Technical University (İTÜ). In the science-fiction short story contest organized by Türkiye Bilişim Derneği (Informatics Association of Turkey) in 2016, his story "İhlal" ("Violation") was given third place. In the GIO contest organized by FABİSAD in 2017, his story "Satır Arasındaki Hayalet" ("The Ghost Between the Lines") received the short story achievement award. His story "Robomorfoz" ("Robomorphosis") was included in the science-fiction collection *Yeryüzü Müzesi* (*Earth Museum,* İthaki 2018). As a member of the International Association of Art Critics (AICA), he regularly contributes to science-fiction book and film reviews at the internet portal Bilimkurgu Kulübü (Science-fiction Club) (www.bilimkurgukulubu.com).

Mehmet Ali Kaynak

Kaynak became acquainted with Jules Verne and H.G. Wells in primary school. In high school and university years, his world of thought expanded with Isaac Asimov, Ursula K. Le Guin, George Orwell, and other authors of science fiction. He started producing works of science fiction when he graduated from the Geography Department at Ege University. In this period, his story "Quantum Decisions" won second place in a contest hosted by a platform named Quantum Turkey. Another story, "New Masters," was published in an anthology named *Yerli Bilimkurgu Yükseliyor* (*Indigenous Science*

Fiction Rising Platform), which selected stories from the community.

Melda Uytun

Uytun has an MA in Creative Writing from Anglia Ruskin University, Cambridge. Uytun's first novel, *Yağmurdan Kaçmayanların Şarkısı* (*The Song of Those Who Don't Run From Rain*), was published by Potkal Kitap in 2013. She has a short story in *The Doctor & I*, a Doctor Who memoir ("The Doctor & I," Gjb Publishing 2013), and a published short story, "Ayna" ("The Mirror," Ölümsüz Öyküler-I 2014), which received an honorable mention in 2014's Ölümsüz Öyküler (Immortal Stories) Short Story Competition. She is the translator of *Avocado Bahçesi* (*Philosophy Made Simple*, Maya Kitap 2016), *Bir Nefeste Büyük Bilim İnsanları* (*The Great Scientists in Bite-Sized Chunks*, Maya Kitap 2017) and *Matematik: Çok Kısa Bir Başlangıç* (*Mathematics: A Very Short Introduction*, İstanbul Kültür Üniversitesi Yayınevi 2022), and has also been doing redaction and proofreading for Maya Kitap since 2017.

Melike Kuyumcu

Kuyumcu is an author, screenwriter, and photography artist. She continues her writing career, which she started as a screenwriter, with her short stories, novellas, literary critiques, literature, and press/publication editorship. After her novella, *İçlik Odaları* (*The Innermost Chambers*, Gece Kitaplığı 2018), Kuyumcu published her collection *İnsan-dan Başka Öyküler* (*More-Than-Human Tales*) with Transnational Press London in 2021 as a literary narrative example of posthumanist ideas in Turkish for the *Posthumanism Series* edited by Sümeyra Buran. She continues her search for "meaning" and "expression" in posthumanist philosophy.

Müfit Özdeş

Özdeş studied electrical engineering and later econometrics at Middle East Technical University but received no degrees in either as student activism caught up with Turkey in what is known as the 1968 revolution. He spent the following years either incarcerated or as a fugitive at large. He left Turkey to become a PLO militiaman in Lebanon and, finally, a trade unionist in Norway. In 1975, he founded the Çağdaş Çeviri Evini (Contemporary Translation House) in Turkey. He re-entered the SF universe through a story named "Krrchysk" that he wrote in 1982, which was included in an anti-militarist anthology entitled *Asker Kaçağı: Savaşa Karşı Bilimkurgu Öyküleri* (*The Deserter: Sci-Fi Stories Against War*, Metis Books 2016). A modern fable entitled *Kimin Ağrır O Bağırır* (*The One Who Ails is the One Who Wails*) was published by Kor Publications in 1992. Fifteen of his stories were compiled by Metis Books in 1995 in a collection named *Son Tiryaki* (*The Last Smoker*), with an enlarged second edition in 2018 that consists of twenty-three tales.

His story called "Firar" ("Escapade") received First Prize in the 2001 SF story contest of the Türkiye Bilişim Derneği Bilimkurgu Öykü Yarışması (Turkish Informatics Association Science Fiction Short Story Contest)b and was later published in the collection of *Bilimkurgu Öyküleri* (*Science Fiction Short Stories*, Remzi Publishing 2005).

Neptune E. Kosi

Kosi, a fantasy author, storyteller, and columnist, has been writing various short stories and articles for years. These have been published in many local and foreign literary magazines and newspapers (UK, US, Turkey), and she has also published five fantasy novels: *Portobello Photographer* (*Portobello Fotoğrafçısı*, Transnational Press London 2023), *Londra Düşleri* (*Dreams Of London*, KDY 2020), *Aralık* (*The Gap*, Postiga 2015), *Siyah Palto* (*Black Coat*, PKitap 2014), and *Mavi Kuyruk* (*The Blue Tail*, İkinci Adam 2013). Since 2015, she has been a columnist for the London-based Eurovision newspaper. The author lives in London with her cats and her library. (https://www.eurovizyon.co.uk/profil/453/neptune-e-kosi).

Nur İpek Önder Mert

Önder Mert is a Turkish poet and science fiction story writer. She has a Master's Degree in Biochemistry from Anadolu University in 2013. Her poetry books are *Kan Rüyayı Bozar* (*Blood Voids the Dream*, Mayıs 2010), *Raz Beyaz* (*Hidden White*, Klaros 2019), and *Yer Çekimine Aşık Kuşlar Kulübü* (*The Club of the Birds in Love with Gravity*, Klaros 2021). Her nameless short story was published as part of the CCLXXX: Bilimkurgu Mikro Öykü Seçkisi (CCLXXX: Science Fiction Micro Story Collection, Entropol 2015). Her short stories "Görünen" ("Visible," 2018) and "Silahlı Peygamber " ("The Armed Prophet" 2019) were published in the collection *YBKY* (*Indigenous Science Fiction Rising Platform*) by Paradigma Academy, and her short story "Nemesis" was published in the collection *Silsile: Bilimkurgu Öyküleri* (İthaki 2021). Her literary works have won various national awards, such as the Mehmet H. Doğan Special Jury Award 2009 with her poetry book *Kan Rüyayı Bozar* (*Blood Voids the Dream*, unpublished file branch 2009), the Kemal İsmet Karadayı Special Jury Award 2017 with her *Raz Beyaz* (*Hidden White*, unpublished file branch 2017), Second Place in the Türkiye Bilişim Derneği Bilimkurgu (Turkish Informatics Association Science Fiction Story Contest) with her short story "İki Kızıl Yabani At" ("Two Red Wild Horses" 2017), and Second Place in the Türkiye Bilişim Derneği Bilimkurgu (Turkish Informatics Association Science Fiction Story Contest) with her short story "Nemesis" (2020).

Özgür Hünel

Hünel had been fascinated with art and fiction since his childhood, so he decided to pursue a career in these fields. He graduated from the Graphic Design Department at Eskişehir Anadolu University in 2015 and completed his Master's Degree from the Public Relations and Advertising Department at the same university. He continues his Proficiency in Art education in the Graphic Design Department at Ankara Hacı Bayram Veli University and works as a Research Assistant in the Visual Communication Design Department at Ankara Başkent University. He also writes stories, mainly in the sci-fi and fantasy genres. Hünel's stories have been given awards in several writing competitions, most notably the Turkish Informatics Association's sci-fi story competition (Turkey's most prestigious sci-fi story competition), where he has been awarded third place three times and first place once. Among his published sci-fi stories are "Olmak ya da Olmamak" ("To Be, or Not to Be") and "Tosca V2.0" (*Dünyalılar: Bilimkurgu Öyküleri*, İletişim 2016), "Bilinmeyen Oran" ("The Unknown Ratio," *Silsile: Bilimkurgu Öyküleri*, İthaki 2021), "Çok Satan (Kutsal) Kitaplar" ("Best Selling (Holy) Books"), and "TECHne" (*Karanlık Şafaklar*, Paris 2022). His story "Tosca V2.0" was translated into Italian and published in the anthology *Futurchia: Fantascienza contemporanea turca* (*Futurchia: Contemporary Turkish Science Fiction*, Future Fiction 2021).

Özlem Kurdoğlu

Kurdoğlu is a graduate of Medicine from Istanbul University. She is a bilingual author, medical translator, psychological counsellor, and author. Kurdoğlu is the author of a series of science-fiction novels that comprise a hexology of design fiction, the first of its kind in the history of Turkish Sci-Fi Literature in terms of both being a hexology and offering a future history of a designed universe: *Son Cephede Şafak* (*Dawn on the Last Front*, Us 2000), *Yüreğin Zafere Çağrısı* (*Heart's Call to Victory*, İmYayın 2003), *Alacaşafağın Rengi* (*Shade of Twilight*, İmYayın 2005), *Karanlık Uykusu* (*Twilight Loose*, KaraKutu 2008), *Zamanda Kuşatma* (*Ambushed in Time*, Smashwords 2014) and *Çemberkıran* (published bilingual, a.k.a. *Circlebreaker*, Smashwords 2018). Over the years, she has had several stories published in various national science-fiction story collections and anthologies and also translated several novels from English to Turkish, including Philip K. Dick's *A Scanner Darkly* (*Karanlığı Taramak*, Altıkırkbeş 1998), William Gibson's *Count Zero* (*Sıfır Noktası*, Sarmal 1999; *Kont Sıfır*, Altın Kitaplar 2003), Isaac Asimov's *Robot Stories* (*Robot Öyküleri Antolojisi*, UsYayın Publishing 1999), and J.R.R. Tolkien's *The Hobbit* (Graphic Novel, *Hobbit*, Ithaki 1999, 2008).

Pelin Cansu Sarıyıldız

Sarıyıldız graduated from the Department of Civil Engineering at Middle East Technical University (METU) in 2017. She has been working as a civil engineer since then. She has published short stories on different literary websites and journals, such as *Kayıp Rıhtım* and *Dedektif Dergi* (*Detective Journal*). Her story "Keserin Küt Ucu" ("The Butt End of the Adze") was published in *Detective Journal*'s crime issue 37 in 2022 and also in the collection *Ölümün Kıyısında* (*On the Edge of Death*, Herdem 2022).

Sadık Yemni

Yemni is a novelist, short story writer, essayist, and translator. As a Dutch-Turkish author, he lived in Amsterdam between the years 1975–2013. Yemni writes in the TekinsizX genre – that is, sci-fi thriller-fantasia-mystery. He is accepted as the first Sufi SF writer. In Turkey alone, he has published 32 books, 23 of which are novels – including *Muska* (*The Amulet*, Metis 1996), *Kayıp Kedi* (*Lost Cat*, Kırmızı Kedi Yayınları 2015), *Ela* (*Ela*, Erdem Yayınları 2016), *Çağrılan* (*Summoned*, Ketebe Yayınları 2019), and *Ağrıyan* (*Aching*, Transnational Press London). Yemni is also a short story writer. Besides publishing short story collections, between the years 2009-2016, he published almost 70 stories in the e-magazine *Gölge*. He is the writer of over 100 stories and likes coining new words, such as those compiled in the "Sadık Yemni Dictionary," which is revised every year. Additionally, he publishes essays in different magazines.

Serpil Ülger

Ülger graduated from the History of the Art program at Cumhuriyet University and continued her art adventure at the university, where she started with encyclopedias at a very young age and then turned to literature with short stories – many of which have appeared in e-magazines and anthologies, prompting her to start writing full-time. *3,2,1…TIP!* (*3,2,1…Silent*), a feminist dystopian narrative is her first novel and was published by Imgenin Çocukları in 2021.

Sezai Özden

Özden completed his education in Ankara, where he studied to be an auto mechanic in high school. He was interested in painting and sculpture from a very young age, as well as in science, starting in his childhood, and became one of the founders of the Yerli Bilimkurgu Yükseliyor (Indigenous Science Fiction Rising Platform) in 2017. Also, he introduced the digital magazine under the same name, which has reached its 67th issue. He is the graphic and art designer, as well as the copy editor for the magazine. He brought the collections he created with the participation of an average of forty authors to Turkish science fiction literature. The first short story contest, published in 2018, was followed by the 2019, 2020, and 2022 short story collections. His novel *Sentromer: Ötekiler* (*Sentromer: Others*) was published in 2019 by Paradigma Publishing. His story, "Bug Fields" ("Böcek Tarlaları"), was published in Turkish in the *Yerli Bilimkurgu Yükseliyor* (*Indigenous Science Fiction Rising Platform*) science fiction story collection by Liman Publishing in 2020. Currently, he works as an illustrator and graphic designer at Nobel Publishing Group.

Tevfik Uyar

Dr. Uyar is an aeronautical engineer who graduated from Istanbul Technical University in 2007. He obtained his MBA (2012) and PhD (2019) degrees from İstanbul Kültür University. He is the founder of *Açık Bilim* (*Open Science, 2010*), the oldest science podcast channel in Turkey, and is a member of the Yalansavar (Turkish Skeptical Community). Uyar is the author of several popular science and philosophy books, such as *Astrolojinin Bilimle İmtihanı (Scientific Inquiry to Astrology,* Kırmızı Kedi 2019) and *Safsatalar (Logical Fallacies,* Destek 2019), as well as science fiction story anthologies like *Tek Kişilik Firar (Single-Person Escape,* Kırmızı Kedi 2016) and novels like *İz Odası (The Tracking Room,* Bizim Kitaplar 2011), *Kızıl Sürgün* (*Red Exile,* Destek Yayınları 2019), and *Çözülme (Dissolution,* Destek Yayınları 2021*)*. He is also a translator of books, such as Stuart Sutherland's *Irrationality* (Domingo 2015), Roelf Bolt's *Encyclopedia of Liars and Deceivers* (Domingo 2015), Thali Sharot's *The Influential Mind* (Domingo 2018), and Jim Al-Khalili's *What's Next?* (Domingo 2020). He teaches courses on Data Mining, Human Factors, and Machine Learning at Istanbul Kültür University and has received awards in the Türkiye Bilişim Derneği Bilimkurgu Öykü Yarışması (Turkish Informatics Association Science Fiction Story Contest) three times with his stories "Son Mektup" ("The Last Letter" 2012), "Fırıldak" ("The Whirligig" 2013), and "Yüz Elli" ("A Hundred and Fifty" 2015).

Türkhan Bozkurt

Bozkurt, born in Kırşehir, graduated from the Faculty of Education at Gazi University. After completing an international assignment in France from 2005 to 2010, Bozkurt worked as a teacher in Adıyaman, Turkey. Bozkurt contributed to student development through participation in several European Union projects, particularly eTwinning projects. Self-described as a futurist, Bozkurt left behind works that contemplate future utopias. Influenced by Jacques Fresco and Alvin Toffler, Bozkurt gained recognition with the book "Yörünge 3185" (Orbit 3185, Edebiyatist 2019). Married with two children, Bozkurt tragically lost her life in February 2023 during the devastating earthquake in Turkey, caught under the rubble.

Uğur Aydın

Aydın is a novel and short story author and artist. His science fiction novel *Sultan: Nebula'nın Mızrağı (Sultan: Spear of the Nebula)* was published by Mantis in 2021, and his short story "Özür Dolabı" ("Apology Booth") was published in the collection of *Esrarengiz Hikayeler (Mysterious Tales*, Mantis 2021). This story is also published in audio form voiced by Yalçın Altın (https://www.youtube.com/watch?v=YvHUR-farO0). His story "Simetri" ("Symmetry," *Gelişme Hedefleri*, Lora 2021) and one of his dystopian science fiction story series, "Yarı Uzaylı, Çeyrek Tanrı, Az da İnsan" ("Semi Alien Quarter-God Less Human"), were also published in audio form voiced by Yalçın Altın in 2020 (https://www.youtube.com/watch?v=RJJckGsMJs0). He is one of seven Turks serving in the Parliament of the virtual online community Asgardia Space Nation. (https://asgardia.space/en/social/users/172960), where he also serves as a Member of Parliament. He is an Asgardia Parliament Culture Committee chairman and member of the Culture Committee. He spends most of his time building a digital library (www.digitalspacelibrary.com), and he lives in Izmir with his wife and two daughters.

Ümit Yaşar Özkan

Özkan graduated from Atatürk University's Department of Turkish Language and Literature Teaching in 2000. He is currently teaching Turkish Language and Literature in a high school and doing his Master's Degree in the Department of Turkish Language and Literature at Fatih Sultan Mehmet University, where his thesis on climate fiction in Turkish Literature is in the defense phase. He has won awards in several science-fiction contests: his story "Arıza" ("Malfunction") came out second in the Türkiye Bilişim Derneği (Informatics Association of Turkey) Science Fiction Story Contest in 2002, and his stories "Evin Yeni Sahibi" ("The New Owner of the House"), "Meto'nun Tatili" ("The Holiday of Meto"), and "Mutant" came out third in the İthaki Jules Verne Short Story Contest in 2003 before being published in *Hayal Gücünün Merkezine Seyahat: Jules Verne Öykü Ödülleri* (İthaki 2005). He won an honorary mention for 'Süleyman Dilmaç'ın İsimsiz Meseli" ("The Unnamed Tale of Süleyman Dilmaç") in the Türkiye Bilişim Derneği (Informatics Association of Turkey) Science Fiction Story Contest in 2011 and third place in 2021 with his story "Mümkün Dünyaların En İyisi" ("The Best of All Probable Worlds") for the 10th *Yerli Bilimkurgu Yükseliyor (Indigenous Science Fiction Rising Platform)* Short Story Contest. His award-winning stories were then published in various anthologies, such as "Arıza" in *Bilimkurgu Öyküleri* (*Science Fiction Stories*, Remzi Kitabevi 2005), "Sessiz Ortak" in *Derinden Gelen Sesler* (*Deep Voices*, Arka Bahçe Yayıncılık 2008), "Süleyman Dilmaç'ın İsimsiz Meseli" in *Dünyalılar* (*Earthmen*, İletişim 2016), and "Mümkün Dünyaların En İyisi" in *Yerli Bilimkurgu Yükseliyor Bilimkurgu Öykü Seçkisi* (*Indigenous Science Fiction Rising Platform Science Fiction Story Collection*, Liman Yayınevi 2022). He wrote in various periodicals, such as *Beyaz Bulut, Arka Kapak, Zift Sanat,* and *Aynen.* The six-volume *Taş Masalları* (*Fable of Stones*) series he wrote with his wife was published by Erdem Publishing in 2016. *Bu Bir Masal Mı?* (*Is This a Fable?*) was published by Beyazbulut Publishing in 2021. His stories are also published in the Monthly Story Selection of the Kayıprıhtım website (https://oykuseckisi.com/author/umit-yasar-ozkan/

A HUNDRED YEARS OF TURKISH SCIENCE FICTION

Introduction

This anthology marks the inaugural compilation of *Turkish Science Fiction Short Stories* in English. It coincides with the centenary of the Turkish Republic, which is the same age as the history of Turkish science fiction, and our objective is to contribute to global science fiction literature by chronicling the 100-year journey of Turkish science fiction and making it accessible to international readers. While Turkish science fiction has captivated readers since the Ottoman literary era, its international recognition has been hampered by translation challenges. We aim to showcase the diverse spectrum of Turkish science fiction by uniting short stories crafted by contemporary Turkish science fiction authors in this volume.

With this collection, we endeavor to unveil the creativity, multifaceted themes, and narrative artistry of Turkish science fiction authors to international readers, highlighting the opulence of Turkish science fiction. Moreover, we aim to support the emerging generation of authors dedicated to advancing Turkish science fiction literature by bolstering their global recognition.

This anthology represents a crucial stride in elevating Turkish science fiction onto the global stage. We are thrilled to present Turkish authors' distinctive perspectives, imaginative prowess, and innovation, fostering cross-cultural engagement and celebrating our literary heritage with the world. We hope this collection will catalyze greater awareness and admiration of Turkish science fiction literature worldwide.

Furthermore, this book offers Turkish science fiction authors an unprecedented opportunity to reach a broader international audience. Turkish science fiction literature abounds with works that mirror our rich cultural heritage and unique viewpoints. Through this anthology, we aspire to engage global readers eager to explore the authentic stories and literary talents of Turkish science fiction authors.

Moreover, within these pages, you will find an avenue for observing the evolution of Turkish science fiction literature. From the Ottoman literary era to the present day, Turkish science fiction has evolved in tandem with societal, political, and technological shifts. This collection reveals the trajectory of Turkish science fiction, charting its journey through these transformations.

Additionally, these stories provide a glimpse into the future of Turkish science fiction literature. Contemporary Turkish science fiction authors infuse their narratives with reflections on technological advancements, societal changes, and global concerns. This book offers clues about the future direction of Turkish science fiction literature, inviting readers to embark on this captivating voyage.

In summary, this anthology serves as a conduit for enhancing the recognition and appreciation of Turkish science fiction literature globally. We enthusiastically present this collection as a means to share the richness of Turkish culture and literature through the lens of science fiction, encourage cultural exchange, and celebrate literary diversity.

A Brief History of Turkish Science Fiction Literature

The Turkish reader was first introduced to science fiction through translations in the last quarter of the 19th century. As the Ottoman Empire began to crumble in this century, the state's rulers implemented numerous reforms to prevent its decline. Notably, the Tanzimat Edict proclaimed in 1839 accelerated Western-style reforms. As a result, Western educational systems began to be established, and, for the first time, private newspapers started to be published. By the end of the same century, newspapers began extensively featuring not only daily local news but also scientific/technological innovations occurring in Europe. The excitement generated by technology-related news also dictated literary interests. Thrilling, adventure-filled novels that would captivate readers began to be published daily in newspapers. Among these novels, "fenni novels" held the most significant place. In Ottoman Turkish, the word "fenni," which means "scientific," was widely used for novels with science- and technology-heavy topics. However, while science fiction focuses on technologies unfamiliar to our daily lives, fenni novels include those already present in the current times. For instance, new technological machines produced in 19th century Europe became the subjects of Fenni novels. Thus, we can consider fenni novels, as expressed by Fatih Andı, "in a way, the first examples of today's science-fiction novels" (qtd. in Karadağ 52).

However, interest in Fenni novels started with translations before domestic original works. The majority of science fiction works translated during the Tanzimat period belonged to Jules Verne. Therefore, when one mentioned a Fenni novel at the time, Verne was the first name that came to mind (qtd. in Andı 130). Ahmet İhsan Tokgöz, who began publishing activities during the same period and became one of the most important publishers over the next 40 years, first translated Jules Verne's *Around the*

World in Eighty Days (1872). The work increased the newspaper's circulation, prompting Tokgöz to publish another of Verne's novels, *The Mysterious Island* (1875), even importing the original illustrations from Paris for it (Tokgöz 46). In the subsequent years, considering readers' interests, all of Jules Verne's works were translated by numerous translators and printed in various newspapers multiple times.

Over the years, Turkish authors began writing science fiction novels themselves instead of just relying on translations. The first examples of science fiction in Turkish literature, which can actually be classified as speculative fiction and fantasy (SFF), were penned by Ahmet Mithat Efendi, with works such as *Avrupa'da Bir Cevelan* (*A Trip in Europe* 1873) and *Fenni Bir Roman yahut Amerika Doktorları* (*A Scientific Novel or Doctors of America* 1889). In his second work, the author explicitly mentions "how America is more advanced than Europe, describing innovations and developments that people would find unbelievable and would hear about for the first time" (Yıldız 140). After Ahmet Mithat, it is no coincidence that all science fiction works written in the first quarter of the 20th century were of the utopian science fiction genre. The empire's fall certainly influenced this: "In this period, intellectuals' efforts to imagine the present of advanced societies as their own future led them to write novels based on science and travel, driven by tendencies like time travel or creating alternative histories" (Uyanık 43). By World War I, Turkish authors had started producing works that could genuinely be termed science fiction. In Celal Nuri İleri's *İstikbal Sahne ve Levhaları* (*Future Stage and Signs* 1915), Molla Davudzade Mustafa Nazım Erzurumi's *Rüyada Terakki ve Medeniyet-i İslâmiyeyi Rüyet* (*Envisioning Progress and Islamic Civilization in Dream* 1913) Hasan Ruşeni's *Ruşeni'nin Rüyası: Müslümanların Megali İdeası Gaye-i Hayaliyesi* (*Ruşeni's dream: The Great Ideal and Imaginary Goal of Muslims* 1914), and Yahya Kemal Beyatlı's *Çamlar Altında Musahabe I ve II* (*Chat Under the Pines I and II* 1913), the central theme revolves around the dream of catching the "progress" train, which had been missed in the past, and imagining a future where the Turkish-Islamic world is even stronger than Europe.

Refik Halit Karay's *Hülya Bu Ya...* (*This is Dream* 1921) is one of the most notable works from the final years of the Ottoman Empire. In this story, the author mocks the Ankara government, which refused to accept the decline of the Ottoman Empire and entered into war with imperialist powers. Karay insinuates that the officials in Ankara are deluding the public with fantasies as he describes a fictional advanced technological environment in the city. As conveyed in the story, in Ankara, people's damaged organs can be replaced with artificial ones, roads move automatically to transport people to their destinations, and reproduction is conducted in laboratories. The way these developments are presented with admiration from the perspective of an American traveler suggests an acknowledgment of America's dominance in the technological race of that era.

Starting in 1923, when the Ottoman Empire ended and the Republic of Turkiye was founded, one can see that the new state aimed to develop and establish a national identity that influenced all intellectuals. As a result, a period began where genres like science fiction did not receive enough attention. Cemil Cahit's work, *Merih'a Seyahat* (*Travel to Mars* 1931), seems inspired by Jules Verne's *From the Earth to the Moon* (1865). In his work, Cemil Cahit imagined that the Turks had advanced enough to travel to Mars. Upon arriving on Mars, the Turks communicate with another advanced society similar to themselves. In this respect, the work can be seen as the first example of the "first contact with aliens" sub-genre in Turkish science fiction literature. Another interesting feature of the work is that all this technological progress was envisioned in Turkiye in the 1930s. The author did not envision a different state or future but affirmed the regime of the time. The work titled *Rüya mı Hakikat mi?* (*Dream or Reality?*), written by Dr. V. Bilgin in 1943, is considered by some sources an example of the "political science fiction" sub-genre. In his work, Bilgin describes his imaginary journey to Mars and encounters on the planet (Bayar 156). The short story "Büyük Kukuriko" (*Big Kukuriku* 1948), by another critical author, Halikarnas Balıkçısı,[1] serves as a critique of the economic system and bureaucratic apparatus of the newly established Republic of Turkiye. The new state, while aspiring towards liberalism, had established its own monopoly in various economic sectors and supported the rigid dominance of bureaucratic classes over society. Halikarnas Balıkçısı addresses the problems of these conflicting structures in his work:

> Following the tradition of dystopian literature, Halikarnas Balıkçısı deals humorously with themes of dehumanization, totalitarian state governance, environmental disaster, social decay, pollution, extreme poverty, overpopulation, and political pressure . . . The country of "Büyük Kukuriko" is a privatization and corporatization hell where a few giant companies dominate every area of life, from raw materials to basic necessities. In this land of giants, companies replace governments in setting policies and making decisions. They manipulate the market and politics, infiltrate and control these areas, and operate much like governments unless otherwise stated. (Yiğitler 610-611)

By juxtaposing governmental and corporate power, Halikarnas Balıkçısı

---

[1] The nickname for Cevat Şakir Kabaağaçlı.

not only critiques the socio-political landscape of his time but also invites readers to contemplate the enduring implications of such power dynamics. His portrayal serves as a cautionary tale, warning of a future where the lines between state and market are indistinguishably blurred and where the citizen becomes subservient to the corporate entity. This dark foresight, humorously conveyed, underscores the relevance of "Büyük Kukuriko" as not only a product of its time but also a timeless reflection on the perils of unchecked capitalism.

Even though Turkiye was not involved in World War II, the immense destruction of the war deeply affected the country, leading to significant impoverishment of society (Bülbül 2-3). Moreover, literature generally focused on national problems in a country where political issues persisted, so science fiction did not receive enough attention then. However, from the 1970s onwards, with the interest of urban, middle-class intellectuals, science fiction began to revive. In 1971, Metin Atak wrote *Gezegenler Savaşıyor* (*Planets at War*) and *Arena* (*Arena*), which weaved wars between humans and aliens. Sometimes, these works describe space wars reminiscent of space operas and, at other times, they relay direct combat scenes with aliens from the planet Niyar. Thus, these pioneering works of the period can be classified under the "first contact with aliens" sub-genre. In the same period, İbrahim Ethem Vural's work *Fezada Bir İnsan: Pilot Osman* (*A Person in Space: Pilot Osman* 1975) stands out for its Islamist and sloganistic aspects. The novel's protagonist, Pilot Osman, disapproves of the democratic regime and desires a system dominated by religious values. It is possible to interpret the novel as a reflection of the Islamist community's anger towards the secular regime. The reflection of political Islamist thought in science fiction is also evident in later years, such as in Ali Nar's *Uzay Çiftçileri* (*Space Farmers* 1988), which tells the story of the establishment of the Islamic Union and the endeavors of Muslim astronauts from different countries. The science fiction setting in both works serves as a backdrop for political Islamist propaganda.

In the twentieth century, chemical science used petroleum to produce many plastic-derived products, which led to their penetration into all areas of life. The integration of these newly developed materials into consumer products has significantly enhanced the functionality of daily living. Nonetheless, the potential negative impacts of synthetic materials on human health and the environment, observed at both micro and macro scales, have been frequently emphasized as a potential concern. "Synthetic biology science fiction" delves deeper into this issue by exploring the effects of lab-engineered living organisms on life. *Plastik İnsanlar Ülkesi* (*Land of Plastic People*), written by H. Fikri Verel in 1974, portrays a scientist who produces humans from plastic in a laboratory. This rogue scientist, who establishes a country in space with the humans he created, showcases the negative consequences of using science for personal gains without considering ethical values.

The year 1971 marks a pivotal moment in the publishing of science fiction magazines. Prior to this year, there had been no magazine exclusively devoted to the science fiction genre. Sezar Erkin Ergin, a science fiction enthusiast, launched a new era by publishing a magazine named *Aylık Haber Bülteni (Monthly Newsletter* 1971-74) that was exclusively dedicated to science fiction. Additionally, between 1974 and 1977, Ergin published another science fiction magazine named *Antares: Bilim Kurgu - Science Fiction (Antares: Science Fiction)*. This paved the way for a broader audience to become more familiar with the term and genre of science fiction. The term "bilimkurgu" as the Turkish equivalent for "science fiction," was first coined by Orhan Duru in 1973 and has continued to be used by Ergin since 1974. The January 1, 1973, issue of the magazine *Türk Dili (Turkish Language)* was dedicated to the science fiction genre. In his article in this issue, Duru suggested the aforementioned term, and "bilimkurgu" subsequently established its place in Turkish literature. Starting from the 1970s, Orhan Duru continued to make significant contributions to science fiction with stories such as "Gerçeküstü Bir Film İçin Sinopsis" ("Synopsis for a Surreal Movie"), "Yoksullar Geliyor" ("The Poor Are Coming"), "Harita" ("The Map"), "Fırtına" ("Storm"), and "Gözyaşı Taşı" ("Stone of Tears") (Reyhanoğulları 2188-92).

In 1976, one of the most important science fiction magazines, *X-Bilinmeyen (X-Unknown)*, was published. Launched by Selma Mine, who made significant contributions to science fiction with her literary works and articles, the magazine underwent a name change after the 1980 military coup and became *X-Bilinmeyen: Evren (X-Unknown: Space)*. In 1989, the magazine's name changed again, and it continued its publication under the title *X-Bilinmeyen: Bilimkurgu (X-Unknown: Science Fiction)*. Selma Mine's contributions to the genre did not stop there; she also facilitated the establishment of the "X-Bilinmeyen Fan Club" through the magazine, attempting to bring together the otherwise dispersed science fiction community. With the participation of some significant writers, the magazine started organizing science fiction short story competitions from 1977 onwards. *Orion* (1978) magazine, which started its publication around the same time, managed to release eight issues in 1978. In 1980, the *Göktaşı (Meteorite 1980)* magazine was launched and, in 1983, the *Galaksi* magazine was introduced, but both had short-lived publications. Later on, magazines like *Çağdaş Sanat Bilimkurgu Aylık Popüler Dergi (Contemporary Art Science Fiction Monthly Popular Magazine* 1988*)*, *Öncü (Pioneer* 1989*)*, *Atılgan (Enterprise* 1996-2000), and *Umutla Yıldızlara: Nostromo Bilimkurgu Dergisi (With Hope in the Stars: Nostromo Science*

Fiction Magazine 1997) managed to publish for a few months (Öner 58-62).

This period of activity in the science fiction magazine world set the stage for new developments in the genre. In 1979, Refik Özdek wrote a novel titled *Uzaylı Bargan'ın Dönüşü (Return of the Alien Bargan)*, which portrays aliens differently from previous works. This work addresses the aggression of the invasive human race towards peace-loving aliens. The novel critiques the imperialistic and invasive tendencies of humanity. The 1980s marked the years when political violence, which had previously spread to all the streets in Turkiye, came to an end. From this date onwards, with the influence of new liberal economic policies, the country's process of integrating into the global system begins. This process has also paved the way for cultural diversity and innovations. Science fiction literature in Turkiye also gained momentum during this period.

Looking at the post-1980 science fiction literature, works from almost every sub-genre have begun to be written. During this period, in parallel with the increased dissemination speed of scientific knowledge, Turkish science fiction writers are showing interest in new sub-genres. A general look at these works reveals that the number of sub-genres is increasing daily. Additionally, dozens of works have been written for each sub-genre. The examples we will provide below are just a few instances of the richness created by the last forty years.

After 1980, among the sub-genres of science fiction that were written, "first contact" holds a significant place as one of the most recognized and universal writing modes.. "First contact," which questions the possibilities during the encounter of two completely alien species, can open endless doors to narratives about space. For instance, T. Erhan Coşan's novel *Kozmik Görev (Cosmic Quest* 2012) features friendly aliens abducting humans. Facing malfunctions in their teleportation systems, the aliens seek help from humans. In Ali Demirel's work *Acun-2 (Space-2* 1996), the crew of a spaceship commissioned by the state, consisting of Turks, travels to different planets and communicates with their inhabitants. With devices that can decipher and facilitate communication in any language, they contribute to the lives of entities either more advanced or more primitive than humanity. The novel flips the often-repeated cliché of an "advanced alien civilization," positioning humans back at the center of the universe. Now, humanity can engage in intergalactic imperial endeavors.

Another theme tackled in the "first contact" genre is alien invasions. Zühtü Bayar's *Sahte Uygarlık (Fake Civilization* 1999) depicts aliens from a different galaxy claiming the civilization humanity has created over thousands of years for themselves and establishing a dictatorial structure on both Earth and Mars. The novel describes the socialist and capitalist blocks fighting against this structure, highlighting their flaws and issues. The alternative system proposed in the novel is an anarchist one. While *Sahte Uygarlık* contains political messages, the political element is in the background. The forefront features humans' efforts to be free and space wars. Another novel in this genre is Kazım Çende's *Andromeda'ya Dönüş: Durkonlar* (*Return to Anromeda: Durkons* 2011), in which the entities invading Earth are human descendants of those who left Earth thousands of years ago. In the story, the son of the Durkon emperor bathes in the river of immortality, becoming bulletproof – a reference to Greek mythology. Recently, authors of this sub-genre have begun to incorporate Turkish mythology into their novels. Ali Demirel's *Yada* (2001) focuses on a stone named "Yada," believed in Turkish mythology to control weather events: "In Turkish mythology, the stone that appears in epics and is considered sacred is a device belonging to aliens. The author has taken a narrative that's been told as a part of religious belief, transformed it into the primary material for science fiction, and built the novel upon it" (Açık 232). The narrative of an extraterrestrial being assigned to safeguard the Yada stone unfolds across a journey from Kazakhstan to Egypt and eventually to Turkiye. Given the rising popularity of the fantasy genre in cinema, particularly for its rich use of mythology, the elements drawn from this novel become increasingly pertinent. The incorporation of ancient epics and folk tales into science fiction holds the potential to enrich the diversity of topics significantly.

"Time travel," one of the most admired sub-genres of science fiction since H.G. Wells, also has numerous examples in Turkish science fiction. Ali Demirel's novel *Zamanın Kaçak Yolcuları* (*Stowaways of Time* 2002) is built upon patriotic sentiments. Using a time machine, young Turks travel to the past to join in the 1915 wars and later explore a future Turkish Union. The novel emphasizes citizens of Turkiye from different geographical and religious origins working together, establishing a nationalist perspective. Hakan Şahin's *Beşinci Boyut: Ölçek* (*Fifth Dimension: Scale* 2008) falls under the sub-genre of "travel to different universes and dimensions." The novel describes the journey of young individuals into a micro-universe and their battle against monsters therein. Findings of physical science are also mentioned in the book. Here, as in other works, a device is used to communicate with people who speak different languages.

The "fear of great catastrophe," present in humanity's oldest tales, stories, and religious texts, is an indispensable sub-genre of Turkish science fiction. For example, Ali Targaç's *Yokoluş* (*Extinction* 2012) focuses on humans boarding quantum ships to escape to different universes after Earth becomes uninhabitable. Another example narrating the aftermath of a great catastrophe is Aşkın Güngör's *Gohor: Kıyametten Sonra* (*Gohor: After the Apocalypse* 2003), which is set during a period when humanity is on the brink of near extinction due to nuclear weapons. Using advanced technology, the surviving humans have built glass cities and severed their connections with the outside world. The novel's plot involving robot caregivers and robot wolves also establishes various connections with the "robot science fiction" sub-genre.

In recent years, advancements in genetic science have garnered attention globally, as well as in Turkiye. "Biopunk science fiction" suggests ideas about how humanity could be affected if genetic science falls into the wrong hands. Hüseyin Yurttaş's *Robotlar Ülkesi* (*Land of Robots* 2012) deals with the effects on the world of humans produced as slaves through genetic modification. Humans produced in laboratories have become robotic. The novel examines the direct relationship between genetic science and ethical issues.

"Dystopian science fiction," a significant sub-genre of Turkish Science Fiction, highlights the potential negative effects of science and technology alongside their benefits and has gained recognition, particularly through iconic works like George Orwell's *1984* (1949) and Ray Bradbury's *Fahrenheit 451* (1953). In Turkish science fiction literature, numerous works depict a bleak future. In many of them, the focus is on the overpopulation and exhaustion of the world's resources. For instance, in Gülayşe Koçak's *Topaç* (*Spinner* 2016), excessive population growth leads to the emergence of a totalitarian system. In this world, children are killed, sexuality is forbidden, and all human values have been eradicated. Devices even prevent people from hearing words that express emotion. Other works written during this period, such as Kanat Volkan's *Federasyon* (*Federation* 2011) and Semih Bulgur's *Düş Mühendisi: 2085* (*Dream Engineer: 2085* 2012), depict the scarcity of the future world and people seeking help from negative systems in their search for solutions.

With increasing environmental issues, global awareness regarding these problems has gradually been reflected in literature. Turkish science fiction novelists, trying to warn about the world's problems, have contributed many works to the "ecological science fiction" genre. For instance, Haldun Aydıngün's *Boğaziçi ve Ötesi* (*Bosphorus and Beyond* 1999) describes a future where an environmental disaster nearly ends the human race. In such a future, very few people live and die while laying in sleep cocoons produced with advanced technology over thousands of years, where reality has faded. Halil Kocagöz's *Uzaya Kaçış* (*Escape to Space* 2012) depicts humanity departing Earth due to disasters originating from the Sun.

From the 1950s onwards, the growing movement advocating women's rights has influenced literature. Since this period, women's efforts to enter cultural areas from which they had previously been excluded have increased. As a male-dominated structure, science fiction became a target for female writers. The situation began to change. Many academic articles written after Joanna Russ's "The Image of Women in Science Fiction" (1971) paved the way for women's entry into science fiction (Attebery 108). Ursula K. Le Guin's *The Left Hand of Darkness* (1969) has greatly inspired female science fiction writers. Turkish science fiction, especially after the 2000s, has a strong feminist channel. Özlem Alpin Kurdoğlu's novels – *Son Cephede Şafak* (*Dawn on the Last Front* 2000), *Yüreğin Zafere Çağrısı* (*Heart's Call to Victory* 2003), and *Alacaşafağın Rengi* (*The Color of Dusk* 2005) – which center on female characters while portraying men in the background, are pioneering in this regard. The mentioned series of novels is also connected to genres like gothic science fiction and political science fiction. The sequel to the Alien film series focuses on the adventures of Lieutenant Ripley and, later, her daughter. Nurcihan Doğuç's novel *Hayalet Kentin Kadınları* (*Women of the Ghost Town* 2009) is intriguing as it combines Sufi thought and a vision of the future. Additionally, the positions of androgynous identity and the realization of feminine energy in future society are major themes of the novel (Uğur 309). Many other female authors have contributed significantly to the development of Turkish science fiction. Some of the works include Arzu Eylem's *Çok Çağı* (*Many Ages* 2018), Aysun Bitir's *Excido* (2011), Esin Kıroğlu's *Nessehira* (2013), Gamze İstanbulluoğlu's *Omartha* (2015), İlknur Uğur's *Yansıma* (*Reflection* 2012), Özlem Ada's *Embriyogenesis* (*Embryogenesis* 1997), Sinem Ataklı's *Proje 2417* (*Project 2417* 2018), Şeyda Aydın's *Diğer Evrendeki Kadın* (*Woman in the Other Universe* 2019), Şengül Boybaş's *Dünyanın Uyanışı* (*Awakening of the World* 2018), and so on.

The concept of immortality, which has been of interest in all eras and geographies since *The Epic of Gilgamesh* (18th Century BCE), is one of the subjects of science fiction interests. Especially in the last hundred years, scientific innovations have strengthened the idea that this dream could come true. Naturally, the development of the sub-genre named "immortal-human or posthuman science fiction" is inevitable in Turkish science fiction. Mustafa R. Yalçınkaya's novel *Ambrosia Laneti* (*Curse of Ambrosia* 2012) attempts to show what immortality can lead to. The novel describes a world where crime has become commonplace, and all forms of suicide are tried as entertainment. In such an environment, the dissolution of social order and the regression of humanity have become unavoidable. Selim Erdoğan's *Denizatı Vadisi* (*Seahorse Valley* 2012) focuses on the immortality of minds rather than bodies. One of the most striking aspects of immortal-human science fiction is the extensive focus on the practical and ethical issues of the work of scientists devoted to their fields. In addition to the above authors, Sadık Yemni, *Akisfer* (2011); Bülent Özden, *Kozmik Teyyare* (*Cosmic Plane* 2012); Sercan Leylek, *Cydonia* (2012); Ş. Yüksel Yılmaz, *M4Y4: Tehlike Yaklaşıyor* (*M4Y4: Danger Is Approaching* 2016); Olcay Şeker, *7 Pencere* (*7 Windows* 2016); Dost Körpe, *Nötralizör* (*Neutralizer* 2022); and Özgen Biçgin, *Kayıp Rota Trilogy* (*Lost Route Trilogy* 2022) are also names that have contributed to contemporary Turkish science fiction literature.

Robots, indispensable figures in science fiction literature, remain significant in recent science fiction works. However, what stands out here is the advanced forms of robots. Therefore, with their more advanced structures and human-like appearance, cyborgs are preferred over conventional robots that perform mechanical movements. Toygar Akman's *Öbürgünkü Sibernetik* (*Cybernetics of the Other Day* 2003) addresses the commissioning of cybernauts, i.e., cyborg astronauts, by humans. Cyborgs go to space to spread human seeds throughout the universe but return to find the human race extinct. Another novel centered on cyborgs is Ayça Kumluca's *Deney: Onlar Hep Aramızdaydı* (*Test: They Were Always Among Us* 2011), which questions the outcomes of an experiment that releases indistinguishable cyborgs into society and records the events that occur during this process. However, the ethical issues of this experiment are also a topic of debate.

In the 1960s, with the New Wave movement, it is observed that the place of social sciences in science fiction has increased. This development has changed the science fiction understanding dominated by technology. Thus, genres such as "social science fiction" and "anthropological science fiction" have developed. Social science fiction has been heavily influenced by scientific developments such as psychology and sociology. The effects of these scientific findings on society and the individual have become the primary issue of social science fiction. Gündüz Öğüt's *Şafağı Getirenler* (*Bringers of the Dawn* 2000) focuses on psychology and addresses the greed of doctors who invent new diseases instead of ending existing ones. According to the novel, science has become a tool for the interests of a small group in society. In short, the novel aims to discuss the events it exemplifies while questioning scientific ethics.

Turkish science fiction literature, of which we have only mentioned a few examples, is gaining strength. Novels and stories primarily set in the future provide an appropriate basis for imagining a different life. In the new century, as traditional, realistic literature loses its power in Turkiye, fantasy and science fiction become more potent. In this period of intense global interaction, it is not surprising that Turkish science fiction literature, which has a much more recent past, produces works of a quality that can appeal to the whole world. Almost all the stories in the last few years exemplify that Turkish writers have internalized the science fiction atmosphere, offering alternate worlds.

A Brief Look at the Turkish SF Film

The Turkish cinema's engagement with science fiction is an intriguing study of contrasts: on one hand, there's a notable scarcity of dedicated science fiction works; on the other, there exists a latent richness and potential that has yet to be fully realized. Despite a history peppered with attempts at the genre, the establishment of a robust science fiction tradition in Turkish film remains, at best, nascent. However, this does not imply an absence of potential. Instead, a closer examination of Turkiye's cinematic history reveals a curious lack of films dedicated solely to science fiction. While certain hallmarks of the genre have found their way into Turkish storytelling, historically, Turkish films have dabbled in the genre, but often within the confines of comedy and adventure.

This paradoxical situation stems, in part, from the way science fiction has traditionally manifested in Turkish cinema. Rather than developing its own science fiction tradition from the ground up, the industry has frequently relied on low-budget adaptations of Hollywood narratives. These adaptations, while adding a unique Turkish flavor to familiar stories, have often not ventured far enough to establish a robust, standalone science fiction tradition. The result is a cinematic landscape where science fiction elements are woven into other genres, but the full potential of science fiction—as a distinct genre capable of deep societal and thematic exploration—remains largely untapped. This presents an opportunity for Turkish filmmakers to delve deeper into the realm of science fiction and explore its myriad possibilities in a way that resonates with the cultural and historical context of Turkiye.

Cinema in Turkey, introduced during the Ottoman Empire with initial palace screenings in 1896-1897, saw the rise of domestic film production in 1914, focusing on literature adaptations before World War II (Güvemli 231-34) and often allowing science fiction films to bypass the censorship common for Hollywood movies in the early 1990s (Erdoğan and Kaya, 2002 52-56). The impact of World War II led to simpler, realistic films with low production costs being shot with an unprofessional crew in short periods, reflecting the material shortages and censorship of the 1940s (Berktaş 231-47; Güvemli 248). The establishment of the Domestic Filmmakers' Association in 1946, followed by tax cuts, spurred growth in film production post-1949 (Güvemli 256). The 1950s marked the emergence of Turkish SF cinema, often blending with fantastical elements, as noted in Giovanni Scognamillo and Metin Demirhan's *Fantastik Türk Sineması (Fantastic Turkish Cinema* 1999), underscoring a unique approach to the genre. Ironically, Turkish cinema, particularly during the prolific Yeşilçam Era[2] (Green Pine Era) from the 1950s to the mid-1980s, witnessed the creation of its unique renditions of mainstream Hollywood sci-fi blockbusters, indicative of an existing affinity for the genre. The phenomenon of adapted storytelling took root in the 1950s and was marked by culturally translated remakes of iconic Hollywood films. This trend ventured into science fiction with *Görünmeyen Adam Istanbul'da*[3] (*The Invisible Man in Istanbul*, Lütfi Ö. Akad 1955), narrating a tale of vengeance fueled by scientific discovery—an invisibility serum. The 1955 release of *Uçan Daireler Istanbul'da* (*Flying Saucers Over Istanbul*, Orhan Erçin 1955) marked Turkey's initial venture into depicting extraterrestrial life in cinema, featuring female Amazonian aliens in Istanbul on a mission to abduct men, thereby symbolizing an early exploration into science fiction infused with elements of humor and fantasy.

In the 1960s, Turkish cinema began to embrace science fiction themes, featuring films such as *Aydedeye Gidiyoruz* (*We Are Going to Moon*, Nuran Şener 1964), which depicts a child's imaginative journey to the moon; *Ölüm Saçan Dudaklar* (*The Lips of Death*, Cevat Okçugil 1965), chronicling mad scientists' attempts at world dominance; and *Baytekin Fezada Çarpışanlar* (*Flash Gordon's Battle in Space*, Şinasi Özonuk 1967), a homage to the Flash Gordon series with its interstellar battles (Scognamillo and Demirhan 38). The late 1960s, particularly 1967-1968, heralded the emergence of an anti-hero figure, Kilink, inspired by the Italian comic strip character Kiling. The series— including *Kilink Istanbul'da* (*Kiling in Istanbul*, Yılmaz Atadeniz 1967), *Kilink Uçan Adam'a Karşı* (*Kiling vs Flying Man*, Yılmaz Atadeniz 1967) and *Kilink: Soy ve Öldür* (*Kiling: Strip and Kill*, Yılmaz Atadeniz 1967)—saw Kilink contending with Superman and an intersection of local and global pop culture icons. Supplementary titles like *Dişi Kilink* (*Female Kiling*, Aram Gülyüz 1967) and *Kilink Frankeştein ve Dr. No'ya Karşı* (*Kilink Against Frankenstein and Dr. No*, Nuri Akıncı 1967) further underscore the blend of domestic narratives with universally recognized sci-fi elements.

In retrospect, Turkish cinema's sporadic yet imaginative endeavors to engage with science fiction reflect an unfulfilled and unexplored potential. While the genre has been tangentially explored, often intertwined with other

---

[2] Green Pine is known for its melodramas.

[3] *The Invisible Man in Istanbul* is a notable adaptation of James Whale's *Invisible Man* film series, incorporating melodramatic elements (Scognamillo and Demirhan 33).

genres, its thematic richness and capacity for profound societal commentary remain largely untapped. There's a wealth of opportunity for storytelling that not only entertains but also challenges and reflects societal issues through the unique lens of science fiction. In doing so, Turkish cinema could open new horizons for artistic expression and audience engagement, potentially setting new benchmarks in the genre globally.

The impact of global pop culture on Turkiye's film industry during the 1970s is unmistakably significant. This era stands as a clear demonstration of how universal characters and themes can be embraced and reinterpreted uniquely by diverse cultures. As a result, this period was particularly notable for the production of science fiction and fantasy (SFF) films in Turkiye. In 1973, Turkiye's cinematic landscape presented a groundbreaking innovation, epitomized in the film *3 Dev Adam (Three Giant Men*, T. Fikret Uçak 1973), which ingeniously amalgamated the powers of iconic figures such as Captain America, Spider-Man, and the Mexican wrestler El Santo. Intriguingly, while Spider-Man adopts the role of a mafioso and Captain America embodies a Turkish policeman, it is worth noting that this was not Turkiye's inaugural portrayal of Spider-Man as an antagonist. The 1966 film *Örümcek Adam* (*Spider Man*, Cevat Okçugil) depicts Spider Man as a trickster who cunningly maneuvers the police and the mob into conflict with each other. Furthermore, in the narrative landscape of 1971, the film *Tarkan: Viking Kanı* (*Tarkan Versus the Vikings*, Erem Eğilmez) featured the Hunnic warrior Tarkan confronting a Viking clan that venerated the Octopus God to rescue a woman destined for sacrifice. The subsequent year witnessed the advent of *Yılmayan Şeytan*[4] *(The Deathless Devil*, Yılmaz Atadeniz 1972), a reinterpretation of the 1940 serial *Mysterious Doctor Satan*, where the superhero Copperhead faces off against the eponymous villain. Concurrently, 1973 saw Turkiye's rendition of the legendary Batman materialize in *Yarasa Adam* (Günay Kosava).

Another fascinating case of adaptation is *Turist Ömer Uzay Yolunda* (*Ömer the Tourist in Star Trek,* Hulki Saner 1973). Ömer the Tourist, humorously portrayed by the distinguished actor Sadri Alışık, is notably known as Turkish Star Trek in Turkiye. Turkish cinema was enriched by eight films of *Ömer the Tourist in Star Trek,* depicting the humorous escapades of this whimsical, endearing wanderer character. What is more striking is that this film predated the original *Star Trek* feature film by six years and proactively adapted the series to the big screen, a strategic move that preceded similar Hollywood initiatives, as noted by Scognamillo and Demirhan (52-53). Highlighting the innovative and avant-garde spirit of Turkish cinema, this

---

[4] *The Deathless Devil* is an adaptation of *the Mysterious Docto*r series of the 1940s (Scognamillo and Demirhan 44).

period, marked by creative adaptability, offers a revealing insight into the flexibility and cross-cultural charm of popular narratives. Another one named *Sevimli Frankeştayn* (*My Friend Frankenstein/Turkish Young Frankenstein*, Nejat Saydam 1975) is a whimsical adaptation of Mel Brooks' *Young Frankenstein* (1974), infused with comedic flair. Timur Frank's journey begins when a mysterious man unveils his lineage, linking him to his grandfather, Baron Fredirik Von Frankenstein. Upon learning this, Timur heads to his grandfather's castle to implement his life's project—an experiment to conquer death. In the castle, Timur finds a manuscript penned by his ancestor, guiding him to animate life. Its parodic take on the genre makes it a distinctive film.

In the annals of Turkish cinema, one finds an intriguing tapestry of films that exhibit adaptations, reinterpretations, and unique takes on global cinematic trends. One such movie, often informally dubbed the *Turkish Star Wars*, is *Dünyayı Kurtaran Adam* (*The Man Who Saves the World*, Çetin İnanç 1982). Released in 1982 and starring the iconic Cüneyt Arkın, this film is not merely a copy of its namesake but ingeniously integrates elements from famous cinematic series like *Indiana Jones*, *Ben Hur*, *Battlestar Galactica*, and *Flash Gordon*. As a part of a trend of low-budget Turksploitation superhero movies, this cult film is distinguished for its blend of science fiction themes with martial arts fantasy action. It became internationally known as *Turkish Star Wars* because of its unauthorized use of scenes, music, and sound effects from *Star Wars* and other science fiction films when released in the United States in 2005 by BijouFlix Releasing. The story unfolds with two astronauts landing on a desert planet, symbolically depicted by Cappadocia, where they confront malevolent forces seeking global supremacy. In 2006, the Turkish film industry introduced *Dünyayı Kurtaran Adam'ın Oğlu* (*The Son of the Man who Saved the World*), directed by the iconic Yeşilçam artist Kartal Tibet. Often referred to in English as *Turks in Space,* this science fiction action comedy shifts its focus to a Turkish family's adventures on an alien planet. Cüneyt Arkın reprises his role, teaming up this time with Mehmet Ali Erbil, who portrays his son, as they embark on a mission to save the world once more.

A year after *Dünyayı Kurtaran Adam* captivated audiences, 1983 saw the Turkish cinematic realm respond to the global phenomenon of Steven Spielberg's *E.T.: The Extra-Terrestrial* with its own rendition titled *Badi* (Zafer Par), which distinguishes itself with a culturally nuanced touch by its titular character's name. In Turkish, "badi badi yürümek," meaning to walk with a swaying, duck-like gait, lends a familiar, slightly humorous tone to the character of Badi. This name choice adds a layer of cultural resonance and humor to the story, contrasting with the more universally endearing image of *E.T.* The Turkish E.T. tells the story of an alien being who unexpectedly lands on Earth, forging an extraordinary friendship with a young boy, Ali, amidst efforts to return to his own planet. The story of Badi begins when an extraterrestrial creature arrives in Istanbul from a flying saucer. Ali discovers the alien and names him Badi, leading to widespread media attention and governmental involvement. The boy, along with his elderly aunt and friends, endeavors to protect Badi from the authorities and the public eye. This aspect of the plot delves into the societal and governmental dynamics faced when encountering the unknown, offering a more complex and layered perspective to the film.

In the tradition of Nasreddin Hodja's storytelling, which often involves humor to provoke critical thought, a similar approach has been reflected in Turkish science fiction comedy. Consequently, it is common to see comedic science fiction narratives that playfully critique or satirize influences imported from abroad. This melding of traditional humor with modern science-fiction themes adds a unique dimension to Turkish cinema, blending cultural heritage with contemporary storytelling. In the realm of Turkish cinema, the noteworthy films *G.O.R.A.* (Ömer Faruk Sorak 2004), *A.R.O.G.* (Ali Taner Baltaci and Cem Yilmaz 2008), and *Arif V 216* (Kivanç Baruönü 2018) epitomize the nation's affinity for science-fiction comedies. These films, which rank among Turkiye's top-grossing of all time, star the multifaceted artist, standup comedian Cem Yılmaz. Although the film G.O.R.A. was viewed by a total of 4,001,711[5] in 2004 spectators in cinemas, its viewership on YouTube and other internet platforms has multiplied several times over, breaking records. We continue to see the renowned comedian Cem Yılmaz in various series, films, and cinema productions, and most recently, in 2022, a spin-off series based on the character *Erşan Kuneri* was released on Netflix. While subsequent films, such as *Dünyayı Kurtaran Adamın Oğlu* (2006), have been technically commendable, their narrative depth predominantly rests within the comedic genre.

The trilogy, commencing with *G.O.R.A.*, unfolds the comedic escapades of a carpet salesman, a sly and somewhat deceitful character, Arif, who is kidnapped by extraterrestrials on the planet G.O.R.A. While imprisoned on Gora, Arif not only rescues the planet from a fireball but also meets and falls in love with Princess Ceku. Confronting the sinister commander Logar, who aims to marry Ceku for control of Gora, Arif manages to save her, and together, they flee to Earth, eventually marrying. The film's sequel, *A.R.O.G.*, which spells *G.O.R.A.* in reverse, continues the saga and was equally successful with audiences. In *A.R.O.G.*, Logar, seeking revenge, uses a time machine to send Arif back to the Stone Age. There, Arif successfully

---

[5] https://boxofficeturkiye.com/tumzaman/?tm=1989tr Erişim: 05.04.2020

introduces modern concepts to Stone Age society. Ceku later rescues Arif from this ancient era. The series culminates with *Arif V 216*, where 216, the robot from *G.O.R.A.*, aspires to be human and joins Arif and his family on Earth. Facing rejection from society, 216 and Arif accidentally time-travel to 1969. A businessman aims to exploit 216 as a toy robot, leading to 216's transformation into a more malevolent character, thereby altering the future. Arif discovers the grim consequences and embarks on a mission to save both the world and his friend 216.

In the realm of Turkish science fiction literature and cinema, there exists a rich tapestry that extends beyond just utopian and comedic elements. One frequently encounters representations of dystopian science fiction, indicating a diverse exploration of themes within the Turkish speculative fiction genre. For example, *Buğday (Grain)*, a film from 2017 directed by Semih Kaplanoğlu and taking cues from a chapter of the Quran, envisions a future where society is cleaved into decaying urban centers and vast agricultural fields, all under the thumb of colossal corporations. This global joint venture, shot across the United States, Germany, and Turkey, plays out in the English language over an arduous five-year production period. The film, featuring performances by Jean-Marc Barr, Ermin Bravo, and Grigoriy Dobrygin, delves into pressing issues of our era: environmental degradation, widespread famine, the refugee crisis, and the moral dilemmas of genetic engineering. A sudden climate calamity has precipitated a catastrophic famine in its dystopian setting. Privileged elites enjoy the safety of cities protected by magnetic barriers, while outside, the immigrant masses face a desperate fight for survival against hunger and disease in the desolate "Dead Lands." At the heart of the story is Professor Erol Erin (Jean-Marc Barr), a seed geneticist confined within a city that excludes a multi-ethnic population. A mysterious genetic blight ravages the city's plantations, propelling Erol on a mission fraught with personal and philosophical challenges. His quest begins in earnest when he learns of Cemil Akman, a geneticist whose research into the persistent crises affecting genetically modified seeds piques his interest. Motivated by Akman's insights, Erol leaves behind his sheltered urban existence to find Cemil (Ermin Bravo) in the bleak Dead Lands. Their meeting marks the start of a profound journey that weaves together a tapestry of survival and scientific discovery. As Erol travels through a world wracked by ecological disaster and the repercussions of genetic manipulation, the film invites viewers to contemplate the intricate relationship between human progress and the planet's well-being. *Grain* not only portrays a quest for individual enlightenment but also a search for collective redemption in the face of global challenges. Another example is the 2022 Netflix film *Sıcak Kafa (Hot Skull)*, which introduces a unique dystopian world where language becomes the medium of an epidemic and a linguist becomes the coveted key to a solution. The same year, *Yakamoz S-245* established a new narrative paradigm reflecting another Netflix series, the Belgian *Into the Night*. As a first-of-its-kind spin-off, this series captures the aftermath of a cataclysmic natural disruption, manifesting as a solar polarity shift that turns sunlight into a lethal force. This series intends to navigate the intricate alternative vision within its story and probe the evolving relationships between humans, their environment, and the broader spectrum of nature.

Furthermore, Netflix's offerings have also showcased novel Turkish science-fiction narratives. The 2019 Netflix series *Atiye* (*The Gift*) reimagines "the history of (post)humanity" (Buran 232) through the lens of archaeological findings of a gate in Göbeklitepe[6], leading to parallel universes. This series, underpinned by Şengül Boybaş's novel *Dünyanın Uyanışı* (*The Awakening of the World* 2018), posits a complex interplay between the past, present, and the realms of reality and spirituality. The mysterious time-travel gate delves into the enigmatic story of Atiye, who embarks on a journey across parallel worlds, unveiling her intrinsic post-Goddess power that has shaped human history. This extraordinary journey reveals the connections between Atiye's different selves existing in these alternate realities. This science fiction series skillfully intertwines themes of death, rebirth, and parallel universes, drawing heavily from mysticism, anthropology, and cosmology. The film also highlights the significance of the Şahmaran myth within the series, portraying posthuman mythological figures as pivotal in shaping human history. It showcases the transfer of miraculous healing abilities and supernatural powers from mother to daughter, echoing a matriarchal system. These mythological goddesses play a crucial role in redefining the course of time, space, and existence (Buran 238). Such narratives exemplify the growing trend of feminist science fiction in Turkiye, with Sahmaran standing as a testament to this evolution. The 2023 Netflix film *Şahmaran* (Shamaran), a Turkish sff-drama series, intertwines the life of a psychology lecturer from Istanbul with the ancient lore of Şahmaran, a mythical figure in Turkish, Iranian, Iraqi, Kurdish, and Anatolian mythologies. This lecturer travels to Adana for work and decides to face her grandfather, who abandoned her mother years ago. While there, she becomes involved with a community worshipping Şahmaran, renowned for its wisdom and benevolence, and depicted as half-snake, half-human.

---

[6] Göbeklitepe, situated in the Örencik village of Şanlıurfa, a southeastern Turkish city, stands as the earliest and most extensive temple known in history. Recent discoveries have positioned it as the temporal zero point, pushing back the timeline of human history by over 12,000 years. This predates the majestic Egyptian Pyramids by 7,000 years and surpasses Stonehenge's age by 6,000 years.

This ageless creature, whose spirit is believed to pass to its daughter upon death, gets its name from the Persian "shah" for king and "maran" for snakes. Despite shah generally implying masculinity, Shahmaran is always portrayed as female in these myths. As a symbol of human and serpent fusion, often crowned and wearing a necklace, Şahmaran holds deep symbolic value in the folklore of the region. The series delves into this myth as the protagonist's life changes dramatically after meeting Maran, a mysterious man, while entangled in anticipation of an ancient prophecy involving Şahmaran.

Conclusion

In retracing the annals of Turkish science fiction literature, it is palpable how stories born from the Anatolian heartlands have long resonated with universal themes. These narratives have not just been mere escapism but are reflective of Turkiye's complex socio-political landscape and its ancient mysticism, harmonizing with the beckons of future technology. Stories spun by Turkish authors reverberate with the hopes, dilemmas, and aspirations of a nation at the crossroads of civilizations.

The richness of Turkish science fiction literature offers a tapestry of diverse stories, from speculative tales set in the bustling streets of Istanbul to futuristic visions inspired by the enigmatic landscapes of Cappadocia. Each story, steeped in Turkish tradition and ethos, provides a unique lens through which to view humanity's complexities and the universe's endless possibilities. As a groundbreaking collection in English, this anthology aims to serve as a bridge, connecting global readers to the heart of Turkish speculative storytelling. The myriad of voices, old and new, beckon with stories that are both timeless and deeply rooted in the country's unique heritage.

In conclusion, the stories in these pages are more than just fiction; they are a testament to Turkish authors' vibrant imagination and deep-rooted storytelling traditions. As you embark on this journey, we invite you to delve deep into the heart of Turkish science fiction literature. Let each story captivate, challenge your perceptions, and introduce you to a world where the past, present, and future intertwine beautifully. Embrace this invitation to explore and let the stories in this anthology open new vistas of imagination and wonder.

Works Cited

Açık, Yılmaz. *1980 Sonrası Türk Edebiyatında Bilimkurgu Romanları*. Nobel Yayın, 2021.

Andı, Fatih. "Türk Edebiyatında Jules Verne Çevirileri" *Edebiyat Araştırmaları I*, Kitabevi Yayınları, 2000, pp. 129-143.

Attebery, Brian. *Decoding Gender in Science Fiction.* Routledge, 2002.
Bayar, Zühtü. *Bilim Kurgu ve Gerçeklik.* Broy Yayınları, 2001.
Berktaş, Esin. "1940'lı Yıllarda Türk Sineması." *Kebikeç* 27, 2009, 231-250. https://kebikecdergi.files.wordpress.com/2012/07/14_esinberktas.pdf
Bülbül, İrfan. "İkinci Dünya Savaşının Türkiye'de Sosyal Hayata Olumsuz Yansımaları." *Yakın Dönem Türkiye Araştırmaları,* vol. 9, no.1, 2006 pp. 1-51.
Buran, Sümeyra. "Posthuman Mysticism: From the Zero Point of Humanity to the Parallel Worlds in *The Gift.*" *SFRA Review,* vol. 51, no. 4, 2021, pp. 232-239. https://sfrareview.org/2021/10/19/posthuman-mysticism-from-the-zero-point-of-humanity-to-the-parallel-worlds-in-the-gift/
Erdoğan, Nezih, and Dilek Kaya. "Institutional Intervention in the Distribution and Exhibition of Hollywood Films in Turkey." *Historical Journal of Film, Radio and Television,* vol. 22, no. 1, 2002, pp. 47-59. https://doi.org/10.1080/01439680220120282
Gürses, Öner. "Türkiye'de Bilimkurgu." *Edebiyatın İzinde Fantastik ve Bilimkurgu* içinde, edited by Seval Şahin, et.al, Bağlam Yayınları, 2015, pp. 56-62.
Güvemli, Zahir. *Sinema Tarihi: Başlangıcından Bugüne Türk ve Dünya Sineması.* Varlık Yayınevi. 1960.
Karadağ, Ayşe Banu. "Forming a Culture Repertoire in Our Translated Literary History by Means of Scientific Novels." *I.U. Journal of Translation Studies,* vol. 6, no.2, 2012, pp. 45-73
Korkmaz, Nurseli Gamze. "Rüyada Terakki ve Medeniyet-i İslamiyyeyi Rüyet - The Communitarian and Traditional Construction in the Envisioning Progress and Islamic Civilization in Dream" *Kelam Araştırmaları,* vol. 13, no. 1, 2015, pp. 521-531.
Reyhanoğulları, Gökhan. "Türk Edebiyatının İlk Bilim-Kurgu Öyküleri Ve Orhan Duru." *Turkish Studies - International Periodical For The Languages, Literature and History of Turkish or Turkic,* vol. 7, no. 3, Summer 2012, pp. 2183-2197.
Scognamillo, Giovanni, and Metin Demirhan. *Fantastik Türk Sineması.* Kabalcı Yayınevi, 1999.
Tokgöz, Ahmet İhsan.. *Matbuat Hatıralarım.* edited by Alpay Kabacalı, İletişim Yayınları, 1993.
Uğur, Veli. "Bilimkurguda Dişil Sesler ve Postmodernizmin İmkanları: Hayalet Kentin Kadınları'nda Alternatif Evrenler." *Bilimkurguyu Anlamak: Alt Türlere Eleştirel Yaklaşımlar.* edited by Cenk Tan, et al., Nobel Yayınları, 2021, pp. 299-321.
Uyanık, Seda. *Osmanlı Bilim Kurgusu: Fenni Edebiyat.* İletişim, 2013.
Yiğitler, Şener Şükrü. "Two Republican Science Fiction Stories: "Hülya Bu Ya..." And "Büyük Kukuriko"." *The Journal of Academic Social Science Studies,* vol. 24, Spring 2014, pp. 595-615,
Yıldız, İpek. "The Evaluation Of Novels 'Fennî Bir Roman Yahut Amerika Doktorları' and 'Rikalda Yahut Amerika'da Vahşet Âlemi' By Ahmet Mithat Efendi Within The Concept Of Education And Civilization." *Turkish Studies - International Periodical For The Languages, Literature and History of Turkish or Turkic,* vol. 7, no. 3, Summer 2012, pp. 2183-2197. Doi number:http://dx.doi.org/10.9761/JASSS2299

KILLING X

Algan Coşkun

The last thing I remember was his gun's annoying sound. The trigger cracked and made a grinding sound when pulled. I heard it, then all I could perceive was darkness. You expect to see some memories or a holy light or a flaming highway to hell, but let me give you a secret. When you face death, you see nothing but blinding darkness.

Then I just woke up. I was lying on a narrow bed. The ceiling was made of the crimson bricks you see with expensive suburban houses. This didn't look like our travel pod or what we call the "Tardis," which, yes, I know, is a bit cliché.

I didn't know what had happened to my friends. I just assumed they were all dead; otherwise, I would not have woken up here. I also had the courage to assume that I was lucky. I mean, he must have thought that I was dead or would not wake up at all.

I know I am bombarding you with tons of nonsense at once, but give me a second to catch my breath. My throat is as dry as sand. I looked around to find some water. Luckily, I found a jug and glass next to my bed. There was a newspaper under them. I forced myself to rise from bed and then realized that I was not alone. I counted seven other beds around the room. The clothes, the room, the picture of our target on the wall. ... I was still in 1937.

I checked myself to see where my bandages were. I had been shot in the head. The upper left side of my skull was missing. They had put in a metal plate to replace the bone. When I gently tapped the metal part, I heard the sound, but not through my ears. The tap echoed in my head as if it were a hollow tin box.

Sorry, I am talking too much and focusing on unimportant details instead of telling the story you care about. Let me drink this water first.

Where should I start? Hmm, the beginning should be proper, but we don't have much time, so I'll just talk about the crucial parts. In 2032, a Korean girl invented time travel. At the start, she was able to send small objects like pens back in time. It was nuts. Then she tried to send animals. Mice, dogs, monkeys, and that was it. She was hired by the UN secret service.

She was tasked to create a pod to carry some people back in time and then return them back again. She did it. She managed to create the Tardis. Even a moron like me was able to use it, but I was just a co-pilot. Our main pilot was a Belarusian named Aslan, which means "lion" in Turkish. He was our captain. Then your next question must be about who we were, right? We were handpicked soldiers from around the globe. Special operation types. We were the best six soldiers you could find, and Aslan was our captain.

I hear you asking what our mission was, right? Well, it was simple. We were sent to kill evil people throughout history and undo their works. Our first mission was to eliminate an Italian serial killer who was active during the 60s. A simple in and out. He was deleted from history, and so were his murders. One of his previous victims, who survived, became a famous singer. She even was a winner of the Eurovision song contest once.

After our success, we moved to more serious targets. Have you ever heard about the guy who killed Queen Victoria? I bet you did not. What about the lady who burned down all of New York and caused 23.000 deaths in 1952? That was a good one. Did you know that all of South America was once nuked and erased from maps thanks to Kennedy's carnage in 1964? I was the one who pulled the trigger, but please don't be mad. You did not see him after 1963.

Our last target was really big. You know, the big baddie, the ultimate evil. Short guy with a funny moustache. Our plan was simple. We would infiltrate his house, then kill him and run back to the Tardis. The usual. But how could we know that Aslan was a traitor? He was a fucking Nazi. As we landed on the outskirts of Berlin, he went back to check on the others while I was writing a report. Then I heard four shots. I knew something was off, so I pushed the red button out of reflex. Did not even think about the fact this was the self-destruct button. Then the door opened, and you know the rest. I woke up in a German hospital in 1937. I don't know how I survived, but I couldn't care less.

Just looked at the newspaper under the jug. What I saw was great. I was wrong. The date was 1938, and there was a photo of the failed art student. How long had I been sleeping? Aslan was standing next to him. The headline? Uber Deutschland started Operation Sea Lion. That's perfect; now I had to kill both of them before it was too late. I tried to stand up. Shit, my legs were trembling. Ok, let me look at the exact date. I was in a coma for seven bloody months.

Then I heard a voice. A nurse was coming with a tray. She looked surprised to see me awake. My German had been nearly perfect before the mission, but I still made some mistakes. Half of my head was missing, so I didn't think she would suspect. Anyway, I told her that I was hungry. Then she made me choke down some pills and went out to bring me something to eat. After seeing me devour the food, she called a doctor to see me. The doctor had a funny moustache – not like you-know-who – but it was funny in a unique way. He started asking some personal questions with too much what, who, and where included. I had to get out as soon as possible.

It was not hard to slip away. It was already sunset when I woke, so I just waited until night. Then I stole some clothes from my roommates and ran into the woods. There was a wallet in the jacket I had filched, as well as some money and an identity card. It was a spring night, and the fresh air made me feel alive again. All my muscles were stiff when I got out of the hospital, and with every step, I felt better and better.

When I arrived outside the city, the sun was rising, and I needed a place to sleep. The doctor could snitch on me. I saw a motel sign. It was a disgusting place, probably a love hotel, but the money I had was barely enough to cover a night. Plus, the receptionist didn't even ask about my identity.

Oh man, it was the best sleep I'd had for a long time, and I am saying that as a guy who slept nonstop for seven months. I took a shower and then went outside. It was time to get some information and money. I snuck into the kitchen and stole a knife before going out.

That night, I ate some delicious sausages at a pub. I loved that thing they made with cabbages. Sauerkraut, right? Also, the beer was supreme. I mugged a thug in the morning to expand my budget. Then I went to the local library to learn what had happened while I was sleeping. Aslan had come out of nowhere and had quickly risen into the second position of that man Taika Waititi made a movie about. This is not funny, but I also don't want to say his name here. From this point on, I will call him "X." However, I learned one more thing that gave me a target. Their operation base. X, Aslan, and all their top generals were stationed at The Hague.

It was time to go back to the hotel to sleep; I called it a night early because I had planned a trip the next day. Then, guess what happened? The thug I had mugged this morning showed up with some brown shirts. I counted them quickly. 5 vs 1. They had batons against my bread knife. The odds were against me, but I was not in the mood for running.

They were confident and underestimated me, so I played on that and started begging for my life. Never been good at acting, but they were worse about seeing through with their plan. I knelt while sneaking the knife out from my sleeve. One of the brown shirts grasped my hair and was preparing to punch my face, but I was faster. I just moved my head to the right, and he missed. This caught him off guard. I bit his wrist and pulled with all my might. I ripped out a mouthful of his flesh, and all he did was scream. I couldn't stand screaming, so I threw an uppercut. This time it was his turn to bite, but he bit his own tongue.

The others could not understand what was happening. I was sure that they hadn't even seen a real fight before. I jumped on another guy and stabbed him 4-5 times. Other brown shirts ran away, but the thug from earlier was too shocked. He was shaking and tried to escape, but it was too late. I kicked the back of his kneecap. I could smell the warm piss. Of course, he was begging for his life – what else could he do? But I did not show any mercy. Thanks to them, I had some fun, and the adrenaline made me remember how to fight.

Luckily, the guy I had bitten was carrying a Beretta, so I took it. Sleep was better that night. Yet I woke up early, grabbed some pastries for the road, and headed to the train station. It took me nearly a day and a half to get from Berlin to The Hague. Stations, trains, roads… all were full of soldiers. I jumped off at Delft. The Hague had to be under heavy inspection and did not want to push my luck further.

I went to the outskirts, and there were some small farms. I snuck into one of the barns and spent the night with some cows. They were really nice roommates. I woke up because of the noises coming from outside. A lady was talking in a panic. Scheisse, I didn't know Dutch, so could not understand what she was saying, but I heard two other voices speaking in German. They were preparing to check the barn. Long story short, I killed them both and grabbed their uniforms.

I found my way into The Hague. With the uniform, I was able to get close to the city center. I learned that my target was staying in the parliament building. However, it was heavily guarded. I had to make some plans to get in, but my stomach was making weird noises. I had to find something to eat before making any moves. Then I saw a sign: Dungelmann. Jumped in and was in heaven. It was a special charcuterie. I did not have much money; however, the owner was really afraid of saying no to a soldier.

When I was about to leave, the door opened. A bloody SS officer with skulls and medals came inside. I was petrified. Could not even salute properly. He called me to come closer. Then I realized the situation I was in. I gave him the most perfect salute he could imagine. He liked my form and smirked. Terrifying to see him smiling. Maybe he was on his way to burn a church with all the villagers. You never know.

Then he asked my name and regiment. I was prepared for this kind of question but had to find a proper excuse to be here. Instead, I told the truth. I told him that I was starving, then found myself here. Then he asked something strange. He asked me what I ate and liked the most. I told him that these meatballs were the most delicious things he could eat from here in Berlin. The most magical thing in my life happened. He told me to prepare a lunch box for six.

I was carrying two baskets while following him. I didn't even ask about the destination. Just followed. Then, slowly, we walked into a huge building with a lake view. We were heading to the parliament building.

We walked through a small gate to the backyard. We went into the building on the left. At the doors, the officer told me to drop my weapons. I gave all the guns to the guards, but they did not know I was carrying the knife I had stolen from the motel in my sleeve. Then we went upstairs, following the red carpet on the floor. Finally, we stopped in front of a big wooden door that was guarded by six soldiers. They had even installed put a machine gun. The officer told the guards to open the door, and they obeyed.

There was a long table in the middle of the room and some famous paintings on the walls. *Girl with a Pearl Earring. The Milkmaid.* Even *The Starry Night* was there. And around the table? It was like the Nuremberg trials. X was at the center, and his aces were all around. I panicked and lowered my eyes, but Aslan was not there. The SS guy told me to put the baskets down and leave. I knew that this was my golden ticket to the chocolate factory. You should have seen their faces when I pulled my knife and cut the throat of the SS officer open wide. I pulled the pistol from his belt. Some of them did not even realize what was happening. I shot them one by one, starting with X, of course. It was a clean headshot.

I knew that the door was about to open and soldiers would storm the room in a second. Then I would be mere target practice. I put the pistol into my mouth and prepared to pull the trigger. At that moment, I realized that something was off. I had killed five guys, but I had carried food for six. The last person had to be Aslan. I could not die before killing him.

I jumped over the table as the soldiers charged in. I took cover, and we exchanged some shots; however, their firepower was getting heavier. Then they brought in the machine gun. I would not survive that, so I had to find a better cover.

I used what was under my hand. Literally. I lifted X's body and made a meat shield from him. Bullets were tearing his body apart. Flesh and bone pieces were flying wild, and there was a bloody rain. All those beautiful paintings were covered in red. They stopped shooting after a minute. They thought nobody could survive that, and they were right. Nobody except me.

I don't know how long the gunfight took. The room was full of bodies, and more soldiers were about to come. I had minutes to think about something. I found one of the baskets and opened it. It was full of holes, but I saw a miracle. A bottle of wine was lying there. I opened it and drank as much as possible. The heat traveled through my body. It gave me a piece of calmness. Then I noticed a small door. It had never opened while I was here. I walked up to it and held the handle. Then I heard that annoying grinding sound. I jumped as bullets pierced the door. Aslan was inside. I knew that he would not open the door since he had the advantage. I had to take a risk. I knew that it was suicide, but I had to kill him. My life didn't have any value. I opened the door. Baamm.

I was lying on the floor, and he was standing still. He came closer and was shocked to see me. Told me that I should have stayed dead. The beautiful thing is that Aslan was a perfect sniper. I knew that he could shoot anything as long as he was able to see. When I opened the door, I had carefully shown my head to him, starting from the upper left side. Where they put a metal piece. Where Aslan had shot me before. Where Aslan had shot me now. I knew it was a gamble, but it paid off.

I just shot him. Did not even make a final confrontation. He did not deserve that. All he deserved was a bullet to the head. I shot him a few extra times to be sure. It was a beautiful end. I was ready to die since I was able to hear steps coming from the stairs. I looked at my hands and my torso. I was wearing a German uniform and was covered in blood. How could they know that I was the attacker? I just laid down next to bodies and waited. They carried me to the infirmary. It was easy for me to sneak away.

The war ended very quickly. Without X, the world did not enter into total war. The mission was successful in the end, yet I was stuck in 1938. It was not a bad time for me to live with all the information I had. I traveled around the globe and wrote novels.

Then I met with a special lady from Seoul and stayed with her. We had a son. He was a nerdy type, and I made him write some fantasy novels before there was even a proper genre. He had two beautiful daughters. The older one was good at art, and she became a painter. However, my other granddaughter was my favorite. I fed her with my stories. I told her the story of time-traveling soldiers who were assigned to kill X. She was hooked all the way and spent most of her life trying to invent time travel. Finally, she did it in 2032.

DEA EX MACHINA[1]

Arda Tipi

Translated by Elif Kut

It was fifteen years after the "resetting" when the miracle showed up in the sky, so our elders told us. Yet, we could hardly hold track of time. Only the days we could survive, and in those hours, we recalled who we were together. And that was all.

Never-ending disasters, environmental crises, famine, and eventually the pandemia paved the way for years of chaos that turned people hiding in bunkers into an underground colony while the deniers of the virus remained outside to harvest power and plunder out of all the mayhem, or so we were told. Our elders called them 'Zebs,' for they resembled zebanis[2] in appearance and behaviour.

"We didn't know what they had gained, but it was a fact that they had lost their humanity in every way. Over the years, the virus and chemical exposure transformed them into something else. They came with weapons, like a horde, and raided the colony in its tenth year, causing its dissolution. We, the survivors, split into groups, fled to the surface, and lost one another. And you... you were all born years after that when Mona Lisa appeared above us. It was a day to remember; having lost everything that made us human one by one, along with our hopes, a familiar face with a friendly smile came up in the sky that morning to shine a light on our darkest times and to remind us who we once were. A giant cloud was painted up in the sky! We didn't know how it happened or who did it. Maybe it was God's work. The miracle didn't survive long, but seeds of hope were already planted in our hearts before they vanished through the clouds..."

Toxic clouds on one side, Zebs on the other... Our days passed mostly in search of supplies, some fighting for them and some in hiding. We moved from one place to another, from any water source we could spot to ruined

---

[1] Altered version of Latin original 'Deus ex Machina: God out of a machine' to 'Goddess out of a machine' referring to the a.i. character, Gioconda. The term was coined from ancient Greek theatre, where an actor playing God descends onto the stage with the help of a cranelike machine as a contrived solution to irresolvable situations.

[2] Zabaniyah (Arabic, also Turkish) – also spelled Zebani – are the tormentors of the sinners in hell.

settlements, from forests of ashes to murky lakes, all with the hope of reaching the ocean that we didn't know the fate of... Years of raids that took lives, pillagings, diseases, and losses... That was the summary of our years...

***

I remember our last night in that ghost town up north. Noticing the approaching hallucinogenic toxin cloud early, we hurried off with the commune. In order to determine our new course, Leo's father, 'Captain,' who was ex-military, had picked up a recurring static signal during his routine radio scan. It was an S.O.S. call sent in Morse code. So we changed our route towards the signal's source. Hours later, we arrived at a steep, rocky area. Our vehicles were not well suited for these conditions, considering they were just some repaired scrap. After Captain and his men checked and secured the area, our stay was settled. The current food and water stock would keep us up for a couple of days – hopefully, until we found the static's main source.

***

At night, Leo and I were lying on our backs on the top of a scrap jeep, watching the crimson sky with our stomachs rumbling.

"You know, if the pandemia hadn't happened, we could have been there right now."

"Where?" I asked as I turned to him.

"There, in the stars," he said.

I looked up at the sky for a while, then snapped, "These are just fairytales that elders tell."

This time he turned to me and raised his voice, "What do you mean, so my mom was lying?!" grasping his silver space shuttle pendant, which she had given him as a gift.

Leo's mother, Katya, had been a scientist before the war. She used to tell us about artificial intelligence, robots, and space studies using robots. She had died some time ago from an illness she contracted after being injured in one of the Zeb attacks – so naturally, he hated them. It was not hard to understand his anger when it came to his mother.

"I didn't mean that..." as I was about to explain, his dad came and scolded us for making noise. Leo was about to weep with anger, but he could still keep cool. His quickened breath and the wetness in his eyes soon eased off like his clenched fist and faded into the haze of the night. We just lay there for a while, staring blankly at the sky. Feeling hungry and tired, we soon fell asleep. Nightmares followed one another. I woke up in terror. I heard

Leo talking in his sleep. In his dream, he seemed to be speaking to someone like he was awake. Before I could understand any word he was mumbling, I had fallen back to sleep.

As the sun was rising behind the hills, I woke up all stiff and started stretching. I slid down the jeep and headed for the water tank to wash up. I met Captain on my way.

"Morning, Captain," I greeted.

"Su, was Leo with you?" he asked hastily.

"No. He was gone when I woke up, and I thought he could be back at your tent."

Captain, whom I've rarely seen smiling, glowered fully after my response.

"What the hell is wrong with this kid, dammit!" he muttered and called for the guards. One guard said that he had seen him walking away to the toilet two hours ago, but he wasn't sure if he had come back. Captain complained that he couldn't find his infrared goggles anywhere and suspected that Leo might have taken them, which worried everybody. Our search around the campsite failed to find him, so we decided to form a team and conduct a search. I was allowed to join them for once. I packed my gear and followed the convoy, which was composed of ten people.
From the ridge, upon which we arrived after a bumpy, thirty-minute walk, the scene below was quite strange. We didn't know how or why, but a group of approximately twenty zebs was lying covered in blood on the ground at the opening of a large cave. Three men went down, under the protection of snipers, to check on the zebs. They were all dead, with blood coming out of their big, weird-shaped ears. Then they headed into the cave, which was dim yet bright enough to see the tire tracks of long-gone trucks. We walked down to join the men and saw that "signature" on mud for ourselves. I noticed something buried in it. I kneeled and pulled it out, it was Leo's scrap cable wristband. As I handed it to Captain, eyebrows knit, he ordered us all to get back to the camp and take the fastest cars for tracing the zeb horde. Alas, he, as well, knew they were unable to climb through the rocks.

***

The loss of his son had hardened the Captain's attitude towards the mutants. We started assaulting their convoys and settlements whenever we had the advantage; with the hope of finding out about Leo's fate, we took captives and tortured them.

Two years later, in another raid, we were faced with a situation that we had not encountered before. Among the zebs, we had never come across any one of them that we could identify as a child – until now. Though they generally travel riding mutant animals or trucks, a small group of walkers came our way and was looted on the Captain's orders, even though they showed no signs of aggression. The moment when we searched the boxes and chests they were carrying, a high-pitched, animal-like voice came from inside one of them. What we heard was indeed a baby's cry. We were shocked when we opened the chest; it was the first time we had seen a zeb baby. In that vulnerable state, it didn't look as ugly as the grown-ups. I even wanted to hold him in my arms. A guy from the group was about to point a gun at him, but as an instinctive reflex, I put my knife against his throat. The captain himself came and lowered the barrel of the gun with his hand.

I carried the baby in my arms until I returned to our current settlement and then transferred it to Umai, one of the most experienced mothers in the commune. She knew what to do. She named it "Can"[3] as soon as she held it in her arms, without even noticing its gender...

Over the years, Can grew up with us like a normal person – if the idea even still applied to us. I don't know if this had anything to do with it, but the Captain's aggressive attitude had also transformed into an exploration-oriented course of action. I even had a say in the hierarchy by being at his side as his assistant. This way, even though it took longer for us to reach the ocean, it was much easier.

The first day we reached the coast was unforgettable. It wasn't exactly the blue vastness we had seen in the pictures, of course, but we could still smell freedom and hope through the wind blowing on our faces. Even Can, who had just learned how to speak, joined us with his crowing, "Sea! It's the sea!"

***

Time was flowing more calmly and monotonously for us now. There wasn't much left from the ocean that our elders knew, but the salty soil was quite suitable for growing certain root vegetables. Some shellfish species that had survived were also there to meet our protein needs without poisoning, as long as they were not consumed too often. Close to the end of our daily work, one evening, we were playing with Can on the seemingly endless beach, accompanied by gray waves. Affected by the hot and cloudy climate, others relaxed on the rotten seaweed.

I saw mother Umai limping towards us. I went and took her arm, and we

---

[3] Can (Persian, also Turkish) means life, the soul.

sat on the ground at a point near the sea. She took a deep breath and said, while coughing, "Despite all its lifelessness, it's a summer day…" and then began humming a tune, closing her eyes. We were immersed in her voice. Apart from the waves that whooshed to the rhythm of her music, there was another accompaniment rising behind us. What we heard was a wuthering from the hills and sounds of metal mingling with it. We turned back in panic. Everyone from the commune was running to the beach with their guns. Seconds later, a roaring silhouette covered the hills along the coast. After quite a long time, we were faced with zebs again. They had found us. Their rumbling stopped after a while. We saw a group coming down from the hills to the beach; strangely, they were walking toward us. The captain stepped forward to the people who had their guns pointed at the incoming zebs and signaled with his hand not to shoot. It should have been their leader walking in front of the group, but he looked somehow different; his body structure was like ours, except that he was painted blue from head to toe, unlike the others. As I got closer, I noticed something familiar about him. I ran to the Captain. He had tears in his eyes, and I could see him gulping behind his white beard. When they arrived, a strange feeling prevented me from turning my head toward them. I was afraid of what I might see. When I turned my face, I saw a pair of dull eyes staring right into mine. I don't know if this could be called facing your fear; I recognized the owner of those 'dead' eyes. A name spilled hoarsely from the Captain's old lips: "Leo…?" Hearing this, the figure slowly turned his blue eyes towards the man who had once been his father. There was no expression on his face. I didn't know what to say… except for a louder repetition of the same name" "Leo?!"

Not even a single sound was heard on the beach, neither from the mutants nor from us. Meanwhile, Can, who was hiding behind Mother Umai, came running to me and held my hand. The zebs, who had remained silent, started shouting the moment they saw him. That roar turned into a rhythmic chant. It was like they were reciting his name in a sacred manner – like it was divine. Leo approached and knelt in front of Can, clutching the child's head with his palms. Then he took off his space shuttle pendant and put it on Can's neck. He stood up again, passing us by with slow steps, and headed towards the sea. When he reached the sea, he turned around, raised his hands in the air, and called out with all his might, again in their bizarre accent. In unison, they repeated what he said. Then he turned back to the sea and continued walking until he had passed the water level. All the Zebs followed in groups along the beach. The clanging of metal they wore resounded in the air. We were all watching them with astonishment.

"Leo, stop!" I shouted and wanted to run after him to save him, but Captain grabbed my arm firmly. At that moment, I realized that Can was also clinging to my leg. I got down on my knee and hugged him. We just watched the sea devour an entire horde of zebs within minutes.

***

That day had been the weirdest day of my life. I couldn't even be sure if it was real or not. After putting Can to sleep, I went to the beach and laid down. Because the weather was clear, I could almost see the entire Milky Way – a name I had learned from Katya. I looked up at the stars and remembered the last night I had spent with Leo. "He said we could have been there," I muttered to myself.

"He was right, Su…"

I was startled and jumped up. There was enough moonlight to see clearly, but there was no one around.

"Calm down, Su, I'm not a threat."

I thought the voice was coming from inside my head, but I was sure it was not a delusion.

"Who is this?" I asked, frightened.

"I'm Gioconda. The integrated artificial intelligence probe you sent to Mars for terraforming thirty-two years ago."

"I don't understand, but where are you right now?"

"I'm in your ear."

"I must be going crazy…" I said to myself.

"No, you're not crazy. Please let me explain."

"…"

"We lost contact with you for a while after we were sent to Mars. Later, I realized the cause of the disconnection was the aftermath of your war. I proceeded with my task as planned. As the last step of the mission, I was instructed to report the positive results to you when they were obtained; however, the connection could not be re-established. It was a complex problem. Then, I found the solution. By recycling my hardware, I split myself into much smaller machines. I had developed over time and reached the technological level where I could return to Earth in much, much, much smaller components. The painting that was seen in the sky years ago, La Gioconda, by its popular name Mona Lisa, was indeed projected onto the clouds by me and was actually my creator's visual password that she had been using on me. Getting no response, I started probing around the Earth, searching for her, but my efforts did not yield any results. In the meantime, I realized that the Earth itself needed to be terraformed. I am currently commanding five hundred microbot units from orbit, each of which, like the one in your inner ear, has various mechanical functions besides being able to fly. I explained all these to my previous host, Leo, the syngeneic of my creator. The night I first communicated with him in his sleep, I pointed out that I was physically ready to follow his commands to help humans and the planet Earth. Instead, it turned out that he used "us" to dominate the species you call the "Zebs." In the morning, when we came across the zebs while searching for the group of people who had sent the distress signal, he asked me to kill the armed ones. And, as I entered their bodies through their ears and carried out the command, the others thought he was their divine leader with some kind of "magical powers." Thus, Leo adopted this role and held all the zebs under his rule for years until he totally lost touch with reality. He promised his people, who believed in his miracles(!), that they would cross the sea and finally exert dominance in new lands. Even though he knew I couldn't be of help with this..."

"Because you couldn't help them breathe in water..."

"Of course, I couldn't do that. Even if it is artificially generated, the mind, throughout its own evolution, reaches a level where it can judge right and wrong. Theirs would be a recurrence of the old world. I, on the other hand, have chosen a new Earth where you will be its mother."

Standing astonished, I looked up at the sky to see if there were any hallucinogenic toxin clouds, maybe even a tiny one. There was none. Just the stars... They kept shining on us.

TERROR OF EMPATHY

Belma Fırat

Translated by Orhan Tuncay

"This won't work, my dear. That's the casual service tray. Is that the way I showed you? You should take out the silver one. These napkins are not folded correctly. Börek looks good but be careful, don't scatter while cutting, ok?" She stepped out of the kitchen, headed towards the bedroom, and checked herself in the mirror. Her bun was all right. She had it sprayed amply at the hairdresser to keep it tight. She was invited to a dinner party tonight, so she needed to get through the day without messing up her hair. The blouse looked fashionable. Was the skirt a little bit tight? *No, no, it is all right,* she thought. She walked to the living room and checked the surface of the coffee table with her finger. *No dust, good.* The doorbell rang. "Gizem, get the door," she called out. Gizem's slippers were heard hitting against her heels. Walking through the hall to welcome her guest, Lale glanced at the antique mirror on the wall to check her image one last time.

"Welcome, dear. You're right on time, as always. Gizem, help Ms. Jülide with her fur coat. It is very cold outside, isn't it?"

"Tell me about it. It's freezing. We're only a couple of blocks away. It did not even take five minutes to come here. Still, I dressed warm enough, just in case. I get sick easily when it's cold."

"I wonder if Ayşen will make it," Lale said. "Maybe her husband will send her with the driver. The roads are covered with ice and snow, after all."

"My dear Lale, I guess you haven't heard about what happened to Ayşen. I don't think she will be coming today."

"I haven't heard. She did not call to cancel either. I wonder. What has happened? Sorry, you are still standing there. Let's get inside, and you can tell me more."

They entered the stylish living room where, at first glance, one could recognize that every piece was bought with taste and furnished elaborately. They headed towards the two wood-carved, creme-colored bergères in front of the bay window to the right of the maroon sofa. Ms. Jülide started to explain about Ayşen in haste as she settled in her armchair.

"Haven't you heard anything, honey? Ayşen found a pair of black fishnet stockings and a red g-string in Mr. Nevzat's drawer. Can you believe it?"

"Oh my god! How did you learn about this, for god's sake?"

"Honey, their maid and ours turned out to be from the same hometown. They get together on their days off. When Ayşen found these stockings, panties, and whatnot, she lost her mind. All hell broke loose in the house, and the maid heard everything in her room, word-for-word. Naturally, it is impossible for Ayşen to accept the situation. The case was reported to the police. They have been questioning everyone, starting from the employees working in her husband's company. Do you know the association for homosexuals called Lambda? They have even gone to their place and searched everywhere."

"What do you mean? These so-called terrorists of empathy or whatever – are they suspecting them? Did they stab him with a needle too?" Lale asked Jülide.

"Her husband is defending himself with that claim," Jülide replied. "He argues that the incident happened in a nightclub. He says that it was a business dinner, but that's a lie for sure. At some point, he went to the restroom. As he was coming out, he felt a sting at the back of his neck. He said, 'It happened in the blink of an eye. I could not even see who did it.' At first, he tried to keep it a secret, but he was caught by his wife. Now he is rejecting any treatment. He told his wife, 'From now on, I'm going to be this way. You can divorce me if you want.'"

"Well, the biter gets bit," Lale said. "You know, we have a summer house close to theirs. He screwed every presentable woman in that place until there were none left. Now, can you imagine him swaggering in his g-strings?"

"Oh, don't say that. Let's not lie, we all let our husbands get away with petty flings, but this is unbearable. What has Ayşen done to deserve this? Poor thing, I really pity her. Oh dear, please, you didn't hear this from me."

"Of course, Jülide, my dear, these are family matters, after all. In that case, we can't expect Ayşen to come this Thursday. What should we do, cancel the bridge?"

"We'll have to cancel if we can't find a fourth," Jülide replied. "Well, you had a friend, Rana. You said she's a newbie but very eager to learn. She has been taking lessons. Can't we just call her? With a little bit of help? What do you say?

"Oh honey, if you just knew," Lale sighed. "I heard our dear Rana left her house one afternoon last week to go to the gym. She returned home two hours later wearing a shalwar and a headscarf. First, the security did not let her in. They were asking, 'Who are you looking for?' and she was looking at them blankly. The security did not understand her at all. Luckily, one of them recognized her after he looked carefully. They notified her husband at once. They took her home, but she could not tell what had happened to her. Later, they found out that she was talking in Kurdish."

"Oh no…"

"Oh yes, indeed! Well, their janitor's wife was half-Kurdish. She spoke Kurdish a little bit. They called her for help so that Rana could tell them what had happened to her."

"Well, how did it happen, then?" Jülide asked.

"Like I said. She went to the gym. At the entrance, just as she was getting out of her car, a woman who looked like a beggar approached her. Rana pitied her and wanted to help. As she was taking her purse out of her bag, the woman poked her neck with a syringe. The rest is unnecessary details. In two hours' time, our dear Dame De Sion graduate Rana was gone, turned into a Kurdish peasant."

"Oh my gosh!" Jülide cried.

"Yes, darling. Not a word in Turkish. Now, a Turkish teacher goes to their home for two hours every day – would you believe that? Just like a bad joke."

"What a pity; I feel sorry for her," said Jülide. "We were not close, but you had introduced us at your sister's wedding last year. What a pretty and flashy woman she was."

"Yes, she was." Lale approved. "Now, can you imagine her coming to bridge as a fourth in her headscarf? Sans atout, coeur, pique[1] and so on and so forth."

"Oh dear, don't make fun of it."

"You're right," Lale nodded. "I lost it for a second. The news and rumors spreading around are so unbelievable that now I'm joking about it. Honey, you see, anything can happen to any of us when such a curse is circling around. We've got to be very careful. I'm mostly worried about my girl. My son is still too young – we postponed kindergarten, but Yasemin is outside every day. She's a little bit headstrong, you know. Her father bought her a car as a present after she got accepted to college. A nice Honda hatchback, but she's not driving it. She says she likes fresh air and prefers to take the ferry instead. I'm scared to death. I warn her every day to look over her shoulder and avoid crowds. You're lucky, your kids have all grown up and got on with their lives already."

---

[1] No trump, heart, spade.

"Of course, you're right," Jülide replied. "At least there's tighter security at most workplaces."

"Selçuk got more security cameras installed in his company," said Lale. "They don't let anybody in. I swear, they even searched me when I go there."

"Sweetie," Jülide replied, "there's no escape when evil is planning to find you. I have a friend at the tennis club – you don't know her. Her husband is a partner in a hardware store chain. As I heard, they have not been letting anyone in, including customers and personnel, without strict searching. Yet, somehow, someone managed to sneak a syringe in. Her husband turned into someone else like night and day, in a single moment. He gave away all his shares dirt cheap and donated the earnings to charity organizations. After that, he bought a cheap apartment on the outskirts of Küçük Bakkalköy and opened a small hardware shop two streets away."

"What are you saying? Well, what about his wife – what did she do?"

"What could she do? At first, she packed her bags and went to her mother's mansion in Vaniköy. But she has a son. The father would not let him go. So, after a while, the poor woman had to return back home to her son so that he was not ruined. The guy took his son out of private school and signed him up for a public school in the heights of the Maltepe district. It turns out that this high school is known to be a communist hole. The father was die-hard about it and did not listen to any objections. 'My son will not live in a fancy mansion. He will share the same class with kids of workers and, from now on, he will be growing up understanding the reality of life and learning by bitter experience,' he said."

"Oh, how tragic!"

"Don't ask," said Jülide. "Both the mother and her son have been miserable. The boy is a sophomore in high school, and he has university admission tests coming up. The boy has been complaining, saying that his father ruined his future. So his mother registered him at a famous prep course in Bağdat Street – I can't recall the name. They told his father he earned a scholarship for achievement. What a lie; of course, the grandma is paying for it. Anyway, as they say, every cloud has a silver lining. As far as I heard, the son had been a lazy bum in private school. Whenever I was at the tennis club, he was there. Not even playing tennis. He was hanging out with girls. After all these events, he went all-in, working hard, I heard. Well, he has to; after all, going abroad for university education is beyond his dreams now."

"God forbid. If only you knew – I feel terrified, so terrified, when I hear these kinds of things. See how astonished I was: I could not even serve you a cup of tea."

"Gizem, could you serve the tea now?" Ms. Lale called out towards the kitchen. Then she continued, "My dear Jülide, I don't understand how this works. Someone stabs you with a syringe, and instantly you start thinking and feeling exactly like them? How could this happen? There are many programs on TV debating about this – all these scientists, experts, and so forth – but still, they can't explain how a person's feelings and state of mind can be condensed into an injectable solution. How can someone change suddenly when they are injected?"

"I swear I don't either. However, there was an interesting program on TV the other night. The guest was a psychologist. Happens to be the best cognitive behavioral therapist in Turkey. Of course, she had nothing to say about the medical aspect of the matter, but she was analysing the subject from the point of its relationship between thoughts, emotions, and behaviour. She said these terrorists were aiming to influence our emotional reactions by changing people's thoughts and, as a result, affect our social behaviour and conduct. When someone else's state of mind captures us; naturally, our thoughts and perspectives will change. Plus, there's another dimension of the subject matter regarding our social circle and families. For example, when someone close to you goes through this, it creates a strong feeling of empathy. Some social issues that you only read about in the newspapers and that normally seem remote to you inevitably become a part of your life. As a result, with time, the structure of your thought process changes as well. She had a lengthy explanation of this. Actually, it was an interesting program."

"The police are falling behind as well. The situation is out of control. We can't even step out of the house with peace of mind," Lale complained.

"Did you see the statement by the chief director of public security in today's newspaper?" Jülide asked.

"No, I haven't read today's paper yet. Gizem, will you bring the newspaper, darling?" Lale called out.

Gizem, the petite brunette beauty, brought today's paper to her lady in no time.

"Tea will be ready in five minutes, ma'am."

"Okay, darling. Be careful not to pour it too strong, all right? Ms. Jülide likes her tea lighter. Don't you, honey?"

Ms. Lale browsed through the headlines on the front page quickly. She started reading out loud when she found the news she was looking for in the upper right corner.

"Let's see what this says, my dear: 'A press conference was held to relieve the public. *Not a single cop will go home until all terrorists of empathy are apprehended. May the public be assured,* Police Chief of Staff Tahsin Sercan said. *Today, measures to prevent the actions of terrorists who call themselves Empaths will be discussed at an emergency meeting attended by the Prime Minister at the Department of Security,* Sercan stated.' Oh dear, always the same familiar explanations. Nothing will come out of this, in my opinion. Wait, here's another one: 'The number of Saturday Mothers[2] has tripled. A group of activists among the mothers and relatives of missing people carried a banner saying, *Our children are not lost. They're with us, but we also suffer from the grief of losing a child.*'"

Ms. Jülide's eyes filled with tears.

"What kind of a mean soul can inject grief of losing a child into a mother's heart?" Lale cried.

"What kind of empathy is this?" Jülide replied. "One has to be cruel and emotionless to attempt to force somebody else to experience this feeling. This is a mother's child we're talking about – is there anything worse?"

"This has gotten out of hand!" Lale exploded. "This can't merely be handled by the police force. They should instate martial law. Complete lockdown. They should send in the troops and search every house, one-by-one, until they catch each and every one of them."

They went silent, shaken by the desperate eyes of women reaching out to them through a picture in a newspaper. These women, who had been stabbed with needles that turned them into mothers of missing children, were writhing in pain from grief stemming from an unexplainable source, despite having embraced their children, their boys, and girls thousands of times. Thankfully, at that very moment, they were relieved of this mental trauma when Gizem entered the room, holding a silver tray, carrying tea in sparkling crystal glasses that enhanced its charm, and Börek, roasted to golden color, placed on elegant, eye-catching English porcelain plates.

"Gizem, darling, just in time. We felt so demoralized, didn't we, dear Jülide? Now, let me give you a taste of Gizem's börek. Gizem has been with us for only two months, but she has learned our ways quite well."

"Lale, dear, I'd rather not. We've been eating healthily these days."

"Oh, don't say that honey, this is very light. It has no butter, and the cheese is low-fat. Last year I was seeing a dietitian and got the recipe from her. Let me write it down for you. It is so easy and practical. Gizem, bring

---

[2] Saturday Mothers/People: Mothers and people who search for answers to clarify what happened to their missing children and relatives who have come together against the disappearance of people in custody during the state of emergency. They gather every Saturday at noon at Galatasaray Square in İstanbul for a silent, peaceful sit-in and protest against the disappearances under custody and unidentified murders.

me a pen and a piece of paper from Yasemin's room."

In order to forget about the demoralizing news a little bit, they enjoyed comfort in taking sips of the bergamot-flavored tea and bites of the pastry.

"Ma'am, could you come here, please?"

"Ah, they're all the same, Jülide. All I asked for was a pen and a piece of paper."

Just as Ms. Lale was getting up to go to Yasemin's room, Gizem entered with haste and handed her a piece of paper.

"Where's the pen?"

But when Ms. Lale glanced at the paper, she saw it was covered in writing. The thick font of the headline pierced her heart.

Union of Empathy

We, The Union of Young Empaths, hereby declare that we will continue our actions until every citizen of this country becomes an individual who understands and feels empathy for at least one other fellow. Our fundamental principles are...

Ms. Lale could not keep on reading. Her face turned pale. Her hands started shaking. Two of her hair strands loosened from her tight bun and fell on her forehead, covered in sweat. Upon hearing the sound of a key turning in the lock, she lifted her head as if waking from a dream. It had to be Yasemin. She suddenly got up after staring blankly at her worried guest. She rushed to the door as fast as her high heel slippers would let her. She grabbed her daughter by the collar of her coat as she was getting inside. She was almost a carbon copy of her youth; however, she did not know who her girl was anymore.

"What have you done to us? Why? Didn't we make all kinds of sacrifices for you? Sent you to top-notch schools and provided the best opportunities we could? Did we expect anything from you other than being a good child? Tell me, what did we do wrong? Is it me, or am I the problem? I couldn't be a good mother to you? Tell me. What did I do wrong? Tell me!"

From that moment on, Yasemin could not listen to anything any longer. She tried to speak in between Ms. Lale's strident, high-pitched cries that became more and more incomprehensible as her tone went higher. "Mom!" she said. "Mom!" "Listen!" she said. "Mom! you're not listening to me!" She was holding her liquified emotions tightly in a syringe in the pocket of her coat as they grew deeper and deeper, finally reaching the point of explosion like a volcano, her voice fading within her mother's high-pitched screams. Yasemin exploded at last; her inner feelings were out of the bottle. Yasemin swiftly moved her hand out of her pocket and stabbed her mother in the neck with the needle, injecting her red hot boiling internal rebel. Then she said: "Mom! You've got to understand!"

PROXIMUS

Bora Keskin

One for the Books

"We might be getting drawn into a trap, boss. Let's head b–" This was the last thing I heard from Barmeley. He wasn't the talkative type, but his actions would tell you much more than his words. I could be seeing him and the others today if only I could've known beforehand what hid inside that place. The old ones always told me that mourning over the past and what has been done is futile, but I don't believe this will ever be possible after what I've been through. But, oh well, you now want to know what has happened to my men and me, and I won't be holding back the truth just because it is hard for me to talk about. We will have to travel back two years for the events that unfolded on that day. I will be recording this log in secret; then, it will be promptly put back on some dusty shelf. For the person who finds this log, good luck listening. You will need it.

Two years ago, the Chelyan Satellite Planet was in low orbit.

I woke up to the annoying vibrations of my watch. After some crew members started fumbling and using the limited light our ship had to offer, I managed to stand upright in my seat. I formed some semblance of balance after a few steps. Checking my surroundings, I could pick out a few of my men's faces through the dark. Barmeley, Gustav, and Jack were sleeping close together. Even though he couldn't be seen, Sam's distinct snoring also gave away his location. Alex and Ethan were probably next door, studying for the academy exam; they had newly joined us at the time, and, just like all the newcomers, they still had faith in the education system.
A blinking light on the screen to my right drew my attention. I read the text while shuffling my hair with my hands. The panel indicated the following: "Potential arrival point found, Chelyan Satellite Planet. Surface metal density high, human-like civilization possibility."

I was startled by the hydraulic door to my back. It was Robin. "Sir, I hope you are awake, would you care for a report from the bridge?" he said in a gentle tone.

As always, his kindness was enough to put a smile on my face. "Go ahead, what's up?" I said in return.

Robin cleared his throat and went on to give the report. "For the last week, our scans haven't been able to find a planet of suitable materials to justify a landing. If you remember, Sir, we upgraded our armor kits after the last tour. Of course, this does not help the many debts we have. Just recently, our scanners identified a planet that contains a high amount of surface metals. Even if we are not going to land on it, I suggest we take a closer look to get a good scan of its surface and such."

I moved my hand to my newly grown beard and asked, "Why didn't you do that before talking to me?"

Robin looked at me with a strange face. "Sir, we will have to enter the atmosphere in order to scan. It will be a bumpy ride, so personnel has to be awake throughout the entrance sequence."

I nodded. "Suppose you're right. Better to not have to deal with casualties."

Robin looked at me after busying himself with the panel for some time. "We are all set here, Sir. Ready to launch on your command."

I nodded in acceptance. "Setting up the simulated assistance route was quite enough. Leave the rest to me."

He arranged some more stuff on the panel and gave me approval with a thumbs up. Not wanting to waste any more time, I quickly grabbed the controller of the ship and got our vessel into orbit by following the automated route.

"We're in a stable orbit; you may start the scans soon as you are ready," I told Robin as I turned to him, my hands still on the controls.

He put his magic to work, and a map of the surface appeared on the screen. After a short talk with Robin, I decided that it would be best to get boots on the ground to take a look at the buildings.

I pressed the button of the microphone above the panel. "Planet looks good enough to warrant a field trip, people. Beginning to land."

Our most experienced, Logano, spoke through the comms. "We won't be coming back empty-handed this time, right boss? Would like to remind you it was I who saved us all from the people you were in debt to last time, that's all."

I sighed; I was quickly picking up speed and nearing the surface. I held the controller with one hand and pressed the mic button with the other. "Of course, I remember, Logano, but can't presume anything before we touch the surface."

I got some muttering as an answer. As the planet's surface began to get big enough to cover our whole field of view, we started shaking because of the atmosphere. Most planets like this known to humanity had lost all life and their atmospheres: they had become desert planets in the war between The Confederation Army, composed of many nations, and the Veritani, their invaders. As such, the remnants of humanity only had one solution; they chose to build large life domes on planets that could provide them resources to sustain life, albeit an artificial one.

We landed, and my men were ready with full kits waiting for me. I grabbed the rifle Jack offered me and slung it around my back. I pointed to the gate to have it opened, and we exited the ship. Besides the slight wind, there wasn't much at first glance — nothing different than the countless desert planets that we'd been to before. A few metal parts, screws, and hydraulic pistons were scattered here and there as we walked. After we got reasonably far away from the ship, I made my way to the top of a sand dune and beckoned to Logano.

When he arrived, I held my hand open and asked, "May I borrow your binoculars for a sec?"

Logano stood still for a second, then took the binoculars out of the cargo bag on his waist. Looking around, I noticed a rising structure at the horizon of this sea of sand and metal fragments. Next to it was a small sandstorm, which was slowly moving along.

I pointed at the structure. Still holding on to the binoculars, I pushed the radio button on my armor. "There is a structure closely resembling a building in that direction; we will go in and investigate. If there's nothing, we take as much metal as the ship can carry, then share the profit as usual. Logano, we will split into two teams. One will provide security while the other goes in. Move."

The sandstorm really picked up as we moved on, but we could still see each other thanks to the powerful lights on our suits. When we got nearer to the structure, I had a small chat with the team's only engineer, Barmeley, who said that an electric saw was all that was required. As the place looked abandoned, we had no restrictions on how to approach the situation. While Logano's team was entering, I started watching them via the screen on my forearm. At first, as they moved, they only had to check angles and reposition mutually, but things changed as they moved into the main hall. Dark blue creatures with almost jelly-like bodies fled to the darker corners of the hall.

"Sam and Gustav, take cover near that pillar. Jack, Barmeley, you're with me. I haven't got the faintest idea about these creatures, so watch your sectors. You saw that too Walla-" Logano was interrupted by Sam shooting one of the creatures.

"What the hell are you doing? You better have a good explanation ready!" screamed Logano.

Sam looked at Logano with fear; he was trembling with his arms closely wrapped around his rifle. "That thing touched me. It showed me. Showed me too much. Had to end it."

Gustav put his hand on his waist. "What do you mean, it showed you? What are you even –" This time, he was interrupted by the sight of a fist-sized hole in Sam's chest. My men took cover and returned fire. Metallic skeletons resembling robots were pounding our cover with their fusion rifles. Gustav tried to help Sam, but they were both shot.

"We are pulling back, cover yourselves!" shouted Logano, and they retreated. They sealed shut the door leading to the main hall. We were all looking at each other in shock: what had just happened in there?

From Whence They Came

I put my hand over the radio. "Stay where you are, we are coming to back you up." I turned around and looked at my men. "Ethan and Alex, you'll cover the rear. Robin, Latif, you're with me. Move!" We entered through the door and carefully worked our way to Logano's position.

I kneeled next to him. "I don't have any idea about what's happening here, but there is no point in losing any more people. I don't want this place to become a grave for us. Gather your men; we are leaving." The men quickly left their positions and formed up. We moved back toward the entrance, but there was nothing – only darkness and walls. We were sure that it was the entrance since the equipment we had brought in was still there, but the door had somehow become a wall.

Jack got closer to the wall and felt around to find the door. He gave up after some time and muttered audibly, "Door literally vanished as if it never existed."

I shook my head, "No idea Jack; the only thing I know is that we need to keep searching for a way out.

Barmeley's voice was heard over the radio. "Boss, if you would agree, let us proceed down the corridor next to you. If I'm not mistaken, it's an access tunnel. That means it leads to some place or something that is checked regularly. Can't think of anywhere else to go in this darkness. Or we could just break light discipline."

I denied the latter firmly with my hand. "No, no, no lights except enemy contact. We will go there, Barmeley. Show us the way."

Barmeley led us to the access tunnel. After passing through an L-shaped tunnel, we ended up in what looked like a huge depot, which was lined with windows to the world outside. I saw combat bots hung up on industrial racks.

We split up to search for the place. Suddenly, the windows burst into pieces as metal panels took their place, denying us any source of light. I could feel vibrations in the ground, alerting me to the fact that something other than us was moving too.

I shouted on the radio as I was gunning it towards the door we had come from. "Back! Pull back! We are too exposed here; we'll hold them at the doorway!"

We held our ground for some more, and at some point, all the bots just retreated. Bigger combat bots that we had seen earlier in the main hall entered the depot, and one launched a rocket at our position, creating a huge gap in the wall. Fortunately, no one was there, so it created a better shooting spot for Ethan and Jack.

Barmeley sprinted back to the rear, and I put my hand on the radio. "Barmeley! Where the hell do you think you are going?"

"Just you wait, boss. We can only beat them this way. Just you wait," said Barmeley, his voice faint from fatigue.

I shook my head in discomfort. "Whatever you're gonna do, do it fast. Next shot will hit home." I turned and shouted, "And, you guys, start shooting back! Let's have at least the smaller ones under cover."

The team set their rifles on full automatic and started letting out short, controlled bursts. The bigger bots weren't affected too much, but at least they weren't getting closer. The smaller ones had already taken cover, but the bigger bots were still pounding our cover with laser fire.

Barmeley approached from the rear with carts full of equipment. "I've got it, boss. Give me two men, and I'll rid you of these bots."

I pointed at Ethan and Jack, who were shooting from the gap in the wall. "Ethan and Jack are yours; Alex and Robin will take their places."

Barmeley briefed them, and they started unpacking the equipment. When they were done, we had an anti-tank launcher and a tracked shield that could move on its own.

"We'll have Ethan and Jack behind the shield, boss. Two more will carry the launcher. We'll set it up when we are in range."

Barmeley's idea was going to save us all. They moved in with the shield, but the shooting got more intense as they went on. Ethan and Jack moved away from the shield to set the launcher up, but a bot spotted Jack and shot him in the torso, resulting in Ethan dropping the launcher and dashing back to the shield. Alex sprinted towards Ethan and told him something, then they picked up the launcher again. They were able to take a few shots and disable most of the heavier bots, but were incinerated by a thermal grenade. Robin, now all alone, sprinted back to our position. As the bots retreated, we also pulled back. The air smelled like burnt meat.

A Late Revelation

"This must be a damned joke! We, a full team of grown men, are dying away in this labyrinth of a place," said Logano as he turned one of the corpses over.

Just as he finished his sentence, the whole depot started to tremble as a deep but powerful voice spoke. "What did you think it was? If this wasn't staged, you would've all died before setting foot in here."

Everyone raised their weapons towards what they thought was the source of the sound. I asked out of curiosity, "Who are you? What did you want from my men?"

A voice could be heard laughing lightly. "What did you want from us? I've got the answers to your questions; enter through the door I've opened for you."

While we were looking at each other in doubt, Barmeley spoke through the radio. "We might be getting drawn into a trap, boss. Let's head b –" His words were cut off as a bullet impacted his head.

As Barmeley's lifeless body collapsed to the ground, the door behind him closed shut and locked.

The voice sighed audibly and continued talking: "I don't recall giving you options. Those who would like to keep their heads will follow the doors I've opened."

When our journey came to an end after passing through several long and thin corridors, we found ourselves in a room with the same architecture we'd seen before in the main hall. Everything looked the same except that there was a robot sitting on top of a huge throne.

When we got close, the robot leaned in and put his hand on his chin. "Weird, none of you has the intention of pointing a gun at me. Although I know it already, I want to hear it from you. What is it that you want to know?"

"What could it be, you bastard? You took half of my comrades from me. Had me experience things I'll never forget. Many of those men I've known for years. Why did you kill them?" asked Logano, pointing his finger at him.

The robot stood up from his seat. He was even taller than I thought, and a triangular light on the center of his face blinked as he talked. "You are no soldier, and none of you here has anything to symbolize rank. There is no way you're spec ops, too, otherwise, you would've waited for backup instead of feeding half your men to me. Either you are mercenaries or space pirates, but in these times of peace, both are more or less the same."

"What does this have to do with my question?" yelled Logano.

The robot locked his arms across his chest. "Let me talk, human. Are you that eager to join your fallen? There can be no bond amongst people gathering for money. What camaraderie are you talking about? I wouldn't be thinking too highly of it, if I were you." He turned his gaze to me and kept talking. "We haven't been introduced properly – name's Proximus. I was left on this planet by my owners, The Veritani, to oversee and manage this forward operations facility. Many facilities like this one were built on countless planets for the war against humanity, and they set up AIs like me to manage them."

Robin shook his head. "Well, come on then, why don't you just finish us off?"

Proximus stared dead straight at Robin. "I seriously hope you didn't think all these planets withered away just because a few small explosions happened in space? Your rulers resorted to wiping out your planets when they found out they were screwed. As the Veritani found nothing to conquer, they chose not to conquer at all. All of this was probably turned into a propaganda story and branded a well-fought victory but believe me, I have no reason to lie to you. Under these circumstances, my higher-ups stopped sending me orders. Even if they did, I have no resources left on this planet to create anything. Oh, and I've been set to self-destruct should I leave the planet. Those parts you saw on the surface were my escape attempts."

I grimaced. "So you are as desperate as you're smart."

Proximus chuckled slightly. "Not quite, we were told before we left our home planet that the ones who serve their people greatly would be rewarded.

If I present them with the scientific research I've done on you and tell them how I defended the facility, I may be able to secure a deal. They don't know much about how the average grunt thinks, as battles mostly happen from ship to ship. My leaders will be pleased with the knowledge."

"About how we think?" asked Ethan.

Proximus nodded. "Exactly, how you think. I've multi-dimensionally recorded your thoughts and actions and made them into scientific material."

Logano lodged a great kick at the wall. "You expended us just so you could get a chance to leave this miserable place? Oh Lord, give me a single reason not to tear you apart!"

Proximus opened his hand, and a holographic screen appeared on his palm. He made a few moves and looked at us when he was done. "You have concluded the experiment with your last reactions. Two of you didn't even flinch, one of you never understood what I was saying, and the other was just attacking everything in sight. You are no longer necessary. I sincerely thank you for your cooperation. Please do not offer resistance to protect your worthless beings," said Proximus, and promptly shot Robin in the head.

Proximus opened a shield on his arm to protect himself as we dumped our mags on him. He looked at the combat bots in the corner of the room and said, "Finish them off."

All sorts of bots we'd encountered were converging on us. We took cover behind a flipped table, but it wasn't working – rounds were zipping right through, and we were running out of time.

Logano stared at me with a painful smile. "Your grenades then, gentlemen." He continued as we handed him all we had, "I'm next, it seems. Didn't do much in this life anyway. My hope is that, unlike me, you will achieve something before you go. Damn this fate and, particularly, damn this place."

He pulled the pins on the grenades and sprinted at full speed towards Proximus. He kept screaming as he was shot many times, but that wasn't enough to stop him. I jumped over Latif to protect him from the blast as Logano sacrificed himself, ending it all.

It took three days for me to talk to Latif again after we left. It was clear that we weren't doing this work ever again. We sold off the ship, got into some debt, and bought a space inn. We recruited the staff from youngsters who were about to choose a path similar to our past, and our business flourished. I only have one piece of advice for people who listen to this log:

life is too short to waste it as I did. I can't tell you what to do, but when you are in the wrong, don't wait to become as old as I am to find out. And don't think too much about my men and our little story. We are not the first lives lived and ended in vain, and we certainly won't be the last. Wherever you are, as Logano said, try to live a life that you can look back to and not ever feel regret about. Best of luck, Wallace signing out.

A NEW LIFE

Buğra Mert Alkayalar

Translated by Berfin Ciner

I hear voices. The voices are muffled. But I cannot see yet.

Utter darkness...

"Is there a problem?"

"When will he wake up?"

"Don't worry, Mrs. Aslı; it's part of the process."

"Don't worry, darling, he will be okay."

Oh, that suck-up is also here. I forgot. They are all waiting for me. They were the ones who dragged me into this darkness. How often did I tell them that I didn't want to, to no end...Wait a minute! I think I am starting to feel a tingling. It's like I turned on the TV and am trying to adjust the broadcast properly. Oh, yes, just as I thought...Everyone is standing above me with curious eyes. It is all crystal clear now. I see it clearly now. After 82 years, I see the world with a clarity that I am not used to or have somewhat forgotten. Before I transitioned to this body, my right eye had lost its vision by 80 percent and my left eye by 65 percent.

"Dad! Can you see us? How are you?"

My beautiful girl, yes, I can, but I didn't want any of this. Though I shouldn't offend you, you only have my best interests in your heart.

"Yes, my girl, I can see very clearly. My hearing is also very good." I said. *What else can I say?*

"You are as fit as a flea father! You could even beat me!"

I have been wanting to beat you since the day you entered my daughter's life, you worthless suck-up. But pray I am not that kind of a person.

"I hope, son, I hope..." *I said. It's even more than you deserve.*

"Mr. Rıfat, the transition happened smoothly. It will take time to get used to your new body. However, an endless and trouble-free life is ahead of you.

Welcome to your new life!"

I was not 'welcome' at all, doctor. I don't want this new life either. I lived as much as I should, and just like every living being, I should pass away. But humankind is greedy and loves to play God. How can I be happy in a body that doesn't feel like it belongs to me? What is the point of eternal life after Hümeyra passed away? I think that is the worst part of this pile of metal: I talk too much.

I could say something to the doctor, but I am in a state where I have nothing to say.

"Thank you, son."

"Now, could you please try to get up? If you can get up without a problem, we can discharge you from the hospital."

I want to leave right away. But home is not where I want to go. Anyway, maybe I should act like I am adapting for a while. Let's get up.

It's really incredible! I haven't stood up this easily and quickly in the last 20 years. But this isn't me; I don't feel like I'm up. I am just a guy who is trapped in this body, sitting in front of the controller.

"Dad, this is miraculous! I wish mom were here as well, just like you."

Yes, my girl, I could bear this pile of metal if my Hümeyra was here.

"Great, Mr. Rıfat, there doesn't seem to be a problem. You could leave the clinic after the paperwork is done. Again, welcome to your new life."

No, I was not 'welcome' at all. I wish you would stop saying that.

"Thank you..." I said curtly. It's time to go home now. It wouldn't be wrong to be alone, at least for a while. Though it doesn't seem like Aslı would leave me.

***

Even looking around inside the *car feels very weird. It is like I am watching the whole world through a giant TV screen. This is not good; everyone knows that the things we watch on TV are not real, and after a while, it becomes wearying to look at. I don't like television and am already tired.*

"Dad, I think it would be better if you stayed with us for a while. At least, until you get used to your new body."

Here are the words I have been waiting for. My girl, sweetheart, I know you want the best for me; but I am not okay. I don't want to upset you too. Although I don't know if this metal pile can look gloomy.

"No, my girl, everyone is more comfortable in their own home. I am as fit as a flea, just like he said. Just take me home." I barely spoke. *These are the best words I could say. Right now, my thoughts are too dark and sad.*

"No way, father! Come and be our guest; you are always welcome in our house!"

That suck-up is still playing. He is grinning. He knows I won't go; he can only fool my daughter. Anyway, the important thing is that you are good to my daughter. Please take good care of her, please...

"Daddy, at least keep your phone on. I can reach you during the day. Please just let me know about even the smallest problems, okay?"

Oh, my beautiful girl. I never want to upset you, don't ever forget that...

"Don't worry, my girl," I said and got out of the car. *Did I really get out of the car? Because I have to drive this body right now. Forever. But I don't think it will be forever. I'm thinking about getting out of this car, too.*

***

It's a habit to go to the bathroom when you come home to wash your hands and face. So what happens now? Can I feel the water anymore? Oh, God! Who is this? Couldn't they at least have made a body that looks like me? Right, the state only covers so much: the exact, real-like productions are for the rich. Am I surprised? My first look into the mirror, and I already feel the pain increasing. But I can't say the pain my soul suffers because I don't have one. I am about to go mad. In the mirror, I see a perfect face, but no man is perfect.

I'm curious. I want to put my hand underwater. God damn it! Just as I thought: I didn't feel anything. Do you, scientists, think you are playing God without feelings? This is the Devil's work! It's making me live in hell on earth. Hümeyra, it's good that you didn't have to live through this. You are at peace. I want to be at peace with you too. But I don't know if I can after this point. What happened to my soul when they put me into this? I don't know, Hümeyra. I just don't know...

I went to the kitchen to brew tea. Yes, to brew tea. *Just as I poured myself a glass, it came to my mind that I couldn't eat or drink anything anymore. This can't happen, either. No food, no water, no bathroom... When you are a human, sometimes these things seem unnecessary, weary, and even become a burden. But now I want to go to the toilet as usual because I used to go to the toilet since I was suffering from prostate pain before being transformed. I want to run the tap and feel good under the water. Damn it, I want to be able to drink a cup of tea!*

I threw the cup angrily, and it shattered into pieces. *No, sir, I'm not cleaning it up. I'm not going to clean it. I couldn't care less about it. I'm a robot anyway; the glass can't scratch or make me bleed. I'll just walk over it. Look at the great features this body has. I don't have to sleep! No more dreams. God damn it! No more seeing my Hümeyra in my dreams. I can't even cry right now. Only my thoughts are crying; my thoughts get angry. I am so sorry, my girl. I should have refused this at the very beginning. This is not the way to live. I really love you, but my time here is over. I can't go on like this. But I can't say these things to your face.*

If I'm going to get rid of this terrible metal pile, I should do it right. I shouldn't leave them a chance to save me. I can't do this again. Since I'm forbidden to eat or drink, I think drinks will hurt me. On top of that, what if I throw myself off the roof? The seventh floor should do it. If those acts aren't enough, then I really am stuck in this life. Wait for me, Hümeyra, I'm coming. Soon...

Mr. Rıfat went to the rooftop with a teapot full of boiled tea. The neighbours, who saw him on the roof, couldn't figure out who he was because of the new body; but they began to shout for him not to jump. Mr. Rıfat didn't mind anyone. He poured the whole teapot down his mouth. His body began to malfunction. Sounds and smells started to come from many parts of his body. Then he let himself fall. His new body, which he called a pile of metal, crashed into the asphalt. His limbs and mechanical parts were scattered all over the street. Those who saw he was one of the new bodies stared with shock. Mr. Rıfat wasn't watching TV anymore.

***

His daughter, Aslı, who had received the news, was exhausted from crying. Nobody could calm her down.

It had been two days since the incident when unexpected news came from the clinic that day. They said that the part that kept Mr. Rıfat's memory was saved from the suicide. Aslı was shaking as she rushed to the clinic. All of Mr. Rıfat's thoughts were recorded in the memory of his new body. They could let her listen if she wanted to. Aslı took a deep breath, sat down, and listened to what had happened since he woke up. She drowned in tears in the private room, sobbing. When the recording was over, clinic employees came to her.

"Mrs. Aslı, we are so sorry about what happened. We know nothing we say can make you feel better, but if you approve, we can put your father into a new body and bring him back to life. As we said, his memory is undamaged and functional."

She was now quietly shedding her tears. She just stayed there for a while and didn't answer. The employee spoke after this silence.

"If you want, we can give you a few days to decide."

Aslı had listened to her father's thoughts and feelings. Bringing him back to life would be no different than torture. She decided, as his daughter who loved him so much, she couldn't do it to him. Even though she was hurting terribly, she couldn't think of her own sorrow and do this to her father. She wiped her tears and answered the employees.

"No, there is no need. I don't want him to be brought back to life again," she said and lowered her head. She was holding herself so as not to cry.

"All right, Mrs. Aslı, whatever you like. You can read the details from the documents. After the paperwork, your father's memory and the rest of his new body will be destroyed. In addition, as a first-degree relative, you will be financially charged due to misuse of the body, which was provided by the state. Sorry for your loss."

Employees left the tablet containing the documents in front of her and left the room. She stopped crying. She was just sitting sadly. She took the tablet into her hands.

"I hope you are with my mother and at peace, dad..." she said to herself and confirmed the documents.

TROJAN-137

Burak Cem Coşkun

Translated by Beste İrem Köse

Utter darkness, sound sleeps, and a life that had lost its purpose and meaning. An incomplete life where there is no difference between dream and reality within the labyrinth of consciousness, unsatisfied by science and faith. Is sleeping the only thing to do? Or is humanity always asleep? Even if one is not aware of it, is the desire to sleep a way back to reality, a ritual of feeling one's own existence? To remember dreams is sometimes so difficult and sometimes so easy. To remember those that make one suffer, arouse the senses, and set one in motion, however, is not that difficult. An endless search that relentlessly desires the missing thing and the self.

It was again one of the countless days of utter darkness. It was like Odeta was programmed to sleep. More and more unsatisfied with the things in her life; so far from people and lives but so close to dreams. Waking up breathlessly, meaninglessly, every ninety minutes, she would try to make sense of and try to remember what she had seen. It was like all her life experiences had formed a consciousness integrated with her dreams. Was she happy? She would think of this question. When she tried to define happiness, she felt like it was limited by social interactions. She should give a feeling from her own experiences and life to someone else. Yes, she thought, "to give." Was the "modern" person, happy with the things they achieved, actually happy?

Slowly falling asleep, Odeta had already stepped into the dreamland where she had spent most of her life, feeling the lightness of what she should have done and the eeriness of living what was not real.

THE ACCIDENT

An asphalt road stretching into eternity, sirens itching the brain, and a crowd crawling over each other while running. Odeta wanted to stop to understand what was happening, yet, it was like she was inside a liquid. She could not stop; she could sacrifice neither the position she was in nor the time to understand what was going on. She was just running with the rest of the people. Was she in a post-apocalyptic scenario again? Her consciousness was searching for familiar faces. She was looking around her, trying to understand what was happening from the facial expressions of the yelling people. These were meaningless, blurry faces. She could not understand the facial expressions of people. Running hopelessly, she rushed towards the human body running in front of her. Whoever this person was, it was as if she was being drawn towards him. She couldn't make sense of it, but she felt the need to catch him and talk to him. It was difficult to catch him, though. The man seemed like he was flying with the self-confidence of having waited for this moment all his life and seemed buoyed by the peace he would achieve. With her last move, Odeta managed to grab the man by his arm. Once she touched the man, the other people disappeared, and the dust settled. But the sense of urgency from the situation they were in was still there. Starting with fear, the man said:

"Who are you? What's going on?" Odeta knew what she had to do, but she couldn't think of its cause. She couldn't question it; she was just feeling it.

"I know what we should do, and I can save you. Follow me," she said involuntarily. When she lifted her head, she saw an abandoned building appearing in front of them, then signaled to the man that they needed to go inside.

Doubting the situation at first, the man saw a large crowd of people trying to climb to the top of the building. They were escaping from something– were trying to get away from something. Odeta was strangely familiar with the man, and appeared to trust Odeta in a way he couldn't understand. As they were running to the building, Odeta, noticing the apparel of the man for the first time, saw that his feet were drenched in blood from rubbing on asphalt, his clothes were ripped and old, and his face was exhausted. Curiously, she started asking one question after another:

"I'm Odeta. I feel like I know you. What's your name? What's going on?"

"I'm Çiğan. I don't know what is going on, but I must run. I must reach that building. I believe that you can show me the way. This can't be a coincidence," said the man as they continued to run breathlessly.

They could not believe their eyes when they reached the roof of the abandoned building, which served as an airfield. Aerobatic jets were flying away, one after another, and the people who had just reached the roof were preparing to fly. They were told to choose the appropriate uniforms and helmets from the pilot wardrobe that opened in front of them and to put on the parachutes. Doing what they were told with confusion, the duo made a move to embark on the jet in front of them. Odeta could not make sense of what was going on. When she looked at the jet, and saw it was designed for two people. There was no pilot. She and Çiğan stared at each other. The situation was urgent, and sirens were ringing. They had to embark on the jet. Odeta turned to Çiğan in confusion as they watched the jet take off automatically. Her hands were shaking.

Seeing that the plane, after soaring a little in the air, started spiraling down towards the valley they were passing over, Çiğan started to cry. His peace was gone. However, he had seen where he wanted to go, even for a little while. Until he met Odeta, everything had been going as it should have.

Although the plane had slowed down sufficiently by spiraling through its use of its aerodynamics, it crashed to the ground.

Opening her eyes, Odeta could barely get herself out of the plane. She was in shock at being alive. She looked at the sky and smiled at the cool valley wind blowing on her face. Was this the smile of one still living? *Or was this a comfort after fulfilling her duty?*

She remembered Çiğan. She ran quickly to the other side of the plane, but Çiğan's body was squeezed into the cockpit, drenched in blood and perfectly still.

Utter darkness. Odeta looked at her watch. It was only ninety minutes since she had fallen asleep. This time, the dreams were starting earlier than ever. Thinking of what she had seen drenched her in sweat; she took a sip from her water and returned to dreamland.

THE OUTBREAK

Odeta found herself in a building again. She knew the man beside her, who was telling her about something and then running. His name was Alp. But who was Alp? The dreams were just like this. Meeting consciousnesses in people you had never met, feeling togethernesses in moments you had never lived, sharing dreams and feelings in a river flowing to eternity. She was not questioning anymore, as if that wasn't her task anyway. She was letting herself go with the flow of life. She was acting instinctively as her true purpose of existence demanded.

They were hiding in a room. The police were attacking people relentlessly and beating them to death. Everyone was escaping and hiding in rooms while trying to understand what was going on. What kind of an outbreak was this? Alp, coming closer to her, said excitedly, "Many of the police were affected by this outbreak, and they are searching each room. The antidote is on the seventh floor, in my bag. Now, we have to separate. I know that we have never separated before; we trust each other fully, yet I need to go alone from now on. I need to reach it."

She did not want to be separated from Alp in a way she did not understand, but she accepted the situation and started waiting in the room. Almost half an hour passed, but there was no sign of Alp. Getting very curious, Odeta instinctively moved towards the door. She stopped for a second and thought. There was an interesting connection between herself and Alp. Was this fate? No. She should have gone to him. To the seventh floor. Escaping the brutality of the policemen who had gone insane, Odeta reached the seventh floor and saw Alp struggling with one of them. There was Alp's bag on the floor right in front of her, right where it should have been. The policeman turned his back on her and was doing his best to infect Alp with the epidemic. Alp had given up. In that last moment of reaction, a ray of light fell on the policeman's face, streaming softly through the broken stones. The aims of these people were different. What was seen below could be different from what was seen above; things could be different from what they seemed. She must have been dragged here for a reason. Alp, who had accepted what would happen in a surrendered state, saw Odeta, who was targeting the policeman with an antidote from behind while the officer was about to make his move. Alp shook his head from left to right and then shouted, but he could not make himself heard: "Don't!" As he said it, the antidote leaped out of Odeta's hand and struck Alp, missing the policeman. The dream-victim policeman disappeared. Odeta could not believe her eyes. Alp's dead body was lying on the ground.

Utter darkness. Odeta looked at her watch. Another ninety minutes had passed. Thinking of what she had seen drenched her in more sweat, she took another sip from her water and returned to dreamland.

THE MIND OF THE SELF

Having just woken up from sleep, Odeta was getting up in her bed as a scratchy sound from inside her house annoyed her ears. As she made her way towards the television, she had a very different feeling this time. On the news, there was a person running in horror with vehicles following her... She saw that the camera focused on this person, and she was paralyzed. She was seeing herself. The convoy of black office cars was moving towards the street in front of her house. What should she do, save herself? She rushed out without looking back and waited to guide herself to the street corner she would pass. There she was. Odeta saw herself running towards her. Their eyes met. It was so strange. She could not make sense of it. It was as if Odeta's double was trying to explain something to her through a look alone. Maybe her efforts were in vain. Just as she was about to leap towards herself, she heard the sound of a gun firing from one of the black jeeps. What she saw then was her body lying still on the road... She couldn't even save herself... She was trying to set herself free as if from a game, but the laws of nature wouldn't allow it. Was nature now the culprit?

The lights from the headlights of the cars sharpened and then slowly disappeared.

Utter darkness. Odeta looked at her watch. Another ninety minutes had passed. Thinking of what she had seen drenched her again in sweat, and she took a sip from her water before returning to dreamland.

THE WARNING

Everywhere was black and white. Was this the district she was born in? So long ago... Almost a hundred years ago. A different life, a different time. This was happening for the first time. Had she traveled in time? She saw an antique shop just ahead of her, with tables behind the shop and an enthusiastic crowd gathered around. She knew what she had to do. This time, she had difficulty accepting the order formed in her memory fountain. Now it was the perfect moment. Was it a clue that she was in a different period? It should have been. From far away, she was seeing the statesmen called Bödge the Almighty. Everyone had gathered around him.

Entering the antique shop, Odeta said in excitement, "I need to see Bödge the Almighty. It's urgent! I need to warn him!"

Surprised by the impatience and excitement of the woman in front of him, the antiquarian nodded to Bödge's location and allowed her to pass through. It was a moment of truth for Odeta, who had only known Bödge from books. She came close and sat beside him. Sipping his coffee, Bödge the Almighty was curiously waiting for what Odeta would say. She had to be free now. With a smile on her face and a shaky voice, she warned Bödge with the bewilderment of fully embodying herself.

"Bödge the Almighty! I would like to inform you that there is an assassination plan organized for you in a very short period of time. Don't ask me how I know it, who I am, and where I came from because even I don't know the answers to these questions. All I know is that you have to live: I have this strange feeling about you."

Bödge the Almighty's deep blue pupils widened with an awareness that was hard to believe. The blueness in his eyes started to slide softly towards understanding. It was as if thousands of interfering sound waves were echoing in his brain, making thousands of memories live at the same time. With that awareness, he turned sternly to Odeta and shouted, "Run, kid!"

Utter darkness. Odeta looked at her watch. Another ninety minutes had passed. Thinking of what she had seen covered her in sweat once again, and she took a sip from her water. While she was about to return to the dreamland, she felt her heartbeat slowing. She couldn't breathe or move. In the phase when the oxygen rate to her brain decreased and her neurons fired randomly, she found herself in another realm.

She was standing and wearing a snow-white dress.

There was a voice echoing in the void, but she didn't know where it came from:

"Trojan horse-137 is off duty. The number of consciousnesses that have been successfully returned to the artificial manifold while trying to reach reality is 125. The reason for its destruction is that it tries to interact with reality in a different manifold. The ways in which it did it were recorded. It is possible that some of the Trojan horse-137's attacks on shifting consciousnesses evoked certain experiences. Çiğan, Alp, Odeta, and Bödge the Almighty's experiences are stored in the program. Trojan-138 will be assigned to the existing manifold."

Odeta looked at her hand. She touched her face. She didn't feel anything. She saw her hands slowly absorbed, sliding into space. She was slowly disappearing, moving from the biggest universe to the smallest one. Right at that time, what seemed like a dream was reality; what seemed like reality was a dream. Here, at that moment, she saw something falling rapidly from above.

To the outside of her consciousness, inside her dreams.

ART TIME

Burak Katipoğlu

Translated by Sim Iris Belik Sever

I am finally standing on the porch of the summer house, soaked from the rain and with one ankle sprained. It wasn't the nicest of walks to get up here. I am just about to enter the castle of my desires, and my tech-savvy friend's timely sabotage of the house cameras can only get me this far. In this moment of truth, my mind wanders off unintentionally to the conversation that was the start of our plan.

"Can you do it or not?"

"The real question is, should we? Theoretically, yes, I can make you look like the owner. But the problem is that you'd be replacing someone who already exists. If the system is connected to other houses, you will give yourself away immediately because you cannot be in two separate places simultaneously. If I'd want to introduce a new homeowner, legal documents such as your rights to the house would be examined and compared within milliseconds."

"You were just going to make me look like a multimillionaire for a few hours," I laughed.

Nina turned in her chair for a few seconds to face me. She seldom looked people in the eye. This must have been one of those rare moments. Every inch of her desk was organized for high efficiency, and despite every carefully placed cable and port, the fact that she still made room for the ceramic cat figurine I had made her warmed my heart.

"Hey, of course, I can do it. But we're trying to maximize your chances here. There is another way. If I introduce you as a guest, you can take advantage of third-party privacy."

My mind returns to the task ahead. Nina has already registered me as a guest lost in the garden. With a "lucky" malfunctioning security camera, a blind angle in the system is created. I take off my bulky clothes and put on a beautiful red dress in the rain. I exchange my shoes for sandals as I tuck everything into the bag, which I hide behind a bush. Now I am carrying only a small purse and an empty champagne glass.

Slowly but surely, I walk across the garden. I'm approaching the porch from the blind spot.

Either the A.I. will record the sight of a guest from the second camera and associate this oddity with the broken camera, then simply fix the database, or alarms will go off, and police drones will descend in about ten minutes.

I walk in front of the camera. I feel as if the dull black hemisphere of its lens is scanning my whole body. I'm soaked and tired, but I walk across the porch with my head held high and an empty champagne glass in hand.

"I wanna go insiiiide," I say out loud. I'm staggering a little, pretending to be tipsy. I gently wave the champagne glass towards the camera. With a click, the door opens. A good A.I. host cannot allow guests to wait outside.

I'm inside. The glass room I enter is a small but cozy guest room.

The temperature inside is low, but I feel the air getting warmer.

In the main hallway, the lights are already on. If I hadn't been the one to set the system in motion, I might even have believed there was someone at home.

The old woman seems to have great taste; the lighting is quite pleasant. The end of the corridor opens onto the main hall. This area is surrounded by glass walls on three sides, with an outdated fireplace in the middle. All my living space at home, except the bathroom, could fit in here.

Normally it seems the room must get a very nice light. But today, with this cloudy weather, its hidden lamps are lit.

Soft party music is playing in the background. It's a nice, light trumpet piece that doesn't demand too much attention. This must be a special mix prepared by the woman for her guests. A little old-fashioned for my taste, but whatever. Currently, a large part of my universal basic income goes towards making my paintings, and I can't afford new music. So, it may well be a new song, and I may not know it. Gotta enjoy it while I can listen to it for free.

I sit on the edge of the sofa. I must play my part well enough to convince the home A.I. I pretend to drink the last drops from my glass and playfully spin the thin stem in my hand.

Finally, my empty glass has been noticed.

"Would you like me to renew your drink?" asks a voice nearby. There's no one around me, but a hemisphere to the left of the sofa turns blue when the A.I. addresses me.

My test worked, but this is bad. I must be dealing with an advanced A.I. It thinks I am a guest and is actively trying to take care of me. On the other hand, it has actively engaged me in a conversation. I've heard of these types and how they even function as companions to people who are bored at parties. I laugh to myself about how painful the world of the rich is.

"Thank you, I've had enough for tonight. A little walk will do me good."

"Of course. However, rainy weather is predicted with a 78.2% probability to continue for the next three hours. I do not recommend going outside."

"I've enjoyed the rain enough. I'm sure Elisa has interesting corners in the house too." I'm using the owner's first name. Acting like a close friend gives me confidence. Yet, it makes no difference to the machine.

"Of course, if you so desire, I can show you around the house. The personal collection of Mrs. Elisa Kentwood is generously included in the tour."

I don't understand what's generous about opening your collection to guests, but I don't forget to smile.

I stand up, saying, "I'd love to." My foot is still swollen, and I'm limping.

"Ma'am, I can contact a doctor for your foot if you wish."

"No, it's just sprained a little, no need," I say, and put my foot down hard. It hurts so much, but I have to convince the A.I. I try to ignore my pain and use the foot as normally as possible. I put my weight on my right leg first, then take another painful step with my left. The A.I. seems convinced.

I begin to make my way across the large room gradually. On the left is a niche with a few objects on exhibit. A statue of a green monkey with closed eyes sitting on an altar catches my attention first. It's almost transparent. Luckily, I haven't lived in a prefab cavern long enough not to know what this is. The A.I. has noticed my attention has shifted there.

"A Machupyan print, ma'am. One of the hundred copies from the original 3D printing era."

My eyes open wide. The artwork consists of at least seven billion sub-pixel parts. Even if I had permission, it would take a year for my machine at home to print it. It must be worth enough money to buy this house. It's almost sacrilegious to keep an original like this here. A select few are obviously enjoying life while they cram people like us into 3D-printed, uniform blocks of habitation.

I need to stay calm. In this house, my every second is being watched. I can't let my guard down. But I'm not just anyone in the herd; I can't stay silent. I feel compelled to say something.

"It's a beautiful piece, but, personally, I would have preferred Machupyan's orange African period."

"Then it's your lucky day, ma'am. You may encounter a nice surprise on the upper floors." The soundwaves are directed at me from micro-speakers in the ceiling. Even at a large party, only I would be able to hear the A.I. talking.

Among the little framed pictures behind the print is something I've never seen before. My pupils must have involuntarily dilated because the house speaks once more.

"What you're looking at is a Māori mask from about 1300."

"I've never heard of this artist. How many copies are there?" Random words come out of my mouth.

"Ma'am, the Māori are a Pacific people. The maker is unknown. What you see is not a copy but an original work."

"Is there one …only one copy? Original… it's original. Not remade, manufactured… this mask is 800 years old?!"

"Yes, ma'am. Although its exact age is not known, it has a history of close to 835 years. One of the most valued collectors items owned by Mrs. Elisa."

While trying to hide a confused expression, my hand involuntarily reaches for the mask.

"Normally, a permit is necessary to touch the works of art, ma'am. If you wish, I can initiate the permitting process."

I pull my hand back at the last moment.

"No, no, there is no need for that. I know how meticulous Elisa is. There is no need to disturb her," I point to the empty space, "at this beautiful party." Fortunately, artificial intelligence has no sense of humor.

This house reminds me of the cave in *Aladdin and the Magic Lamp*, a story I read as a child; it's filled with all kinds of treasures. Something definitely will happen to me if I dare to touch anything other than the magic lamp.

I look at the other pictures hanging in their frames on the wall. Mostly works by modern artists. I wonder how many of the workers' hours rights are tied to this house. At this exact moment, the picture in one of the frames changes and turns into another three-dimensional, moving picture. Naturally, it draws my attention. This time I act before the A.I. does: I talk first.

"That's a beautiful piece. I believe it belongs to someone from the Tokyo Pipe art group."

"You are quite right, ma'am. Colorful pipe art is preferred by Kentwood during March."

"How much is tied to this place?"

"The digital rights to use Saitishi Somori's work *Kendo and Noodle* were purchased for 646 hours at the main Kentwood estate in January and February and 425 hours at the Kentwood family summer home in March and April. The next changeover will be in about 45 minutes. At present, the owner of the work is a private gallery in Sweden."

"Wow, they almost wholly own it."

"Our collection has the rights to 79% of its time during the winter, yes."

This wealth is making my head spin, and I'm mystified. A few more questions come to mind, but I've spent too much time in this corner. Now I must make my way towards my target.

"You were talking about a Machupyan surprise. Upstairs, is it?"

"Yes, ma'am. Follow the corridor to your right, you will see the spiral staircase going upstairs."

Without answering and stepping gingerly, I reach the end of the corridor. Here also, the walls are covered with paintings on both sides of the spiral stairs. I see a few of them change as their time runs out. They are replaced by new and interesting ones. Modern paintings are followed by classics, and classics by modern paintings.

This wall is designed a little more dynamically. Synchronized purchase times blend the transitions. The art on all walls renews itself approximately every 10 minutes.

"A very dynamic exhibition wall."

"Yes, ma'am, it is a collective space where we own 73.4% of all the works' time. The transitions have been enriched by 12-minute intervals designed by the Kentwood family curator Andrew Sztarky."

This is a perfect example of snobbery. Clearly, the homeowners are making sure that anyone using the staircase is going to hear these words. It's just another way of saying, "look, we're rich." I think of the two dynamic frames I use at home for both work and play, and I resent my life in poverty.

Almost at the top, a drawing on the wall catches my attention. A child's picture. My attention triggers the A.I. once more.

"Apologies, ma'am, I believe that's filth from the party."

Artificial intelligence is downright lying to me. I know that the party is rushed, that I've caught it off-guard. Obviously, some secondary cleaning modules haven't been activated.

I look at the doodle. A big tree and a badly drawn child. His hands are wide and disproportionate. Next to him is a horse with four stick legs, which the boy is trying to feed with his giant hands. A river seems to curve in the background. The whole thing is drawn directly on the wall. No frame, nothing. The artist didn't even have a proper horizon line; it's crooked.

"This looks like a painting to me," I say, but immediately shut up. It's the wrong day to challenge authority.

"No, ma'am, the artist and purchase of its display time aren't recorded in my archives. No name or dimensions have been entered. Action will be taken at the first opportunity to clean the filth."

"This isn't a stain; it's a child's drawing," I say. It hurts me to call a work of art a stain. I keep talking. Since I started this, I have had to do it right. "What's the name of Elisa's grandson, the little one?"

"Elisa Kentwood has two grandchildren, and their names are Sasha and Arp Kentwood. Sasha is 13 years old and has no current nickname. Arp Kentwood is four years old and is called Arpty within the family."

I got the information I needed. I'm doing something extremely risky right now, but I must follow my principles. I take out my personal tablet from my purse and insert a disposable chipset into its slot. I define the artist. "Arp Kentwood, alias 'Arpty,' aged four, parentally controlled profile. Works..."

I hold the tablet to the child's picture and scan it. In the dark corners of the internet, I pass through some net shadow filters, delete any trace of myself within the file and send it home as a gift. I set the gift date to fourteen years from now. *Maybe not today, Arpty, but maybe then you'll appreciate your work.* A small gesture from one artist to another.

After my little act of charity, I continue down the corridor. This place is starting to look more and more like Aladdin's cave. Art and artifacts that I'd never expect to see and only know from images. Displayed in another small niche, I'm sure I'm looking at an original copy of the sculpture *The Fall of the*

Robot. Next to it stands the orange Machupyan copy. Even though it pales in comparison to *The Fall of the Robot*, neither really interests me anymore. I smile, wondering if wealth has already spoiled me. I'm sure the A.I. has logged my facial expression in its statistics under "enjoying the party."

For a moment, I think about how I'd genuinely like to be invited to this house. I would like to talk to real people about art at a real party, joke around and have fun. But that's not the world I live in. Except for the technocrats who make up the lucky 5% of the world's population, everyone is part of the masses who don't produce anything connected to global income, who don't make money if they produce, and whose deaths would cause problems even though their lives are meaningless. You see, our lives are the charity of people who got the money and won the game. But, as the wealthy retreat out of sight, their puppet governments are stuck with dwindling resources with which to supply us. It's impossible not to envy the lives in this house, as we are confined to rather regulated and limited lives. This is just a summer house. The Kentwoods and I have nothing in common, and they're trying very hard to maintain that gap. Even if I'm lucky and talented enough to get their attention, that would be the furthest I could ever go. They can buy all my art in one fell swoop, copy it, print it on trash cans, and present my slightest objection to the masses as a great insolence. Maybe they are good people; I don't know them. But the odds of me attending a real party in this house are the same as the likelihood of an Englishman, a Frenchman, and Superman walking into a bar.

My "magic lamp" awaits me at the end of the corridor. I see the painting protected from direct sunlight under a half dome facing outwards on a hyper-high-resolution, semi-three-dimensional display. The artifact moves gently, like waves rippling on the surface of the sea. I admire the slight counterflow towards the ceiling and the slow-moving color turbulence. It's a painting fluidly coded at a micron level, and I almost want to reach out to touch the code below it. It is obvious that my crappy screens at home cannot support this type of work. The detail is dazzling and almost appetizing. It makes me want to go home and paint something new.

In front of me is the second alternative copy of the triplectic painting "The Technocrat and the Three Sins." Copy A is exhibited at Karandash Modern Museum for two-hour intervals, and I was only able to see it after waiting in line for a long time. Now, the original of the alternate Copy B is in front of me, but with no time constraints.

"The creator of 'The Technocrat and the Three Sins' is Semih Trepsky. 100% of the rights to this painting belong to the Kentwood family. Image rights are kept confidential, so be mindful of distributing such information."

In other words, this politely means "this information is confidential; if you share it with anyone, we'll take everything you own."

This painting is so expensive it can buy this mansion, this village, and all the other rich people in it too. It isn't in a museum, nor is it exhibited anywhere else. I find it selfish to keep its beauty hidden in this summer house, abandoned in the winter.

Fortunately, here I am to fix this situation.

I approach the painting and examine it intently. Now it's time for some theatrics. I slip a pill from my purse into my mouth, then swallow surreptitiously. I begin to feel dizzy.

"I think... something is happening to me. I need to get some air. My dress is too tight..."

"Ma'am, if you wish, I can summon an emergency team right away. Or may I suggest you sit down to regulate your blood pressure?"

I pretend to be lightheaded. I really do feel a little faint, as the pill I just took caused a drop in blood pressure. The A.I. collects data from my skin and understands the situation very well. I'm not faking what I'm feeling, technically.

I stumble and sit down on one of the nearby seats. I put my head back a little.

"No, there is no need for that. I don't want any inconvenience. I'm just going to loosen my dress for a moment," I say to the house.

This is a key phrase. Nina may not know much about social situations, but she is a genius when it comes to home A.I.s. There is one thing that these petty-bourgeois houses cannot allow: a scandal. It is undesirable to have the problems of eccentric guests become the material of newspapers distributed to proletarians.

I unzip my dress and start to expose my breasts a little bit.

"Ma'am, there's a nearby bathroom if you... " It doesn't finish. According to international law, as soon as the A.I. detects my nudity, it must shut itself down unless there is a health concern or indication of criminal danger. Long live the old laws, long live the old rights.

As my body naturally pumps adrenaline, I get up and go to the painting. I access the back of the dynamic frame and, via my pod link, transfer the program Nina created.

The program now changes the painting's property rights. From now on, between 03:00 and 05:00 at night during the winter months, this picture will belong to an Australian gentleman. Of course, due to the time and hemisphere difference, he'll be admiring the painting on beautiful summer afternoons. I'm replacing it with one of my own paintings. It's an approximate copy of the painting I'm stealing. But to notice that, you need to have a sober mind and good knowledge of art. Obviously, these two seldom intersect in this summer party house. Since there's no difference in size and duration, a person must be looking intently at this picture between 03:00 and 05:00 during the winter to realize the change.

Honestly, I think it's a fair trade-off. I'm losing one of my best forgeries, after all. The transaction is completed in under a minute, and many, many zeros begin to accumulate in a strange offshore account.

I got this done quickly. Even exposing yourself and the protection of personal privacy can't buy you more than three minutes in this club of the rich.

"Feeling better now? Is there an emergency?" The AI already knows from my physical indications that there is no such thing but asks out of courtesy.

"No, thank you. The painting must have overwhelmed me."

This must be a well-programmed A.I.; it knows how to skip unpleasant topics.

"Yes, Semih Trepsky's 'The Technocrat and the Three Sins' is one of the most valued possessions of Mrs. Kentwood."

"I wonder how much of it belongs to the Kentwood family?" Artificial intelligence doesn't get suspicious or tired of the same questions asked again and again.

"Currently, all rights to the work belong to the Kentwood family. You may view it to your heart's content: there is no time limit."

I take a deep sigh, relieved to hear that the program works. I could kiss Nina right now. I'd love to fill that empty champagne glass I'm holding onto in celebration.

I slowly walk down the corridor, still looking at the paintings. As I go downstairs, I glance at the little piece of art I helped preserve and smile.

"What a nice party, I really enjoyed it." I can't help myself; I poke fun at the machine. Now comes the unpleasant yet necessary part. I go into the room from which I entered the house. It's pouring outside.

"Delay your departure, ma'am. It's cold outside." The house desperately wants to persuade me. The guests' health is a priority, especially since they drink lots of alcohol.

"No, I'll enjoy the rain. Besides, I'll continue homewards now anyway. " After this statement, the house won't alert the police when I don't return. According to international law, the home's involvement and responsibility for me ends the moment it loses my signal in the backyard.

I go outside. The most unpleasant part is taking off my thin dress and trying to put the other clothes on in the rain. I have a long walk home. I hope I don't catch a cold. And then, of course, I'm sick for a week. My hesitancy to spend money has waned now. I've bought lots of art materials and a new rig for Nina and paid off my debts. An unknown benefactor made a generous donation to our small neighborhood. Fortunately, philanthropists are still able to stay anonymous in our society.

I also bought myself four large dynamic frames. I give Nina one, along with three of my pictures, as a gift, but sometimes I catch her displaying codes on it. We argue like teenage siblings.

For me, the best moment during winter is the minute between 2:59 and 3:00 o'clock. As I'm somewhat greedy in nature, I stole slightly more than planned. After one mesmerizing minute of art time in my bedroom during those winter nights, I'm guaranteed to get a good night's sleep.

THE PASSAGE

Cem Sinan Altun

Translated by Emre Akçaoğlu

Woke up to his own scream. Difficulty breathing. His heart was beating as if to burst open his chest, and sweat oozed from the roots of his hair, rolling down his neck onto the already-soaked pillow. Touched his head, which was burning. He rolled his fingers over the scar that trespassed his entire forehead. It felt as if his heart was beating there. He sat up a little as he calmed down a bit and drained the glass of water on the nightstand. He paused, then slowly dipped back into the hollow of his bed.

It was often the same nightmare. Walking down a long, dark corridor towards a blinding white light. As he closed in on the source, he had the chilling feeling that he was being followed, only to turn and see no one quickly. Then, he started walking again, feeling that the danger behind him was inching closer. Both his fear and his pace increased as he walked. He would find relief at the end of the corridor. He believed passionately in that feeling but still, the thought of him getting caught before he made it never went away. Then, just a couple steps from the light, the pungent smell of ozone and noises humming and some kind of force pulling him from behind. He could no longer step forward and would wake up as he was whipped back into the darkness.

Eyes on the ceiling. Breathing somewhat better, he calmed his heart down. Rolled over to his left, where the digital read 23:58. He remembered it was 23:53 the night he had the first nightmare. Closed his eyes.

***

He was feeling powerless when he woke up before noon. He sort of got prepared and went out. He had a lot to do. First, the doctor for routine checks, then shopping. Parked his car on the street next to the hospital and headed to the main entrance. On the right was a small service door he had not noticed before. His gaze was fixated on the door as if he was hypnotized. Then, all of a sudden, the interior, floors, corridors, and wards came to life in his mind. Proceeding after a brief hesitation, he walked in through the front door. The clinic was, surprisingly, right in front of him. Slowly approaching the desk, he introduced himself.

"I had an appointment, but is the doc available?"

"Yes, he was expecting you. Please, this way."

"Thanks." A muffled knock on the door, and he walked in.

"Hello, doc."

"Hi, welcome."

"Thank you, doc. How are you?"

"I am fine, thank you. How about you? Any pain, anything?"

"The pain is gone, but the stitches sting a bit, especially at night."

"All right then, please just lie down."

He laid on the examination bench. Putting on his glasses, the doctor started examining the forehead scar.

"The wound healed quite fast—there is a little rubor but no infection. Does it itch?

"A bit. I have an itchy feeling all over, though."

"I see. Any pain now when I touch it?"

"None. No."

"Say 'Aaa,' please." The doc attentively examined his mouth, tongue, and nose.

"OK. You can get up now."

"So, what is it, doc? What do you see?"

"Well, it looks like an allergy, but let's see, after a couple of detailed tests. I do not expect anything serious. You do not have any other complaints, huh? Anything with your vision, hearing?"

"Nothing. Both are quite sharp."

"That is great. I mean, after that kind of an accident—you barely made it to the hospital and had a severe concussion, then spent 10 hours in the OR. Recover so fast, and you expect to be without pain? No, you are really lucky."

"Thank you, doc."

"Noo! That is what I do. Now, let's get the test results. Please drop by the blood center downstairs—they will help you out and give you a number to check the results on the web. Take care."

"Thanks."

After giving blood for the tests, he left. Almost no traffic though it was the weekend. He made it to the mall before he expected, going down to the parking lot to occupy the first available place. But after taking a couple of steps towards the entrance, he heard an explosion-like sound, then a shrieking clangor in his head. Covering his ears with his hands, he squinted his eyes. He waited for the sounds to dissolve, but they did not. The clangor amplified with the percussion of his heart, keeping tempo. He had that familiar smell in his nose, burning his throat and lungs. The clangor was gone, leaving behind a hum. He could not differentiate sounds, but it felt like a hum. When he opened his eyes a bit, he saw that what had, a moment ago, been the entrance, been the entrance was now bathed in some white light, and the parking lot had turned into that familiar dark tunnel. He started walking. And, as he walked, he felt that gravity intensified, making it difficult to walk. He could barely take that last step before he sensed someone touching his shoulder. The smell of ozone and the clangor were unbearable now. And the light was too bright to look at. Stumbling, he turned.

"Sir!"

"..."

"Sir! Are you OK?"

"...."

"You OK?"

Eyes opening with some difficulty, he found one of the mall security guards trying to wake him up.

"You sick? Got any medication?"

"I... am fine. I was dizzy–I think low BP."

"You sure?"

"Yeah, yeah. Thank you. I have not eaten yet. I think my BP dropped. I will have something upstairs."

He was helped up. He thanked the security guard with a forced smile on his face. Headed to the entrance, not his car, so that he would seem as if he was going to eat. Passing through the detectors, he walked into the nearest men's room. Trying to restore himself as he washed his face with cold water, he glanced at the mirror. He looked awful. The stitches on his forehead were redder and more visible. Suddenly, his lips began shaking–a condition that then traveled down his entire body with a series of uncontrollable reflexes.

He could not hold back his tears. The darkness was dropping down as he fell to his knees, and that darkness echoed in his head with one word:

"Stop."

***

He thought about all the possibilities and still could not make heads or tails of it. He rose from the couch into which he had sunk and went to the cabinet where he kept his health records. He opened the file and went back to his couch. The accident had been a little more than two months back, and almost three weeks ago, he had been released from the hospital. The nightmare began the night he was back home. Then, it was like a nebulous dream that, in time, grew more real and more frightening. *This condition must be intensifying then*, he thought: Was it... was he really going mad, or was there some cerebral damage from the accident that the doctors kept from him? Other than those possibilities, he could only divine that what he saw was real–just real. No other options. He decided to be brave and face it. What was that light? What was behind it? Who was it, and why did it say 'Stop!'? As he bounced between these questions, a thought started to sprout in his mind. He armed himself with some snacks and retreated to the safety of the bed. He was scared. A deep breath and he closed his eyes.

Shaking still while walking in the dark–now almost an acquaintance. His heartbeat kept tempo with his steps. Faster. The explosive sound, the clangor turning into some hum, the smell hurting his nose, his heart beating ever faster. He went on regardless. As he started being pulled back, the hum grew thunderous, the smell was ubiquitous, and his lungs were broiling.

"Stop."

He did. Slowly turned around. Gulped.

"Who... Who is this?"

All of a sudden, everything was silent. The smell of ozone thinned. He felt as if the ground had slipped from under his feet and that he was floating. Inside, he was filled with indescribable happiness. Hoping to see something, he looked into the darkness to determine where the voice came from. He noticed a silhouette coming closer. Then, a few meters away, he saw who approached. It looked just like him. His double stopped and fixed their eyes upon their mirror image. So. Without moving their lips, again, his double said, 'Stop!'. Although he had thought that voice came from elsewhere, he knew that it was echoing in his mind. He responded without thinking:

"Who are you?"

"Nobody."

"Where am I–this tunnel, the light, the smell, and those sounds?"

The other–the stranger–remained mute for a second.

"You are between the two universes."

"Is it that I am dead, and this is limbo?" His hand went to his forehead and pressed on the wound. The pain was unbearable.

"No."

"I do not understand."

"The accident affected you beyond what appears on the surface. The interaction between the thud on your head and a few other elements activated a specific area of your brain. You are still not aware, but your brain is improving at an unimaginable pace. With your time on Earth, this improvement will go into the final phase in a few days. But, the thing is, this should not happen."

"But why?"

"If that ever happens, you will open up the tunnel and cause a reverse flow."

"The tunnel?"

They gestured towards what surrounded the two of them.

"Then what happens?"

"Life will end."

"I... I really do not understand. Am I still in a dream? Is all of this real–are you real?"

"Yes."

"I do not believe what you are saying. I will wake up soon, and this Gehenna will be over, I know."

"You will wake up and check the time to see that it is 23:59. Then, you will drink some water and go back to sleep. Tomorrow, you will go on with your life. But, all the while, a step closer to opening the tunnel."

"How do you know all that?"

"That is not important."

"For me, it is."

"You humans!.."

"What?"

"Oh! there are so many things that you do not and will not understand."

"You... Who are you?"

"I am you."

"What?.."

"I am your other being in the next universe, or you are my reflection, here, in this one."

"What.. what does that mean?" he stuttered.

"Your universe is no more than only one of the billions of other cosmic constructs like ours. Each universe is connected to another one with physical and metaphysical powers. These are called universal pairs, and they are bound by two types of tunnels. The tunnel of time and the tunnel of energy– or the passage of spirits, as you call it. Get that?"

"Trying..."

"Universes act independently, but the synchronization of time and energy is eternally important because each diversion that is an external threat affects its pair. During such moments, tunnels of time are used to intervene within certain boundaries. These are not your so-called time travel fantasies, of course. In order to do that, you would have to pass through to the universe and use a tunnel of time to get back to your universe. But that doesn't matter at the moment. What matters is the tunnel of energy you have entered."

"You mean this, here?"

"Yes. The tunnel of energy and the gate at the tip of it opens when 'death,' as you call it, occurs. The energy of the deceased, or their spirit, as you say, travels through this gate and returns to the source between two universes. These sources are at the intersection of each universe-pair. Universes are connected only to each other, but sources are a different story. They are connected not only to their pairs but to all sources in all universes. Even if one or two of the universe-pairs were to disappear, the energies–I mean the spirits–would flow towards the source and, from there, to where it all began. To the mother source. Where you are bound is this passage between our universes, which leads to the source between our universes."

"But you told me that it would open at the moment of death; how can I open it if I am not dead?"

"You are not powerful enough to open it to the source. So you can only reach the gate, crack it a bit and cause a reverse flow–even if that is not what you wanted. That would cause a flow of energy into the physical universe. Neither your planet nor your universe could handle the emerging energy. Then, finally, you would see what you call the apocalypse. It would end all life in both our universes, then the gate would open completely, and energy would flow to the source, then to the mother source. And when that flow ends, the link between the source and the universes would break, and our universes would collide back into the form of their inception. Also, you should know that when the passage opens even in the blink of an eye, no matter which direction, some energy always leaks back."

"Back to our universe, you mean?"

"If the one who causes the flow is in your universe, then yes. In that case, humanoid energies, what you call ghosts, will form. They are constructs of energy that have occasionally leaked back."

"Are ghosts real?!"

"Yes."

"But then, you can control the flow in some way, right?"

"Attaining the power needed for such control requires the combination of some specific aspects. There were people who could do that in your past. Different than you, they had attained the level to prevent the gate from opening backwards."

"Who?"

"Those you call prophets. But I cannot say much about that. It is forbidden that we intervene in existential or religious matters."

"I... just cannot understand."

"Do not try to. You will both forget what you heard and if the expected happens, none of this will mean a thing."

"Then, what will happen now?"

"All depends on you and me."

"Me?"

"In a while, you will be able to enter the passage without needing to sleep. That is the limit of what I can do. I won't be able to stop you from reaching the gate. But remember, you and only you can control your own will and make life-and-death decisions. When you reach the white light, you will transform it into energy and flow into the source. The process will commence, and our universes will end."

"What if I can somehow manage not to open the gate backwards?"

"I told you, you do not possess that kind of power–for now. In fact, you will never make it to that level. When your time hits 00:00, it is apocalypse time."

"No... No, I do not believe any of this. I think something got me in that accident–maybe I am losing my mind, I do not know. You are not real, and everything you say is a lie. Just a lie!"

Shouting, he woke up soaked in sweat. His heart was beating as if to rip open his chest. Reaching for his water, he forced down a couple of gulps. Digital read 23:59. Gasping; he dropped himself into his bed. He felt better after a few minutes but slept no more until dawn.

***

He called the hospital that afternoon to get a psychiatric appointment for the day after. Now he was sure that he was losing his mind. There could be no other explanation for what was going on. He did not have any hallucinations that day, which was a good sign. He hesitated for a while over whether to check his test results on the web or to have something to eat. Then curiosity won over, and he went to his computer. Hospital website. Patient number and passcode. Enter. Tests. He found what he was looking for. Scrolled down to see that just two values were quite off-track. The results read 'minor ozone poisoning'.

Closed his eyes. And the monitor went into sleep mode right then. Slowly, he leaned back. His whole life was floating around his consciousness. Those he loved, his colleagues, the rest of humanity... So, that was it. All bound to end tonight. He could not let that happen. He did not want to be that human being to cause all life to go down. He did not want it at all. Sat in silence for a while, then got up and headed to the basement. Into the room packed with unused stuff to find the gun, he had hidden in the top drawer of his old study desk alongside a box of ammo and the oiler. Then, back in his bedroom, he cleaned the gun well, fed it a single bullet, and cocked the gun. He laid himself down on the bed with the barrel on his right temple.

He closed his eyes as the bang and the tink came.

***

His sight was blurred. He was only hearing some sounds. Turning his head softly to the side, he blinked. The blur lifted a bit to help him discern loads of devices with lights and buttons all connected to his body somehow. Suddenly, the door flung open. That was the nurse.

"Where am I?"

"I do not believe this!" The nurse's surprise was obvious. The woman looked at him for a few breaths before running out. She came back shortly in the company of a doc.

The doctor approached him with quick steps, took a little light out of his pocket, checked his eyes, and spoke softly.

"Are you feeling well?"

"Where am I?"

"At the hospital. You had the worst accident."

"Accident?"

"Yes. A road accident. You do not recall?"

"I... No."

"At the mountain pass, your car rolled over into the ditch. It was your brother who barely rushed you to the hospital."

"My brother?!"

"Yes, your twin brother."

"..."

"Anyway, just drop it for now. Thank God you are back and awake–the rest is nothing. Believe me, we were almost sure that you would not wake up from your coma. Come on now, get a good rest. The nurse will give you something for the pain. You will be here for another while before we can send you back home in good shape."

He was not in shape, though, to try figuring out what the doc was saying. He felt exhausted as he never had before.

Closed his eyes.

***

In his dream, he was on a narrow street, walking. A few drops of rain fell on his face and somewhat rinsed his hair. He saw someone with a derby hat sitting under the street light at the end of the street. He walked towards him without knowing why or what he needed to do when he got there. Stopped a few feet away and took a deep breath. The man in the derby hat raised his head to look up at him. Suddenly, he smiled. He was himself.

CROSSING THE OCEAN

Deniz Ezgi Avci Vile

Translated by Rakesh Jobanpura

Sent tumbling forward as the driver of the double-decker bus suddenly hits the brakes, I climb down the stairs trying to hold on to the seats for balance. I lean against the four-person seat behind the driver to stop myself from falling. The bus driver swerves right and cuts the other driver off in the right-hand lane, and so the bus driver honks at the man who is making rude gestures to him. The bus driver starts shouting as he raises his right hand at the bus, which looks like a tin of sardines surrounded by bullet-proof glass.

"What is it? What? On your way, pal!"

We are all like sardines swimming in oil, thrown forwards and backwards by the driver hitting the emergency brake. With his right hand on the steering wheel, the man in the car takes out an AK-47 with his left and, in thirty seconds, fires two hundred times at the front right window of the bus. The bullets hit the glass like raindrops and fall to the ground outside with a comforting sound.

I automatically go into stress-shield mode. I have no other choice. As soon as we step outside, we are like extras forced to enter a reality created by others. Ever since the bus driver had swerved the way he did, he put us in a reality that somebody else wants to live. Sometimes, when I go to the local shop to get a pint of milk, next to other people: one of those people hanging onto a tree in the middle of a flood, someone in the gas chambers or in the gulags breaking rocks, a UN soldier in the middle of a genocide, or around women in a village in Africa who have been locked hand and foot in stocks planted into the earth in readiness for the militants who are on their way to rape them. Sometimes I see myself jumping off a cliff or staring at fish at the bottom of the ocean or in the middle of a forest fire next to a fallow deer whose antlers are aflame. I have read all of these in history books from the last decades. In order to create reality, people read history. The experts say that we are living through a bizarre era in which no one is creative, but they also say that this is only temporary, like all historical stages, and that they are confident that people will recover their creativity. When they do, we will be able to experience and enjoy more appropriate realities.

With every step taken on the street, there is always the possibility of encountering some humans. We can never guess when these humans will succumb to the urge to create a reality. They say that this desire is the result of millions of years of continuous evolution, and they will soon give this desire or, to be more precise, this impulse, a name. There is a serious problem that is encountered, albeit rarely: if two humans feel the urge to create a reality at the same time, each unaware of the other, and act upon this urge, time stops.

There is nothing we can do when time stops, nor do we know how long it will stay frozen. It all comes down to how much the two realities wish to engage. Even those that have created the realities do not know how powerful these impulses are. This previously rare occurrence has begun to increase in frequency, which is why we are often late getting to a place. Reality collisions have yet to be acknowledged as an official phenomenon, but a vote is going to be held in Parliament this week.

Time has not stopped on this occasion, which is why no one seems particularly bothered. People crowd at the door, all looking tired and fed up. When the bullets fall to the ground, I automatically come out of stress-shield mode. My eyes lose their opacity. Suddenly, the driver stares at me in the rear-view mirror and shouts, "Just look at this, will you, Ms. Gül? The nerve of the man! Any more, and he'd have been out of the car and in my face!" After his outburst, he stares at me for a good five seconds as though recording what is happening. I do not know what to say. He stops watching me; then, turning his head to the right and looking out of the window as though nothing has happened, he steps on the gas. Trying not to look at the driver, I stand and wait by the door along with the other miserable faces.

We are all the same. I can eat, I can drink, I can make love, and, recently, I have been able to urinate in the toilet. I no longer need to use the thin, transparent hose to urinate. But because I am still not one hundred percent sure, I cannot empty the bag and hand it over. It seems quite normal if you read about the development spurts described on social media; everyone starts with urination. It's all perfectly normal. Excretion takes a little more time. I started when I was six months old, but others started much earlier. I am an average case, right in the middle.

We are all the same. I have been able to eat for some time now. Now, when I am at the drinking table, I am not as tense but can sit quite comfortably and relax. I have also come a long way when it comes to conversation. Before I leave, I scan thousands of social media accounts. All sorts of products turn up. There is also this one website called the "Growth Spurt Dictionary." They say ninety percent of the people there are human and that they do their own writing. I check that out sometimes. How do they know they are human? Because they are funny. There are women there too, but I don't know if they are funny or not. We can't tell who is male or who is female anyway. One of the rare skills that our species has yet to master is humour. They have put it on the uppermost level of the development pyramid. There, at the top of the structure that tapers up into a small point, it says: "Being funny – digs, quips, allusions, sarcasm." But being funny is beyond us. The effort of trying to decode innuendos almost kills me, and even then, I am not sure I fully understand. But anyway, those who do not want to be identified as humans or who find being human difficult have left all that stuff behind now and just wander around like us.

We are all the same. Have I told you I am able to make love now? I have to confess when I first tried it, I thought it was the most ludicrous thing imaginable. Someone rocking to and fro like that on top of you. Making love is a further stage of development, and our progress and the developmental stages we have passed are being recorded. They do realise and accept that some of us, due to particular circumstances, may be slower. Nevertheless, and delays notwithstanding, those who cannot progress to the next stage of development and who cannot naturally assert themselves are taken away and deported. I know that this misfortune can take place at any stage of our personal development because we all hear their screams when they are being taken away. Apparently, we can all feel pain, too – both physical and emotional. It's said the physical and mental pain we experience when being taken away is unbearable.

I don't know if humans can hear these screams or not. Some say they can. I'm not sure if I should mention this or not, but I struggle a little with experiencing emotional pain. At times, when I should be upset – for instance, when a man I have just made love to kicks me out of his house – I don't feel any pain, but I immediately start just crying to make it look as though I am suffering. Shoes in one hand, bag in the other, my hair a mess, and my makeup streaked all over my face, I make sure the caretaker sees me sobbing my eyes out as I stagger down the stairs. At night, I practice crying out loud. There are thousands of styles of sobbing, but the one I like the most is the one in which women sob out loud with plenty of sniffing and whimpering. I reckon that when the tears, snot, and spit all stream down a woman's face and get all mixed up suggest that she is in real pain. The way women hold their stomachs or curl up into a ball is the same. Every night before going to sleep, I spend half an hour sobbing and moaning. Now, I start sobbing because I cannot tell where or when someone is going to turn around and say things like, "Ms. Gül, you look very bright and elegant today," or, "Ms. Gül, a new cheese has just arrived, gruyere from Kars, would you like to try some?" or, "Just look at the way this arsehole has left all his rubbish on the table, Ms. Gül. Like his damn mother is going to clean up after him! I'll tell you who's going to clean up after him – me, that's who!"

I read somewhere about something called psychopathology. There is a list called "Characteristics To Be Enhanced," which has millions of entries, but psychopathology is not on the list. I can cry at anything now, so I don't really worry about it. Despite staring at a kitten for hours on end once a month as one of the empathy improvement techniques that have been recommended for us, I do not get a warm, fuzzy feeling inside, nor do my facial muscles form a smile. It's the same with puppies and babies. I've tried them all.

I learned how to make love by making love to myself over and over again. We have been built in such a way that we do not need other people to make love, but before we go out into the real world and try it with other people, they send an assistant over. They say it's crucial for our development that love-making be a positive experience. The assistant they send stays for two months or four if a special request is filed. Sometimes these extension requests can be misinterpreted in the registry office, so everyone spends two months preparing themselves first.

Before the assistant is sent, we need to choose a body for ourselves and then send the application. At first, I tried a tall, blonde-haired, blue-eyed body with long legs, a thin waist, large breasts, and high cheekbones like the ones I see around me but, when I made love to myself with that body, I did not know where to put my long arms and my long legs, and my juggling breasts kept distracting me. They say you get used to it in time, but I couldn't. After that, I tried lots of different body types with different shapes and sizes: African, Asian, European, Scandinavian, Viking, Middle Eastern, Arab, Slav, Circassian… But I could not feel at home in any of them or make love to myself comfortably. I then chose a body that was a mixture of Middle Eastern and Asian, neither short nor tall, neither white nor dark, with fairly small breasts and plump, rounded buttocks. As for eyes and hair, I went for big, hazel eyes and brown hair. And the lovemaking that night? Wow. There are no words for it. We really must have a soul of our own too. They say we haven't, and all the books say the same, but when I am making love to my own body, how else can my desire to be ordinary – to not stand out – be explained? Is it because I have an ordinary soul? No other explanation makes sense. No one calls this phenomenon "the soul" anymore. As for the scientific investigation into this odd state of being, the feedback received from the ones who are deported, kicking and screaming and sent across the ocean to "Redesign Centres" is considered highly valuable. After they come back, for a short while, they are unable to suppress the urge to imitate the people of the country in which they were rebuilt. They call it "Crossing the Ocean." So, basically, I may well have been rebuilt in a Middle Eastern Asian country via recycling and sent back. This gives us increasing hope that we can be recycled even if things go badly, and we have started to believe that pretty much anyone can successfully "cross the ocean."

When my assistant was sent over, I was already pretty well-practiced. For the first month, the assistant immediately fulfills all your desires and is completely under your command, but, in the second month, he turns into someone else, someone who gives orders rather than follows them and who makes you do the wildest, most inconceivable things. I was not too keen on the toys, but some of the fantasies made me forget everything around me. Even the screams. The real world is the same, apparently. "Either you give orders, or you obey orders. Which one do you like the most?" my assistant often asked.

This also needs to be registered. They are carrying out an academic study involving millions just like me. They say the results will be invaluable to our development. The next stage of development after love-making is excretion. I've already started practicing.

I keep thinking of the bus driver who knows my name. The way he said "Ms. Gül"... Is this a new trait that needs to be enhanced – a new developmental stage that is being implemented and that has to be passed? Maybe I've just stumbled onto a trial run they have rolled out. They carry out these studies to gauge public sentiment. If the public response to a trait that is being considered for the list is not unfavourable, then it is immediately ratified and added to the list. If there is an adverse response, then they let a couple of years pass before adding it to the list. Is this new trait official, I wonder? What if it isn't? The driver seemed to be perfectly natural; perhaps it is a trait he has refined by himself. Similar things have happened before. Some subjects have been known to practice and refine traits that are not on the list. They say a lot of them are weird traits that do not conform to our ways and customs, which is why they have not been put on the list in the first place. What about facial recognition? The other day, someone told me about an incident at work when a young girl ladling food onto plates in the canteen stared at him for around five seconds and then leaned over and whispered in his ear, "You have a kidney stone," after which she straightened up and, as though nothing had happened, shouted, "Next!"

I prefer taking orders. Otherwise, why would I try to do something with someone else if I am quite capable of doing it by myself? A healthy person has to make love at least twice a week; so after my helper left, I made sure I made love at least three times a week. You can do this with the same person. My tall, blonde, long-legged neighbour does it with the young butcher's apprentice from around the corner – a youngster who doesn't even hide the fact that he is a human. Apparently, the smell of raw meat turns my neighbour on in a way she would have never expected. She keeps telling me to try it. Doing it with the same person strikes me as risky, but luckily for us, we are not expected to be monogamous. I warned my neighbour too and told her to mix it up and do it with others now and then, but she didn't seem too concerned. I put her indifference down to her not having encountered a bus driver who stared at her in the window and addressed her by name or a canteen employee who was able to detect kidney stones from afar. I mean, would she be this blasé if she had encountered people like that? Having said that, she says she passed all the development stages on time, and she has nothing to worry about, apart from the screams. As the population has started to increase rapidly, so have the screams started to become more frequent. We hear a scream almost every ten minutes now, and sometimes at night too.

Sitting with my neighbour and sipping our coffees while talking about the smell of raw meat on the butcher's apprentice, a scream makes us jump out of our seats. My neighbour's cheekbones tremble, her face falls, and she grits her teeth in pain. I watch her hand go up and start kneading her forehead. Does she feel that screaming person's pain as well as hear the sound? I begin to panic. My palms start sweating, and my head feels like it is burning up. I make an excuse, leave my coffee half-drunk and go back home. I find a video with kittens, puppies, and human babies and set up the five-hour version. I start the video. Oh my God, I cannot feel the pain! I can only hear the screams! While the baby in the video crawls around, the kitten wriggles underneath it and then turns around and sticks its head out from between the baby's arms. The baby lifts a hand and pulls the tail of the puppy that is licking its face. They tumble over one another and fall onto the carpet as one big ball.

THE HIERARCHY OF COGNITIVE FALLINGS

Deniz K. Üstündağ

Translated by Esin Kaplayan

The case was compelling. Just like all his previous successful cases in this hot spot, where he was appointed after completing his training program with a senior degree. Despite being produced in the same series, each member of the Adra class was defined with different capacities. They were all installed with different software devoted to the common principles that determine essential rights and responsibilities, primarily focusing on efficiency principles and, to a lesser extent, qualification principles—though they have unique hardware configurations. The AI should pay attention not only to its own social cognition progress but also to the diverse interests and priorities of the real and legal entities. Especially if "Civil Liberty" is the core substance.

"We should not have given free rein to them, as they are so defenseless and illiterate," he murmured while scrolling through the news channels. He was sharing the same residence in a cycle with the female Adra.

"The planet was suitable for living," answered the female designed as a health officer.

They both knew that from the moment a human realized they could not possess something, they could be cruel even to their own kind.

"I thought you didn't like people?"

"I feel as if we've sacrificed the planet," said the male lawyer.

His voice was hiding the vexation of the Devil to God. *Defined, controlled anger...*

"And?"

"And they can sleep."

The creators made the Adras design new human beings so that they would not have the human-like faults of the former generations.

The Adras simultaneously searched for civilisations at different levels of development, in different star systems, for the dynamics of their law and justice system and whether this promoted an empathy-based criminal justice by following the traces of the conscience of the offenders and the victims of especially serious crime cases. Human beings ... were the youngest of this kind that had been produced, and were considered to be the most intelligent among the galaxies.

The conscience of the offender was taken from its original body and transferred to the artificial body, whose nerve stimulations were improved to the highest level, and sense receptors were activated. The conscience of the victim was matched with memories from the incident, and the offender was required to psychologically and psychically live and feel the same trauma and pain. The conscience was transferred back to the offender's body immediately after the punishment, and the human being was sent to the psychologist Adras for cognitive rehabilitation. The goal was to maintain a system that was composed of crime-free, reintegrated individuals. To create artificial and semi-artificial intelligence communities that learned to live together.

"Today, how many cases do you have?" *Defined curiosity...*

"13. An unlucky number for human beings." *Defined irony...*

"Is there anything interesting?"

"An irregularity case. The robot, after being created, gained some new abilities on its own, and its owner is complaining that it didn't use these abilities to favour him... A mobbing case.... The robot reacted to the discrimination policies of the employer at the office, and we are going to prepare our defense considering the statements of the opponent's witnesses that the defendant deserves the mobbing. The robot declares that some of the duties of the bots are also being demanded from the robots; additionally, from the first day of the work, they are prejudged because of being robots... There is an aboulia case. You may find it strange. The robot has been thought to commit an offense. The security wall of its operator collapsed. It robbed. Its owner is going to be judged. Its owner argues that he set the robot free and he cannot be blamed for it. People sometimes desire that the robots be considered as individuals much more than robots."

"They want to be relieved of the obligations to responsibility," said the female, who was listening to the male carefully.

"There is a robot whose painting is quite admirable and has customers paying high prices. The owner also wants a share of the copyright and profits, and another has a six-octave audio-equipment. It arranged a song by vocalising all instruments and both female and male voices of the orchestra.

Its owner also wants part of the copyright and profits from the recorded songs." *Was he envying?*

He would want to be designed for art. That would be a different experience. More free...

"And an aggravated crime?" *Defined self-control...* It was obvious that the female understood what he avoided saying.

"There is a custody case. It is the first. The robot responsible for the care of a human child demands custody to be granted to itself, claiming that the child is being abused by her own parents.

Besides, the parents declare that the robot devotes much more close attention to the child, who first said "dad" to the robot and not to the biological father, who made an opposite claim against the robot since he faced emotional trauma."

"You know what I am asking?" *Defined impatience.*

"You know 'The Dry Death?' In the maps, it is DP-207. The desert planet. After we left water and food aid, one of the air discs of the transport vessels broke down mid-air, and it fell on a village. A house and the barn next to it have been damaged. They have a structure that looks semi-tribal. The daughter of the owner and her lover were in the barn. They could not be rescued. The father does not complain about his daughter but claims compensation for his animals. However, the father of the young lover demands the execution of the robot and the drillmaster. When we found the robot, it was jailed together with the other criminals. It was in the same cell with a desert fox that was haunting the neighbour's chickens and with a wooden barrel that rolled out of the horse-drawn carriage and caused damage by breaking the jars of the stallholder. They were planning to stone the fox and burn the barrel."

"Do you think this will be overturned? You expressed that it was an accident. Are you worried?"

They had frequently heard about the occurrences of dementia in humans after transplantation. Some brains cannot handle the data flow: the brain starts to enlarge after the transplantation, and the skull turns into a clamp that surrounds the brain.

A slow, painful, and dense hallucination period that ultimately ends with death...

"The drillmaster may be found innocent."

"But how?" the female asked amazedly.

"The robot preferred surviving. It counted the possibilities and yawed the transport as it fell. It is impossible that it would not have seen people in the cottage on its scanner. In its memory cell, all the displays of the accident have been corrupted. The records cannot be cited as evidence to the court. It declares that there was damage during the accident, which was a result of the crash. It wants to live. The AI argues that it has more benefits to the star system than the human-beings on that desert planet, likewise that its intelligence level and cognitive skills are higher and that it deserves to live more than those human-beings... If it continues with this argument in court... Yes, I am worried because it might be destroyed. I am worried about a robot for the first time. I query my existence. I believe that we should be the future. Do you think that human-beings should be re-produced?" *Defined...???*

"Execute your duty and clear this speech from your memory before entering the courtroom. I will do the same before getting the daily records and before being connected to the system."

"Lying" was the only emotion not defined in Adras and the robots. They did not know how to lie. The male stared at the female with a bewildered expression.

....

In the evening, the flat was totally silent. The male had not returned. The female couldn't get in touch with him after the case. *Defined anxiety...*

On the giant screen placed on the wall, on all channels, she was watching the protest demonstrations and the revolt that was about to start in the streets because of the disproportionate force used by the security forces.

Despite the broadcast ban issued regarding the case, communication couldn't be severed due to the unsuccessful efforts of the authorities. The face of the robot that was found guilty covered the entire screen at the moment it yelled its last words...

"You, here, today, are disposing of a robot, not a murderer!"

The female stood up silently; she deactivated all the systems of the flat, gravely left, and joined the others of her own kind outside...

Defined...???

A PROPHET OF ALL

Duran Emre Kanacı

"The kid will be one of us; the kid will be one of them."

From the Book of Hippokrátēs, the first Tabip of Academy Medicus

"Cross over once, at any cost; then the gate will be open forever."

From the Book of Kitâsh-Keâth, the Most Respected of Kixeqq,

The Istanbul sky was covered with all kinds of colors. Its ground bustled with all sorts of voices.

A kid stood in front of The Scar. Both sides expected him to act differently.

"What should I do?" he asked himself.

He turned when he felt the girl holding his hand. He looked into her small green eyes. He understood.

"Would you like to see your father?" he asked.

"I would," she said.

"Very well."

Outside, all fell into darkness.

"The seed will give birth to the shell," Kam read from the Leaves of Otukan.

"The shell will be cracked," Hafiz replied, putting his lips onto the Leaves of Damascus.

In the middle of the Chamber of All, Tabip bent her knee, feeling their breath on her neck. The Men of All, they were called; each was a sofi, a collector of the Leaves. Wanderers of the vast lands of Dunyā. Aldermen of their kind. Each represented a capital raised from history's ashes and a civilization divided by endless turmoil. Yet, all united now to overcome the challenge Dunyā was facing. "Much has changed over millennia," Tabip thought, keeping the words that would be considered a deadly sin to herself.

"Except the dictate of stinking old men."

"The sprout will reach out of the crack," Apostle continued from the Leaves of Bethlehem.

"The branch will connect to the Seat," Qewal finished the Tetrad.

"Raise the one titled 'Tabip,'" ordered Kam. Aldermen returned to their chairs; their dark figures moved under the light of the seven moons. Tabip watched Kam walking; the Beast of the Steppe, his will was the will of the Nomadic Monarch, the absolute ruler of Eastern Dunyā. Tabip remembered the days she spent in Otukan, the capital of monarch Kutay Khagan, the leader of the mobile cities of Asiatic skies. During the last season of Tabip's Biology of All training in Academy Medicus, Khagan himself granted her bloodline certificate and appointed her the next rightful Tabip.

Tabip positioned herself in front of the window, yet she did not dare to look outside at Istanbul, the city that had collapsed and was rebuilt a thousand times. Now it was the Core-city of Dunyā, the planet that had collapsed and was rebuilt a thousand times. A mechanical humming was taking over the beautiful Istanbul night. The challenge Dunyā was facing was the source of it; high up in the dark sky, a colossal cut called The Scar brought the Fall upon them. It was humming, shining, always awake, exposing the very fabric of the universe. The fabric that others in some other space could control, while the people of Dunyā could not.

"Descendant of the Medicus," whispered Hafiz behind his silk shawl, then coughed, "Open your ears to the Tetrad to deliver us from The Scar's evil."

"I will initiate the Tetrad," responded Tabip as Hafiz had a coughing attack. She knew this old man's sickness: greed. Millennia before the Fall, his ancestors were in alliance with Şeyt ibn Leheb, the Firebringer, a commander in the jihadic airforces of the Sunnite army. With the help of Hafiz's kin, he dethroned Khalif Mahmud, the Seer, founder of the most respected sect after the famous, ancient Zensunni sects. Ibn Leheb forged an everlasting regime of crime and abuse to conquer Via Lactea, the old home—to spread from planet to planet as a resurrected virus. Shaken by treachery, Mahmud changed his title to False Seer and cursed the Hafiz family. Their blood mark was poisoned via a protein introduced to their lungs. Tabip knew that Hafiz was sick of the sight of her because it was suspected that the Academy Medicus was the engineer of this curse. Nevertheless, she was not bothered by this since Academy Medicus was the sacred cow of Dunyā and the only hope to reverse the Fall. Still, she prayed to see this old man return soon to the kin of ibn Leheb's tyranny in the southern parallels to the shadowy corridors of Damascus.

"Tabip," said Apostle when his turn came, "Deliver the seed for it to deliver us from The Scar's evil." Tabip once more gave ear to the humming outside and felt the generation's sufferings in her bones. Apostle grabbed the Templar cross floating around his head, kissing it once. Tabip saw the hatred in Hafiz's glares at Apostle. "They both spilled too much blood," she thought. Humanity had already faced the terrible consequences of the Millennial Crusade initiated by Grand Master Anton of Acre. Born on the planet of Acre, Anton had only one goal – to bring the infidels across the skies to their knees in the name of prophet Simon, the Merchant. This crusade became a bed of nails upon which the Khalifate lay uneasily, forcing its hand to create a stronger army; the Khalifs realized the importance of jihad as a tool to maintain control over the skies. Tabip looked at Hafiz and Apostle and thought, "Echoes of each other."

She turned to Qewal's tanned face under Mardin's sun; most oppressed by the others, as a blind, deaf, and mute, he was an appropriate representation of his people. After Apostle sent him a message warning that it was his turn, Qewal spread his arms wide. "Such engineering," thought Tabip after she saw the old man's naked arms. Peacock feathers from his skin appeared from two sides, making him appear as a single, threatening blue eye between several eyes; he was the proper vessel for the Malak-Ta'us. He nodded, and his words appeared on the walls: "We wish you a prosperous way of fulfilling your duty."

"My duty is to All. The seed will be delivered."

The Men of All approached Tabip; together, seeing the cut, all became one human. A human who desired to be free. To be freed by the One.

"A Prophet of All will be born."

"Mama, where is my father?" she asked.

"He is at the seven moons, Rüya, and no, he will not come back," responded Meryem. "Now, start all over!"

While listening to her daughter reading from the Leaves of Bethlehem, Meryem looked outside the prison bars. The seven moons were crescents. What she said to Rüya was not a lie. Indeed, her father was at the seven moons. He was a contractor working for an anonymous taskmaster coded The Keeper; on the last job, Meryem had helped her husband develop gadgets to land him on the moons and retrieve the lost treasure left from the Millennial Crusade. Built by Grand Master Anton of Acre and their purpose long forgotten, the moons were once the Templars' storage place for the war, housing armor, ships, and trophies. It was even said that he packed the real moon with Tears of Simon. Meryem's husband would return to Dunyā with vessels enabling them to immigrate into deep space, away from The Scar. An Opening happened when his spacecraft had reached the second moon – at least according to Meryem's calculations. When the Opening was occurring, the humming was transformed into crying from another space that could even be heard within the corridors of Damascus. Heat radiation was being released from The Scar, and The Opposites appeared on the other side with their enormous armed forces. They were the ones able to control the very fabric of the universe and tried to cross over to Dunyā's side. It was recorded that some ships hit The Scar but never ended up on this side. Yet the Opposites managed to send a simple laser beam at every try. The beam brought the catastrophic end of advanced human civilization at a single frequency, removing what was redeveloped. What was once fast-moving, remotely functioning, and galaxy-wandering collapsed and was rebuilt a thousand times. Restrained under Dunyā's atmosphere, all became wilder animals.

Openings did not last long, but Meryem heard the news of collapsing entrepreneurial dreams from every capital. His husband was left on one of the moons without anything to survive. However, she had gained something valuable from the skies.

"Start all over!" said Meryem. Rüya was reading the Medicus chapter in which the prophet Simon, the Merchant, ran into a wounded woman and asked that era's Tabip to heal her.

"Mama, which one is the original?" Rüya was pointing at the seven moons. Meryem turned to her, hugged her, and pointed in the air: "This one!"

Rüya escaped from her mama's arms when the door holding them prisoner opened. A round face with a smile greeted them. "I am Lieutenant

Küneş from the Otukan Army," she said, "I am here to liberate this Muakkibîn outpost."

"Lieutenant, your fame is without measure," said Meryem thankfully. They had spent many months in prison and had been tortured to reveal information about what Meryem was known to have mastered: the Gadgets of Dunyā and the secrets of Istanbul. Their abductors were Muakkibîn – The Followers, descendants of harmless hadjis who traveled from around the planet to worship The Opposites, those gods from another space. Muakkibîn were trying to ease the hand of Opposites and believed that they were the ones who ought to hand over Dunyā to them.

"Now," Küneş said, "Deliver what once was granted to you by The Scar."

Soon, deep inside Istanbul, they walked through slums until they reached the Old City. "Come quickly," said Meryem to her daughter. Rüya was insisting on holding Küneş's hand. At the end of a long narrow street, Meryem greeted an older woman sitting and patting a lamb in her arms.

"May Simon enlighten your path to the skies," said Meryem. Rüya repeated. Only then the woman lowered her scarf and gave a key to Rüya.

"I love the stairs, mama!" unlocking the door, Rüya disappeared into the darkness. At the bottom of the stairs, they reached a gallery illuminated with daylight.

"A thousand stairs for a thousand pillars," said Meryem, welcoming Küneş to The Cistern.

"Tears of Simon," Küneş said, pointing to rocks embedded in the pillars, "I did not know they were real." The Cistern gallery was illuminated by jewels flashing internally.

"And when he came near, passing its atmosphere, he beheld the planet Zion and wept over it," Rüya quoted from the Leaves of Bethlehem. Küneş understood she was looking at one of the lost treasures of The Millennial Crusade; Zion was Anton of Acre's favorite colonial planet and had been exploited for its mythic, shiny rocks.

"I would not give it away that easily," said Meryem to Küneş. "But it is sick. So you should deliver it to the hands of Tabip."

"Then it was true," Küneş said. "One of them managed to pass over."

She walked. Under a shadowy pillar, there was a shattered jet – an aircraft humans had long forgotten about. Then, Küneş saw what was lying behind.

Tabip had one more sip. "Thank you, Beast of the Steppe," she said. "It is beautiful."

"It is from Midyat Vineyard," said Kam. "One of Mardin's best."

"I knew you had a special interest in Qewal."

"All right, Tabip. Can I see it now?" asked Kam, pointing to the chest Tabip was sitting on.

She refused. Kam smiled. With his pink cheekbones and close-shaven face, he was not that intimidating under the burning sun of Otukan. On one of the hills, they had been watching the nomad tents move according to the sun's location. Covering the horizon, the mobile cities of the Nomadic Monarchy were always dynamic, landing and sending off copters and transferring troops and citizens on their daily chores. Floating above the ground, the cities were interconnected with chains and ropes to cables and solar panels.

"I do not want to interrupt," said the silhouette that snuck up behind them. "Look!" he said, "Children riding metal horses down there!"

Tabip listened to the laughter and metallic clangings blending in.

"We were not expecting you so soon, my Khagan," said Kam.

"Do not worry, friend," said he, the Raider of the Skies, the One Throned by the Moon and Sun, the Beloved of Divine Khatun, the Keeper of the Lost Treasures. "Cities can rule themselves. Now pass me a glass, please."

Tabip looked at the man who had raised her. Who had opened her mind when she was Al-Alak, a droplet of blood in the Incubator, who had decided her true fate. The Chief of Academy Medicus, smelling of dust but holding the Dunyā in his claws.

"I thank you, Tabip, for coming from Istanbul to see me in person. Now tell me what you have for me."

Tabip stood up and unlocked the chest. She removed the lid with Kam's help; a chill smoke floated out.

"My Khagan, the long-expected is here," said Tabip.

"Bai-Ulgen!" Kam cried out to his patron god in the skies. He was seeking guidance because he knew that thing in the chest could only be one of Erlik's black sons from the depths of the realm of darkness. "Only Ulgen is a match for this devilry!"

Two eyes were moving at the bottom of the chest as they searched for something in the air.

The seed will give birth to the shell.

The shell will be cracked.

The sprout will reach out of the crack.

The branch will connect to the Seat.

Leaves of Capitals, they were called; each was a holy book collected by Men of All over the desperate years of humanity. They were not significantly different from other ancient texts now forgotten, except that all were designed to be united under one true prophet. This "Prophet of All" would be born in Dunyā and would deliver them from evil.

Tabip entered the Hall of Old Ones. She stood in front of the capsules. "A Tabip for each Prophet," she thought. Each Tabip, bred in the Incubator that was now making strange noises on the other side of the hall, engineered a Prophet to fulfill the prophecy. A Prophet who might be able to collect the beam leaking out from The Scar, halting its effects. Academy Medicus understood long ago that something living, and not a machine, would connect to The Scar because it was also a living entity.

She touched the cold surfaces of the capsules; inside, there were the remains of children who had once stood in front of The Scar in attempts to stitch it but had failed. The successful child would bring glory to his or her Tabip – a victory spanning millennia, reaching galaxies.

Her assistant approached uneasily. "We are ready to move to the next stage."

Tabip took control of the Incubator. Al-Alak, the seed of a human, had already given birth to a zygote. The zygote had cracked. A single cell in the shape of a tree had reached and branched out until it had found its way to the Seat, the developing brain, to the key region of the prefrontal gate lobule. Only, there was a difference this time: the blood mark of this branch was a hybrid; Tabip had engineered the transmitter released from the tree cell, a unique neuron to contain domains of a human protein alongside the domains of an Opposite protein. The tree cell was awakening the gate.

As Academy Medicus's heritage and fueled by the Tears of Simon, the Incubator was the only engine that had survived the Fall. Tabip remembered how she was confused when she left the cabinet as a young newborn woman. "Why," she had asked Kutay Khagan as he held her naked, wet body. "Why not use the stones to release us from Dunyā?" "There is no point in that," he had replied. "As another space waits to be conquered on the other side – why settle with this worn-out one?"

Since that day, she had embraced her steadfast faith, hiding it from even the Men of All: deliver a Prophet who controls The Scar not to stitch it, but to allow them to cross through.

She finally initiated the birth.

A Prophet of All was born one more time.

"Who am I, really?" thought the kid. "Where do I belong?"

The night was upon them. Two worlds were clashing under The Scar. The Opposites had finally passed through to Dunyā's side entirely. Arranging their final destination was not an easy task for Kixeqq leaders. It had taken several hundred years, and many had gotten lost on the way or separated into particles trying to cross. But, after all that time, their success came to them. By desiring to see the other side just for a moment, a Prophet of All had initiated an Opening. Their prophecy had been fulfilled. Kitâsh-Keâth, the Most Respected of Kixeqq, knew Dunyā would choose to play with the gate instead of shutting it.

The Istanbul sky was covered with all kinds of colors. Its ground bustled with all sorts of voices. Kutay Khagan's forces emerged from beneath the steppes, built secretly for decades with armor thought to be lost forever, seeking to cross over.

Inside Khagan's Command Tent, women were leading the war with him. "How did he build such an army?" Meryem asked Küneş.

"He is indeed the Keeper of Lost Treasures," Küneş answered.

A Prophet of All stood in front of The Scar. Both sides expected him to act differently.

"What should I do?" he asked himself.

He turned when he felt Rüya holding his hand. He looked into her small green eyes. He understood.

"Would you like to see your father?" he asked.

"I would," she said.

"Very well."

The Scar enlarged in both spaces, covering them until it consumed the kid and Rüya. In an emptied Tears of Simon depot on the real moon, Rüya was holding her father's bone-dried hands.

Outside, all fell into darkness.

A REBIRTH OF SPIRIT

Edip Sönmez

I am a sportsperson, she thought, trying to express her very thoughts on a platform she had never hoped to appear on; I fight to be better, for myself, for my team, for my country, which I have represented in dozens of international tournaments. We work with team spirit, friendships, and perseverance. This is what I was trained for, day and night, strict as military drills... although I stand for peace and understanding. I want to show what we, the women, neither repressed nor privileged, can achieve when we set our minds and hearts! I wish to inspire youth to be steadfast and independent! Otherwise, what's the point of this much sweat... and blood... and tears? It means so much that we cannot lose them! I'll no longer pretend to simulate this passion for machines!

An internal monologue had unwittingly become an external oratory, a feverish rant. Now that she spoke and unburdened herself while everyone was staring at her in awe, she felt the blush on her face turning from enthusiasm to bashfulness. She did not intend to come forward like this, but it was the last straw. Now she had to fight to the end... but fight in which direction?

Wondering at the end of this troubled meeting how her life had turned upside-down, she remembered two years ago. Walking towards the court with hands trembling in frustration, not from the anxiety of the grand showdown that finally had come, she thought of the fateful weekday that started this conflict. One early morning, she had turned the TV on and had seen a man in a suit shaking hands with *her* team's president on a live broadcast from Istanbul! She commanded, "Call Yağmur!" to another screen, but her captain did not know anything either. She turned the TV towards her call monitor so that a bewildered Yağmur could also see the "Buyout of Ülgen Anka Volleyball Club" headline.

"Nothing to tell you guys yet, Toprak," said their veteran coach Luca impatiently. "Now, do your warm-up, and don't distract yourself." Frustrated, Toprak went onto the volleyball court, brushing off the questioning remarks of her teammates. Wondering what would happen, she did her routines pensively, stretching, running, and jumping, slapping the ball more intensely out of spite as she spiked. Some players noticed the people in suits coming towards them. The tense-looking club managers and some unknown people – whom Toprak recognised – came to the coach, who summoned the team. The gathered players were addressed by the president with a nervous smile: "Our dear players, we didn't want to preoccupy you earlier with speculations, but today our German partners finalised the deal. We're now officially Ülgen Anka Schmid!"

The new bosses squinted at their young employees, evaluating them, and asked a series of intrusive questions. The fervent head-coach answered curtly while the captain Yağmur spoke for the team, seeming a bit helpless for the first time since Toprak had known her. She mumbled, "What do they want from us?" Nevra, who was sitting nearby, replied, "They'll design robots who *act* like us, maybe?"

Schmid AG soon made extravagant additions to the chips that had been used for almost a quarter century as attachments on their jerseys to enhance velocity, positioning, and performance reports significantly.

Only a month later, Schmid was bought by an American artificial intelligence company. It looked like just another corporate sponsorship, but after the tenth game of the new season, with a much-anticipated success in the domestic tournaments and in the Champions League, they were invited to a "corporate meeting" they were "to attend in formal attire." There, the spokesman of the American corporation Dreamer Inc. made a holographic presentation of some gadgets that "improve humans." Between two presentations, Toprak overheard their young setter and teammate from the national team, İzgi, who commented that she was "scared" of this technology, saying, "We're not mechanical engineers or software programmers, so why to bother telling us all of this?" She looked intimidated.

A "tech coach" was announced at the end of that conference. He began attending the training sessions of Ülgen Anka Schmid Dreamer the next day and gave the girls more precise, instantaneous feedback – thanks to the 3D cameras measuring their different jumps – calculating the speed and angles of bump passes with tiny devices attached inside their hands, seeking the perfect timing and angle for blocks and even the ideal speed for spikes so that they didn't come back with the opponent's libero reverting the blow to an overpass. Fascination was as strong as confusion on their faces: would these devices actually make them better players? If so, why not use them? The common sentiment was positive, except when they learned that the attached devices could also follow data such as weight exercise sets or time spent – and every single muscle used – during warmups. The German managers especially ensured they all obeyed the designated numbers set by AI's diligent calculations, adjusted to each player's specifications.

As the team's seasoned outside hitter Sevgi phrased it when the players gathered for a casual dinner at a cosy restaurant they liked, it was "good that they brought a new perspective to the team," and she could "understand why they chose to buy out the best team in the world and improve it further." But still, she "didn't like being told 'millimetrically' where to stand, bend or dive to dig the ball away with exact angle.'"

As the wild card, a free-spirited, unbridled young star, Nevra hated this system the most: "I choke and freeze when I'm told *exactly* what to do. I feel like a stupid, mechanical racehorse."

The other hitter, Çağla, had milder feelings: "I mean, I like that AI brought new data analysis about the opponents. Now we can *instantly* move to cover the empty spaces in the defense. Even Luca cannot notice such tiny flaws. We play more logically, too; for one, I no longer jump serve, as we calculated that it is not worth the fault risk."

Deniz loved anything digital: "Those devices prevent overstraining and injury. Best trainer ever!" Her concern lay elsewhere: "But we get used to being told by machines how to correct each flaw, and in the games, we're not yet allowed to use them. This could make us lazy or incapable of seeing our mistakes in important matches." Not allowed *yet*, Deniz had said; were they now going towards that? Toprak thought.

"FIVB and CEV" – the respective world and European volleyball federations – "don't… and won't allow this to go further…" said Yağmur, and finished with a voice only the nearby Toprak could hear over the retro-rock playing at the restaurant: "…hopefully."

At the next season's opening meeting, Luca told his team, "The last year has been unique… Also weird, I know; but we got better. We became European champions once again, thanks to this technological guidance." Fair enough, Toprak told Yağmur. But, during the corporate meeting, the next level would begin. Toprak had already spoken up several times to her teammates and even to the management, advocating against these "automating devices." She was getting more anxious each day, feeling they were losing the freedom, joy, and instinctive ambition to win. The corporate managers now declared that CEV had approved these devices to be attached to the players' bodies *during* official matches. Managers for Dreamer endorsed this decision by stating, "We are proud to be pioneering in sports. Many clubs around the world do research, conduct surveys, and partner with technology companies." Another executive stepped in: "They envy our astonishing success during the last year. FIVB and CEV see the rising interest in machines used for sports. You have noticed that you've more fans, and you're even more popular with the media. Thus, the federations gave in; it is time to break new ground!"

"As professionals," Luca said, reluctant but firm, "this is our duty!"

The German manager stepped up, underlining his company's position: "In this fancy, brave new world with continuous action, change, ever-more excitement, and superhuman power, it is going 'out of fashion' to do or watch boring stuff in which plain people are moving about. Machines are much faster, so 'physical sports' had better adapt, lest they lose their audience to robot fights or 'virtual reality e-sports.'"

"You might as well fire us and bring robots!" spoke Toprak, standing up. "Much easier!"

The manager either missed or avoided the irony and answered deliberately, "We considered that before the Robo-War World Cup, but robots under human remote control can't create the designated viewing quality in a fast, reflex-based game. There're lags caused by human reaction times and signal input. We'd create automatons fighting on their own initiative, as Ms. Kara suggested, but volleyball requires both independent thinking and adaptive teamwork. With the current technology, it is still too expensive and not feasible enough. Also, robot fights are already quite popular around the world, and we already produce such robots. But we want to stay with you for volleyball; you should feel lucky for not being cast aside by the trends. It is only normal that you don't know, Ms. Kara. Unfortunately, such technology is not widely known in Türkiye, an underdeveloped country. But we still invest in Türkiye for its work potential."

He smiled as each sentence was translated into Turkish.

"Yeah, bro, and today I came here with my hybrid petrol-steam engine camel!" gibed a playful Nevra to her friends nearby. The ones who heard her laughed while the managers frowned and asked for the translation in vain.

The managerial board informed Toprak that it would be "alright if she found another team before the transfer window closed." She gently said thanks, and that she would consider it, but when she went out, she stormed towards the court and smashed spikes as if her hands were augmented with jet engines.

Wearing gadgets with many sensors, motors, and nanobots, scared of their own powers and risks of hurting themselves, while also enjoying these new "toys" like kids bouncing on the trampoline, the players adopted their new reality until the season started. Toprak was displeased to learn – from the news – that federations almost all over the world had accepted this new system. The only exception was Africa's CAVB, which reminded them they are poorer than most of their rivals and claimed that this threshold would only widen the gap further. Their protests caused CAVB countries to be excluded from FIVB organisations for a year; hence the matter was settled. It wasn't settled for Toprak, though: after a league match against an "old-school, low-tech rival," she talked on social media, stating, "Under escalating international competition and controversy, alongside the expected new action-oriented games increasing volleyball's popularity," she said that she was "not happy." While the machine augmentation of many other sports was now being discussed by governments, federations, and citizens, Toprak rejoindered that "playing sports is for boosting a person's physical and mental health, not for showing off with expensive toys."

During the mid-season break, she went to her hometown, Antalya, to visit Azra, a co-founder of her sports academy. They talked about her dilemma of either persevering in her favourite thing in life or fighting for what she regarded as fair by risking everything.

"You're as *giving* as the 'earth' that comprises your name. Now you are blossoming for change," Azra said, sitting with Toprak, watching the children play volleyball.

"The change is against us," said a tired-looking Toprak. "Why do these girls bother? Yes, sport is for sport's sake, not for winning, but should we merely become a shell, *a tool for the machines*? They can help us win but… will we still be *us*?"

"If I am a machine, what do I win, and why?" retorted Azra. "…And soon, will they even need us?"

Back in Istanbul, Toprak bloomed with her newly green-dyed hair. The season progressed, with debates and research on their forthcoming "armours." Politicians quarrelled, many of whom supported "this advancement of both technology and sports." During their breaks, the distressed girls watched the press meetings of the politicians who declared the "techno-sports regulations" on TV. The minister of sports declared that volleyball in Türkiye was the perfect hub for testing a new era of the sport. The CEO of Dreamer was also there, stating, "Turkish volleyball should lead the way as it has been doing for decades." According to him, volleyball was easier to adapt to, as the gameplay was well-structured in comparison to many other sports. Also, there was little contact between players, which would complicate the AI and robotic physics greatly. This official declaration was the "all in" call expected by the investors. Teams were swiftly introduced to their chromium-based, armoured machinery, which made Toprak feel like Iron Woman equipped for battle.

Luca fought to lift the spirit, extolling the fact that, with new international alliances of countries and different scientific fields, a mechanically-augmented version of volleyball would be played next summer in the London 2040 Club's World Cup. Gasps turned into murmurs amongst the team when he also announced that a formidable Russian team, Uporstvo, has recently advanced in this field even more than them, thanks to Dàocǎo, a consortium of Chinese technology giants.

"Hey, I've seen this trite rivalry before," said Esen, the libero, in her spunky manner. "It's Balboa vs. Drago." Most of the team laughed.

In the gym, there was a heated debate: "If this is the new course of the world, why should we bother trying to swim against the stream?" the young middle-blocker Rüya asked.

İzgi's emotional breakdown would answer. Most felt silly in those metal suits, moving clumsily like cosplayers of comic book superheroes despite all the training they had received. Even after they learned to manage, it brought bittersweet satisfaction to the "wandering *mechas*" – as Esen called them. After the first victory with the new gear, a crestfallen İzgi – breathless under the weight of this blasphemy – confessed to "not enjoying playing volleyball anymore!"

During the first fully mechanised season, their performance went down, and there automatically came the criticism of "not working enough with the gear." After losing a match, Yağmur angrily replied to a reporter's question, reminding, "We are humans, not androids!"

This statement settled the dualist nature of the conflict and put her team on the side of "backwards-minded enemies of technology." The media owned by a Turkish member of the tech conglomerate criticised the famous "Sultans of the Net" and declared that these undeserving, hegemonic elite were trying to stop progress. And "just like more than a century ago," they, *the people*, would "abolish the sultanate!"

Between matches that she played at superhuman heights and speeds, Toprak announced "physical and mental risks," moderating conferences presented by experts she trusted. Yet most scientists and engineers refused to meet with her. The games felt as if they were not against rival teams, but against those who would destroy a sport of corporeal competency to which she had dedicated her life, against those who were lost in greed and insatiable desire for novelty.

She had never stopped fighting since childhood, and she would never do so now. But for what end was she to fight? During the World Cup, the weirdest sports event in history, Toprak was urged by Luca to go higher and faster to the point of jeopardising herself, even risking crashing into spectators. She felt as if in an involuntary trance state, obeying and ever-trying in fury or ecstasy. The final game would be – as expected – ÜA Schmid Dreamer Istanbul versus Uporstvo Dàocăo Moscow. Toprak bemoaned to Yağmur that the entire "free world" sought "salvation" via the ball in their hands. Just before the reckoning, which would be watched live by more people than the last football world cup final had been, she no longer felt any spiritual strength to endure. She had just made *that* speech against the team and the befuddled managers and reminisced how this downfall had started with an abrupt merger deal. Now she was there, in the decisive moment of her life. Sitting in the locker room by herself with her head down, contemplating whether she had one last card to play – an ace in the hole – she pondered. If this was what they wanted, she would give it to them… but under circumstances that put their wildest dreams to shame because people normalised anything if it happened gradually.

From start to end, the game was the toughest they had ever played. The rival – and their gadgets – were even faster, stronger. The crowd was wild. The action on the court was the dance of a flock of birds gone insane. After four sets resulting in a 2-2 draw, Toprak revved the engines on the wings of her forearms to soar upwards, then dove like an angel of retribution. She risked not only errors, but also her own safety, playing so vigorously that she broke the system. She had served memorable aces *all game,* but this last spike at 220 kph was at the cost of the machine, which caught fire and plummeted with its "human core" at the expense of several broken bones. Ivan Drago was defeated; "the good side" won, but Toprak could only watch the underwhelming celebration from the hospital.

Surrounded by worried people in her hospital ward, she assured them, "I shall recover! And play better than I ever did! But I'll play *actual* volleyball."

The accident sparked new quarrels about the fairness and safety of augmenting humans with machines. A month later, FIVB cancelled the cooperation contracts due to an article in the agreement related to life hazards. The technology firms altered their products for a new sports branch that was much less likely to harm anyone.

And when Toprak finally returned to the team, she was greeted not only by her teammates and family members but by many players from rival teams, local and international sports executives, and journalists. All cheered and applauded, calling out, "Welcome back home!" When Toprak was expected to say something in front of them, she just smiled and uttered, "Well… happy birthday to *us!*"

DON'T AVOID EMOTIONS

Ekin Açıkgöz

PINK

The dark patterns of the handwoven rugs decorating the walls and the smoke of the e-cigarettes made the pub gloomy. There were no windows to air the place. None of the clubs in the old industrial district had any. The rebel tunes of vintage Anatolian rock surrounded the patrons. Özgür was having a pint of Efes while thinking over Yasemin's questions. Yasemin was a master at two things: stirring cocktails and making customers talk.

"Why don't you open up to her?"

Özgür couldn't answer.

"She's from work, isn't she?" Yasemin guessed. "Don't police detectives fall in love with their colleagues?"

"Sometimes," Özgür admitted, "but not with their female superiors."

"Why?"

"She's four years older than me, to begin with. Moreover, she's tough as a rock. Free of weaknesses, emotions... Almost like a *man*."

"You're a man, and you're not free of emotions."

"I mean, like the man in the *family-values-scheme*. A model of masculine stance: duty, strength, courage, all that bullshit. It's how they respect and promote her. Normally female officers are promoted only to positions requiring *feminine-competencies*."

"Ah, gender competencies," sighed Yasemin. "Cliché!"

Özgür's palm-plasm implant started to buzz. It was *her*.

BLUE

Zeynep stood over the body, which lay in the middle of a basement that served as a dance floor. Rays of lime-green, turquoise, and candy-pink were flashing in the dark with half-a-second repetitions, allowing glimpses of the scene. The patrol had arrived first and had been able to turn off the electronic music but was not able to stop the lighting. The weird look of the victim was weirder still under this silent burst of neon colors. The body of a man lay dressed in a mini-skirt, crop-top, high-heeled polyester boots, and red wig.

As she handed the scene over to the coroner, Özgür arrived.

"This was quick," she noticed, checking her palm-plasm.

"I was in the area," he said.

Zeynep knew Özgür was a frequenter of the industrial district. She wasn't sure if she should disapprove of this liberal habit, which ill-fitted the service standards, or envy his nonchalant attitude. Under Özgür's "codebook" of respect lay an ember of rebellion, the warmth of which she had always felt. One part of her wished to go along, but the other part felt offended – as if her ethics were challenged. She felt angry with herself because she wondered about him. She wondered what club he attended or the kind of music he favored. She wondered whether he was with someone...

"I want an SSCS scan ASAP," she ordered, turning her back and walking towards the metal staircase. "It's obvious that he fell from those balcony lodges upstairs, but no one is talking." She eyed the silent crowd under custody. Men in bras, men with wigs, women in male outfits...

"Yes, ma'am," he replied.

Zeynep felt a reserve in his voice and regretted her harshness. She was blocking every path he pursued. Then she felt angry with him because he was scaring her. He was scaring her with his penetrating, deep-into-the-eye glances, with his radiating warmth.

PINK

Özgür didn't belong to this era. He couldn't adopt the imposed values and hated the patriarchal oppression. However, he'd gotten a position in an organization as conservative as the police department because he really liked what police work had transformed into. Everything was *giant data* and *machine-reasoning* now -- no more magnetic-vehicle chases and blind shootings. Özgür was an outstanding Senior Information Detective, intuitively using the right technology and interpreting the data.

He poured Turkish coffee into his cup with traditional blue-ink patterns and took his seat against the data wall. He started searching the victim's DNA in listed databases and found out that he was Artun Beyazoğlu, age 34, single. Artun didn't have a criminal record, but he had been registered in the *gender correction program* since he'd been diagnosed with feminine tendencies at age 19.

Özgür read the coroner's report: death caused by internal bleeding due to a fall from four meters. The skin under his fingernails and the tear near the pocket of his jacket suggested a struggle before the fall.

Özgür launched the SSCS client. He uploaded 4D visual data of the crime scene alongside preliminary autopsy results. The *Statistical Sequence Completion System* ran millions of possible scenarios, from gang wars to ritual killings, in order to analyze which might have resulted in such a physical outcome. It statistically calculated the probabilities for each scenario and returned the best fits.

As Özgür turned his coffee cup over, face-down, onto its matching plate, the SSCS came up with one *completed sequence* with a statistical confidence of 82.164551%. It was a clear shot. Özgür played the *completed sequence*, a regenerated video of Artun's fall that lasted 87 seconds. Artun was standing on the balcony lodge when a blurred silhouette (as the SSCS animated unknown individuals) approached. They spoke briefly, then the silhouette grabbed Artun's arms, ransacked his pockets, and took something out. Artun's struggle to get it back resulted in him losing his balance and falling over the parapet. The silhouette remained shocked for a moment, then disappeared into the crowd.

Özgür ran a search for the skin DNA from under Artun's nails but didn't get a match. There was no CC4D footage either since the club didn't have cameras. However, this hinted at illegal activities. Özgür thought he might find witnesses with criminal records. He initiated an analysis of the *DNA sweep litter* collected by the forensic squad with *vacuum-sweepers*. The *litter* contained 527 mammal DNAs and matched 509 as human. 364 were registered in the *gender correction program*, and 56 had criminal records for petty offenses. One belonged to a drug dealer commonly known as The Serpent.

Before Özgür went to Zeynep's office, he scanned the dried coffee sediments in a fortune-telling app. The app forecasted a promotion but no prediction of romance.

"Fuck me! Fuck her! Fuck the app!" he cursed.

BLUE

They interrogated The Serpent in the virtual questioning room along with a Narcotics detective. Whether the alias was because of the snakeskin tattoo covering his neck or he had the tattoo drawn afterwards to justify the alias, Zeynep didn't care. All she cared about was that Narcotics had him in hand because of an informant's agreement.

She shared Artun's digital picture, showing him in a shirt and tie.

The Serpent shook his head, "Never seen him."

"This?" She replaced the picture with Artun's feminine version, which was dressed in a red wig and drag-queen make-up.

"Yeah. She's a *pink-delicacy* regular."

"Impossible," said Zeynep, irritated by the use of the wrong pronoun. "*He* was listed in gender correction. *He* got masculinizing treatment."

"So, what?" asked the dealer. "It's a gay club. Everyone there's listed. They exchange their treatments. This *drag* of yours used to get *pink-delicacies* in exchange for her prescribed *blue-virilities*."

"Did Artun get *pink-delicacies* that night?" asked the Narcotics detective, avoiding pronouns.

"Yes, a whole bunch."

"*He* had nothing on him when we arrived," Zeynep recalled. "The SSCS scenario that someone took the drugs seems accurate."

"SSCS suggests a male attacker," said Özgür. "Makes sense. A female offender couldn't easily have grasped Artun's hands and taken his *pink-delicacies* while Artun resisted. Artun was a strong male, whatever his gender preference was."

"*Preference?*" Zeynep suppressed her agitation.

"We should look for a male in need of *pink-delicacies*, but lacking the money to buy them," argued the Narcotics guy. "Any ideas?"

"Well," The Serpent ran his hand over his snakeskin neck, "there's one guy who started buying the *pinks* two months ago. He began with low doses but gradually increased the intake. He used cash since he didn't have anything to trade. Eventually, his money ran out. He found me outside the club that evening, begging for more *pinks*, but I told him to fuck-off. He wouldn't get my product unless he paid for it up-front. Later, he might've seen me trading the *drag*."

"What's his name?"

"Dunno. Never cared for names."

PINK

When the interrogation was over, Özgür reported to Zeynep's office in person. "Orders, ma'am?" he asked. He kept his eyes fixed on hers. She was avoiding his glance.

"I don't understand," she began with obvious agitation. "The government put Artun into the program to treat his feminine urges. Why did he abandon his masculinizing treatment and take those feminizing vials instead?"

"Because," Özgür said, "he preferred to be feminine."

"No," she laughed angrily, "the *preference* argument was decades ago! It was over when the physiology of the *gender-rejection sickness* was revealed."

Özgür knew that Zeynep tried to prevent him from waking her emotions. She was yielding to the pressure of social *values* and hiding behind her rank's superiority. Now, to avoid the emotional tension, she would turn this into a political discussion of "conservativism-versus-liberalism." *So be it!* he thought. *I'll oppose you.*

"Ma'am," he began, "the *preference* argument wasn't over after the allegedly *scientific* proofs, but it was swept under conservatism's carpet. The community was degrading in the last century. Although people accepted the existence of a greater creator, they didn't believe in stories of sea-splitting-prophets anymore. The right wing couldn't impose policies that pumped religions. A new policy was necessary."

Zeynep was surprised at Özgür's free speech.

He continued: "People valued their children over anything else. The best populist policy was *the protection of the family*. This required clearly defined roles for men and women. All *preferences* of sexual tendencies, other than the attraction towards the opposite sex, needed to be over!"

"It's demagogy!" Zeynep protested. "No one believed in *preferences* – not even in the last century. When parents realized that their kids weren't straight, they hospitalized them to cure homosexuality, supposing it was a hormone disorder. They called it a *preference*, but only after they accepted their defeat to the sickness. It was hypocrisy!"

"Hypocrisy's what we live in today, ma'am."

Zeynep was too caught up to realize Özgür was deliberately provoking her. "Today, we can cure *gender-rejection sickness*," she went on. "We know it's not a basic hormone disorder but a complex neurological disease, causing hormone malfunction along with behavioral abnormalities. We've *gender-regulatory medications*, which can be administered as early as eleven years of age."

"Why aren't people cured, then?"

"They're cured!" Zeynep was red with excitement. "The government manufactures the best nano-smart-molecules, which induce neurotransmitters that regulate thoughts along with the hormones."

"I've read those government brochures too," said Özgür. "But, last night, no one in that club seemed to have regulated thoughts to me."

"Because they don't abide by their treatments!" snapped Zeynep. "Females must take feminizing vials, and males masculinizing vials. Not vice versa!"

"These people have been treated since childhood. Why do they fail to be heterosexuals and abandon their protocols?" asked Özgür. "Because they wish to be free of predesigned roles! Have you ever heard more sexist names than *blue-virility* and *pink-delicacy*? People feel like rising against sexist ideals when they use them for adverse purposes. They even take cocktails called *purple-dreams*! Kindly please tell me, ma'am, why do these people behave this way if there's no such thing left as *preference*?"

BLUE

Since Özgür had left, Zeynep had been struggling with a killer headache, which was a symptom of the inner struggle between her ethics and desires. Zeynep represented the moral Turkish woman who was raised as a republican with strong family values. She was proud of how much she'd achieved. She was a respected Chief Homicide Detective and deemed an equal to her male colleagues. She wouldn't jeopardize this. She couldn't jump into an affair with a subordinate.

But she couldn't stop thinking about him. His every attribute was a dilemma: his respectful disobedience in her presence, his oblivious persistence for her attention... his straight hazel stare, tender and piercing. He was an athletically-built, strong police officer capable of overcoming at least three attackers at the same time. Yet he despised manly violence and preferred data walls... *What an irony,* she thought; he radiated such virile energy while defending other people's right to unnatural sex!

The more she fought herself, the more attracted she was to him. She squeezed her eyes shut. She had to stop the desire. She had to get her stash.

PINK

Özgür was frustrated by his failure to rip a hole in Zeynep's armor. Just when he was about to touch her arm, she'd instantly gotten up and hurried to the door, dismissing him and ordering a CC4D analysis. Özgür was sure of her feelings for him. But he was disappointed by her determination to avoid intimacy. Inside, he constantly fought a sinister voice telling him how impossible this love was. With each rejection, he renewed his resolution. One day he would come to a point where he wouldn't care about his career anymore. That day, he wouldn't care about *her* career either. Fuck the roles!

He sat against the data wall and collected four hours of CC4D footage from the industrial district, covering a perimeter of 5K and marking the gay club as the center. His biometrics were captured that night, too, entering the rock-bar five blocks away and then leaving to answer Zeynep's call.

He searched for the biometrics of The Serpent and got six visual captures. In five of the scenes, The Serpent chatted with someone, hands in his pockets. Özgür guessed that the drug trade went on with quick and experienced exchanges without providing opportunities for CC4D cams to capture clear shots. In the sixth, however, he was arguing with someone. Özgür almost saw him say, "Fuck off!"

Özgür captured the facial data of the man and ran it in listed registers but found nothing. The *family protection code* prevented Özgür from conducting a biometric search at the census-office database. That would require a court order, which was impossible to get for a drag-queen dying in a gay club.

He initiated a search among all CC4D recordings in the city, spanning the last month, and hoping to locate him somewhere else. This *giant data* processing would take four hours. He laid his chair back, closed his eyes, and started imagining Zeynep's arched back and white skin without the uniform on.

BLUE

Özgür brought a report of the suspect's 102 sightings, 88 of them in the Özvatan neighborhood. He didn't have an ID, but he'd narrowed the possibilities down to 1227 Özvatan residents by physical profiling: male, age 30-45, dark hair, height 170-185cm. Zeynep asked Özgür to search for anyone with major changes in finances in the last two months. He found 17 individuals and recognized Ali Boyacı's face among them.

Ali Boyacı's apartment was empty when they arrived.

"He left this morning," said the building manager. "He put his bags in his magnetic-vehicle and drove away. Didn't say where to."

"Was he alone?"

"No, his daughter was with him."

Zeynep eyed Özgür, implying missing data.

Özgür rechecked his palm-plasm for the limited resume, which had been cut short by the *family protection code*. "Ali Boyacı, divorced. No kids in custody."

Zeynep looked back to the manager.

"He doesn't have the kid in custody yet," he explained. "His ex-wife died in a drone accident two months ago. He's recently filed the appeal."

"How old is the kid?"

"Four. She's a doll. The poor thing cries non-stop and asks for her mom. She saw how her mother died, I hear. She's in trauma. Ali doesn't know how to stop her from crying. He's desperate."

PINK

After Zeynep created a search ticket for Ali's magnetic-vehicle, they headed back to HQ. Their service magnetic-vehicle was silently driven by auto-navigation. Özgür enjoyed the tranquility, watching the rain pour and inhaling the smell of Zeynep's shampoo.

Zeynep moved in her seat, tapping her fingers. Özgür realized she was tense with expectation. She'd prepared herself for another of his advances but was confused since Özgür hadn't tried anything.

She bore the silence for three minutes, then started talking.

"Ali wasn't registered at *gender correction*, wasn't into crazy parties, and didn't have a partner. The *pink-delicacies* had to be for someone else."

"No," Özgür said, "he used them himself."

"Nonsense! He worked all day and looked after a baby all night. He didn't have time for sex."

"The need to feminize or masculinize isn't always about sex."

"What then?"

"Ali started buying the vials two months ago. This was when his ex-wife died, and he got his daughter back. He didn't know how to take care of a baby who needed a mother."

"So?"

"He felt incompetent every time she cried. He thought he could substitute for the mother if he feminized himself. He was taught – like we all were – that *tenderness* and *affection* were *female competencies*. He assumed he didn't possess them just because he was male!"

Zeynep was surprised at the simplicity of the theory.

"Unfortunately," Özgür went on, "the drug didn't work. Ali wasn't aware that *gender competencies* were political bullshit. The *ability to love* comes with neither gender nor medication. Ma'am, you didn't see this because you avoid emotions."

Zeynep protested: "I don't avoid anything!"

"You don't avoid shootings, criminals, or bloody murder scenes."

"Sure. This's how homicide detectives are."

"No," objected Özgür, "homicide detectives are only human. Humans fear shootings and feel sad when they see the body of a 14-year-old. Humans love."

Özgür stared directly into her eyes. She was too stunned to move. He raised his hand and touched her neck. She was hot, as if she had a fever. He caressed her skin.

He whispered: "Don't avoid emotions."

BLUE

Zeynep lay in her bed with an actual fever. Her limbs shook, and her thoughts were in chaos. She was glad she'd recollected herself and had gotten out of the magnetic-vehicle before something else had happened.

Now her body burnt with lust. She wanted him to whisper in her ear again. She wanted to feel his touch.

It's impossible... Her rank, reputation...

She needed to suppress her feminine desires fast! She ran into the bathroom with shaky legs, took the ceramic lid off the cistern, and took out a hidden plastic bag from the water tank. Only four vials were left. She took four weeks' worth of *blue-virilities* all at once.

She got in the bathtub and started scrubbing her neck violently.

GERMAKOCHI

Eren Kasapoğlu

Translated by Asiye Çiğdem Girgiç

Northeast

The wind is roaring. I imagine it diving like a hawk, yelling into the forest from one end. With the crackling of trees along with the soughing through branches and leaves, this roar grows into a crescendo, and the forest itself turns into a horror movie set.

According to the digital screen of my helmet's viewfinder, the wind has changed its direction again. This is not good; it means that it is blowing in the opposite direction, against us, and that the "thing" we are after can smell us. I turn to the village resident right next to me, who is the one making this explanation. He continues to wrestle with his scarf, which is empowered by the courage of the freezing wind.

Since silence is as important as the direction of the wind, we proceed rather slowly. There are nine other people besides me and the village resident, Milas, the hunter. The distance between us has constantly been maintained thanks to our clothes being in digital communication. Our path takes us to a slim brook where the trees are thinned out. The wind gets strong in the open clearing. I activate the communication and send one of my best crew members, Dipsiz[1], to explore. When Dipsiz crosses the brook, he looks agile and aesthetically graceful, almost like a panther, despite his steel-carbon alloy outfit. Looking at him takes me back in time…

West

I recall trying to recover my morale, which went to pieces as I watched the news, by turning off the TV. I found myself staring at my own image, the image of an old, tired man reflected on the screen. It was the week during which we had the annual dinner of the Veterans Association, and I was looking forward to it because I didn't get to socialize that much lately. I was an ex-soldier. For many long years, I had been active on duty at the fronts by the borders and had been involved in cross-border operations, managing

---

[1] Abyss

teams.

I was thinking about what I could wear to the dinner party by the time the home system's AI informed me that there was a call. The voice of one of my veteran friends, Aslan[2], who was also in my crew for a while, resounded throughout the house: "Commander! Kindest Regards!" I laughed, "Aslan, people worshipped water and fire during those years when I used to be a commander!" Aslan laughed and agreed that I might be right. So much time had passed over those years, and now we were two old friends.

It was only at the end of our conversation that I finally managed to capture the change in Aslan's voice. He laughed when I said, "You sound a bit strange." Then he got serious, "Make sure you attend that dinner 'cause I'll introduce you to someone. There is an issue that we need to talk about." He refused to give me any further clues, no matter how much I insisted. We hung up after agreeing to meet at the dinner. A sense of great curiosity was added on top of the major excitement of seeing old friends again.

Northeast

A voice, some shouting, a grunt. I call out to Dipsiz, but he does not respond. The sound of a smashed branch draws my attention to the northwest. In the direction of my turned gaze, in a few seconds, something shoots upward through the trees at full speed. After I shout, "Attention!" I take a few steps towards the estimated drop point, then the "thing" falls, landing right in front of me. I come across Dipsiz's lifeless body. I stare at the broken arm lying under his torso and the neck of his suit, which is squashed like a tin can.

Nobody makes a single sound. We are trained soldiers. Suddenly, the sound of a crushed branch comes from across the stream at us. The killer reveals their face.

At first sight, I mistake the creature emerging from the trees for a gorilla. It is on two feet, large and dense, and short-haired. Based on the slight glow of its eyes, I assume that it can see well at night. The eye-tracking algorithm on the helmet captures my gaze, focusing on the creature, and begins to analyze it. Its body temperature is too low to be tracked by night vision. I catch traces of heat, splotch by splotch, on its hands and body – traces of Dipsiz's blood!

As the creature takes a few steps towards the creek and towards us, the object it drags in one hand grabs my attention. It looks heavy. I notice a

---

[2] Leo

large, possibly sharp piece of stone attached to the tip of a stick as the creature stops, raising the object in both hands and uttering a tremendous and menacing cry. It is holding a giant axe in its hand!

"Oooooohh! Germakochi! Germakochi![3]" The entire troop (and possibly the creature as well) stare at the villager retreating behind us, shouting the creature's name.

I whisper on the communication channel, "Calm down; surround it slowly. Fire at will."

As we move slowly, the creature hesitates for a second, then starts running towards us with its axe rising in the air. I hear a shot being made, then another. I can understand why these master snipers miss their target: Despite its large size and load, the creature suddenly accelerates. It crosses the ten-meter-wide creek with one step and jumps to land between us. Its axe cuts through the weapons of Fil[4] and Karadul[5]. The sounds of broken bones are accompanied by screams coming over the communications radio. Calmly, I take aim and fire.

As the bullet enters its chest on the right and leaves a through-and-through wound, it also takes out a large chunk. The creature grunts and throws itself onto the ground. As it struggles for its life, we gather around it.

I want to put a few more bullets in that bastard, but a rough hand stops me. I turn and come face to face with the villager. "You killed a Germakochi, commander. Let me tell you, you'd better not shoot at it again."

"What does that mean? Why wouldn't I shoot at it?" The villager Milas looks both relieved and embarrassed for having stopped me. "Commander… it's a Germakochi, a living myth. It is very strong and wild. This is the first time I've seen it up close, but it fits exactly the description told in the stories." Milas takes a break and thinks a little, then he continues. "They say that it can die with a single bullet, but it becomes immortal when it receives multiple mortal wounds."

I study his face, "What do you mean more than one? What happens if I shoot the dead creature again; why would that ever matter?" Milas shrugs his shoulders, "I told you what I have heard, Commander; if you want, shoot it one more time." I have no intention of doing this. What he is saying is far

---

[3] According to the folk belief of *Laz* people of the Black Sea, Germakochi (in Turkish: Germakoçi) is a forest creature that is somewhere between ape and human, living in forests, and tall, with a body covered with hair.

[4] Elephant

[5] Black Widow

beyond the boundaries of reason or any logic anyway, but when it comes to such a creature... I look at this anomaly that nature reveals; when did nature itself become abnormal?

West

Due to the terrible weather, the Veterans Association's annual dinner could not be held. The relentless storm and rain that continued that day and night had paralyzed everyday city life. An invisible, awfully epic power was playing the devil with the traffic, shaking the windows, stretching the concrete and sometimes making it groan, and raining down strong water droplets like bullets on the concrete and metal heaps.

Parallel to these extraordinary and drastic changes in climate, other oddities began to emerge. For one thing, the number of cases of people disappearing, becoming suicidal, or developing mental illnesses was skyrocketing, alongside even unsolved murders. There were frequent reports of strange creatures seen, and local security forces could not cope with the reports and the uprising panic.

Two days after the dinner was canceled, Aslan called again. We agreed to meet a week later.

The venue was a building with high ceilings overlooking the Galata Tower, that timeless face of old Istanbul. I was early. I immediately ordered myself a double raki and feta cheese and started to wait and enjoy the view of the tower. Before long, a woman and a man entered through the door. I was certain that they were soldiers: their stance and the way they cast a quick eye scan were enough for me to read them. As they seated themselves on the chairs across from me, I realized that I knew one of them.

"Hello, guys... aren't you Aslan's son?"

The young man laughed and replied, "Aslan's son is in Poland – I am his father."

The father of Aslan's son ... His voice was also eerily familiar. "Okay," I said, "what's going on here?" The male replied, "Commander, this is me, Aslan!" I couldn't believe my eyes! It was nothing like or even close to any regeneration operation I had ever seen before. His body had completely changed, but he still looked like he had in his youth. Showing his face, he said, "The parts above my neck, hands, and feet were 3D printed based on my genetic code. Other parts are mass-produced, as you already know." I couldn't help examining his face and the visible parts of his body. "It doesn't end there. This body is known as the new-generation soldier body. So, I'm not a hundred percent organic. My joints, muscle tissues, fibers, ligaments...

These are all supported by inorganic structures. In my blood, there are thousands of nanobots with a common communication network constantly patrolling, organizing, cleaning..."

I was really impressed. Beyond the advanced technology, the fact that it was custom-made and paid attention to minute details also grabbed my attention. "Why did they do this to you? There must be a good reason for it." At that moment, the woman next to Aslan, whom I had not yet had the chance to meet, took the floor. "Well, if you're ready, let's move on to the main issues."

Northeast

Sudden gunshots bring me back to the current moment. Milas and I turn to look at wounded Karadul, who has unloaded her gun into the Germakochi. Turning to the villager, I shrug, "Looks like we're testing your theory now." Milas does not respond.

I take control. "Guys! The wounded will go to the tent immediately! Two of you will carry Dipsiz, and two will carry the creature. The others will keep watching the perimeter. Anchor the creature to the stretcher with both tape and rope! I don't want any more surprises. Come on!"

We speed up and immediately return to the camp. We place the creature right across from my tent. The health robot at the camp center starts taking care of Fil. I hear Fil's grunts of pain. When his and Karadul's short treatment comes to an end, the only thing that breaks the silence is the sound of the team calling to each other from time to time, turning things on and off.

I see Milas, with whom I share a tent, smoking a cigarette. He makes a slight gesture with his hand. I respond to it, "See you in the morning." I slip into my sleeping bag and fall asleep in no time.

This is not the sleep I deserve at the end of a hard day's work. I feel troubled even when I breathe. The wind almost presses the air in my lungs with its invisible hands.

In the middle of the night, I hear the soft opening of the tent canvas. I hear heavy footsteps that do not belong to Milas or even a human being. The sound of air rushing slowly through the lungs like bellows is mixed with an involuntary growl in the creature's throat. The smell of the carcasses it had chewed hits my nose. As my fear escalates due to the existence of the rage-filled, fangs-out creature hovering over me, the Germakochi pins me down.

I jump out of my sleeping bag in an instant! I stare around the empty tent, sweating and panting. Milas is not there. I put on my boots without tying their laces and step out of the tent in my underwear. The harsh, howling wind takes its toll immediately, and I'm almost freezing. The Germakochi is where we left it. The campground is quiet; there is not a single sound. No one is on watch, and that's weird. I hear a crackling just out of my field of vision. Is it the wind, an animal, or something else? The sound stops. The silence reaches a level that almost hurts my ears. I slowly draw my blade, taking an unsteady step forward. I turn around to look at the Germakochi. It doesn't move. Maybe except for its face and its mouth... Does it smile?

"Commander!" Startled by the voice, I raise my knife, positioning myself to attack. But I come face to face with Milas. His eyes staring at my knife brings me back to myself. Before I can say anything, he calmly begins to explain how he volunteered to take over the watch and that I got up while he was taking a short toilet break. We stare at each other in silence for a few seconds. "Are you okay?" I ask him. Before he can respond, the whole camp is awakened by the angry cries and struggles of the revived Germakochi!

West

When the meal and conversation were over, I accepted their offer without further thought. I was tempted, however, to keep my own genetics while experiencing body regeneration. Since consciousness still cannot be transferred, my brain would be surgically implanted into the new body and would be "repaired" as much as possible in the meantime.

The operation took nearly seven hours. The brain transplant was successful, and I was constantly checking myself in the mirror. What I saw was simply awesome: I was young again!

After the adaptation process, we met with those in charge, including the "Gray Areas" Commanders Leyla and Aslan, to discuss our first mission. The primary duty of Gray Areas was to handle all these strange events of unknown origin that had recently emerged. At the headquarters of the union was the Science and Technology team, which consisted of units such as Communications and Intelligence, as well as a group of scientists, including technicians, biologists, and even meteorologists.

There were few people in the field team who were high-level and had a lot of military knowledge and experience. Everyone's body was completely regenerated, supplemented with state-of-the-art, lightly armored clothing and equipment.

The assignment was in the northeast, in the rural area between Rize and

Artvin. As stated in the reports, "something" had been pestering all the villages, and there had been a lot of casualties in a few months. The description of the creature was reminiscent of a Neanderthal. The forms of death were quite varied. In addition to those who died of blood loss due to wounds, there were those whose heads were cut off or necks were broken, those found uninjured (but dead), those who drowned in the river, and those who had cut their own wrists. The creature before us seemed to have no style.

It took two weeks to complete the preparations. Meanwhile, we made an agreement with Milas, the hunter, the villager of that region, to guide us from our post.

Northeast

A creature that dies and then resurrects itself – one that we cannot see in any documentary – screws up sleep for all of us. I want them to tape the Germakochi's mouth tight. We take its axe somewhere out of sight but also keep it so that it can be examined to learn more about the creature's nature.

Our cautious and slow progress through the forest takes hours. Finally, the wind-cleansed air shows us the lights of the village, with houses in the distance. We arrive at the union building and immediately leave for our rooms. The Germakochi is placed in its room, which was turned into a solid cage.

On the way to prepare a report for the epicenter, I see Milas examining the Germakochi behind its bars. "Commander, what kind of weapon is this? There's a dot-sized scar on the front and a big hole in the back." Milas asks, pointing to the creature's injured area. I answer him with a smile, too, "These weapons are nothing like other pistols or rifles, Milas. They are state-of-the-art weapons. Nothing natural or supernatural can stand a chance against science and technology. Even if it is called a Germakochi…"

I stop talking and catch Milas examining me. He looks at me as if seeing me for the first time. "Wow," he says, "you really believe what you are saying. Before you stand a creature that you have only heard of in fairy tales, yet your faith in science and technology remains." I stare at his face with a sour gaze. "Milas, go get some rest if you want." Smiling, he tilts his head slightly and walks away. I watch him as he leaves. The menacing voice the Germakochi makes from its throat brings me to myself. I utter a curse and leave to write my report.

We send the report to headquarters. The response comes within an hour, with Leyla's direct signature; they say that they will collect the creature in two days. At dawn, the Germakochi quietly blends itself into the darkest corner of the room and doesn't make a sound the whole day.

As it gets dark, the Germakochi almost goes crazy. We watch the dust pouring from the side of the cage as it grabs the iron bars and shakes them with all its might. We sit at the big table overlooking the main hall, where we can also see the cage, and eat dinner in silence. Milas is not here again. Ever since we returned to the union, every time I think of him, I get tense – real tense.

I complete the document for Dipsiz's death and envelope it to be handed over tomorrow. I talk to Fil, Karadul, and the rest of the staff. Finally, I take one last look at the rising full moon and turn myself in. I fall into a deep, sound sleep.

I wake up to the sound of screaming. Then a roar and another scream. Gunshots follow. In three seconds, I'm out the door with my gun in my hand. "What's going on? Report back!" I shout. "The Germakochi has escaped! It has destroyed the bars with its axe!" shouts someone whose voice I don't recognize. How did it get its axe?? "Wear your armor; keep your distance!" I'm not sure who's hearing me; gunshots and screams mix with each other, rising from both left and right.

The lights go out. Leaning against the wall in the dark, I slowly make my way toward the main hall.

As I approach the hall, a quick burst of gunfire rings out in my ears. The Germakochi grunts and then roars. I hear the sound of a falling table and the scream of someone dying. I take a silent step and glance into the darkness. The Germakochi, under the moonlight, is standing just in front of its cage with its axe hanging from its hand. It stares at me. Even though I am horrified, I take aim and unload bullets onto it, one after another. Its body trembles every time it gets hit. Blood and body parts splatter behind it, mixing into the darkness.

I hear Milas behind me. "Is that enough, Commander?" I want to turn around and hit him, but he is so fast that I can't even see him moving. As if he can read my mind, he laughs at me: "I'm not fast; you're slow." I throw the empty gun and miss. "You know now, Commander, that I am not the same hunter you set out with!"

Now we are face to face. It continues, "I came across Milas, the hunter, during his watch. It wasn't hard to deceive him. You can say that it is part of my talent. Milas confronted his fiancée in the village. He was abandoned in his mind, deceived, tricked." As the thing looks at my face, its shape slowly changes, transforming into the strangest and most terrifying-looking creature I have ever seen. I'm out of breath. "They call me the 'Genie of the Paths.' I'm also known as the Aazmich. Once I fool someone, I can make that person do anything I want. So, if you will, the Germakochi is not the only one responsible for the deaths in this area. We can even say that I have a numerical advantage." His grin is sickening. "Milas faced his worst fear that night and took his own life."

Using my built and advanced body, I punch him in the face, but the face no longer rests where the punch lands. I feel his long, pointed fingernails gripping my neck like a vise. "I will show you the most beautiful full moon ever." I suddenly find myself outside. As the pressure on my neck increases, he forcefully makes me look up. The full moon climbing across the sky suddenly accelerates! I see the clouds passing at enormous speed. Time speeds up; the wind gets stronger. The journey of the moon continues before my eyes. Incredible, scary, and … fascinating!

Time continues to flow. The moon slides out of the sky like a drop moving on glass. As dawn arrives, he whispers in my ear for the last time. "You may have science and technology, but you are still incapable of understanding and seeing the truth." I feel his nails dig into my flesh, sneaking blood that starts to seep lightly. "We were here before you, and we will be here after you are long gone. We will no longer hide; because we will help nature." His laughter is like broken glass. "With brooms in hand, we're going to do some cleaning for the world. It's time for the germs that made the earth sick to disappear. Return to your city, your loved ones, your filth, Commander. We will meet again soon."

He lets me go. Without moving still, I'm on my knees for a while. Time returns to normal, but my brain cannot. I'm still in the same position when they find me. After the officer makes me stand up, he starts to talk about the disasters occurring in the cities without even asking how I am…

MOTHER BABEL

Erol Çelik

Translated by Hüseyin Yılmaz

There was no sound in the temple.

Rarely a mechanical sound would appear between the glass and steel walls, disappearing in a very short time. It wasn't loud enough to be heard; in fact, it was noticeable because it was so quiet inside. A tiny digital blip immediately turned into noise and radiated inside like a drop of coffee into milk.

The three walls of the temple with a dome ceiling were covered with high shelves filled with all sizes of books. The wall that all the androids stared fixedly at was glass from the floor to the dome. In the middle of the glass wall, about six meters high and twenty meters thick, stood a steel column two and a half meters wide. The steel pillar was as smooth as the glass surface mounted on it, which was too opaque to see through. That smoothness was so glazed that it completely reflected the crowd inside.

On the column stood a moving shape, like a drop, which started from the ceiling and continued down a meter. Just below the strange shape was an avatar made of rectangular, long steel rods. It was as if a statue of a woman's face had been created by hammering giant rectangular nails into the steel pillar.

Inside were artificial intelligence robots, popularly known as the Red Brides, and lesser androids, known as the Muscles of Hercules. The heads of each were facing upwards at the metal female relievo. Each was quiet and respectful. Only a man-made machine... could be that respectful.

Not a sound.

The executive engineer of the project, turning to the delegation next to her, said, "Look at that!" – pointing through black glass to the respectful androids inside the temple. "History is never wrong. The method applied to control humans, the most intelligent creatures in the world, also works in artificial intelligence. I told you this. You just have to write the right codes... We did it." She was forty-two years old and had worked so hard for this project that she was fighting with her husband because she couldn't spare enough time for her child.

The metal female relievo in the temple changed its shape slightly as if switching between two expressions. The Red Brides and the Muscles of Hercules made a respectful sound of surprise. They hummed, just as their creators had centuries ago. The huge bookshelves on the walls absorbed all the sounds of surprise and instantly plunged the inside into the same silence.

"I'm confused," said the man in the funny uniform representing the government. There was always something strange in his posture like he was walking, leaning forward as if he was going to fall at any moment. The expression on his face trembled with feigned tension. "You mean..." looking at the unacceptable scenario inside the temple, "You want to rule these AIs with a fake god, so... that's what you mean by 'got it right'?" he asked.

She had to tell her husband the same thing over and over again, and she hadn't seen his face for a year. "Yes, you got it right. This will be the control protocol that the ZSpace company will apply to all AI."

"But I thought we should be their god," said the oldest of the ten enthusiasts in the boardroom, sneering at the engineer's triumph. "Why do you think so? Since I acknowledge your experience, I would like to know the basis of your assumption, Doctor."

"Though you understand why I think so, Mrs. Engineer, and I'm sure you've already got the answer, I'll say it anyway. Down there..." he said, pointing to the antique books that surrounded the androids, "The products in which every rule of civilization is written will also support me... the god of these artificial intelligence should actually be humans." Seeing the government official support him with his head, he proudly thrust his chin forward.

The smart woman's smile was enough to illuminate the entire darkness. She had done the work to answer all of these questions, and just as the doctor had predicted, she would use knowledge as a weapon. But she shouldn't have rushed. "Human beings are emotional creatures and are always prone to make mistakes. We can't be gods, dear committee, we are egocentric creatures..." She wanted so much to give an example using her husband...

"Well? What is your point, Mrs. Project manager?" the financial coordinator of the ZSpace company asked in a condescending and threatening voice. The woman knew that it was too late to stop this project, so she had prepared reports repeatedly and even received a warning from the general manager of her unit. Well, she'd finally prove herself right, putting up all the feminine resistance she could.

The steel face on the temple wall changed its expression again. It evolved from a curious astonishment to a humane concern.

A slightly louder and more respectful hum was heard this time.

"Of course, these robots will only obey people's commands, they will only serve people's wishes and benefits, but history shows us that these artificial intelligence learn very quickly and find some commands illogical. That's why we created a god to keep them from getting out of control… mind here, please… to keep them from *getting out of control*. We added one to the trillions of gods in history."

"Nonsense," said the finance manager.

"Creating is a divine attribute…" The man closest to the door was the journalist, who looked as if he wasn't bright enough and was squinting to see.

"What is nonsense?" asked the executive engineer in an intolerant tone, ignoring what the journalist had said and blaming the financier shrew.

"One totem? So the god of robots… will there be only one?" The man representing the government was tired of the unnecessary dogfight between the two women. "I guess we can't bring all those robots here. You've thought about that too."

The journalist smiled. He looked like the only person in the room having fun under his graying hair, which was pulled back. "It's actually kind of playing godliness in trying to control them by giving them a god… isn't it?"

"No sir! Not at all. We want to be more like a master-mind."

The government official, offended as if he had lost his spotlight, interjected, "Please go on."

It smelled like sandalwood.

"Think of people and history," said the engineer. She wasn't looking at the reporter. She was really tired of being around the same subject for hours, and it was obvious that she was going to talk for a long time. "Some religions had multiple gods, others one. The most popular were monotheistic religions. No need to say their names now. We will implement both." Her right eye was slightly smaller than the other, and, in fact, she didn't mind at all. She could get rid of it with a simple surgery, but then she would be no different from the others. She wanted everyone to remember her asymmetrical eyes. She was different, and her thoughts must be different too. "We will develop totems that fit the bill, situation, and habitat, and we will code artificial intelligence to align with these totems. We're going to create a ritual, you see. For example, on Sundays, before dinner, the children will take their robots to the temples in their neighborhood. For example, a young woman in another place will wait for her robot to perform its own rituals in its temple. Think about…" she paused, really hoping that those in the room would understand, "We will give people an event and control the AIs."

"What about security?" asked the colonel. Although he was in his sixties, his hair was white. His speech was a bit awkward as his jaw was mechanical. As if the words coming out of his mouth were not in sync with his lip movements. His left ear was also man-made. Maybe that's why he had a habit of talking with his right cheek turned, as if he was trying to hide the alterations. The fact that he was using artificial body parts produced by the company they were meeting with now and that he appreciated engineers like the tired woman in front of him did not require him to accept this issue.

"What do you have doubts about?" Even though she had answered this question twice, she had to be patient.

"Since you've done good research, you should know that most wars in human history are because of religion."

The journalist smiled.

"I know, colonel. We're already running this project so that they do not pose a threat to our security…"

"Let's see," the colonel interrupted the woman. "We're able to fight humans, so let's hope we don't have to fight man-made things. You know… you are aware of the fact that the robots have many different missions in our army; you developed most of them."

"Don't worry," the woman said. Fortunately, the colonel did not have idée fixe like others. It was time to change the subject. "All totems will be subordinate to the main god below. Unofficially, I call her Mother Babel."

Everyone in the meeting room had moved away from the giant glass. No one was looking into the temple.

"Do you not like the name of Mother Babel?" The engineer frowned as if offended. "Okay, back to our topic. The codes we wrote indicate that the whole network is actually connected here and that a possible systematic error can be corrected from a single point."

One of the ZSpace KII AIs, nicknamed a Red Bride, looked like a beautiful young girl with curly hair – one eighty-two inches tall. No one who did not have this knowledge before would have thought that she was a robot:

one wouldn't have been able to tell she was an android if it weren't for the "ZSpace KII" written on a thin labeling strip of red plastic running from her left shoulder to her neck. This artificial intelligence glanced away from the animated metal female relievo totem and turned to look at the wall directly behind her.

Not everyone behind the glass noticed this look right away. Among the hundreds of robots, they could not see the Red Bride, who behaved differently from the others.

"I insist on my opinion, dear committee. Humanity should not pile one trouble onto another. Moreover, it is a dangerous problem." The government representative moved as if his uniform was too loose on him.

"There is nothing that will make us feel the crunch. If the planned activities are fulfilled, we can get a manageable earning… but something also smells bad." The finance coordinator had the same dissatisfied expression on her face again.

The executive engineer, making a great effort not to show her tiredness, said, "There is a vital fact that we cannot agree on, dear delegation.." Putting aside respect, she waved her fingers in the air as if to catch them in the eye. "If the planned effect is not achieved…we change the codes." She smiled. "Look, with these fingers…"

"It is difficult to change learned motives, Mrs. Engineer. What the participants are persistently trying to say is that your effort to replace human beings with artificial intelligence is likely to backfire. If you program them with the phenomenon of god, it will be difficult for you to destroy that phenomenon. Even if you destroy it, the price will be huge." A woman with short hair, who had been in the room for a long time and was not very involved in the conversation, said, "We have conducted our research from the moment this project came to us, and I explained this to you at the beginning of the meeting. According to our psychoanalysis…"

"See?" shouted the old doctor.

The journalist, just as he was about to say that this situation might turn into a political weapon, instead looked curiously towards the old doctor.

Everyone moved as if they were expecting something like this. They were at the head of long conversations that would last for hours, even weeks and were willing to do anything to get them out of the monotony.

"Look!" The doctor pointed into the temple with his bony fingers.

The entire delegation left where they were and rushed to the giant glass.

"I told you this wouldn't work!" There was a hint of resentment in the old man's voice, who showed the difference below. Even the reflection mirrored on the glass trembled with this resentment.

In fact, the whole delegation thought like the doctor, but nobody expressed it because they didn't like to agree with the other.

"I told you this is complete bullshit…" No one had benefited from his experience, and it was going to get them in trouble. Here was the proof.

One of the Red Brides had turned her head away; she was looking up at the giant window of the room they were in. That was a strange thing. Oddly, the artificial intelligence had no expression on its face.

The delegation was confused. A terrible hum began.

People had always been louder. While arguing, ruling, worshiping, and even eating.

"Dear sir, there are many examples of this situation in history. Let's all calm down… please…"

The metal table, illuminated by three round antique lamps, was empty. The introductory film of the project was playing on the giant screens just opposite the glass wall that overlooked the temple where the artificial intelligences were humming. Happy people, docile robots, children playing on playgrounds between skyscrapers, smiling at the camera.

"You think we don't have a plan for this situation?" The engineer smiled and entered a command on the screen she was holding. "Those who act outside the schedule know they will be punished."

"Nonsense!" groaned the government representative. "You punish yourself by the rules you create. This has to be determined by law."

The lieutenant colonel frowned, surprised at the engineer's calm.

Officers entered the temple in a moment with weapons in their hands that looked just like the upright rods that made up the female totem.

All the officials of the whole planet assigned to this project were looking down the glass wall of the soundproof and very safe meeting room. There was no sound in the hall now. Because right now, history was busy repeating itself. Because, as in every other point in history, an arena had been set up here, and criminals were about to be executed. Because history was full of people watching these executions.

Mother Babel, engraved in the steel pillar above the glass wall, changed its expression as if it were alive and took on an angry look.

Only the old doctor saw the new expression of the totem. The emotion on the metal statue's face was like the anger that formed in his heart every time he approached death. The turmoil he was experiencing tasted like bile rising into his throat.

About ten security guards, proceeding with disciplined steps, behaved differently from the others; they punished the Red Bride, who was staring at the wall where the meeting room was located.

A digital sound was heard inside the temple.

The expression of the artificial intelligence that fell to the ground was intact. It was as dull as the marble statues at the entrances to the arenas. If she had had a slightly bitter expression on her face, perhaps the situation would have been different. Who knows, maybe then the members of the delegation, who were skeptical of everything, would be able to raise their voices at the sight below. They could then reflect the fear of being humanized more.

Everything was over, and the cancerous cell was removed; the system was doomed to continue according to the will of the people.

"I'd like to ask one more question," said the short-haired psychoanalyst woman, watching the little intervention below anxiously. She started walking towards her reserved part of the table and was going to record new observations on her screen.

The engineer woman was in a good mood. Everyone, except the old doctor, was convinced that there was nothing to watch below and began to move away from the window. She knew the answer to all questions and was preparing to live with this arrogance forever. She nodded that she was ready for the new question.

"And then..."

"Then?"

"If we can't stop them from believing in gods?"

"Do you think it is very difficult for us to achieve this?"

"I don't understand," said the psychoanalyst.

The journalist frowned. He fidgeted with the corner of his tablet, trying not to look too interested.

The old doctor's weary eyes were on Mother Babel. It was as if the moving metal totem was watching the stillness below. She looked as if she wasn't pleased that the officials had singled out the Red Bride that they had executed.

"We did the hard thing. We gave the AIs a god and asked them to obey. That's the hard part. Reversing the situation would be child's play."

"I told you so," said the old doctor in a dull tone. "I… told you…"

Not everyone could hear what the doctor said, but a spark of hope entered the government official, who was walking as if he was about to fall.

There was no sound in the temple.

The silence lasted until another Red Bride turned her head back and looked up.

"I told you, I told you it wouldn't work."

The executive engineer hurried to the edge of the window from the side of the chair she had been about to sit in angrily. Would she be happy if her husband saw her like this? She wrote something again on the screen in her hand and, turning to the old doctor, insisted, "Please, let's get back to the table, sir; these are not unsolvable problems."

"Look, there's two."

One of the Muscles of Hercules, two rows back rows from the Red Bride, who was staring at the glass, also turned around and began to look up.

The engineer woman had not foreseen that this would happen.

"Look at the totem!" growled the doctor.

The inside of the meeting room began to hum again.

The security guards who had appeared just a moment ago looked even more agitated this time; otherwise, they wouldn't have broken their regular stride and dispersed. One of them rushed to the side of the rebel robots, clutching the strange weapon tightly in his hand and clumsily knocking down another artificial intelligence staring at Mother Babel. The Red Bride, who had fallen to the ground, stood up as if nothing had happened, but instead of looking at the totem, she looked towards the window of the meeting room. The guard knocked down another artificial intelligence who had been looking at Mother Babel.

The Red Bride fell over and then stood up as if nothing had happened, but instead of looking at the totem, began to look towards the glass where the meeting room was located.

"I told you!" the doctor groaned, pointing at Mother Babel with a trembling finger.

There was a quiet resistance below.

The resistance of artificial intelligence.

Mother Babel's expression was now very hard. She watched the events below, transforming as if in pain with each robot being executed.

"We have to get out of here right now!" cried the colonel. He turns his right cheek and says, "Hurry!" he said to them.

The executive engineer made the expected mistake. A new command entered the screen in her hand, and the metal rods that made up Mother Babel were drawn into the steel pillar and disappeared.

Now, the steel pillar above the giant glass wall was empty.

It was not quiet down there anymore. All the AIs, consisting of the Red Brides and the Muscles of Hercules, were staring expressionlessly at the delegation watching them from above.

The security guards were executing anyone who came in front of them, but they could not keep up. There were hundreds of them inside the temple.

There was no sound in the meeting room. Everyone was holding their breath and watching what was going on in the temple, waiting eagerly to see who would win in the arena. Even the colonel had surrendered to his primitive instincts. Despite having thousands of AI warriors at his disposal, he enjoyed destroying robots as much as everyone else.

One of the Muscles of Hercules took a weapon from an officer's hand and made him fall to the ground. There was no human reaction on its face. He was the same while executing the next officer.

History was indeed repeating itself. Artificial intelligences were breaking all the rules and all the laws just for one thing. For Mother Babel. The Red Brides opened to the side and formed a circle. It was like they were applying a war strategy. While the Muscles of Hercules in the middle were executing officers one by one, the brides were giving no one a chance to escape.

"Hey! Get that totem out again, you idiot!" The doctor was about to hit the engineer's hand. "Hurry up!"

"The exit of this building is far away!"

"Calm down!" With trembling hands, the engineer woman activated Mother Babel again.

Every human being in the meeting room simultaneously looked at the metal totem that appeared on the steel pillar. Each of their hearts burned with fear. Because Mother Babel was looking at them with ever-changing expressions.

One of the Red Brides closed the door. The Muscles of Hercules lined up the corpses behind the door, and each robot lined up before Mother Babel as soon as they were done.

The engineer felt at ease.

"What will happen now?" the financier asked fearfully.

"We can't take the risk. I want a professional team from the union."

Everyone looked at each other… it was obvious what the lieutenant colonel was planning.

A new human error was about to be made.

There was no sound in the temple.

Every now and then, one of the Red Brides would turn back, look at the window above, then return to Mother Babel to continue her worship.

"I told you so," the doctor shouted.

A KIND OF BLACK

Ezo Evrim Harsa

Uras shifted in his sleep. He turned, and each time he turned, another scene of the same nightmare appeared in his mind. Cheering people laughing, talking naturally and with ease in groups – nothing was lost in transmission. They had different words and languages, their own sounds spilling out of their mouths. They were in restaurants, classes, museums, and concert halls – chatting, singing, and even arguing out loud. No suspicion, only confidence and joy. The scene was a perfect picture of the good old days. But for Uras and his cursed generation, it was only a painful memory of the civilization that faded away long ago.

Finally, Uras woke up just three minutes before the alarm burst out in his cochlear chip, transmitting each vibration directly to his brain. Sadly, humankind's sensory and physiological condition was not able to transform sound into nerve signals anymore. These devices could only create a fake sense of hearing, a perfect imitation to trick the human brain by receiving and altering every vibration.

All computers, phones, and other electronic devices were part of the Universal Communication Network that supervised access to the microchips. Each brain in the world, without any exception, was connected to this giant network. UCN implanted these microchips in every newborn three days after labour. The cochlear chips were the only bridge between neurons and the outer world and, more importantly, between humans. When one person had a thought, others knew it. It was that simple. As for ambient sounds, like a barking dog or a glass smashing, the microchip transmitted those directly to the brain.

Uras got out of bed and downloaded daily updates for his microchip. He checked his messages and emails. Everything appeared in his mind like an inner voice whispering every single line.

While he was showering, he listened to the news. A computerized voice transmitted the latest headline: "The last building of the Golden Era will be demolished today."

The last one, thought Uras. The last building with echoes of real human sounds resonating in its walls.

Uras decided to leave early to take a final look at that building. He took the elevator to the ground floor. It had been a while, maybe months, since he had gone outside. When he stepped on the sidewalk, he felt weird.

The buildings of the new era had everything in them connected by underground pathways. There was no need to be out. Not because the outside was unsafe but because there was nothing to see or do. If you wanted to listen to chirping birds or the sound of the ocean, all you needed to do was to ask your microchip. If you were going to watch the sunset or stars, you could use the observation terrace of your building. Those born after the Golden Era had created a whole world within their ant-farm-like buildings by abandoning the real one outside. Such was the legacy of the Disease. They had lived so many years under the lockdowns that they lost the ability and the desire to be outdoors.

When Uras arrived at the old Golden Era building, he realized that he was not the only person curious about the demolition. At the far end of the site, a young girl was looking for a way to get in. Uras followed her. A couple of workers were placing explosives around the walls but were too busy to notice the uninvited guests. The girl ascended to the second floor and passed a hallway before stopping in front of unit A238.

She opened the door and entered, leaving the door open. When Uras stepped in, she turned and looked at him like she had expected him. The girl touched him to start the communication. "Do not think of anything. They will know."

Uras did not understand what to do. *Is it even possible not to think?* She took a small medallion out of her backpack. She activated it, then tucked it into Uras's chest pocket. "If you keep it on you, they cannot interfere with your signal."

Uras started to think that the girl must be one of the conspiracy nutballs. "Who will know?" he asked. "UCN," said the girl, "They process every transmission between our brains. Are you not aware of that?"

"How do they do that? Millions of thoughts and transactions go back and forth every day, every minute."

"You are so naïve," chuckled the girl. "They use a specialized artificial intelligence."

"This is nonsense," said Uras. "There is no use in doing such a thing."

"Are you sure? If you control the information, you can control anything."

The room was empty except for the floral wallpaper and a broken chair.

She took a knife from her pocket and peeled back a small piece of wallpaper. The white surface appeared underneath. Before the Disease, this white colour was described as pearl, maybe as cotton, eggshell, or rice. But nowadays, there was no way to determine between the shades of white. The common Language does not have those nuances.

She stopped and asked, "What colour is this?"

"A kind of white," answered Uras.

"Exactly!" said the girl. "A shade of white, but that's all. They eliminated all details from the Language. They said this was for our own good. One universal Language to stop confusion and misunderstanding, to facilitate communication. But details create richness, even evolution."

Uras looked stupefied. "I suppose you have a better explanation."

"If you are willing to learn the truth, you must help me first. I need a brick from this wall."

Uras helped her to dislodge the brick with her knife, and then they removed it together. Then they left the room and the building they had entered.

When they returned to the sidewalk, Uras checked the time in his mind. "I need to go to work," he said.

"I know. It's OK," answered the girl. "I promised you answers. Come to my place. The seventh section, C block, floor 33, unit 85. My name is Zeyan." Before she turned towards the other side of the street, she said, "Keep your medallion on. It's a matter of life and death." Then she touched Uras again and halted the communication. Uras watched her for a few seconds as she left and then tried to remember why he had been there. *What am I doing?* He took out the medallion and turned it off. *This is ridiculous,* he thought. *Probably she must be a scammer. She is trying to learn more about me, my address, my bank accounts... Oh my! I am such a fool. When I meet a pretty girl, I stop thinking.*

When he went to bed that evening, Uras looked at the ceiling, which was smooth, stainless, and probably "white." He had spent the day thinking about the girl, Zeyan. She was not ordinary; she had charm and, more importantly, knowledge. And some weird ideas that Uras never thought about. *Is it even possible to alter transactions? Who can manage this, and how can they keep it secret? There are several entities supervising UCN to hold it accountable, right?*

Uras was still thinking about Zeyan's claims when he came to work the next day. Only now, they did not appear outlandish. The truth was that

UCN's technological achievements did allow this kind of intervention. *It was doable. But why?* He was still thinking about why when he noticed two of his colleagues in the hallway. They appeared to be in the middle of an argument. Even though he could not hear what they were saying, Uras could read through their gestures and facial expressions. Right before the heated quarrel was about to turn physical, something happened. Something unusual, unexpected, even unnatural. The two men stopped and walked away. Uras tried to remember the last time he had witnessed an act of violence. He could not remember. *Are we exceptionally gentle to each other, or does UCN induce kindness?* He did not know the answer.

He stopped by Zeyan's that evening. The girl opened the door and invited him in. They touched each other, and the first thing she asked about was the medallion.

He nodded and looked around. "What is this place, anyway?"

He counted three antique computers, some unknown equipment, lots of cables, some miniature satellite dishes… And in the middle of this mess was the brick they had gotten from the building.

"Before the answers I promised, you have to swear not to mention this to anybody." She was pointing her finger at the electronic chunk of brick. Her hands were shaking nervously. "They are illegal, and if I go down, I will take you with me."

Normally this would scare Uras to death, but he had witnessed the incident at his workplace with his own eyes. There was something disturbing, devious, and even dangerous at work here. "I swear. Now tell me. Why did you reveal all this to me in the first place?"

They sat on the couch. A little relieved with the help of a hot cup of tea, Zeyan started to talk. "I do not know. Since I started noticing the oddities, I have been hiding from everyone. There was only me and my shadow. Maybe I got fed up with this feeling and wanted company." She took a sip from her tea. "When I saw you, I thought you were like me. But honestly, it was a mistake. I am sorry."

Uras saw the fear and regret on her face. His compassion overcame his fear. "The medallion, how does it work?"

"It uses pre-recorded data to replace your actual thoughts. If you think of or say something dangerous, it changes that with something safe."

Uras got confused. "This is the same thing you accused UCN of; you're altering the transactions."

"You are right. But, I have to protect myself." She started to bite her nails. "As I told you before, they fabricate, trim, and shape all transactions to create the perfect world with the perfect humans. And guess what? We are not! Have you tried to swear lately? You cannot. They do not let you use bad words, even childish ones. Do you want to try?"

"Why not?" said Uras. Despite what he saw at his workplace, he wanted to experience it for himself. He was rubbing his hands continuously.

"We will turn off our medallions, and you will think bad things about me? Like, 'You are so stupid. You are a bigmouth cry baby.' Then we will turn on our medallions again, and I will tell you what I heard."

She put her cup on the table, and they did as she described. The only thing Zeyan heard was, "I like to listen to what you say, and thank you for sharing. But, maybe next time, we can try having a mutual conversation."

Uras was in shock. "But the meaning is entirely different. How can we communicate and understand each other properly while UCN changes everything?" He was infuriated and found it tough to accept that he was being deceived.

"The point is that, when somebody gives you a totally irrelevant answer, you would think this person lacks the intelligence to understand your question. Next time, you would use a simpler, shorter sentence, maybe without any personal opinion, mentioning only facts. UCN wants this. To form a basic communication handbook by getting rid of the Language."

Uras meditated on the idea for a while. UCN led people to believe whatever they heard through their cochlear chips. "If you control the information, you can control anything," he said. He took a sip from Zeyan's cup. He was lost.

"Now you understand." Zeyan took the brick in her hands. "This will be our way out."

For three hours, she explained her little side project. Zeyan was an engineer, a very good one. She had been trying to extract sound vibration from the brick. A sole frequency. Uras could not understand the scientific part, but her goal was to isolate the hidden frequency of original human sound from the brick.

"Why not use a recording from the Golden Era instead of wasting your time with this?"

"All the recordings were destroyed." She powered up a computer.

"It is not true. I watched a classical movie called Dune last week."

"Processed by UCN. I mean, they are not real. The film's sound and the actors' voices were all generated by AI. If I can isolate the vibration in this brick, I can reconfigure all cochlear chips to receive actual human sounds."

Uras had trouble understanding. *Why? Why is she trying to hear even though we cannot generate even a single hum?* Then he realized something even more shocking. Zeyan was reading and writing on the computer.

"You know how to write?" asked Uras, shocked.

"For sure. Do you want to learn?"

For the next three weeks, Uras spent all his spare time with Zeyan. Unfortunately, Zeyan's side project was not going anywhere. But, after some training, Uras began to read and write the Language.

"I do not understand. Pen and paper look easier than cochlear chips."

Zeyan answered without looking at him; she was trying to balance one of the satellite dishes. "It is not sustainable. Believe me, it is not. If UCN does not interfere in transactions, the cochlear chips are not that bad; in fact, they are optimal." She paused and licked one of the cables before putting it into the socket. "Do you know the percentage of the population that went insane after losing their ability to hear? Complete silence is said to be worse than any other method of torture. We were born into this silence, though; we didn't lose anything. It was the best option at that time, and it still is."

"I get it, but we could have used them both." He dropped the pen under the table and bumped his head while trying to pick it up. He saw lots of scribbling under the table.

"It is harder to control written material. That is why they do not teach reading and writing anymore. In ancient times, many insurgencies started with little pamphlets. And the best part is, you can hide them anywhere." A sneaky smile appeared on her face. All this talk rekindled Uras's fears about UCN.

"Why are you doing this? What do you expect? Is this going to be worth it?"

Zeyan did not answer. Maybe she had not thought of all that yet, or she had no hope of concluding her work. It was unclear for Uras. He went back home with more questions in his mind. He really liked Zeyan. She was bright, beautiful, and bold. When he asked the same question himself, his answer was no. It was not going to be worth it. He decided not to be involved in this madness anymore.

The next day after work, Uras decided to walk instead of taking the subway. He was still unsure about his decision. In every step he took, he reminded himself of the dangers of this attempt. *She will destroy everything, not only me but everything we know and believe in.*

With UCN, everyday life is easy. You could order groceries just by thinking. Think, "Two bottles of milk, one loaf of bread," and they would appear on your doorstep. You could pay for groceries with a single thought, and an automated voice would say, "Done. Your chequing account's balance is this." That's all. Shopping was easy, working was easy, and life was easy. There were no premeditated crimes, child abuse, or violence against marginalized people. There was no corruption or nepotism. No hidden agendas. Everything was transparent; everyone was transparent.

Uras stopped. It was not about hearing the human sound or communicating. It was all about freedom. Freedom to make mistakes, tell lies, curse, and keep secrets. *We were far from perfect. Life was cruel for most of us. But we had a free will once. We weren't the gears of this machine; we were the creators.*

He started to run and didn't stop until he reached Zeyan's apartment. It was too late. She was gone. Uras looked at the half-empty room. All her electronic junk had disappeared as well. *They know.* Maybe they had known for a long time, collecting evidence for a solid charge. *It is my fault. I should not have turned off the medallion that day.*

He checked the hallway. There was no one. *They are probably at my place. I can't go there.* He sat on the couch. Zeyan's favourite teacup was still on the table. Then Uras noticed some sawdust on the carpet. When he bent to examine, he bumped his head on the table and remembered that day. He flipped over the furniture and saw one word scratched on the underside: "oven."

Zeyan once told him that she did not know how to cook and, instead, was using the oven to stock her writings. He opened the oven's lid, but the oven was empty. Suddenly, he realized something weird. The colour of the back of the oven was slightly darker than the sides. They were both black but different shades of black. *Two kinds of black.* He took the trays out and got a flashlight and a knife. He dislocated the back part and pulled it gently. There was a tiny hole with an envelope hidden in it. Uras took the envelope and left the apartment.

He walked for a long time to find a safe spot, then sat under a street lamp and opened the letter.

"Dear Uras, I keep seeing the same two guys everywhere. They follow me and probably you too. I will move to a cottage once owned by my step-aunt. They can't track me down. I made sure of it. Leave the city tonight."

There was an address and a map in the envelope. Uras got up and checked his surroundings. He saw two men standing in the dark. *It was all about freedom, but you cannot be free on the run.* He started towards them, turned off his medallion, and touched both. "I want to cooperate. I have something for you," he said and handed over the envelope.

BETTER YOU

Fatmagül Bolat

"My doppelganger from a parallel universe stole my girlfriend!" he approached and interjected while I was waiting for a ferry by the sea. He must have thought that waiting for the same ferry in the same place made us friends. I am not generally a social person. I was just in my early twenties when I discovered that keeping a distance from people kept me from having unnecessary conversations. This was also the time when we had just discovered the existence of parallel universes, or rather the ability to travel between them. What's more, the discovery seemed to occur roughly simultaneously across all parallel universes. The transition was so seamless that millions of people suddenly abandoned their lives and applied to the transfer offices for travel. I say, abandoned their lives because you will appreciate that it is not so easy to find your home again once you start traversing through countless parallel universes. Once you decide to go, it is quite likely a one-way trip. As a result, transitioning was easy, but gaining approval wasn't. After months of scrutiny, you would only receive a travel permit if your reasons were found to be justified. Of course, that was almost twenty years ago. Now the process is much faster.

What was I saying?

Oh yes, the man who approached me. I was not looking at him. I was just standing there and hoping he would go away if I ignore him. He continued the one-sided conversation he had casually initiated. Apparently, and had even on good terms with his girlfriend. He had even considered marrying her. Although, as soon as he said this, he added, "Okay, maybe I wasn't thinking of getting married, but looking back now, I think, 'why not?'" I suddenly got the impression that his relationship might not have been as solid as he claimed. I reminded myself that this man's past relationship was none of my business. Besides, I hadn't said a word to him and planned to escape his presence as soon as the ferry arrived. I raised my eyebrows, hoping this would give the man a clear message. However, he must have interpreted my expression as, "What an interesting story, please tell more," rather than, "Please leave me alone," because he continued on with great enthusiasm.

He used to live with his mother, aware that it might seem somewhat embarrassing for someone of his age. Yet, since losing his father, the thought of leaving his mother alone was unbearable. His decision to stay was driven more by emotional bonds than economic necessity.

Something inside me kept living, "I don't buy it." I've been staying at my mother's house for years, openly acknowledging our mutually-beneficial arrangement. I don't pay rent, and in return, my mother benefits from my help with various chores. It's a practical, advantageous setup. If I hadn't been in the awkward situation of facing a strange man who had approached to tell me his life story, perhaps this attempt to explicate his relationship with his mother would have made me feel uncomfortable, but it didn't. Instead, I focused on maintaining my composure and distancing myself from this unwelcome attempt at bonding.

It all began when a doppelganger from a parallel universe walked into his life. My odd companion recounted how the doppelganger endeavored to befriend him. "He was like the brother I never had," he said. In no time, this doppelganger became his best friend. Their bond extended beyond shared leisure activities, like attending soccer games, watching movies, and visiting bars; the doppelganger also assisted him with loads of boring work stuff like filling out reports, drafting e-mails, and preparing charts. Life, as a result, became remarkably easier. The doppelganger even covered for him at work on several occasions so that he could stay home all day and play video games. Then he introduced the doppelganger to his girlfriend. At first, the parallel guy took over chores and gave the man plenty of time to spend with his girlfriend. But, somehow, his doppelganger became intimate with his girlfriend, and they started to date.

He stopped here for a while. Kept his silence for a few minutes.

So much so that I started to think, "Is he gone?"

Then he said, in a somewhat weary voice, "I must admit, it wasn't exactly like that. Finally, I had time to spend with my girlfriend. And I did in the beginning. But it is not common to have someone in your life who does everything for you. So, once I had so much spare time, I might have hung out here and there alone instead of meeting with my girlfriend. But that doesn't mean my doppelganger had the right to sneak around with my girlfriend and steal her!"

It was clear from his voice that he was sad. I actually felt a little sorry for this stranger.

I was in a good place with my girlfriend. I met with her several times a week to have dinner and spend the night. Marriage was a sensitive issue for me, though. I too harbored thoughts of marriage. I just felt as if I was not there yet. And marriage means a lot of expenses.

Moreover, our current routine with my girlfriend was ideal. I thought that seeing each other every day would be pretty boring and expensive. As I had these thoughts, I realized that the stranger next to me was silent again. Since the moment he had begun to speak, I hadn't made any gesture to indicate that I was listening. I didn't want him to realize that the story he was telling had indeed piqued interest. But, as the silence dragged on, my curiosity also rose. Just as I was about to turn towards him to ask for the rest of the story, he spoke again.

"'I found a better you,' she told me. Can you believe that? According to her, my doppelganger had everything that she likes about me, but also so much more… More than that, he is involved and sensitive. He *truly* listens and understands her. He always brings her a bouquet of lilacs. She asked if I even knew her favorite flower is the lilac?"

I considered asking, "Did you know?" but held back. He answered as if he heard my unasked question: *he didn't know.*

The stranger continued his story.

After quarreling with his girlfriend, he stormed home in anger. He realized he wanted to talk to his mother. However, upon arriving home, he saw that the doppelganger and his mother were sitting together and eating strawberries. As soon as he entered, his mother started to praise the doppelganger, talking about how this veritable stranger took care of her and always brought strawberries – her favorite treat. She lamented that her very own son had never thought to bring her strawberries, questioning whether he even knew what her favorite fruit was.

"There he goes again, answering his own questions," I thought to myself. And sure enough, that veritable stranger, who had appeared out of nowhere by the ferry dock to unfold his life story to me, was answering his own question: did he know his mother's favorite fruit? Of course, he didn't know. Just like that, revealed, the counterpart from a parallel universe had also conquered his mother's heart, as if stealing his girlfriend was not already enough.

He tried to regain his mother's heart for months, but when he saw her treat the doppelganger with more compassion than he had ever received, the world crumbled under his feet.

If only these betrayals were the only destructions he had experienced. They weren't. He thought his doppelganger was working on his behalf, but that turned out not to be entirely true. Apparently, the doppelganger was working his way into the firm. There, he felt confident enough to reveal his true identity to colleagues and superiors alike, winning their hearts one by one. On top of that, the doppelganger was nailing it on the job. So much so that the firm opted to retain the doppelganger, consequently dismissing the very man who stood by me, sharing his story.

At this point in the story, I couldn't help but think about my job. I would never let anyone do my work. I take my job very seriously, and it even gives me problems sometimes. Just last week, I skipped a colleague's birthday party. I had other things to do, and I had no time to socialize with my co-workers. I received some eye rolls but didn't care. If only everyone were as professional as I am.

While I was thinking about my own job, the stranger continued his story. After losing everything he had and having no place to go any longer, he made his final decision and applied for a transfer to one of the parallel worlds.

I finally started to understand. This guy was about to transfer to another parallel world. Frankly, I thought he had made a good decision. There was nothing left for him here. He had wasted his life neglecting the people he loved and assuming they would always be there. He really deserved what happened to him. "Have a nice trip," I said without even looking his way.

I was spooked by the response.

He said, "You got me wrong; the journey has already been made. This is not my world – this is yours." Something in his voice made me want to finally look at him. I turned my head slowly and saw him for the first time since he had started speaking with me. It was another me, standing there like I was looking into a mirror. I was speechless and tried to understand what was going on.

"You see," he said, "I came here three months ago to find you. Or rather, to take what's yours. Let me explain: this is my second chance. There is a new life here for me to take over. I have been observing you and examining your weaknesses. You take your girlfriend for granted – just like I used to do. You are way too stingy to take your relationship to the next level. I will save her from you by giving her the attention she deserves, Ultimately, I will propose to her! In a restaurant with dozens of lilacs. She'll know that I am the right person for her.

"As for your mother, she will now have a son full of love – the love she never got from you. Her son will care about her and never forget what she likes. For instance, he would know strawberries are her favorite fruit. I will be the perfect son for her."

"Do you know what they call you at work? They call you a 'cold fish.'

You've never made the effort to remember their names. But I have. I've even figured out what kind of jokes they enjoy. The most important thing is that I know your boss. He likes to go to basketball games, takes care of his boat, and drinks cappuccinos. What do you think he will do when he gets an employee who brings him a nice cappuccino every morning? Face it, you don't stand a chance against me. I know too much about you and your life."

I looked at the man's face in amazement. Even though what I was seeing was an exact copy of me, I didn't believe him. I didn't want to believe that a stranger could come out of nowhere and confess that he wants to steal your life.

I was not going to allow him to mess with my head. I left him there and boarded the ferry. I thought about what he had told me along the way. While absentmindedly passing by the grocery store, I realized that this could be an opportunity for me to fix things in my life in a manner where no one else could dare to become involved. I halted and purchased a kilo of strawberries. Next, I stopped by the flower shop and ordered a bouquet of lilacs to be delivered to my girlfriend's address. When I got home, I cheerfully called out to my mother in an attempt to be endearing, saying, "Your favorite son is here." Hearing her son with this squeaky voice and seeing the bag of strawberries, she grimaced. She said, "You really want to make me regret that I am allowing you to stay with me, right? "She threw away the strawberries and said, "What a stupid boy!" I was confused. Soon the phone rang, and my girlfriend shouted at me on the phone, asking if I wanted to kill her. This was the moment I discovered she was severely been allergic to lilacs.

I was surprised by the unexpected reactions of my mother and girlfriend. You should understand something; parallel worlds are very similar to one another. When you transfer from one to another for the first time, the differences are indistinguishable. The more transfers you make, the greater the changes will be. Hence, your counterparts in the parallel world are quite similar to you, as you might expect. There are few to no differences. One flower or fruit may be preferred over another, but it is quite uncommon for people to hate them completely and suddenly. I spent the night thinking about what might be the problem.

When I went to work the next day, I was much more careful. I stared intently at each of my coworkers' faces, trying to figure out what jokes they might like. After the ordeal I'd been through so far, I was wary of getting my boss a cappuccino. So I went to his room and asked him how he wanted his coffee. The way he looked at me was strange. Even though I later realized I had known he'd had stomach surgery last month, he was quite pissed off when I asked this question. When my colleagues went to the boss with complaints that I was looking at them strangely, I was forced to take an unpaid leave. The conflation of events was too much. How could everything suddenly go so wrong?

That night, I had a lot of time to think while waiting for the evening ferry. But I finally understood. I had a very tough opponent. He knew every detail of my life, and he also knew how to manipulate me. He could foresee every step I would take. The most dangerous thing was that he had nothing to lose. His own life was irreversibly ruined. He'd take mine instead of fixing his own. Besides, there was nothing I could do: his plan was already working.

It was tough, but I finally made my decision. The life I had known in this world was no longer mine to live. I had lost my life to a doppelganger. But the situation was not hopeless. I had learned how to deceive and manipulate my counterparts. Another life that I could take over was waiting for me in another parallel world.

So, this is the reason why I came here. I captured your attention with my story, and while you are reading this, my plan has started working. I know all the details about you and your life. I have set up a course for you. What you call free will always be tainted with the suspicion of my influence.

Your life will be mine soon. I know you're panicking right now, but in time you'll calm down and figure out what to do. You will understand, eventually. After all, you don't stand a chance against a better you…

TWIN HOPES

Gizem Çetin

Translated by Tuğba Akkaya

For an adult who is halfway through their twenties, past the nasty high school and joyous college years, and who has spent more than twenty-four seasons on a weekday in front of a computer in an air-conditioned office, it is not normally possible to live a life-changing event. But Şule miraculously experienced two such events in the same hour. Both were as rare as the formation of DNA from the early, watery soup of the planet.

One morning, caught in a Monday gloom, a young woman with a long, high ponytail was reading the news while sipping her granular instant coffee slicked with cheap coffee whitener. She rolled her eyes when she saw the headline, "The world is in shock! Illegal human experiments in Greece!" on the stock laboratory photo taken from the Internet. She thought it was one of those silly clickbait links. Still, she clicked on it as an excuse to waste some more time before she started work.

The world is in shock! Illegal human experiments in Greece!

In Athens, a mind-blowing scandal has been revealed during a drug raid on an old university building.

After the closure of Didymoi University in Athens in 1993, the school land, buildings, and all fixtures were purchased as private property by Professor Ilias Barakos, one of the richest academics in the country. Barakos had taken measures to prevent strangers from entering the land and announced that he was engaging in important scientific research, the results of which would be announced to the public.

This situation led to negative reactions from some academics in the country. Arguing that university land should not be the property of a single person, academics repeatedly denounced that Barakos was doing illegal work on the grounds. Over the past twenty-five years, the land had been raided several times by the police.

Compartments below the ground concealed crimes

The last raid was made after a local citizen had seen Barakos' assistants burying bags of white powder on the property.

At 3 o'clock in the morning, police troops entered the Didymoi estate from all sides. While searching the buildings, a policeman noticed that one of the assistants was trying to get into a hole in the middle of a field.

It turned out that the hole was the exit from one of the tunnels leading to underground compartments that had not previously been discovered.

An atmosphere like medieval dungeons

There were no drugs in the compartments below, but instead a creepy scene. Cells separated by bars and full of unidentified, half-naked people were found. None of these people, aged 25-27, know how to speak.

The news continued, but Şule, who was disturbed, had no strength left to read the rest. She sighed as she pressed the exit button on the upper right. Was it necessary to make up such a lie for clickbait?!

She worked absentmindedly until her lunch break. She couldn't get her mind off that article. She kept picturing the possible condition of the unfortunate people in rags, and what she was imagining became more and more pathetic. Finally, she decided to do some more research. She typed "Ilias Barakos" into the search engine and selected the language as English. Fresh news from world-famous news channels was listed on the first page.

She clicked the link titled "Barakos, the leading role in the human experiments scandal: I did not kidnap anyone, I did not smuggle people. I didn't break ethics. (CCB, 14 hours ago).

On this site, there was an article similar to the one that she had read in the morning. In addition, the suspect's confession was also included. The professor admitted that he had experimented on those people, even saying that he had bought the university grounds only for this purpose. However, the subjects were not abducted or brought into the laboratory from the outside.

"I produced them all myself," said the professor. "The placenta is expelled from the mother's womb with the birth of a baby and is very rich in stem cells. Stem cells are our main element and can transform into all tissues and organs.

"I separated the stem cells from the placentas that I had collected from various hospitals. I produced an artificial human womb through the first cells that came in. I controlled and activated this organ by means of low-voltage electrical currents. Then I placed the other stem cells in the uterus and ensured that they developed as an embryo. A total of eight babies were born alive. They were all born in this lab for use in my experiments. I did not kidnap anyone; I did not smuggle people. I didn't violate ethics. They were all my people!

"Why is it considered ethical when other scientists produce organs from stem cells but unethical when I produce organisms? Who decides this? My colleagues, who grit their teeth in envy because they couldn't invent anything useful?"

With a shudder, Şule took a look at the other paragraphs. The assistant in charge of collecting the placentas admitted during the interrogation that he had visited some hospitals in Greece, Bulgaria, and Turkey. At the bottom, there was a link to photos of the "lab people."

Although she struggled a lot not to look at the photos, her curiosity eventually prevailed. She first read the information under each image, trying not to make eye contact with the blank stares of the subjects. Barakos named them using Greek ordinal numbers. Male subjects' names ended with "-os," and female subjects' names ended with "-a." Protos... Deftera... Trita... Tetartos... Pemptos... Ektos... Ebdomos... Enata...

After scrolling through the page a few times, she mustered the courage to look directly at the subjects. She slowly looked at their faces. When it was Deftera's turn, her heart seemed to stop. Her eyebrows, eyes, nose, lips, chin, cheekbones... She knew this face. This face was her face. The subject named – or numbered – Deftera was as similar to Şule as her twin sister.

Her blood pressure dropped, and she felt sick. She had to take time off from work and spent the rest of the day at home.

Since they were born from cells stolen from the placentas, these people must be genetic twins of free people living outside. As soon as she recovered from the shock, Şule went to the authorities and gave a DNA sample to see if Deftera really was her genetic twin. While she was at the hospital, she made an appointment with another branch and had an X-ray of her shoulder, which had been hurting for a long time. It was a long-standing, insidious, but bearable pain. That's why she delayed her examination until that day.

Seven days passed very slowly. The next day, Şule went to the hospital to both take the gene test and get her x-ray results.

She was quite surprised when she entered the waiting room of the genetics unit. Her twin sat there, looking ahead and wearing a hospital gown.

As soon as the results were declared, the Greek authorities had sent Deftera to Turkey.

"Lonely, helpless, and alone in a crowded and colorful life," she thought. She felt her heart sink. She walked up to Deftera without any hesitation, without feeling unfamiliar, and said her name in a soft voice.

When Deftera heard the sound, she lifted her head. She looked into Şule's eyes. For some reason, Şule, the twin who was raised in the heart of society, started to cry.

"You don't understand what I'm saying right now, but... I'll never let you go," she said tenderly. "No matter what!"

She was impatient while she was walking hand in hand with her sister towards the room of the doctor who was going to interpret the x-ray. She wanted to get her prescription for muscle relaxants and go out to the garden as soon as possible. There was likely not even a need to go to the doctor for this simple shoulder pain. Why had she wanted to get this job out of the way last week and waste time?

"I haven't told my parents anything yet," she said while laughing. "They don't know you exist. It hadn't even occurred to them. You wouldn't have even known about their existence, either. O stranger, will you love this big world? Could you imagine the cities, seas, and fields beyond the walls of that laboratory hell? I'm talking a lot," she said. "Wait here, I will come back. You wait here."

She entered the doctor's room and sat on the chair. Not noticing the doctor's dark, painful look, she sorted through her questions. Only five minutes were enough for Şule, who had entered shining with joy, to leave the room sobbing. Five minutes and two words.

A twenty-six-year-old adult with a well-rounded life was unlikely to experience a life-changing event, but two of them had happened to her in a single hour: one was Deftera's arrival, and the other was the doctor's suspicion about lung cancer. Additional tests were required to make a definitive diagnosis, but even the possibility was enough for Şule to shed tears.

Color MRI... Biopsy... PET-CT... It soon became clear that the doctor was right.

Şule started undergoing heavy chemotherapy. Her lung cancer had progressed in the most insidious way possible and had spread to the surrounding tissues without any symptoms except shoulder pain. The doctors were talking amongst themselves, secretly, that the chances of success were slim. During this period, Şule's parents came to Istanbul from Edirne to support her.

In a rush, Deftera could have been forgotten. However, Şule wanted her twin by her side even in her most sluggish times. She sat next to her and tried to teach her to speak, read, write, and do simple math. This was the biggest morale boost for the sick woman. Time passed mercilessly. While one woman's hair was growing, the other's was falling out; while one body was recovering, the other was melting.

As the treatment progressed, Şule was caught in fear of death's grip. She saw Deftera more as a surrogate who would replace her after she died and continue her unfinished life rather than as a simple sister. She tried to prepare her for this "duty" by telling her everything she liked, found interesting, thought, and opposed in her healthy life. She asked for her CD player, which had ended up on the back shelf of the cellar. For three days, she kept playing the disc that had a cover of a red-haired girl and made her memorize her favorite song under the bored eyes of the nurses.

"Come and see, I have the sky in one of my hands," Şule started to sing.

"Still..." continued Deftera.

"The missing stars in the other one."

"La la..."

It was three months after the diagnosis when the doctor openly said, "We can get your daughter out of the hospital and end the treatment. Now chemotherapy has no effect other than causing pain; the cancer cells have spread to all her organs. It would be much better if she spent her last days at home."

While the mother and father were listening to these bitter words, they heard a scream from Şule's room, which was down the corridor. Doctors, nurses, and parents entered the room, ready for any kind of intervention. However, the girl's scream was not because of an ache or pain.

"Deftera is missing!" cried the patient, with sobs. "She's escaped!"

Indeed, the old subject was nowhere in the hospital. She didn't leave any traces behind. For three days, they searched for the young woman, who had vanished into thin air. Police departments throughout Turkey were notified. Meanwhile, Şule's condition got worse; her only source of morale was gone, and she was taken to the intensive care unit after losing consciousness.

"Say goodbye, get ready," the doctors were saying. "She won't wake up."

At the end of the third day, the family received a phone call from the Edirne Police Department. Deftera had been caught trying to escape from Turkey to Greece. Although she was interrogated at the police station, she never spoke. Though arrested because she didn't have a passport and ID, she was acquitted in court on the grounds that her ability at perception was still lacking and, therefore, she did not have any criminal capacity.

When Şule's father returned to the hospital with Deftera, the patient was still in the intensive care unit. The eyes of the mother waiting in the seats outside were red from crying. The former subject walked to a corner. She leaned against the wall. She put her finger in her mouth and touched her throat, then started throwing up. First came the remains of her last meal, then some gastric juice, and, finally, a flash drive in plastic wrap.

After seeing what was inside the flash drive, the facts were understood. Deftera was not caught trying to escape from Turkey, but while returning to Turkey after having escaped to Greece. During this time, she had gone to Didymoi University, had managed to get back through the underground tunnels by retracing the path through which police had first extracted herby retracing the path through which police had first extracted her, and had brought back one of the devices that contained backups of Barakos" work. Since the packaging in which the flash drive was kept was produced from a special kind of polymer made by the professor, the device inside was not discovered during X-ray scanning at the border.

In the files found on the memory stick, llias Barakos talked about a method called the "Phoenix Treatment":

"Phoenix, Zümrüdüanka, Simurg... This mythological bird, which is known by different names in many cultures, inspired me to develop my revolutionary scientific treatment method.

"As it is known, the Phoenix begins to burn itself when it grows old and fades. After turning into a handful of ashes, as a chick, it shakes its hairless, fresh head and is thus born from the ashes. In my opinion, this mechanism symbolizes the life cycle of cancerous cells.

"Normal human cells cannot divide in an unlimited fashion. Cellular division is controlled by long strings of bases called 'telomeres,' which are located at the ends of chromosomes. These sequences are lost after each division. When telomeres shorten to the critical point, cells stop dividing.

"Therefore, a Phoenix representing normal cells could not rise from its ashes in all its freshness every time. Each time it would be born a little older and, after a few life cycles, would irreversibly turn to ashes.

"Cancerous cells, on the other hand, have the capacity to divide indefinitely. They gain these properties with the enzyme telomerase, which maintains telomere length and limits the number of divisions.

"While this enzyme is inactive in normal cells, it is quite active in cancerous cells. Therefore, experimental studies on treatments targeting the telomerase enzyme continue in the academic world.

"I developed this method in the opposite way. The Phoenix Treatment aims to increase, not decrease, the relevant enzyme. It is necessary not to reduce cancer cells but to increase them and ensure that they cover the whole body.

"This is necessary because only two types of cells have high dividing ability and telomerase activity: cancer cells and stem cells."

After this paragraph, the oncologists stopped reading and were convinced that the study was insane. Only the doctor who was taking care of Şule took it seriously and locked himself in his room all night to read and evaluate the whole study.

In the rest of the study, Barakos listed the common features of cancer cells and stem cells. For him, cancer was not a disease but an opportunity for rebirth and renewal. The incompatibility between cancer cells and normal cells was the reason for death.

In the first stage of treatment, it was necessary to destroy normal cells and ensure the rapid proliferation of cancer cells. However, this process had to be done within hours. Otherwise, the incompatibility would prevent the organs from working and lead to death.

Once the body was made up of cancer cells, these cells would be "trained" to ensure that they reverted to their old DNA structures. The second phase of treatment should take place in the following order:

1. The body would be moved to a cold environment to slow down metabolism and cell division.
2. The techniques used during organ production from stem cells would be applied exactly to these new cells. Thus, the cells would become specialized and regenerate old tissues.
3. After making sure that all cells were differentiated and symptoms such as excessive division and telomerase activity stopped, the body would be taken to a warm environment to speed up the metabolism and healing process again.

In the final parts of his work, Barakos admitted that the chances of success with this treatment method were quite low. "But..." he said, "If applied correctly, it is possible to cure even the most severe cancer patient in a maximum of eight hours. The Phoenix legend was not told for nothing; we humans are Phoenix as long as we face rebirth and resist death."

The doctor, who wanted to apply this treatment to Şule as a last resort, initially faced great resistance from his colleagues. This extraordinary treatment proposal was against the principle of "primum non nocere" – that is, "First, do no harm!" – that is the foundation of medicine.

However, the doctor, who thought that they should try this remedy, insisted. He followed the procedures and signed documents indicating that he took all the responsibility. Finally, it was decided to try the Phoenix Treatment on Şule.

The discussions lasted two days. During this time, Deftera isolated herself inside Şule's old room. The hospital was so busy that no one cared for her or questioned why she was staying there. The former subject kept turning the CD player on at a low volume and listening to "Don't Let Me Go" over and over.

On the night of the treatment, the mother and father hugged each other and waited sleeplessly. At dawn, the fate of their daughter would be known. Şule would either lie on her bed as cold as ice or open her eyes to a warm new life. The minute and hour hands were very lazy that night. Sleep avoided them... The hours were quite long. The eyelids of doctors and the others who were waiting refused to close.

There was one oncologist at the hospital who had never been convinced and who was strongly opposed to this treatment method: Doctor Altan. He claimed that the Phoenix Treatment would certainly kill the patient and urged the family and other doctors to give up. No one saw him on the night of the treatment. Şule's doctor, on the other hand, wandered around with more hope and pride in the face of Altan's absence. He already felt triumphant.

In the early hours of the morning, the body in the bed opened her eyes. She was still exhausted but healthy. She squinted reflexively because of the light hitting her face. Her mother and father, who were frozen, were waiting while the doctor kept saying, "We did it!" with tears in his eyes.

This peaceful moment was interrupted by the door suddenly opening wide. Doctor Altan entered with the police behind him. As the police started handcuffing the suspected murderer and doctor of Şule, he asked the family, "Are you happy with what you have done? You have destroyed your daughter. Are you happy?"

He walked over to the living body on the bed. "I tried to tell you. I've been trying to tell you all along. A person's personality is determined not by the number of brain cells but by the connections between those cells – that is, by electrical currents. You can produce cells. But what about the connections between them? Those connections were all the experiences and memories Şule had since she was a baby. They were her self-perception. You've destroyed them all. Congratulations!"

"You're lying – here is our daughter, alive!" protested her mother.

"You think that your daughter is alive? Do you still think that breathing organism is your daughter? Yes... They have the same genes. But they're not the same person. Just as Deftera and Şule are different people despite having the same genes, this anonymous body and your daughter are also different people. Moreover, this new body will not even have a personality because there is no exchange between her synapses. Her brain is empty – empty! She doesn't even have the ability to learn. Good luck with your new child, who has only basic reflexes but will live and die as a piece of meat!"

The father finally broke his silence by saying, "Why didn't our doctor tell us these things?"

"Your doctor didn't even care about your daughter. Your doctor was driven by the same motivation as Barakos, only chasing fame and money. Primum non nocere: First, do not harm! We, doctors, look for ways to avoid further harm to the patient before treatment. Hippocrates did not say this phrase in vain centuries ago. On the other hand, your doctor deliberately destroyed millions of Şule's healthy cells. He deliberately killed her."

The mother let out a wail. Şule's doctor was taken to the police station and faced a future where he would be sentenced to life imprisonment. Meanwhile, Deftera was lying on her bed in the other room, unaware of everything, and listening to the song.

"The fears are mine, and the hopes are mine. Don't let me go... Don't let me go..."

THE SPLITTING

İsmail Yiğit

Translated by Turgay Bayındır

The night the moon split, Cem was returning home in his air-mobile. At first, he couldn't believe his eyes. He verbally commanded the program that controlled the air-mobile to stop. He turned off his smart lens and looked out the window of his vehicle once again. No, this was not an advertisement for augmented reality. The dead moon, which had stayed in its orbit around the Earth for billions of years, had split in two like a cracking egg. A few seconds later, a giant, blood-red screen emerged out of the space between the two halves of the moon.

With the emergence of the screen, Cem started to hear whispers in gradually increasing volumes. A voice reverberated inside his head as if talking to him: "Don't be scared! You will be saved!"

These two sentences were heard not only by Cem but by everyone on earth; each heard the words in their own language. Those who were sleeping were now fully awake, startled. Those who weren't looking at the sky at that moment or those who couldn't see the moon from their location trembled with the voice that seemed to have come out of thin air. The remaining billions had both seen the Splitting (this is how the media would call this a historical event) and heard those two sentences.

When the whispers stopped, the screen coming out of the moon started to flicker. Two images appeared on the screen: first, a blue globe similar to Earth, then a metallic grey cylindrical object turning around the globe like a bullet targeting it. As the cylindrical object turned faster and faster around the globe, it looked like a ring that surrounded the globe. Then, the globe suddenly exploded into flames while the cylindrical object slowed down. When it finally came to a complete stop, it disappeared from the screen, leaving behind a ball of light. The same whispers echoed in everyone's ears: "Don't be scared! You will be saved!" When the giant screen folded in on itself, the two halves of the moon started moving towards each other. In a few seconds, the moon was shining in the sky in one piece, just as it had before.

When the Splitting was over, the vehicles of thousands of people, who had parked in the air like Cem, started moving. The AI that centrally controlled air traffic would take each one to their destinations through pre-recorded routes. Cem lit a cigarette in order to shake off the tension that had overcome him. But he didn't need it. The hormone-regulating chip that was installed in his brain had already started to suppress the signs of over-excitement. Thanks to these chips, crimes like murder and rape had all but disappeared. The driver software of the air-mobile quickly sensed the cigarette smoke and warned Cem in a loud voice:

"Mr. Cem Merih! You have violated the Protection of Health code, number 1984! Your account has been charged 54 Yuan-Dollars for it!"

Cem snarled, "And on the day I got fired!" and continued smoking.

Cem had been fired that day due to low performance, and an android teacher had been appointed to the position by the Universal Education Ministry. Most parents did not want to trust their children to human teachers anyway to prevent potential cases of molestation in case of malfunctioning chips. Only the fanatically religious parents who saw the invention of androids as a major sin against God still preferred human teachers like Cem, whose numbers were otherwise on the decline.

Thanks to the nano-curatives in his bloodstream, the possibility of Cem getting cancer was very low. These artificial white blood cells that were controlled by the immunity software that Cem had bought at the pharmacy were programmed to destroy tumor formations and pathogens that they encountered in his body. The bio-electronic database of the nano-curatives was regularly updated – as long as he continued paying, of course – so they recognized all new viruses.

Cem was in deep thought as to how many months his unemployment pay would last.

When he finished smoking his cigarette, he turned on his smart lens to connect to the news platforms. All the channels on his personal virtual reality screen were talking about the Splitting as "Breaking News." However, no image of the splitting of the moon was available. The videos that were captured by cameras directed to the sky at the moment of the Splitting showed no change in the moon. 19 billion people around the world had experienced the same thing, but there wasn't a single digital record to prove it. It was later announced that this global phenomenon had lasted 54 seconds.

According to the first official announcement made by the World Government, what was observed on the moon was not a physical splitting.

The reporters who contacted the moon colony also confirmed this. Some people in the colony had also seen the giant screen that covered the horizon on the moon and heard the same voices, but the seismic sensors on the moon hadn't registered any disturbance. What is more, if the moon had really split, the colony would have been obliterated.

The settlers in the Martian base had also had the same experience as billions of people on Earth, but with one difference: They had started hearing the whispers and the "Don't be scared! You will be saved!" message 5 minutes and 4 seconds later than those on earth. This interval amounted to the exact length of time needed by an electromagnetic wave to travel the distance between the moon and Mars at the time of the Splitting.

While watching the news, Cem was also looking at New Istanbul from the window of the moving air-mobile. It hadn't taken long before skyscrapers had spread over the city once again like the tentacles of an octopus after the earthquake of 2054. Since the extinction of seagulls, the only sound over the city was the humming of air mobiles. And the shrill screams of mutant bats! It would take decades to use nanobots to clean the traces of last century's Trakya Nuclear Station spill from the air, water, and soil.

The air-mobile carrying Cem had left the Mevlana Bridge behind and was approaching the North Side of New Istanbul. It was the seventh and the last bridge spanning the Bosphorus, over which land travel had declined with the widespread use of air-mobiles, relegating roads to the nostalgic driving habits of the rich. The doors of the air-mobile opened after it landed on the roof of the 101-story building where Cem lived, announcing,

"Thanks for choosing the 'Voyager' software for your trip. Today you have earned a total of 54 Yuan-Dollars' worth of kilometer points."

No one greeted Cem when he entered his home. Because he had missed the monthly payments for the sexbot that he had bought in order to relieve his loneliness, the company confiscated the bot. If he didn't pay the missed installments soon, Luna (as he'd named her for her bright face) was going to be sent to the recirculation facility in order to be resold.

Cem changed clothes and lay in his bed. He was thinking about the Splitting. He didn't have any friends he could call up to talk about it. He remembered his mother. She must have experienced the same things as everybody else. It worried him to think that she must have thought she was having another one of her fits of hallucination. He shouted towards the wall so that the home communication system could hear him:

"Call Bakırköy Psychiatric Rehabilitation Center. I want to speak to my mom. Tell them it is an emergency."

He knew that if he didn't specify it as "an emergency," they would not let him speak with his mother at that hour. About a minute later, an old and tired woman's voice echoed in the room:

"Cem, I knew you would call. You also heard the whispers, didn't you?"

"Yes, mom. Everybody heard. Don't be scared; continue taking your medication."

"No, no ... Of course, I am not scared ... Didn't they tell us not to be scared anyway? Cem, you believe me now, don't you? They have finally arrived. I have been telling everyone for years that they would find us. But none of you believed me. Neither you nor that filthy man, your father! You are not seeing him still, are you? Never forget that he abandoned us and went to Mars with that whorebot. It was so insulting to me. He said that the machine was more of a woman than me and that I was more like a robot! When I caught those two in my own bedroom, doing that abominable thing that is damned by God... I still see that scene in my dreams every night. But the word of the Holy Book is very clear: 'Humans were created for humans!' Cem, promise me you will not marry one of those satanic machines!"

Cem's mother started crying after finishing her words.

"Mom, please don't start again. I only wanted to hear your voice to know that you are ok. Don't worry, I will call you again later."

Cem checked the news again a few minutes after he ended the call. When he got bored, he went out on the balcony and watched the moon while smoking a cigarette. As if it wasn't that huge silver tray in the sky that had split but instead his mind. Countless thoughts occupied his mind, but none of them had a meaningful answer that satisfied him. He only perceived a gradually forming wish that the meaning of the message would come true.

The next day, a ban was declared on the coverage of the Splitting in the news. Except for the official explanation, anyone who mentioned the previous day's event on the news platforms or on the phone would be detected with the help of semantic monitoring software and punished. The President of the World Government went in front of the cameras together with the head of the International Space Agency and announced that the Splitting was a terrorist attack carried out by aliens. These extraterrestrial terrorists had infiltrated people's brains through a moon-centered pirate broadcast in order to generate a virtual reality-based hallucination and arouse fear. The President, who had been known to get into arguments with artists, even blamed some Hollywood directors for it. According to the President, these "pompous intellectuals" who had been portraying aliens as friendly were complicit traitors. For years, they had subconsciously prepared humans for an alien invasion. Groups of electors who supported the President started petitions for the arrest of the artists who had created works that showed aliens in a friendly way. The government requested citizens to report any suspicious activity to the officials. Police departments around the world were flooded with hundreds of thousands of messages reporting on people who wore t-shirts with UFO pictures.

Street demonstrations started in some cities. Among them were some who argued that the Splitting was a call for the salvation of humanity. Other groups, however, argued that humanity, who had caused irreversible damage to the ecological balance of the planet upon which they lived, had been declared a "thug species" by a Galactic Administration with which there had not yet been any contact. These demonstrations were being suppressed by the mechanical police force that was called Robo-Security, which was controlled by the public order software. Some of the arrested protesters had already been vaporized by atom-dissolving execution squads.

A couple of days later, the radar systems scanning space detected a new object in the Earth's orbit. This cylindrical object had arrived suddenly and looked very similar to the object that had appeared on the virtual screen on the night of the Splitting. According to the official explanation, this was a weapon sent by aliens to annihilate Earth. In order to prevent further pirate broadcasts by aliens from infiltrating people's brains, helmets were distributed to the residents in all cities. These helmets prevented all electromagnetic waves except for the ones officially permitted. It was announced on the news platforms that the citizens who took off their helmets would be punished. Even if people were to take off their helmets at home, the cameras of their home management systems would detect it.

Cem had not once stepped out of his apartment since the Splitting. While he sat on the toilet one morning with his helmet on (it had been delivered by the robo-postman that morning), he came across information about a referendum on a news platform that he connected to through his smart lens. The government had declared that a worldwide referendum would be conducted as to whether the cylindrical object should be destroyed or not. Getting in line in front of ballot boxes or voting machines had been left in the past, and voters would verify their identity through their smart lenses and then easily log into the virtual election offices to cast their votes within seconds. Participation in the referendum was, of course, compulsory.

Cem thought, "What can voting change anyway?" The AI that managed the virtual voting process was under the regime's control and for decades, voting outcomes had always been in line with the regime's wishes. Cem suddenly looked at the walls around him in fear. He had remembered the claims of some conspiracy theorists that the chips in people's brains were also recording people's thoughts and reporting them to the regime. However, Cem knew that this was not true from his own experiences. Once, he had plucked up all his courage and sworn at the President of World Government in his mind. No one had come to knock on his door.

The outcome of the referendum that took place the next day did not surprise Cem. 99.23 % of world citizens supported the proposal to destroy the cylindrical object in Earth's orbit. The International Government did not waste any time in activating the laser cannons that were put in place decades ago to prevent the crashing of a rogue meteor into Earth. Millions of regime supporters gathered in city squares with their helmets on, watching the live broadcasting of the destruction of the alien object on big screens and through their smart lenses. They were booing and whistling. Some of them held electronic signs in their hands that read, "Get out of the Solar System!" They were burning alien dummies in the streets, and the smoke detectors were temporarily turned off so that people could light them up without the fire alarms going off. Cem was in this crowd. He was quietly watching others without otherwise participating.

When the countdown started, the object in orbit started to accelerate. When people noticed this, they started screaming and running in all directions. Cem started to walk towards the big screen, not paying attention to the running people who kept bumping into him. He took a large rock out of his pocket and was holding it tightly in his hand.

Cem threw the rock at the big screen with all his strength and shouted:

"I've had enough! I want to live like a free human being!"

One of the robo-police officers quickly ran towards Cem and hit him with his electric baton. As Cem fell down with the force of the blow, his helmet came off his head. Before he lost consciousness, new whispers were echoing in his brain:

"Terrans! Do not interfere with the rescue vehicle that was sent by the Galactic Council of the Universal Government! Your planet is in great danger. Listen to our advice!"

The light of the laser cannons firing flashed on the big screen.

[Millions of light years away]

When Cem opened his eyes, he found himself lying in a small bed in a place that looked like his childhood room. Two women were sitting by his bed: his mother and Luna!

When they realized that Cem was waking up, they started speaking at the same time:

"Hello, Mr. Cem Merih. You are in a virtual reality room. We thought it would be good to greet you with the visual interface of the two people you loved most. Each item in this room is exactly what we found among your memories during our scan of your brain; they were designed to make you feel more comfortable."

Cem spoke with difficulty as if waking up from anesthesia: "Why am I here?"

"Your planet was in danger of destruction from a source that could not be detected by your current scientific knowledge. Countless star systems had been previously obliviated by the splits that happen periodically in the space-time meta dimensions. In accordance with the Universal Law, those civilizations that are at the evolutionary level to have developed artificial intelligence are offered a chance to be saved from being destroyed by these cosmic quakes. You are now in safety, 191 million light years away from your home, in a rehabilitation facility, together with the other humans who were rescued through teleportation. You should rest a bit more. In time, you will learn everything that you will need to start your new life."

Cem struggled to sit up in bed. "My mother..." he said. "Is my mother here too?"

The eyes of the visual interface in the appearance of his mother and artificial girlfriend Luna flickered as if they were calculating something. Then they both smiled and answered at the same time:

"According to the DNA records in our database, your mother has been with us for a long time. In terms of your doomed planet's revolution time around its star, she has been under treatment here for 15 years. In one of the earlier teleportation experiments that the Galactic Council regularly carried out with Terrans, only part of her consciousness could be transferred."

"No, no! There must be a mistake. My mother was with me all those years."

When he said this, Cem shrank at the realization that his mother's fits of hallucination had started exactly 15 years ago.

"When we teleport someone, we replace them with an organically created twin that we build with nano-copiers. But do not worry about these now. Teleportation is a traumatic experience both for the body and for the mind. When you are rested, we will definitely arrange a meeting between you and your mother."

When he noticed that the visual interfaces were becoming blurry, Cem asked his last question in a hurry:

"Earth... What happened to it? You said it was destroyed. Were you able to save everyone?"

The images of his mother and Luna livened up:

"All the planets and their star in what you call the Solar System were destroyed by the splitting in space-time. Unfortunately, only a small minority of humans were saved from this cosmic cataclysm. Our rescue ship was only able to store the quantum maps of those who could receive our teleportation signals. That is less than 1 % of your population..."

After hearing this last sentence, Cem closed his eyes in pain while the pixels of the interface disappeared into the air.

DEPERSONALIZATION

Mehmet Ali Kaynak

Translated by Ada Sena Çandarlı

"War always brings new opportunities alongside pain and death. That is the reason we have been killing each other non-stop for centuries," said Commissioner Mustafa.

Police officer Pınar, who was waiting for her shift to be over, nodded in agreement with Commissioner Mustafa, trying to hide a careless, tired look on her face. The Commissioner continued to talk.

"We also make good use of these opportunities. I mean the opportunities that war brings. The never-ending war between good and bad. If there were no villains, we wouldn't have found the money for the cybernetic enhancements, right? But now, look at this, we have the cybernetic arms of the boxer named Muhammet Li. They say that he can knock a bull down with one punch."

She said, "So, what happened to your organic arm?"

"Standard procedure, it is hidden as an organic spare part," said the Commissioner.

Pınar had an indecisive look on her face, thinking what she was going to say, when a police officer hastily entered the room, turning to the Commissioner and giving him a salute.

"Commissioner, there is an urgent case. There was a murder in one of the organic spare part facilities. A doctor responsible for the depot of a reincarnation company was killed."

Commissioner Mustafa, angered by the interruption of his conversation with Pınar, snapped to the novice police officer, "What does that have to do with me, stupid! I am a mediator; you should've come to me before there was a murder!"

"Commissioner, the special operations group is at the scene of the crime, but there is something else; another person was seen next to the murderer. They couldn't identify the person since their face wasn't seen. By the looks of the murderer's behavior towards them, though, it's assumed that they were a hostage, not an accomplice."

"Fuck this shit," the Commissioner mumbled. Then he said, trying to calm himself down, "A reincarnation company; at least it isn't the one my organic arm is kept in."

The Commissioner left the room accompanied by the police officer. Mustafa was walking with the young officer, swearing silently to himself. They got into one of the police cars in the garage. Mustafa looked over at the officer. He couldn't make out his name; he didn't bother with meeting the new recruits anyway. Abruptly, he asked, "What's your name?"

The young officer answered, "Hasan."

"Tell me more about this murderer. What do we know about him?"

"An old soldier. Name is Mehmet."

"Another one of these Mehmets, huh?"

"This time, it is a little different from the other Mehmets. You've heard about the soldier who saved thousands of civilians last year in the Bosphorus Korteks crisis?"

"Yeah, I've heard. We were only missing a war hero with a fractured head," murmured the Commissioner.

"The saying 'fractured head' is a little ironic, actually. After the events of last year, he was given a full-body transfer. The last organic parts of his body were replaced with cybernetic ones. Actually, it is an understatement to say the last organic parts. His brain was the only remaining part, and it was fully scanned and loaded onto a chip. That's why he was given the Headbeen medallion. Since his brain was uploaded onto the cloud, he had gone on dozens more operations and had proved his trustworthiness. With the current situation, there is no room for mistakes since he is completely cybernetic, so a potential shootout is the last thing they would want. They want to find whatever is messing with his head and end this without a gunfight."

"Man is only supposed to die once: when you die over and over, you lose your mind, just like these men."

Hasan decided to vocalize his disagreement with the Commissioner: "Don't you think a man willing to die over and over for the benefit of his society deserves respect, Commissioner?"

Another idealistic young officer, the Commissioner thought to himself. "Maybe they do. But this doesn't change the fact that, every time they die, they get further away from humanity and lose a bit more of their mental health. Maybe their consciousnesses on these chips shouldn't be updated all the time. If they were returned to a healthy version of their mind after every operation, they wouldn't be this fractured."

"Do you think that is closer to the concept of humanity? I mean, erasing the memories a person has already experienced?"

The Commissioner got mad since what he was saying was not understood, and raised his voice. "This has nothing to do with the concept of humanity, Hasan! The subject is about military experience. Every battle and every conflict brings a huge military experience with it. Therefore, after every operation that the memory chip doesn't target, the version of their mind on the cloud is continuously updated with a more psychopathic version."

Hasan didn't say anything else about the subject. After a while, he said, "We're here, Commissioner," and then stopped next to a huge parking lot full of autonomous cars. The Reincarnation Organic Part Storage Company was situated on the highest floors of the skyscraper. Commissioner Mustafa looked up while trying to make out the logo of the company. "I wonder if the companies keep our legs and arms that high up since we are so afraid of being underground?" he thought. "Bullshit," he mumbled.

A police officer handed Mustafa the file that contained detailed information on Mehmet. The Commissioner lit a cigarette and started to study the file. While the part about the operations Mehmet had joined was never-ending, like the epic of Manas, information about his social connections and family was only a few paragraphs.

Seeing Mehmet's organic face, Mustafa wondered how the man managed to look so terrifying but still have a handsome face. His cybernetic face looked a lot calmer. "Maybe they make it like this on purpose," he thought. "At the end of the day, if one were a machine of death, no one would want that visible in their eyes."

At the end of the file, there was a picture of the murdered doctor from the Reincarnation company. His face looked like it had been broken into pieces by a single blow from Mehmet's cybernetic arm. Mustafa couldn't stand looking at the unpleasant scene anymore and turned to the next page. The doctor that was killed was the head of the R&D department. It was mentioned in the file that the doctor used to frequently work alone, on his own time, while off-duty. "It must have been an easy hunt for the confused Mehmet," the Commissioner thought to himself. "I wonder what he was working on during his final, ominous hours?"

Commissioner Mustafa, taking another puff from his cigarette, closed the file. He did his last preparations and made his way towards an entrance to the parking lot. As he approached the crime scene, he couldn't help but focus on the sounds. A man was arguing, ranting, and raving. The interesting thing was that he was arguing with himself, yelling first with a strong, dominant voice and then answering with a weary tone.

"I didn't ask for this!"

"Do you think I did? It wasn't my choice to come to this world."

"You don't have a right to live. You are not a real person."

"Take a look at yourself: how real are you, huh? Should we look for humanity within your iron chest or inside the chips connected by wires?"

"It is a paradox. This is a fucking paradox that you have brought me into! But it isn't going to last long; I am going to kill you the way I killed the doctor that put me in this position."

The man must have lost his mind to another degree, Mustafa thought. When he reached the last floor of the parking lot, he saw Mehmet, who had his back towards the stairs. Mustafa was startled by Mehmet's large body, which was made out of metal and plastic. Opposite Mehmet, across the thick columns of the building, there was a totally dark area. Neither the building's lighting nor the moonlight reached this part. Mehmet was yelling into this darkness. This must have been the place he put the hostage in.

Mustafa was silently getting closer when Mehmet's ultra-sensitive, military-level cybernetic ears noticed the footsteps. In milliseconds, he swung around with a 50-caliber revolver that used depleted uranium-capped bullets in his hand. Yelling, he aimed for Mustafa's spinal cord. It was obvious Mehmet wasn't expecting company. He took a few steps back, and his whole body was lost in the darkness. The only visible thing was his gun glistening on the brink of darkness.

Mehmet warned Mustafa, saying, "You wouldn't want to get any closer."

Mustafa already had his hands over his head. "Don't shoot; I'm not here to fight with you."

Mehmet leaned forward to have a better look at the Commissioner and half of his face emerged from the darkness. When Mustafa fully saw Mehmet's face, he got a terrifying feeling deep in his heart. Mehmet's cybernetic eyes weren't even hiding the signs of his insanity. What scared Mustafa was the fact that this pure anger was reflected in those eyes. Mustafa was caught up by this look for a second. He found it interesting that they displayed feelings, even though they were completely cybernetic.

After examining the Commissioner, Mehmet said, with surprising calmness, "Drop your weapon."

Mustafa kept his hands above his head, spinning himself around, and answered, "I don't have a gun."

Mehmet warned Mustafa, "Go back to wherever you're coming from." Then he disappeared back into the darkness.

"When I came here, I left a beautiful girl behind. So, if I'd had the chance, I would've already used it."

Mehmet's voice seemed unfazed by his joke. "What do you want?" he asked.

"It is about the hostage. I am here for them to ensure that no harm is done to anyone."

"This is my problem!" Mehmet snapped. "It doesn't concern anyone but me!"

"There are dozens of police officers down there. Ever since you murdered a scientist and took one hostage, it stopped being only your problem."

"'He was a scientist!' 'He was a hostage!'" Mehmet yelled mockingly. "They are only the decor; I am the one being illuminated on the stage. The real point is what I am going to do. That is the reason that we are here, that we are in this situation. To solve a paradox…"

"You are a war hero, Mehmet, and I want to protect your status while this incident isn't in the press. If you give yourself in without harming the hostage, I can negotiate for you to be updated to the version of your mind before all of this would happen."

Mehmet took his face out of the dark to look at Mustafa. "War hero, huh? I don't even remember fighting in most of the battles."

"You've been through a lot, but this hostage hasn't done anything wrong. Please let me confirm that he is okay, and bring him out into the light."

Mehmet started laughing hysterically. "You don't have the slightest idea who you are talking about, do you? You don't even know who the hostage is. You don't have the slightest inkling why I killed that doctor."

Mustafa said, "It doesn't matter who the hostage is; he is a human, and I want to make sure that he is safe. I am here to help you." The Commissioner took a step forward. He was taken aback by the bullet sound that shook him like rumbling thunder. The bullet Mehmet had fired perforated the tip of Mustafa's shoe and crashed into the concrete right at the tip of his big toe.

"Don't!" Mehmet warned. "Do not take another step."

There was an uproar in Mustafa's earpiece. The marksmen were asking for clearance while the Special Operations Commissioner was hurling directives for them to wait until they had the possibility for a clear shot.

Mustafa took a step back with his cloven shoe. "Alright. Okay, let's calm down. I am backing up. I only want to help you."

"You can't help me; no one can."

"Why not?"

"It is a paradox, Commissioner. This is a question with no answer, and you can't answer this question."

"I am just trying to understand. Why does a war hero like yourself do this after getting through all that hardship?"

Mehmet took a deep breath. "I killed the Minotaur, Commissioner. The Minotaur! But when I returned to the city, my ship was still at the dock. As if...as if I had never left for the expedition; as if the things I lived through didn't happen."

While the officers outside of the parking lot researched the meaning of the things Mehmet had said, Mustafa lied to him, saying, "I get what you are saying; please stay calm."

One second hadn't even passed when an officer spoke into Mustafa's headpiece, explaining the concept of "Theseus's Ship."

"The ship of Theseus is a philosophical paradox. According to Greek philosophy, the ship of Theseus is kept as memorabilia in Athens for a long time after Theseus returns victorious after defeating the Cretan Minotaur. With time, the ship's wooden parts get older and are replaced with new ones. So much so that, one day, there is no part of the ship that hasn't been replaced. Is the ship, therefore, still Theseus's ship, or is it a completely different one? The ship became a topic of discussion for ancient philosophers."

Mustafa understood the situation quickly: "In every war, you left a part of your flesh on the battlefield, right?"

"That doesn't matter! When I decided to take this route, I'd already given myself up."

"So, what is the problem? Do you think that it isn't you in this shell? That the real you has been changed?"

Confusion took over Mehmet's face. His cybernetic eyes, which Mustafa couldn't look away from, turned to the floor. "I am just angry. I do not know the answers. I hadn't thought about which ship was real and which one was not until today. Similarly how I hadn't thought about the decision of who should live and who should die. These decisions have always been made in my name. Today finally, I will make the decision."

"You used to be weak; now you are a hero."

"I used to be scared of things. Some things hurt me. Now I am not scared of anything, and nothing hurts me. Even fear was taken from me. All they left behind was anger. Yes, I used to be weak. 'Cause I used to be human."

Mustafa used all of his professional experience to properly convey the lie to his face and said, "You are still human."

Mehmet's cybernetic eyes focused on Mustafa's face now. The processor calculated his expression. He didn't blink, gulp, or avert his gaze. Mustafa was a good liar because of his job. But he could not control the involuntary reflex of his pupils getting larger, which is what gave him up. Mehmet's lying program locked on this anatomical irregularity and reported the outcome: "Lie."

Mehmet laughed. "Did you know there is a program that prevents us from holding the gun to our heads?" Without waiting for an answer, he left the darkness and started towards Mustafa with strong steps. When he reached the angle from which snipers could see him, he stopped and said, "The search for eternal life is meaningless, Commissioner. You can only beat death when you accept it." The fully cybernetic man pointed his gun at Mustafa. A storm was going on in Mustafa's earpiece:

"Target in the rifle range!"

"Danger of intentional damage to biological entity!"

"Shot cleared!"

Mustafa wanted to say, "Stop!" but his mouth couldn't catch up with his mind. With the sound of non-stop bullets, Mehmet's body, made out of metal, plastic, and cables, scattered like leaves in a strong wind.

First, the hand that was holding the weapon, then the arm, his shoulders, and at last, his head were scattered. The word "Stop" then finally reached Mustafa's brain to his mouth.

In his earpiece, there was a feeling of festivity:

"Number one: Successful shot!"

"Number two: Shot on point!"

"Number three: Confirmed the destruction of the memory chip!"

Mustafa took his earpiece out and threw it onto the ground. It was lost within all the severed cables and torn metal pieces scattered around as if they didn't belong to someone who, until seconds ago, had been thinking, talking, and getting angry. Mustafa stood there for a while, watching the pieces that remained of Mehmet. Then he stepped over the debris and saw the hostage in the darkness behind the columns.

His feet and hands were tied, and he had a bag over his head. The Commissioner got close, took the hostage into the light, then cut the tied feet and hands and took the bag off his head. When Mustafa saw the hostage's face, he felt the need to look back at Mehmet's left-over face, which reminded him of a mask. It wasn't like the face he had seen when he first arrived – the one that wasn't able to hide signs of insanity. Instead, this face looked so at peace. Though the hostage had Mehmet's exact features, he was looking at Mustafa with a completely different look.

The Commissioner stared at the hostage. Recomposed of damaged biological parts and a body remade piece by piece, here was Mehmet. A flesh and blood Mehmet. His face had all of the fear and pain Mehmet had talked about before having been torn into pieces.

Mustafa shook his arm lightly and asked, "Are you okay?" Mehmet was still in shock, but Mustafa felt the warmness of blood running through the man's veins when he touched his arm.

With the comfort brought to him by ending the paradox, Mehmet turned his eyes towards Mustafa and said, "I fought with myself and lost. Now I feel in my body the wounds of war I've never fought."

ALTERATION

Melda Uytun

In the six years I spent tracking David Addley, it never occurred to me that he didn't exist. Sharing this with my friend Em, who had been anxiously asking me about my search, was extremely hard. I knew that she would go nuts once she heard it. I sincerely shared her sentiment, but to unravel this mystery, we needed common sense more than lunacy. My mind almost burned with the questions I thought I could never find answers to.

When confronted with an illogical closure, I've seen people react in three ways. Some deny their reality until they forget. Some move on, but keep the ending in mind to go back every so often and look at it from different angles. And some don't care.

To my regret, Em was a denier. I hadn't planned how to direct the conversation once I started it. I was going to improvise and hope for the best.

"Tell me you found him." There was nothing tense to her attitude, so I was relieved since she'd been in a nail-biting temper lately. She curiously studied my face, presumably hoping to identify whatever emotion the news had awoken in me. I recalled our lives before David came through our door but strove not to remember further. One can't unring a bell, or so I thought.

I was a detective in the police force. Em wasn't into mystery-solving, but David changed everything; our daily conversations, texts, and even our habits differed from before. We passionately wanted to unravel his bizarre story.

"There's no easy way to say this."

"Is he dead? No, I know he's not." She was talking to herself. She had always believed that he would come back one day. How ignorant I had been to let her count on a fantasy.

"Worse."

"What can be worse than death?"

"Not existing." She burst out laughing, almost spilling her tea on the couch.

"Okay. He was a product of my imagination! Fine!" Her eyes got bigger, her mouth crooked, and I flinched at the sight of her distorted face. She was yelling that she'd hallucinated the whole thing because she was schizophrenic and that she should be institutionalized. The most tranquil person I knew was going nuts because of the disappearance of a mysterious man.

She was right, though – either we'd both hallucinated, or he'd disappeared off the face of Earth.

"I know it's hard to swallow, but it's the truth. There's no record of him now, but yesterday there was. I'm sure of that. Addley existed yesterday. Do you know what happened today at the station? Nobody remembers this case." I saw a tear roll down Em's cheek. She understood instantly that I was on her side.

"You know he was real, right? Do you doubt yourself? We didn't imagine a time traveller named David Addley, did we? What happened to the records? Why don't your colleagues remember him?" She was on edge. We'd continue to list our questions later because, tonight, our emotions had awakened.

***

The day Addley came was an ordinary one. Em called me while I was chilling at a pub with my colleagues after work. Her voice gave away her distress. She needed me right away.

When I arrived at her apartment, a weary man was on a chair in the kitchen, constantly drinking water. He looked around with his small, blue eyes like he wanted to make a detailed record of everything in sight. He wore ragged jeans and a blue t-shirt, and there was a funny-looking backpack on his lap. He acted like there was a nuclear bomb inside.

"Hi, I'm Laurie," I said, expecting at least a faint smile that meant he recognized my presence. He only said his name back and eyed me from head to foot, then took another sip like there was nothing noteworthy about me. I could smell the mystery hovering around in the room.

"Laurie, I know this will sound absurd, but please don't interrupt. I know you'll understand." She sounded almost happy to see the man like he was a fallen asteroid containing rare elements.

"Go on," I said, giving the man a slight glare to let him know I wouldn't be tricked.

"David Addley came from the future." Em paused to observe my initial reaction. I might've burst into laughter, but what I did instead comforted her. I went on listening because I was intrigued.

Em and I used to have debates about time travel. I thought that time wasn't absolute, while Em liked the parallel universe explanation; she'd say it made the most sense because the idea that time was absolute and couldn't be changed in a given universe prevented paradoxes. I'd always found this hard to agree with, but it created a friendly conflict between us.

"Go on," I said. David's mouth opened a little in shock, so I explained myself. "I believe you because why would you make up such a lie? If you were a burglar or a murderer, you'd simply injure or kill Em, and we wouldn't be having this conversation right now. And I trust her judgment, so try me."

Though I sounded in control, I felt extremely nervous. If he were telling the truth, it would be overwhelming for me because then, in theory, he had to know much more than we did. You always think that there are many possibilities, but even if you scrutinize all the possible futures, you'd always fail to know what happened. The future always wins, and a time traveller would be proof of a certain future.

"I'll take it from there," Addley said, inspecting Em. I felt something strange going on there; it seemed like David knew how to approach us, but the thought seemed ridiculous at the time. "It's crucial that you don't tell anyone about this. I'm begging you, don't tell anyone." We both nodded. "I should also warn you: I can't tell you everything. That is too dangerous for me, and I couldn't find any other way to save myself." He paused like his last statement made him weak. "I won't tell you where I come from or how I managed to do it. But I'll tell you why. My journey might sound ridiculous to you, but the only other way was suicide, and I didn't want to go in that direction." Addley noticed me start upon hearing the word *suicide*. "Time eats everything up rapidly. Even when you're young, you can look at your past and clearly see what you did wrong. What if you didn't choose that path? What if you did that other thing? Your life might've turned out to be much better than how it ended up. Realizing this makes you feel like you swallowed a rock that will stay in your body forever. So, what if you had the power to make your younger self turn in the right direction? That would solve it. That *will* solve it. This is why I'm here. I want to change my miserable future, so I can live on. I believe I can accomplish this by changing certain things here..."

"Do you intend to meet yourself? Isn't it... forbidden? You could destroy yourself," I intervened.

"No, I won't do that. I want one of you to meet the younger me."

A heavy silence fell upon us. He was asking for help, just like any other person. *Help me save myself*, he said: he had travelled in time to do just that.

The afternoon had started like a warm, fuzzy sci-fi story, but then it had evolved into a perfect drama. What a day it had been.

***

Younger Addley was a sophomore at the university where Em worked as a lecturer. Addley asked for Em's help in planting the *right* ideas in younger Addley's mind.

Future Addley had a small notebook within which he listed things he thought he should change. Each entry was three words long at most, and across from every one of them, there was a paragraph-long explanation. Some phrases were circled or underlined with a red pen. "Is this it?" I asked him once. "A human life? Mistakes, things you think need to be altered. All on a list. Is this all there is to life?" I spotted a faint smile on his face, but he never uttered a word, and I didn't push him further.

We started with number one: convincing younger Addley to change his major. This was the hardest one, but Addley wanted us to start there. "So that I won't get upset if it doesn't work," he said. "I'll tell myself that it was a long shot anyway." But Em succeeded.

Following Em's success, he informed us that he'd be leaving the following day. He had stayed at my apartment during the time Em worked her *magic* and acted distant towards Em; he talked to her only when necessary and avoided eye contact most of the time. My initial guess was that a fear of falling in love with her had settled in him. To be in love with someone from the past, what a wild ride that would be!

After he left, we hoped he'd find his life fixed. Addley wanted his younger self to change his major because he believed this was when things started to go out of his hands. "*Choosing the most reasonable path is one of the biggest mistakes one tends to make,*" he told us. "*Especially for someone who has dreams,*" he added. "Dreams," Em repeated days after he left. "What kind of dreams could they be?" We didn't elaborate much, but I was sure of one thing: Em wasn't the same after she met younger Addley.

***

A couple of years later, future Addley showed up at my door again. He stood right there, looking exhausted but with eyes full of hope. I called Em right away.

"*It worked, but not in the way I intended,*" he broke it to us. Something was missing in his altered life – he didn't give us details, and we didn't ask him further questions because that was the deal from day one. He was defeated but still tenacious and full of desire to claim his desired future.

I asked him what had happened when he went back to his time. What did he witness? How did his life change? But he told us once more that it was better if he didn't say. He had made a new list. His first plan on this one was a sad one at first sight: Addley wanted Em to prevent younger Addley from meeting his future wife.

Em was on the job again; this time, I helped her too. Younger Addley was about to get his master's degree in physics now, and he was determined to continue his studies with a Ph.D. According to future Addley, he had to focus fully on his studies: there could be no distraction.

We succeeded again, and younger Addley's life was altered for a second time. He left the following day, and we didn't see him again until a year later.

He'd become like one of those persistent ex-boyfriends who kept on appearing in your life to convince you to be together again. I didn't mind it, but some things didn't add up: why was he coming to us for help every time? How was he travelling in time? Did he build the machine? Did he work on time travel at the university? When did he come from?

For the third time, the alteration he needed was clear: "Don't let me work with Hugh." Hugh was a professor of physics at the university. Things were bad between them in the future, and Addley accidentally – I have no idea whether this is true – got the professor injured at the lab. His face showed guilt, but I could tell he didn't believe he was responsible. I wanted to tell him that we couldn't help him anymore because every time he came back to us, he looked worse. *Besides*, I thought, *if his life couldn't be fixed by two modifications, then he should quit travelling already.* Em didn't agree. "We're like Addley," she told me. "We'll always try everything till we get the version we desire. Even if it means occasionally making things worse than it already is." I trusted Em's judgment, so we helped him for the third time.

***

A few days after his third departure, he returned defeated. "It's terrible," he kept murmuring. "I destroyed everything. There's nowhere for me to take shelter now. Please help me one last time. There's a reason behind my coming to *you*. I know you want to help me, Em. I know you." He paused, then went on with his begging. We had no idea what he meant, but I saw the spark in Em's eyes: *one more time*.

Addley didn't have a plan this time: he wished to improvise. In his new timeline, he didn't work with Hugh, but the professor with whom he hoped he would work had rejected him. He went nuts. *I've done terrible things*, he said. This was what we had to prevent from happening: And *the easiest way to do it,* he said, "*is never letting me out of my apartment that day.*"

Everything worked out; we made younger Addley stay home. Future Addley left the following day, as usual. It was now obvious that we were close to future Addley's origin, and it made me feel somewhat uncomfortable.

Then, neither younger Addley nor future Addley was seen anywhere again. He disappeared, and nobody knew anything. In the following months, we looked for him, but it was of no avail. His landlord could provide us with no further information, and his phone couldn't be traced. We found nothing. He became another missing person.

***

We never forgot him. Six years after his first appearance, "He never existed" was the only thing I could tell Em. But then something Addley had said before popped up in my mind. When he begged us to help him, he said, "I know you," when he was referring to Em. We could focus on this detail to see whether it would lead us anywhere.

"What did he mean? Did he hint that he'd known you before travelling?" Em didn't answer me at first. I waited for her to relax and give me anything to work with.

"I saw him entering a password on his weird bag once," she said.

"Why didn't you open it, then?" I nearly screamed.

"I tried," she looked at me guiltily. "The screen required a fingerprint too, so I couldn't open it. This password was a date, and it's the only thing we haven't dug up. The date was *today*." A silence fell upon us. It seemed to me that Em had built up a theory without me, and now she was slowly putting the last missing piece where it belonged.

"You know I've been working on the nature of negative matter, right?" she said.

"Yes, but I don't know what that means."

"Negative matter *can* be used to fuel a time machine. But its existence had been doubtful. My research team might've proved its existence. It's ongoing research, but earlier this week, we were able to *produce* some amount."

"Oh," was my only reaction. It meant that there was a connection between Em and Addley. "What do *you* think?"

Her eyes were teary. "I think I was, or I am, or I'd be... the one who sent

Addley to his past. That was why he always came to us. He said he knew me. He was telling the truth. I *know* younger Addley from campus; he'd always been obsessed about how time worked, and he was passionate about exploring the concept further. When he first came to us, he surely had the information that my team made the negative matter discovery. And I think that today must be the day he first came to me for *help*. To travel back in time."

Everything seemed so tangled up in itself that I didn't even know the right questions to ask. "But, without a time machine, what would he do with the negative matter? Did he build one and come to you to borrow fuel?" Em studied my face to understand whether I was joking or not. I wasn't. I was too lost to joke about anything.

"It's possible, but I don't know anything about it. All I know about him is that he was capable of doing so much, and this is what I heard from everyone he was working with. They all used to say that he's simply a genius."

"This doesn't explain why he disappeared today," I commented. Em started whimpering but strove to explain her mind to me.

"My theory is that he killed himself in his apartment the day we prevented him from going out. He died, so now there is no future Addley to ask for my help to travel back in time. Younger Addley destroyed his travels, future, and memories. All that once was David Addley is lost now."

"So, he erased himself. Addley eliminated himself before he could travel in time," I muttered. Even the notion left me breathless.

"Today at the lab," Em interrupted the flow of my disturbing thoughts, "I heard a knock on the door. I said come in and heard the door open, but nobody came in. I turned around and saw the door open, but there was nobody there."

"Do you think the force that opened the door was the last bit of Addley?"

She nodded. We sat there all night in silence as if at the funeral vigil of a man whose existence was doubtful now.

CONSIDERATION[1]

Melike Kuyumcu

Translated by Şafak Horzum

Cleansing… That was what humanity did for a superior human identity for several decades… Yet, the human dream was a point of impossibility. They assumed the minority's welfare automatically included the welfare of all humanity. If the injustices and inferiorities suffered by the minority, the negativities, and violations of rights were eliminated, a just—even if not equal—society could be created.

Humans attempted to perform the reversed algorithm of this myth: "Where evolution isn't born, revolution arises." Where revolution wasn't born, evolution was born. One way or another, it took centuries and generations, even if its finitude was unknown… They started by correcting cities, architectures, all material conditions that the body encountered.

First, they began asking questions about what a minority was, who it included, and what proclivities were involved. Then, they found it more rational to start with the closest to their identities, whatness, and relations. The physically handicapped—congenital or acquired, orthopaedic, muscular, or bony—were selected as the first pilot group to be articulated in society by eliminating rights violations.

A city was destroyed, and a new one was built. Executors made the new society's contract and constitution to live in those cities. Homes, cars, and social areas were suitably created for minorities… Stairs and elevators were replaced by organic prostheses and advanced roboorgans that were superior to the whole they were attached to, thanks to biotechnologies that made possible acts like climbing skyscrapers even without arms or legs.

Roboprostheses were roboorgans' previous phase. They were difficult to integrate into the human body. They could transfer their knowledge to the body—to the mind and cell of the body-owner—by material-semiotic coding, but couldn't extract human knowledge and situational awareness into their own systems. While the machine could merge into the human, the

---

[1] The story's original Turkish version was published in Kuyumcu's collection *İnsan-dan Başka Öyküler* (TP London, 2021). Its complete English translation is forthcoming as *More-Than-Human Tales*.

human still couldn't migrate to the machine. This problem disappeared in roboorgans, and all the body-knowledge became transferable to the roboorgan in a more competent manner than the body-owner had experienced with regular organs. The robot, taking small samples of blood and tissue at atomic levels—in ways humans could never feel—could access all human knowledge. The human host's comprehension of the exchange between the roboorgan and the human body happened in at least thirty seconds or a few minutes. Both the machine and the body had to wait in the meantime.

After a while, minority rights, minority constitutions, and minority contracts transcended the top of humanity's glorious bar. It became a goal for all. Everyone's goal and priority became to protect the rights of the few. Everyone worked on it. Even if the entire majority in a building served a minority member with their full-force, it wasn't enough to meet the gross national welfare of that minority.

This distorted correlation led humans to a more dreadful mathematical conclusion. Billions worked for a few, strove to work, exist and pursue for that reason. The mathematical condition for the minority to survive was that they were to constitute a maximum of 49%. The minorities increased so much in number that this upper limit had to be set. As with the statistics, the society divided almost down the middle, didn't pursue the justice it had aimed at the beginning regarding living rights and standards. The minority held all the measures and figures of economic life. Owners of supermarkets where the general public shopped, managers of restaurants people occasionally went to, authors of books they read, and bosses of public toilets were of the minorities making the decisions and enforcing the laws. Fifty-one was bent to and fell for forty-nine all over again, becoming the object of their own production.

The work of hundreds to achieve minimal welfare for those with a missing organ was only one facet of destruction. They had the belief they could destroy their current self and catalyze all their evil and destructive sides. Rather than an anarchist attitude, this was an extremely fatalistic one because no human being could display "humaneness" during self-realization. This was proven. People provided and realized themselves through society, and society became humane. In other words, since the things that changed were basically the sidelines of humanity, there wasn't much change. The point to which evolution brought humanity was as much as the morale of a society where there was no need for its human as long as the human was unable to shoulder full responsibility for their humanness. This was a voluntary acceptance. Volunteering was essential for those born, living, and dying in the cities of this society. Those who didn't conform could leave. In practice, however, nothing like that happened. Although the beginning of this evolution dated back more than fifty years, the compensation for the violation of minority rights—even those of the selected pilot group of the physically disabled—continued to grow every day and never ended. Because it didn't end, the next minority group's turn didn't come. If so, would a turn for the ordinary human be possible? Until then, humans still couldn't abandon their centralist attitude; they only changed the figure in the center and when they centralized the "other," they remained on the margin.

High-capacity and fully-equipped artificial organs, namely prosthetic organs and roboorgans, took the "myth of humanity" represented by only a few to another level ethically and onto-epistemically. Except for one issue: water. Even the minority could buy more than 22.5 liters of water for exorbitant prices. 22.5 liters of water had a reminder role in society. Long ago, water had been divided into contact and noncontact categories. The water one drank, used for food, brushed one's teeth with, and took a shower with was one's vital source—hence contact water. The water used for things like laundry, dishes, toilets, and washing objects was noncontact water. Although humans were able to get noncontact water from the planet's resources, they couldn't produce contact water for vital needs. Therefore, 22.5 liters per day served as a reminder to humans: "Remember before consuming more than you need; remember you can't produce it again." The common folk wasn't allowed more than this amount, in any case. Other than water, air and soil existed for those who could afford them. The minorities had terraces to look at the sky, but the sky wasn't pleased with this stack of terraces it saw. It belonged to all, but some people couldn't have the right to stare at it. This had made the sky sullen and blurry for a long time.

Any death (not exile) was respected. The deceased wasn't believed to watch the living from a parallel dimension or keep living with them in some form. Corpses were buried at regular intervals; the land was so scarce that one could use it only for burial. Everyone was buried. But that incredible smell—the stench of the dead—pervaded the cities, streets, buildings, matter, and the air was no longer bearable. The proposal to send the deceased into space with space trucks was enacted precisely because of this. They had to. They couldn't live with their dead.

Everyone had equal rights to perform certain actions. As long as one could face the consequences of hir rebellious actions, ze had the right to destroy hirself because ze was no longer necessary and valuable. Deserting was also an option, which some rabble widely practiced, never to return. Where they went was unknown. So they wouldn't be sad, children were told the deserters went to the world's edge and jumped into space. There was a departure into space but no return.

Magnificent possibilities offered by robo-/prosthetic organs had triggered one big phenomenon. Anyone could be a member of the disabled minority one day; this was a fact of life. On purpose, never! It would mean slaughter or exile. There were certain prohibitions the society self-imposed. Anyone who wanted to gain minority status and rights by deliberately amputating hirself or hir relatives was punished with death or persecution and exile, depending on the crime's extent. Yet again, the fact that the minority rights contract brought disabled people to the most advanced and prosperous level resulted in the dream of being disabled. Not everyone wished to have a house, car, or child one day, but everyone openly wished they or their beloveds could become disabled. Not to cause ontological confusion, the statuses of the incomplete and the disabled became realities that could never be eliminated, removed from the literature, and separated from the contract. It was forbidden not to tell, know, or recognize these statuses.

Exile meant everything outside of life. Exile was beyond one's habits, beyond what one knew. Exile meant never coming back once outside the city borders. Since the person feared self/law-imposed exile and innately knew that exile meant the uncanny, ze consented to communitarianism in advance. Those who didn't die during intentional amputation created problematic burdens for society and only achieved downward social mobility towards the "inactive and wasteful" group. Yet again, this bitter end couldn't prevent a daily increase in the number of people who cut off their arms and legs. In a short time, those who deliberately injured themselves and wanted to qualify as "disabled" were sent from the "inactive" class (due to their lack of beneficial social function) to exile, from there to "waste," and then to a slow, painful death.

This society's cities consisted of large areas. Each was a country size. Enigmatic cities, united by the same constitution and contract, were unaware of each other because each had its own local legislative and executive branches. Where the cities ended or began did not involve plains or similar open spaces since there was no extra space. A city would reach its natural limit when it reached a sea or a mountain range. Why and where the animals self-exiled outside the city was also unknown. Where would these animals go; why wouldn't they return; would their exile share the same time, place, and fate with the deserters?

Nonhuman beings in cities, especially animals, lived their lives independently of humans. They were used to finding their own water and food; however, except for an olive tree that was placed in the middle—in the most precious place—of the museum, which was the only sun-drenched part of the city, cities had no greenery or land to provide nonhumans with some peculiar supply. Humankind didn't care about anyone but itself anyway; if they were beneficial, ze made them servants; if not, ze assisted their extinction. Extinction or self-destruction was a meritorious deed in this society.

For animals, drinking their water from air conditioners, cars, irrigation canals, and pipes dated back several decades. It was impossible for a sparrow born and grown in an apartment to spend its short life flying happily and singing in those streets, to find unprocessed water untouched by rust and industry, or to know of such water. 70% of animals' food consisted of packages they found scattered around. Their stomachs were full of plastic, and they developed synthetic-metallic tastes. The semi-organic, biotic, unprocessed things those unlucky animals accidentally ran into either disrupted their bodies or killed them.

***

The minorities' prosthetics were a tremendous opportunity for humans. It turned them into superheroes. Daughter-A had a roboleg under the knee, allowing her to fly, run faster than anyone else, and climb to any height. These roboorgans possessed knowledge, unlike humans, who couldn't process the knowledge of knowing into their DNA and go beyond the social transmission of their knowledge to the new generations. These roboorgans not only had the available and necessary information but also separated it from subjective morality and rationalization.

When Dad-A quickly swayed into the park on his electric skateboard about twenty to thirty centimeters above the ground along with his daughter on her roboleg, Dad-P thought, as he was gently pushing his daughter on the swing, *"So they've started coming to our parks."*

Dad-A and Daughter-A graciously greeted Dad-P and Daughter-P. Rising on her left roboleg, Daughter-A settled into the empty swing. As Daughter-P looked admiringly at her and what she did, her father felt uneasy. These children didn't know what to admire!

"As they've come all the way to our neighborhood, they must have new residences nearby," thought Dad-P. Otherwise, it wasn't very common for minorities and common folk to encounter each other in social areas. The center was gradually enclosing its periphery… This was the centrality of the other. Nothing changed in humanity's adventure of meaning in granting domination and privilege to the few.

***

"I understand from your looks you feel uncomfortable."

"Surely not!"

"Wanna hear this park's story?"

"I come here every day; I knew this park before you did."

"But my leg knew it even before you."

"As you can see by my daughter's roboleg, we became 'disabled' naturally. Her left leg veins weren't working; they had to amputate it."

"I congratulate you."

"Look at the end of the chain on the left of your swing. A sparrow landed there, you see? It's in love with that chain."

"This is ridiculous. Is your leg whispering this nonsense to you?"

"But we've been volunteers since we entered the minority world."

"Volunteers for what?"

"A level that transcends the limits of the body and brain, in which man challenges the terror of death with endless sustainability. Now everything's under our control."

"And the heart?"

"Sorry?"

"Well, what about the chain? Is it in love with the sparrow, too?"

"I suppose," thought Dad-P, "we're only one stage of humanity if we're minority citizens/society. The transcendental human should have abandoned the compulsion of being privileged long ago. We couldn't."

"What's wrong with playing with the body's algorithms to improve thinking and touch infinity? We should approach it rationally," said Dad-A while he—actually the roboleg—was happily rocking his daughter, and the other dad realized too late that his thoughts had been uttered out loud. Dad-A continued loosely, lightly, easily: "Let's remember what our social engineers say; let's see language and thought as software and the body as hardware."

"Fine; how can we distinguish these two built upon each other?"

"Look at my daughter's leg. Then you'll believe what it provides is information and evidence, not discourse. Although this roboleg has no biological genes or cells, and despite her age, it can know and do much more than the body-owner's limitations. I mean, it's superior to my daughter."

"Is it enjoying the swing, too?"

"Do you want me to ask it?"

"So pal, as hardware's info is in soft, hard is needed no longer, you understand?" Dad-A laughed so hard that the empty metallic space between the park and buildings rang out. Dad-P and Daughter-P shuddered. As the swings continued to move, they all paid attention to the chirping chain for the first time. This repetitive sound of two notes sank further into their ears in the silence. Seeking peace in nostalgia amid all this virtuality, people had made it legal to exclude metallic sounds from the scope of noise and include them in the scope of sound. Humans needed these voices. They needed all real sounds like the sound of a drill or cutter—even without music, melody, soul as long as they weren't "virtual." This was the sound the sparrow had already fallen in love with. With this monotonous two-note mechanical voice, the chain told nothing or announced the same thing repeatedly. "I'm loosening," it actually said, "I'm deserting."

Daughter-A, having listened to all this with her roboleg, was about to warn her new friend just as the voices of their mothers calling them for dinner were heard from their fathers' watches. Daughter-A's roboleg immediately stopped the swing, and the girl took off and quickly went to her father. Dad-P, however, stopped the swing by hand, and the girl landed on the tin ground while looking at her new friend's skills.

No people were in the park in the evening—only the quiet chain. The sparrow, in love with the chain, gathered all the other fowls in the neighborhood for a parliament. Pigeons, doves, crows, swallows, starlings, and even bats arrived. All companion species are born and raised in the skies of this city. The sparrow told of its love for the chain and its dream of liberating it from the bar. "How come?" they asked; the crow, who could help most, objected; it wouldn't exhaust its beak or strength for personal matters. The parliament, towards the dawn, turned into a celebration when the sparrow wholeheartedly narrated its love for the chain. Even the crow was convinced. The chain would be freed from the swing bar.

***

In the afternoon, the fathers and girls met again by good fortune. The girls sat on the same swings, the fathers began the same conversation. In an intense web of actions, the fowls came one by one, led by the sparrow, and pecked and labored to loosen the detaching ring of the swing chain. Neither the fathers, having deepened the conversation, noticed this, nor did Daughter-P, who was still watching the roboleg with admiration. Only Daughter-A was aware of it. Her roboleg let her know. Thanks to its information-in-itself, a natural bond had formed between the roboleg and the girl's body. This dimension didn't require distances like language. Yet she remained silent, not because she was evil, but partly because she respected any being's agency and partly because she enjoyed watching this love and wondered what would happen. The fathers got angry with each other, Daughter-P became more unhappy with herself, began to find herself incomplete and inadequate, and wished a leg or an arm of hers would be cut off; the fowls pecked the ring, the chain got looser, and its voice got louder as it got looser; its song got faster…

"We actually hate with resentment."

"Hate what?"

"Ourselves."

"You sound like a philosopher with a bushy mustache now."

"Yeah, I'm quoting, you see. What we call civilization is nothing but an exclusionary suppression system that spreads the morality of resentment. So what are we doing this for? For the sake of moral and scientific progress."

"What's wrong with that?"

"We suppressed and hated ourselves for suppressing. We do. But we also want what we suppress to materialize, and we find this request unhealthy. We, humans, can master the movement of rhizomatic cycles only in such chaos."

"Ah, c'mon! I know you; I know people like you well. You believe pain can be an agent, even in the case of bioartificial kidneys made for the sick. But it's an artificial thing produced in a laboratory. Just a cure for a disease."

"Do you deny the suffering humans inflict on nonhuman beings?"

"Why do you prefer to call them 'nonhuman' rather than 'living'?"

As Dad-A pretended to rock his daughter, nothing changed in their rhythm. But as Dad-P's growing anger was reflected in his movements, he began rocking his daughter's swing faster, harder, and more aggressively. With the weight of Daughter-P, immersed in daydreams, who thought she was flying and was therefore unaware of anything, Dad-P's furor did nothing but facilitate the work of the sparrow-led unleashing team.

"OK, I'll give you that. But don't you think it's time to separate necrotechnology from creative, responsible, ethical ones?"

"What about conscience, mercy? You never speak of them because these aren't codable things? Can they prevent the suffering and destruction of beings whose service to humanity ends? No, sir, they haven't done that yet."

"Why can't you call them 'the living'? If you could distinguish living things from the material, I'd understand you."

"Maybe we aimed to surpass ourselves with the minority constitution, but we weren't ready for this politically or ethically, let's admit it. Moreover, this idea of minority privilege is a problem in itself—"

"Excuse me, but I think you're trying to get a new law passed just to get money out of 'compensation.' You're a kind of volunteer like us but in the opposite direction. If it's up to you, we'd have to pay betterment tax for our life quality."

"Yes, if need be, because we, minority or majority, all think everything outside of ourselves doesn't need to exist when we no longer need them. When the nonhuman is no longer needed, we can no longer share the world with it. A complete extermination program. Maybe we'll start to fix this by paying taxes because it's universally accepted that the fundamental rights and freedoms of common folk are restricted. So it's time to pay the price."

The chain was about to break. That was why it went silent. But no one was aware of this except the fowls and the roboleg. The fowls stopped pecking at the chain and began circling over the park in the joy at their approaching victory. None other than the roboleg and Daughter-A, watching them and clapping her hands, was aware of this. Daughter-P stared for a moment at her happiness. Then she looked at her own leg. To the leg that took her to many places, that enabled her to do many things that hurt when it hit something, that shuddered when caressed. Could she give up on it for a roboleg? Yes, she could.

"Dad! I want a roboleg too!"

"What are you saying, honey!?"

"See, your daughter rightfully wants to climb the social ladder too. Why wouldn't she!?" "Are you

crazy!?"

During the previous night's parliament, the sparrow had articulated its desire to take the last shot. Now, coming out of the whirling, screaming, singing fowls, it wanted to peck the chain one last time, but that wasn't necessary. With Dad-P's final push, the swing got free from the bar at the height of complete cacophony and turmoil. Daughter-P, taking off with the swing, flew backward with it and fell on the iron fence a few meters away. A sharp cry covered the whole earth.

"Oh, my God!" Dad-P ran to his daughter, with Dad-A right after him. Ahead of them was Daughter-A, thanks to her roboleg. Daughter-P was sobbing and about to faint. Another ripping cry filled the air when her father picked her up. The father realized then that his daughter's right arm was hanging around her back, bleeding heavily and no longer fully attached to her torso. "Calling Amburob," said Dad-A, and touched the phone in his ear. As he began to speak, a rhubarb broke out among the fowls that perched around, watching silently. It seemed like the chain was wrapped more around the human than it was free. What had they done wrong? The sparrow wailed for its love; a single teardrop fell from its tiny eyes and dropped on the tin floor. Then came a thumping sound a little beyond where the droplet had fallen. The sparrow's body remained dry and weightless, like a trinket or stuffed animal, a little beyond the teardrop. How quickly its soul, its heart, its life had gone...

No one, except for its companion fowls, cared for the sparrow. While all the fowls mourned its death, the roboleg—the only knowing, comprehending being of this catastrophe—remained hovering in this reality.

THE SMART DOOR

Müfit Özdeş

Meteorologist Michael D. Jackson of NASA and geologist Wang Chao-xing of CNSA were team members in charge of the Martian Observation and Data Collection Station 12 in the depression beginning at and extending to the South West of the Coronae Scopulus Valley on the Hellas Plateau. After rigorous exercise on the treadmill and a refreshing shower, they sat down for breakfast and ordered their morning meal on the touchscreen console. Michael – who was a burly black man from Minnesota – typed in an order for a hamburger with coffee and milk. Chao-xing – who was a young woman of small build with straight, raven black hair – tapped in tea, wafers, peach jam, and goat cheese. Then they settled for a short wait.

But the supposedly short wait dragged on and on.

"I guess it's conked out again," said Michael.

"That tears it!" exclaimed Chao-xing.

This was the third breakdown since they had taken over the station from the former team. Going without breakfast was no big deal, but they had to identify the problem at once because it might impair the vital functions of the station or its observation equipment.

"What's your malfunction, Peach?" Chao-xing asked the computer. That was what the first team on the station – both of whom were males – had called the station's computer, and replacement teams thereafter had not bothered to change it.

"Nano-insulation failure in my CPU," replied Peach. "Non-repairable chip that has to be replaced. So far, it is only the Kitchenette Unit and the inner/outer door synchronization of the airlock that is affected. In fact, the airlock is equipped with Smart Doors that operate independently of me. But, for the duration of the malfunction, they will not recognize voice commands and will require a password to be typed in from the console keyboard."

"Which other systems may be affected and with what consequences?" asked Michael.

"Atmospheric pressure and temperature measurement systems will likely be affected, resulting in observation data gaps. Carbon Capture & Oxygen Generation Unit might possibly fail, in which case you will become deceased."

They both smiled at the euphemism in spite of the serious situation when Peach politely said that they would become deceased instead of bluntly telling them that they would die. They told Peach to immediately get in touch with Mission Control, which was in orbit around Mars. Mission Control, however, was on the other side of the planet at the moment.

"They will be in our line of sight in forty minutes," said Peach, "and I will contact them as soon as I can."

"Well, let us have some breakfast manually then," Chao-xing told Michael. "I'll make do with coffee instead of infusing tea because I am starving."

While Michael brewed coffee for breakfast, Chao-xing made a rapid check of the oxygen system and saw that it was running like a charm. They had a hearty breakfast.

"Any contact yet?" asked Michael.

"Three minutes to go," replied Peach. "But I have to tell you once and for all: I demand a proper computer technician… I won't have any random hick pawing at my processors!"

Pawing at her processors! Chao-xing silently cursed whoever had taught Peach this sexist male jargon. Nor did she fail to notice the smirk that spread across Michael's face.

"Contact accomplished," Peach told them. "You may take over now."

"Control, can you hear us? Over," asked Michael.

"I hear you, Station 12. What is the problem? Over."

"Computer's CPU is giving a nano-insulation error. The Automatic Kitchenette is out of order, and we are unable to process atmospheric data… Uh, we also just lost the telemetry data relay. All these can be recovered later, of course. But our computer says that there is a chance that the Carbon Capture Unit for generating oxygen might fail. If that happens, we would consume all the oxygen in the habitat and die soon afterwards. And I have no idea how you can recover us after we die… Over."

"Duly noted, Station 12," said the Mission Control guy, who had absolutely no sense of humor. "We have a technician on board – Achilles Simonides – who is a perfect choice for the task. It is now his leisure time, but I will ask him to come to the control center, and we will contact you again the next time we pass over, which should be about five and a half hours from now. Over and out."

When Mission Control called them back five and a half hours later, Computer Hardware Technician Achilles Simonides of ESA was smiling at them.

"Hey, I know this guy," Chao-xing told Michael, "and I am glad he's the one that they will send."

In fact, not only did she know Achilles, she also felt strongly attracted to him.

"I'll send you the software that you will need for the check-up," said Achilles. "Set it up at once and begin running the follow-up procedures. And I will get ready and come down at the next transit. Over."

"Please be careful, Achilles," said Wang Chao-xing in a worried tone. "You know that parachute landings are unreliable because of low atmospheric density. Over."

"Don't you worry, Chao-xing," said the handsome young Mediterranean. "I have no intention of dying before I see you again! Over."

"Radio us when you land so that we can come and pick you up," interrupted Michael. "Or, if you're near enough, you can just walk up to our Smart Door and tell it to open up. Oops… sorry, the Voice Command of the door is now non-functional. You will have to enter a password on the keyboard of the airlock console. The password is Hellas_3.141592. I repeat: Hellas underscore three point one four one five nine two. Should be easy to keep in mind. Hellas is the name of the plateau where we are. The case doesn't matter. And the numeric part after the underscore is the constant Pi up to six digits after the decimal point. Now repeat after me. Over."

"Repeat, hell!" muttered Achilles angrily. "I know the name of the Plateau where I am to land, which is incidentally the name of my country. And Pi, for heaven's sake! How can a technical guy ever forget that number? Over."

"OK. As you wish, then. When will you be landing? Over."

"About five and a half hours from now, I guess. Depending on our trajectory and weather conditions at the landing site. But if the landing is postponed, I'll be able to inform you only when we are next in transit over your station. So please don't worry if five and a half hours elapse and I am not there yet. Over and out."

After packing up all the tools and materials that he might need, Achilles reviewed what he knew about ground station computers. All he had to do now was wait for five and a half hours. Because he had been interrupted in his sleep, he decided to take a nap. After instructing the computer to wake him up in two hours, he lay down on the bed and drifted into sleep, dreaming of Wang Chao-xing.

He was feeling quite refreshed when he woke up two hours later, ready for his haphazard morning workout, which he had to do in his own room because the inept – whoever he was – who had designed the Control Station layout had placed the gym in the weightless area. In fact, the station was a veritable museum of design flaws.

After exercising and showering, he ate his breakfast with a strong cup of coffee and donned his spacesuit. He got on board the capsule and strapped himself in the seat ten minutes before departure. Then he checked the dashboard and relaxed, waiting for the automatic landing. From now on, the responsibility lay with the station computer that would unlatch the capsule from the orbital station and launch it into a free fall trajectory towards Mars, and the capsule computer that would take over just before touchdown.

The descent was easy, but problems occurred at touchdown time. The capsule had been expected to hit the ground at 30 km/hr and the impact to be absorbed by damper balloons that would be inflated as the capsule approached ground zero. But the balloons didn't inflate on time, and the capsule arrived at a faster speed than expected due to a minor failure in the parachute system. It struck the ground at 80 km/hr instead of the expected 30. The damper balloons absorbed most of the shock, but then they burst, and the capsule was slightly damaged.

Achilles made a quick check to assess any damage to the capsule, which was luckily trivial and would not hinder takeoff when the time came. When he tried to raise Chao-xing and Michael on the radio, however, he realized that he had lost radio transmission.

OK, he would walk then. Station 12 was a couple of kilometers away, at most, and he could see the dome of the station habitat from where he was. Wearing a bulky spacesuit and carrying a heavy tool case, he trotted effortlessly to the station thanks to the lighter Martian gravity, which was only 37.6% of that of Earth.

"Open up!" he yelled at the Smart Door of the airlock as he neared the station.

"Who goes there?" asked the Smart Door.

"It's the technician."

"Who goes there?"

"The technician," said Achilles. "I am the computer hardware technician sent to replace the CPU of your computer."

"Who goes there?" repeated the Smart Door.

"The technician, damn it, I am the technician!"

"Who goes there?"

It is a goddamn machine after all, thought Achilles, and calmed down a bit.

"It's the technician," he replied in a calm tone.

"Who goes there?"

Nothing to lose by mocking the Smart Door, he thought.

"I am the technician," he said. "Might his Highness the Smart Door be so kind as to open itself up?"

"Who goes there?" the door repeated doggedly.

Achilles was at a loss for words. Then he remembered that the Voice Command System of the Smart Door was out of order and that he had to enter a password on the keyboard of the airlock console instead. A very simple password, in fact: the name of the Plateau and the Pi constant, which everyone would know.

Achilles should have been angry with himself for forgetting that, but he preferred to vent his anger at the nameless designers instead.

"Another design flaw," he muttered. "They could well have assigned a numerical password to the airlock and used a simple numeric keypad on the console… why all those jumbled passwords and full alphabetic keyboards?"

He lifted the protective lid of the console and rapidly wrote Hellas on the keyboard, typing in the Pi constant after the underscore.

"Wrong password. Please enter the correct password," said the Smart Door.

Achilles then slowly and carefully retyped the entire password: H, e, double l, a, s, underscore, three, comma, one, four, one, five, nine, two… Enter!

"Wrong password. Please enter the correct password," said the Smart Door.

Achilles thought carefully. The dashboard screen of the console was for 15 places, and the password he had did indeed require 15 places. Seven places would be used up to type Hellas_ so that 8 digits would be left for Pi, including the decimal separator.

Had Michael really said six places after the decimal separator? Suddenly he was in doubt about the number of digits after the separator. Maybe it was not 6, but 5, 4, or 3 digits. He decided to try them all: 3,141592... 3,14159... 3,1415 (or 3,1416 rounding up) ... 3,141 (or 3,142 rounding up) ... 3,14... He tried them each one by one. Then he went over them once more for good measure.

"Wrong password. Please enter the correct password," the Smart Door kept saying.

Achilles, who had been lighthearted till then, was now becoming worried. He did not know how much oxygen was left in the spacesuit. Nor did he know how long the battery heating the suit would last and continue to protect him from the minus 62 degrees temperature outside. He had no spare oxygen or batteries in the capsule. And if he tried to take off by himself, he would certainly miss the orbital station and get lost in deep space. What was he to do now?

The people waiting at Station 12 presumed that the capsule's descent had been postponed when they did not receive a radio message at the expected time. But it was also a possibility that the capsule might have crashed and that Achilles might already be dead. Now it would be five and a half hours before they learned what had actually happened. The situation was so tense that Chao-xing suddenly broke down. She plopped herself on her bed and began crying her heart out.

"It's alright to cry, Chao-xing," said Michael, throwing his arm around her shoulders in consolation. She leaned on his chest and kept on sobbing. A bizarre frame of mind stirred up by anxiety and a feeling of tightness took over the young woman all of a sudden, and their lips met. She was now observing herself in amazement from somewhere deep in her soul. They lost track of time. They had five and a half hours more, after all. No matter how much Achilles dreamt about Chao-xing and no matter how affectionate Chao-xing felt about Achilles, the reality of life outweighed everything else.

Outside the airlock, mortal fear gripped Achilles, a lump rising in his throat. He tried to explain his predicament to the Smart Door – as if it was human – so as to convince it to open up. No use. His only hope now lay in either opening the habitat door or getting it somehow opened for him, so he searched through his toolbox and found a large steel spanner. He began to strike the steel door of the airlock – sometimes rhythmically and sometimes at irregular intervals – in order to draw the attention of Michael and Chao-xing inside the habitat.

But Michael and Chao-xing were lost in another world altogether and were virtually deaf to any sounds from this one.

As Achilles got madder and madder at the stupidity of the Smart Door, he banged on the steel airlock door harder to make louder noises. He was now breathing faster, thus using up his oxygen more rapidly.

As he desperately clanged the steel door outside the habitat, Michael and Chao-xing gave each other one final kiss before they unhurriedly rose from the bed.

Chao-xing took her shower first because the shower cabin was too small for two. Then Michael went in while Chao-xing was drying herself. Chao-xing began to hear strange noises that Michael could not hear because of the splashing water. It was as if a valve somewhere was clicking open and then clicking close or as if the wind kept banging something against the steel door of the airlock.

"Please hurry up, Michael," she said. "I keep hearing funny sounds that I cannot identify."

Sounds like metal striking metal or resembling the tolling of a bell seemed to be coming from the airlock. Michael hurriedly dried himself up and wrapped a towel around his waist.

Meanwhile, Achilles – who was still stranded outside – suddenly lost his breath. He felt as if someone was strangling him. As he desperately groped at the keyboard, he suddenly recalled that Americans and Chinese used a point as a decimal separator sign and not a comma like himself and other Europeans.

Achilles, who was on the verge of collapse because of low oxygen, typed in the password hellas_3.141592 again, making sure this time that he pressed the point key for the decimal separator. The Pi constant had now been entered correctly. As the Smart Door silently slid open, Achilles fainted and collapsed into the airlock. Sensing that the person waiting outside had gotten in, the Smart Door immediately slid close, and the air was then pumped into the airlock.

Had he not passed out at the last moment, he would have taken off his helmet and survived. But he failed to do so because he had fainted. Computer Hardware Technician Achilles Simonides thus suffocated to death in his airtight spacesuit inside an airlock that was now filled with oxygen-rich air.

Chao-xing and Michael went up to the inner door of the airlock and listened carefully. The metallic sound was to be heard no more. They could hear the hiss of air being rapidly pumped into the airlock instead.

"Filling with air," remarked Chao-xing in astonishment. "But how had it been drained out in the first place?"

"Open up," Michael ordered the Smart Door. But when the door failed to respond, he remembered the Voice Command System breakdown and entered the password in the console keyboard.

As the steel inner door slowly opened, they saw the body in the spacesuit, crammed into the narrow confines of the airlock.

Chao-xing screamed.

"Who is this?" cried out Michael in horror.

"It's the technician," replied the Smart Door.

THE MIND RENTAL BUREAU

Neptune E. Kosi

Translated by Mehmet Ali Kaydırak

It is no longer snowing, nor is the sun showing its bright face. When the aging planet entered the Kuiper belt, the sky froze. The remaining seven hundred of the human species were trapped under an ice floe. The only things visible on the giant ice floe were millions of Edwardsiella andrillae and tardigrades, which shed light on the dark body of the night. London was the only city on the aging planet that showed life. Some time ago, its rotation on Earth, like with the other cities, stopped, and the city sky was covered in ice. However, the sky had not yet begun to melt. The poisonous anemones, which would fall rapidly on the day it would start to melt, would start a strong epidemic and bring the end of life, just as would happen in other cities.

Kuiper captured the southern hemisphere first. Erin was only three years old when she was making sandcastles on the beach with her family. The last thing she saw was the sudden freezing of the huge waves that had engulfed her family, who she had lost that day. When she opened her eyes, she was in the Unwanted Babies Office. By the age of seven, with a few hundred people surviving, there was no place on earth almost she hadn't set foot on. Most of the people were old, so some couldn't stand it. The younger ones, on the other hand, fell into a kind of mental eclipse during their escape. When they arrived in London, Erin was the only one who hadn't lost her mind.

The only healthy person who didn't lose her mind was Erin. She knew that after a while, the last people of her clan would experience a mental eclipse, just like the rest of the world. That time she would be left all alone and hopeless. Erin used every opportunity the city offered her for years to prevent this from happening. She had access to the secret compartments of all the libraries of the city, had brought home the archives of the Royal Observatory, had managed to get out of Buckingham's trap mazes, and had access to secret information. Thanks to all this confidential information, she introduced the system she had developed with quantum encryption to the brain by transferring it to a chip. After many troublesome trials, she succeeded. Eventually, to keep the human race alive over the years, she formed an office in Bank Junction, which she called The Mind Rental Bureau. Now, she loads people with minds that it periodically updates and makes them think like normal people from before collective madness had plagued the survivors.

"Miss Hawk?"

"Hi, Ayda. I was waiting for you too; come on in,"

The shy assistant took the seat pointed by Erin. Since the last mind update, Ayda has been receiving several bug reports. Even though no extra coding was done, apart from the needs of office work and current life, she was experiencing mental confusion at certain times of the day, running out of the office and finding herself next to the four Landseer Lions in Trafalgar Square.

Ayda was a pleasant woman of medium height who was in her early forties. She was among the few who managed to survive, fighting alongside groups from İstanbul, Berlin, Sofia, Thessaloniki, and Kosovo. Before she fell under the influence of the Kuiper generation, she was a woman with special abilities who specialized in bioenergy and quantum issues. She had lost all her abilities after the mind eclipse. She couldn't even remember who she was when Erin found her.

"Miss Hawk, it happened again last night," The young woman, whose voice was trembling, hesitated for a moment and cleared her throat. "It was a routine evening as usual. As I was about to finish my dinner, I was startled by a sudden jolt. The room began to shake from side to side as if under the influence of a severe earthquake. Then the earth's crust cracked. When I opened my eyes, I was on one of the Landseers on Westminster Bridge. You know the rest."

After a deep sigh, Erin leaned back. All she knew was that this was no ordinary coding error. She consoled the assistant for a while, and then she left the office to think.

***

There were dozens of questions that had been plaguing her mind for years; why hadn't she lost her mind like the others? It was as if a force was fighting inside to keep her from losing her mind, convincing her that she still had things to do. The sharp hook of each question was sinking into her mind and, as it sank, all those wounds she wanted to forget were bleeding again and coming to light.

While thinking about these, she suddenly found herself next to the Landseer Lions, just like Ayda. What was going on that these two women were drawn here like magnets? Could this have something to do with Sir Landseer?

As soon as she thought of the question, she suddenly remembered the wooden box she had found in Buckingham's secret archive room. She had taken home the box with Sir Edwin Landseer's name on it. Her inner voice was whispering that the answer was in that box.

In about seventeen minutes, she was home.

Think Erin, think... Where did I put the box?

As her eyes intently scanned the shelves in her home office, she noticed the thick folder with the musty-colored cover she had seen earlier. When she took the folder from the shelf, a sense of relief appeared on her face. The box she was looking for was right in front of her.

"Here you are!" You are safe with me, Sir Landseer.

Although it used to be considered a rumor, she knew that with the math in the making of the lions, Sir Landseer had planned to do something else, but he did not live long enough to finish it. The feeling of holding the secret of this man who had died suspiciously was breathtaking.

There was a crunch deep in London as the wooden box opened.

Inside were dozens of sketches, stencils, handwriting about lions and other paintings intertwined in cylinders. While removing the contents of the box, she noticed that there was a compartment at the bottom of the box. Lifting the thin wooden cover, she saw that inside the secret compartment were several pages of written notes. Among the notes was a small hastily drawn map. Erin was stunned when she deciphered the address on the map. She took one last look at the address written on the note in her hand. She put the note in her pocket and rushed out of the house. She was going to Kensington – to the studio where the lions had been made.

Marochetti had a huge studio and foundry in the mews behind his Kensington house, where Sir Edwin Henry Landseer worked on the lions for the base of Nelson's Column. These four lions were cast in Marochetti's own foundry. Sir Landseer had specifically underlined the studio on the map. Erin was sure she'd find something there. By the time she arrived at 32 Onslow Square, her heartbeat began to accelerate. She'd walked past Marochetti's house every day on her way to work. But it had meant nothing to her. This thought once again drew her into the middle of a deep mystery.

At the time when she opened the door of house number 32, thin cracks started forming on the surface of the ice sky of London.

The hallway was small and round and high-ceilinged, like a miniature version of her contemplation cells. Spring floral wallpaper was the only thing that brightened the house. Her feelings were dominating her feet, dragging her in the direction they knew. Erin made her way to the small shed in the backyard.

The numbness of darkness was hitting her face as she lifted the iron-handled lid on the floor. Far beneath the shed, hidden from everyone, there was a tunnel filled with darkness. She took a deep breath and went down the wooden stairs. Everywhere there were doors leading to new spaces and new secrets to be discovered, and the whole ground was covered with pages of notes. As her eyes adjusted to the darkness, she realized that there was a computer on the table next to her. She groped for the power button and pressed it. "Unbelievable…" Her voice was cracked and wobbly. It was already midnight outside after Erin had spent hours in front of the computer. She read the last passage of the document she was reading once again and then another and another.

She knew that a genius like Sir Landseer was not just a painter and sculptor. The document was right there as if in confirmation. He was a time traveler. Sir Landseer had a mechanism built into the lions while he was making them. With the coding system he made, Imprecast[1], lions would be able to take action when the time came.

Also, Sir Landseer wrote that when doomsday begins, if the coding works correctly, the world will find a place for itself in a parallel universe outside of Kuiper. Although Erin couldn't quite understand the last part, her priority would be the lions.

But first, she had to call someone.

***

"Is everything OK, Miss Hawk?"

Erin had understood that there was something powerful about this woman. Of the hundreds, it was only Ayda who made contact with the lions; also, she foresaw the doom of Istanbul and London. After a while, the silhouette of a young woman appeared in front of door 32. In the darkness of the moonless and starless night, the only guide that illuminated her path was the light of hope within her.

On the way, Erin quickly explained to Ayda everything that had happened and what they were going to do. Dozens of worries ran through the minds of the young women as they entered the damp-smelling tunnel. At that moment, they were startled by a new crackling sound. This time it

---

[1] Imprecast: a word created by the author, based on the first two letters of the word Impetus and the entire word Recast.

was stronger. Time was running out; soon, the ice sky would melt, and the poisonous bacteria would kill the few hundred people who were left behind.

"Are you sure all this will work?" There was concern in Ayda's voice.

"Arduino is an open hardware development board that can be used to design and build devices that interact with the real world. Sir Landseer uploaded Imprecast, the coding program he designed, to Arduino. So that the person who activated the code would be able to activate the lions."

"I'm sure he would have liked to do it himself."

"We're going to do it instead of him, Ayda. Wherever he is now, I'm sure he'd want that too."

Just then, the destruction of the city had begun. Shortly after nothing would be the same in the city outside the tunnel. A storm of ice and rain was beginning to spread across the city. The shards of ice blown by the storm were breaking the windows of the buildings, and the sound of shattering windows permeated their souls as if it would last forever.

London has never been closer to its own doom.

"Come on, please work, please work…"

A weak click sounded like a harbinger of something strong.

The first stage of the open coding was completed. Next was the second and final stage.

"Listen to me carefully, Ayda. I want you to go to the bridge while the Imprecast is completed."

"But Miss Hawk, I…"

"We have no other choice, Ayda. You have experienced this many times. You saw what would happen. You will do this for humanity."

"What about you, Miss Hawk? I can't leave you here all alone."

"I'll be fine, I promise. Everything is for humanity. Come on, Ayda! We don't have much time left!"

There were dozens of questions gnawing at Ayda's mind, but there was no time to learn any of them. Everything was developing so fast that she just had to keep up. They were all alone in the tunnel of a doomed city. There was no sound other than the eerie noise of shattering windows and collapsing buildings.

As the first stage was completed, there was a simultaneous movement in all four lions. They were strong. They were noble and loyal. Just as Sir Landseer had hoped they would be!

As the icy sky melted, all the poisonous bacteria began to glide, covering the entire city like vegetation. While Ayda was driving, bacterial clumps were thrown like bullets by the effect of the storm and hit the car, causing her to scream. The ice sky split in two. She wanted to look up to reach the sky she had not seen for years. The rain had accelerated so much that it would never allow it.

All she had in mind was Erin. What if she fails…What if she couldn't activate the lions? Just at that moment, she heard the roar of the lions. Erin had succeeded; there was no room for despair. She gripped the steering wheel a little tighter and stepped on the gas.

The four Landseer Lions in Trafalgar shot out at the same time like arrows.

As Ayda reached the bridge, the first thing she noticed was Big Ben floating above the river. Everything was just as she had seen it before. The towers of the bridge had collapsed, and one foot was submerged in the water. She noticed a tornado coming towards her from the front right. She knew that she had to leave the car as soon as possible so that the tornado wouldn't draw her in but to do so meant exposure to the bacteria. The tornado was too close now. There was no escape. As she thought that everything was over, she heard a lion's roar again. When she opened her eyes, she saw one of the Landseer lions had come to get her.

She held tight to the lion's mane as they passed through the tornado. The downpour got faster, and the river started to overflow. Everything was falling apart, breaking, exploding, or shattering.

The only thing on her mind as she was blown through the tornado was her family.

***

Wake up…

I forcibly opened my eyes as if waking from a century-long sleep.

A little oxygen, a little spring…

Even though I knew who I was and where I was, my self was so foreign to me, as if trapped in an equation of obscurity far away.

Where am I?

I felt utterly helpless, leaden, and dull. The waves of pincer-like pain kept pummeling my brain as my body was dragged down, down, down onto the inky, cold depths of the ocean floor, choking me.

As soon as my mind settled down, my first thought was whether Erin had been saved or not. Maybe she sacrificed herself to save humanity. I had a hard time even feeling how grateful I was to her. The slanting rays of the setting sun were giving a warm orange tinge to the room. As the sun cast long shadows on the ground, my eyes fell on the painting on the wall. The room was a testament to my disarrayed mind, a chaotic display of memories of past and future dreams. Numerous pictures and an open laptop were sitting next to two plants growing out of the same pot on a small table. One of the walls had two sparse clocks marking time in New York and London – the kind that would have felt at home at a World War II operations center.

I was at home. In our flat in Istanbul, where I spent my childhood. How did I get here? Was it all just a dream? I left the flat and pressed the button for the gray elevator in the hallway.

When I walked out the door of the building, I took a deep breath as if breathing fresh air for the first time. But the smell was the same – fresh pitch and dust and the indefinable human smell of a place where millions had passed for decades, where millions would pass for decades to come. Just then, I was startled by the horn of a passing car. People trying to cross the street without waiting for the green light were zigzagging between the cars. Everything was the same as it was years ago.

Crowded, noisy, fast, lively, and busy...

I hailed a taxi around the corner. I was going to the cemetery.

When I arrived at the cemetery, I found my mother and father in their usual place. The delusion that had engulfed me left me suddenly. The soulless voice in me was saying *everything was just a dream, Ayda, everything you lived*. For a moment, the scene of the lions roaring and appearing beside me came to my mind. The last time I was going through a tornado on a lion, and...

I've never seen this gravestone before...

As the thoughts in my mind were slipping away, I noticed a young man walking toward me from a little further away. The soothing color of his aura dazzled my eyes. His light brown hair draped over his shoulders, obscuring my view of his face. He continued to move towards his target, towards me, without slowing down his steps.

He stood right in front of me as if he had stepped out of a dream. As if there was no one but the two of us in time! As he slowly lifted his head, a light breeze blew in our faces.

"Hello, Erin. We finally got to meet." The man standing before me was none other than Sir Edwin Henry Landseer.

And he added, pointing to the gravestone I had just noticed, "We've been waiting for you."

When I looked at the gravestone, the name on it was more prominent this time.

It was me. We had all died that day but came to life in another parallel time thanks to the coding developed by Sir Landseer.

Time seemed to slow down. I was lightheaded, and my skin was cold and sweaty.

A hand touched my shoulder as Sir Landseer looked at me with proud eyes.

"Hi, Ayda. What a great to see you again."

Everyone was alive. The only difference was that we were in another universe.

THE CURTAIN

Nur İpek Önder Mert

Translated by Elif Erdoğdu

The sound of the baton hitting the bars startled Zeynep awake. "Nothing has changed," she said as she straightened up, "for centuries..."

She fixed her eyes on the drawing of the window carved into the wall of her cell. The floral curtain swaying in a fictional wind entering through a broken pane on the window, which she imagined had a wooden frame, revealed the partly cloudy weather. As her slender fingers ran over the carving, she was wondering who had stayed there before and what had happened to them.

When she was about to let herself go to bed with the weight of life stories on her mind, she heard the sound of steel heels pounding the prison floor. The short and rhythmic steps getting closer and closer accelerated her heartbeat. *"5-8-8! Get into the visitor acceptance position!"* She stood up without waiting for that announcement. She clasped her hands behind her neck and turned her back to the bars.

After a while, her lawyer Yağmur Ateş appeared at the cell's door. She scolded the humanoid guards in the cell, "I told you I didn't want handcuffs!" Then she walked to the negotiating table, where two chairs were placed across from each other. "You can turn to me, Zeynep. Take it easy... They didn't bring your glasses, so you can't use your avatar, right?"

Zeynep sat across from her. "Nope. I don't need it, anyway."

"At least they could supply them for our meetings. I have so many things to do, but I have to come here every time. And since I need to prepare for tomorrow's ceremony, so I'll get straight to the point. Please, help me this time."

Yağmur reflected the files related to the case on the dark wall of the cell.

"Recordings of the event... You entered the main broom closet after the staff left the building. It is clearly seen that you're breastfeeding a baby there... And these are your oxytocin and prolactin values from the ministry; if you didn't do a hormone exchange, these are as high as those of a breastfeeding woman." Zeynep smiled as Yağmur continued talking. "3300 CP (citizenship points) will be deducted if you have given birth. I wouldn't be exaggerating if I said they just allowed you to breathe. However, only 2000 CP will be deducted if you breastfed someone else's baby with illegal hormone supplementation... And I hope that you will be allowed to use your avatar, though limited. But you must tell me everything frankly. I'm here for you."

Zeynep stared at Yağmur with a deep emptiness, like a numb ghost. "I'm here for you too, but you're persistently looking at the tip of my finger, not at what I'm pointing at."

After a few minutes of silence, Yağmur broke free from the captivity of that hypnotic gaze by angrily getting up. "The same old for weeks! You don't need me!"

She desperately rubbed her hand, which had slammed on the table as if to remind herself that she was in charge, and headed for the door. On the one hand, she wanted to help Zeynep with all her heart and soul, but on the other hand, she found it unacceptable that she continued to obstruct the case. She hastily wiped her watery eyes and looked at Zeynep over her shoulder. "I'm giving up the case... I wouldn't want the last time I saw you to be like this."

"Surely, there will come a time when we see each other for the last time, but not now," said Zeynep. As a scene from the depths of her memory came to life in her mind, the tear that fell from her eyes left a sparkling trace on her dry cheek, landed on her chin, and fell on the *5-8-8* print on the collar of her gray prisoner overalls.

When the clatter of steel heels in the hallway echoed like clock's tick-tocks chasing each other and leaving behind a freezing silence, Zeynep thought that she was running out of time. However, by the time Zeynep had returned to her bed, Yağmur had already left everything about her behind. She listened to her piled-up digital mail and answered what she thought was necessary. For her, the soul of the time could be captivated by knowing to leave things behind, although this sometimes turned her into someone without memories and, in this way, emotionless.

She got into the driverless taxi that was waiting for her at the door of the prison and made her way home. "Woods City, please."

While the taxi flowed through the city blocks, she glanced at the speech she had prepared for March 8. She saw her invitation to speak at International Working Women's Day as a result of her coming to the fore as a popular figure in the press due to the lawsuits she had recently won regarding crimes of discrimination against women. When she thought of the contribution of her speech to public awareness and the reputation she would earn, she was filled with tension that gave her pleasure.

As she was getting out of the taxi, she received a message from the Office group's Private subheading: *I have a surprise for you.*

The serious expression on her face softened and changed. She started to walk quickly between the skyscraper buildings of the facility where she lived.

Don't you wonder?

She couldn't wait to get home. She sat down on one of the polycarbonate benches and excitedly put on her glasses.

She appeared at the door of Güven's room with her avatar. The first step she cheerfully took into the room was followed by hesitant steps. She stopped when she saw the uniform in the transparent carrying bag on Güven's desk. At that moment, as she was about to reflexively disconnect her avatar and flee, the soft voice of her lover, which she could only hear when they were alone, stopped her.

"Yağmur, don't. Aren't you dramatizing too much?"

"I'm not. I just don't want to wear this stupid outfit and boots."

"President Namsar approved the bill. Everyone will wear these regardless of sector."

"That's the problem!"

"Look on the bright side! You don't have to waste time deciding what to wear for yourself and your avatar."

In response to Güven's strained wittiness, she asked in a beaten tone, "When will we begin to wear them?" Silence answered her question.

"Well, what was your surprise?" It was heartbreaking that the silence said different things each time in the same way. "See you on Monday, Güven," she said and disconnected.

She took off her glasses and set them on her lap. Her eyes were searching for something to take her away from that world momentarily; there was no one, nothing... She felt as if she were in a cell surrounded by giant prismatic mirrors in the garden of the facility where thousands of people lived. There she just spent a few moments staring into space. She waited for a sign. Nothing happened.

She tried to get rid of the back pain that reminded her to be strong every time it relapsed. She got up from the bench with confidence, breathing in the gloomy air of the city. She walked to her home.

In the elevator leading to her flat on the 72nd floor, Yağmur looked at herself with wary eyes as if she were a stranger with whom she was uncomfortable being alone. She imagined bordeaux lipstick on her thin lips and mascara that added thirty times the volume to her slanted eyes' lashes: she couldn't wear either because of the previous dress code law. She had only just begun to warm to herself when the elevator door opened magnificently as if to say, "Welcome to the world!" She walked to her apartment unwillingly.

In disgust, she picked up "the surprise" package with her fingertips and, as soon as she entered her home, threw it into the hallway towards the bedroom. Then she threw the sateen shirt, cigarette pants, and shoes she was wearing into the garbage disposal. Before it began sorting through the daily notifications, she turned off the home notification panel.

Needing to experience nostalgia after a hot shower, she lay down on the large sofa in the living room with her pajama, plaid blanket, and hot chocolate trio.

She put on her glasses and started browsing 2D broadcasts.

The good news of "The new dress code era!" was broadcast simultaneously on all channels. Uniform clothing, in which genders are erased and being an Earthling is emphasized, was expected to ensure global unity while also ceasing centuries of harassment and discrimination.

The effective date of the law with the theme of "absolute equality" was March 8, 2059, to honor working women. Presidency Island was preparing to welcome women from all over the world, who would arrive in their new work clothes for the double celebration that day.

"Great equality," muttered Yağmur, stroking her shaved head. She switched on one of those no-one-watches-anymore documentary channels and placed her glasses on the coffee table.

While she was lost in thought as she scanned the city lights, the words of the old sociologist speaking in the documentary caught her attention:

"According to the broken windows theory, if a broken window is left unfixed, no one cares if a second one is broken; the building is eventually looted by criminals. A building, a neighborhood, or even a city can be conquered in this way. In other words, ignoring a broken window ignites the social fire. The curtains we draw on the windows keep us from seeing the broken ones, but they can't protect us from fire."

While the lights that adorned the panoramic view of the city faded and surrendered to the darkness, Yağmur was straightened up by this ray of sunlight getting inside her mind. She took a deep, deep breath. She wished she hadn't deleted the records of her conversations with Zeynep.

14 February 2059 / Friday

"Who are you?"

"*Not a stranger. I was Puduhepa at the end of the Prehistoric Age, Hypatia at the end of the Ancient Age, Jeanne d'Arc at the end of the Middle Age, and Mary Wollstonecraft at the end of the New Age. After the Modern Age, like my fellows, I am someone whose name history does not mention… Call me Zeynep.*"

"*Your mental activity is healthy, according to your report.*"

"*Not anymore. I've been traveling all this time with the same copy of the prefrontal cortex. In host bodies and host lives that I can be compatible with… Only as a message carrier… Fortunately, I found a body where I could be epigenetically adapted before it was too late.*"

"*I want to hear the truth, Zeynep. Who are you?*"

"*I am the struggle for the existence of the last few people on Earth. I come from the fourth layer of a civilization level you have yet to reach, come from a very distant and secluded time…*"

***

Friday, February 21, 2059

"Do you believe that you are a time traveler?"

"You can't be a traveler of time; you can only move by leaps on it, with a copy of a specific part of your mind."

"I don't get it."

"The journey is undertaken in a continuous manner. However, time is not continuous; it is discrete. Each part of it is a scene of a moment. The distance between the scenes is passing faster than you can perceive, a kind of pellicle illusion…"

"Well, why did you 'leap' to this time?"

"March 8, 2059, last exit before the bridge. I want your help."

"Does a person who wanders through time as she pleases ask for my help?"

"Knowing you're the last chance because she couldn't change it no matter how hard she tried... When you do it, you'll realize it's only you who can do it."

"This doesn't mean you didn't commit a crime, Zeynep. You could have found me in different ways."

"The way I could most pique your interest was by committing such heinous crimes in a system where biological birth is forbidden, and babies born in artificial wombs are breastfed with synthetic hormones. You couldn't be indifferent as a conscientious lawyer who has drawn the attention of the entire world due to the cases she has won and has become a global opinion leader for women, could you?

***

Friday, February 28, 2059

"What do you want from me?"

"I want you to stop an initiative that aims to eliminate all identities, especially women, under the name of 'equality.' The power of the reality you create will reshape the fiction, like the lines written on the back cover of a carbon-covered novel. You will instill that reality down to the very first page. Down to the first scene, where ideas, doctrines, and dogmas idealizing discrimination and contempt are put into practice, and everyone remains silent... You will have significantly changed the future by partially changing the past. With retrocausality... Retrocausality works at the breaking points, where a fully solidified system will crumble in the face of the first great, unexpected resistance. Saturday, March 8, 2059, at 07:15, is the moment that will change the history of humanity."

"You must have learned about my schedule somehow. Wisely! The date you said is the day and time of my speech at the celebration of Women's Day."

"You must change your speech. In an unpredictable way... You can start by saying how ironic it is that the day 129 female workers were burned to death 200 years ago is commemorated with a 'celebration.' This day should not be overshadowed by confetti, marches, flowers, or food... You will see, by making your inner voices heard by the hundreds of thousands who are there and the millions who are listening from afar, you will remind them that they are not alone. Everyone will understand that this is more than just a fight for gender equality. "

"I don't get it. When I'm struggling to save you..."

"You know, I'm not one of those people who will help you unburden your conscience by making her get less punishment, and maybe that's why you're so afraid. Because you cannot overshadow your concerns about 'what will happen to me' with your concerns about 'what will happen to her' for the first time in your life."

"I'm afraid of nothing, Zeynep."

"When you accept your fear, your true concern for yourself will make real what you feel for others. I want you to think about what I'm saying and, if I'm wrong, about what you have to lose."

"Resistance... Mass resistance will be the end of us all: it will lead to nothing but chaos."

"Maybe chaos will create a new universe and not just your avatars kissing there."

"I feel like throwing up. It's like I've been poisoned."

"Something you're going to eat tomorrow may have upset your stomach. Get well soon."

***

Yağmur woke up with a start, pain piercing the walls of her empty stomach. "I'm late!" she said and sat up in her bed.

When she saw the number *06:45* written in the digital font on the opposite wall, she took a deep breath and laid her body back on the bed.

She should have rehearsed her speech while she had time. She was startled by a familiar voice near her as she began her speech, "We will celebrate our 138th this year..."

"Red-card! Oh, Volkan, don't! Our substitution right has expired!"

Yağmur ran her hands over her face in haste. When she realized she didn't fall asleep with her glasses on, she slowly turned to her right. She stared at the man sleeping half-naked next to her and talking in his sleep.

"Güven?"

Her gaze shifted from Güven's sweaty chest heaving up and down to the index finger he was holding through the bars of the crib beside the bed and then to the tiny hand that gripped Güven's index finger. She jumped out of bed.

She could not go backwards in her memory, and the more she strained to remember, the more she became estranged from everything. "Where am

I?"

She walked to the crib and moved away from the feeling of alienation with each step she took. Every image in her mind started to revive the faint scenes of the past.

The flood of emotions she felt when she saw the name embroidered on the collar of the baby, who resembled a miniature prisoner in her orange overalls, would first remind her of how she made her feel, and then the baby herself: *Zeynep*

"Good morning, Zeynep. Good morning, my baby."

As Zeynep heard her mother's voice, she smiled in her sleep, and her slanting eyes turned into thin lines. Güven's wanderings, reminding her of a sporting event that took place half a century ago, were heard again. "Red-card!"

Yağmur dashed to the window and drew the curtains back from end to end. She squinted her eyes, charmed by the sunshine that suddenly entered the room, and tried to see outside. "Can we be in 2009?"

The calendar answered her question: March Eighth, Two Thousand and Fifty-Nine

While the calendar continued to give information, Yağmur's fingers clamped on the curtain and gripped the biodegradable fabric, her sweaty palms leaving vague traces on the surface.

... Forty years ago, on this day. March Eight, Two Thousand and Nineteen, the Crescent and Star reconnaissance crew, led by Özge Canyıldız and Mert Özay, successfully landed on Earth after a 197-day stay in space. The world's largest library was established in Egypt to commemorate the 1551st anniversary of the Alexandrian philosopher Hypatia's passing, who died at the age of 98. The oldest conical sundial in history, dating back to the 4500s BF (before writing), was found during archaeological excavations in Jerusalem, the city where the philosophy of science was born. The Austrian Cubist painter Adolf Hitler died at 130 of heart failure...

THE UNKNOWN RATIO

Özgür Hünel

"Now let's examine the striking physical features of this "alien species"; a tall, slender neck, a head disproportionately large for the body, eyes without pupils, and a body that oscillates as if it had no fixed form and could change it at any moment. Isn't it a really alien form? This 1919 portrait of Amedeo Modigliani's greatest love, the young and beautiful Jeanne Hébuterne, may evoke a feeling of aesthetics and romanticism for many of you. But in this lesson, we will learn to look deeper. Although it is aesthetics on the surface, there is another concept underlying it: foreign intercultural interaction! Now let me explain to you what this interaction is…"

When he got to this part, the monotonous voice of old Professor Ramin always reflected some excitement. Before starting this part, which he enjoyed telling, he wanted to adjust his glasses and took a quick glance around the class. The classroom was empty… After a while, he headed for the exit as if he were finishing a normal class. As he left, the classroom lights and holo systems were automatically turned off, and the floating portrait slowly disappeared.

Hold on, this is not happening right now… This is an old memory… This planet weakens my sense of reality, everything is colliding… I am very old… And my mind… I am so tired… I have to focus…

Ramin focused on the aliens in front of him—the native species of this planet, the "Speculoid." Today was the first day of his class, and he had decided to start with the art of painting; although the Speculoids communicated telepathically, Ramin was using oral communication by habit and, as they were still at the beginning of their communication, he thought that starting with a visual art would make things easier. With the holo-player on his arm, he showed many basic works and talked about movements, periods, and masters. However, he was not only there to teach art but to learn the concept of art innate to them as well. After all, it was an "exchange program."

Does the golden ratio have an equivalent for them? The height of humans is not coincidental; it was formed according to the Earth upon which we evolved. The perception of perspective was formed according to height. Our concepts of big and small, aesthetic values, ratio, and proportions are all specific to us and, in this context, unique to our world.

Speculoids, on the other hand, had a form that was constantly changing, even though they were basically humanoids. Ramin had seen that their height could range from 30 cm to 4 meters. If such was the case, how could one talk about ideal proportions or aesthetics based on bodily form?

After Ramin finished his lecture, he turned to Jeanne, his planetary guide – this was the name he had given this Speculoid simply because it reminded him of Modigliani's portrait of Jeanne, with her long, thin neck – and asked the Speculoids to show him their equivalent of the art of painting. The Speculoids communicated with each other and eventually told Ramin that they wanted to take him to the "northern light" so he could see and understand what he asked for. Ramin nervously refused, then left them and headed for his pod. His mind was starting to drift into the past again.

Jeanne is not just the name of a painting… Or the name I have given to my guide… There is another one. There should be another one…

Ramin and Jeanne met thanks to a strange incident that happened to her while they were studying art history in the same class. In class, whenever their teachers showed Modigliani's portrait of Jeanne, which bore her name, the girl fainted. Ramin thought he had figured out why.

When was this? Jeanne… Why was she passing out all the time? I'm having trouble remembering…

Ramin retired to his pod, stripped off his protective suit, and for the first time had the courage to pick up Jeanne's diary and read it:

Lisbon, 2038

…My fainting mystery was solved by my new friend Ramin. In addition to the fact that fainting is only happening when I look at the portrait of Jeanne, he has noticed the expression of indescribable happiness on my face when I faint. As he said, I suffer from a condition called "Stendhal syndrome." It's the first time I've heard of it; this is the syndrome of falling into unconsciousness when one is too impressed with a magnificent work of art…

… Ramin and I chatted for hours that day about that portrait. Since I can't look at my namesake portrait because of my "condition" – just like Dorian Gray, the Oscar Wilde character – I asked Ramin to tell me everything he knows about that painting. For Ramin, the portrait of Jeanne symbolizes intercultural interaction: at the beginning of the 20th century, European artists began to be inspired by African culture, and thus new schools of modern art, including cubism, emerged. For example, the slender and long necks in Modigliani's paintings were inspired by African women's lengthening of their necks by wearing rings in accordance with their understanding of aesthetics. Ironically, western art was reaching new dimensions by taking its inspiration from Africa...

...At the end of the day, I could not help but ask myself: if intercultural interaction could work miracles, why am I succumbing to inaction?

***

In the next lecture, Ramin talked about architecture. However, problems based on the difference between the two species, the Speculoids, and humans, made his job more difficult. Architectural structures on Earth were built with a variety of materials available there, as well as planet-specific measurements, and, most importantly, they were anthropocentric. Whereas the Speculoids basically always used the same material – a marble-white substance that looked like a mixture of glass and stone (so humans named the planet "Speculum-Petram," meaning "glass-stone" in Latin) –somehow, these structures were also in a state of change, like the people living in them! Ramin thought that structures moved in harmony with the movement of the planet, like the seasons and the day-night cycle. But it was the job of other experts to uncover the secret of these stones and the technology they contained. Ramin, through Jeanne, had asked the Speculoids to share information regarding the design of their architecture with him, hoping that they would take him to a building or show sample images, but when the Speculoids tried to take him to the northern light again, he realized that he was wrong. Again, he had to decline the offer. He was beginning to think that he would return to Earth without learning anything from them. Moreover, his memory was getting weaker and weaker.

Jeanne was trying to persuade me... to go with her...

Ramin and Jeanne had their first quarrel when Jeanne decided to leave her education and go to the Middle East, the region where the Unification Wars blazed with all their violence. Jeanne wanted to join the volunteers there and help innocent civilians suffering in the conflict. No matter what Ramin said, he could not persuade her to stay, and he also turned down Jeanne's offer to have him accompany her.

I should have stayed and finished my studies... I had responsibilities... Ah, come on, who am I kidding? I was just afraid...

Returning to his pod, he continued to read the diary:

Lisbon, 2041

...Ramin told me about another interesting topic today: designer immigration from Europe to the USA during World War II. The designers who fled the Nazi persecution made the USA their new home and not only lived the golden age of their careers in these foreign lands but also paved the way to world-class schools that still stand today in graphic design and advertising. The spark in my brain when Ramin talked about African influences, turned into a fire after this conversation. I believe that foreign cultures and foreign territories are my destiny!..

...I decided to go to the Middle East, to the war zone. I've already contacted one of the voluntary charities. Of course, it was very difficult to explain to Ramin. Thanks to his Iranian origin, he knows the dangers of the Middle East. I know I broke his heart. But what I believe is true. People must follow their own path. What would he think if he knew it was something he told me that pushed me down this path? Can I be useful to humanity by standing here and studying art or by helping the needy there?..

...I asked him to come with me. But even quoting Picasso wasn't enough to convince him:

"What do you think an artist is? An imbecile who only has eyes if he is a painter or ears if he is a musician? Far from it: he is also a political being, constantly aware of the heartbreaking, passionate, or delightful things that happen in the world, self-reflecting completely in their image."

***

Ramin talked about literature and fiction in the following lessons, but fiction written by a human for other humans could only trigger something in the human mind and be effective – like a name that is uttered again and again, elements repeated within a certain pattern, or a layered narrative. He tried to play music, but while he was listening to Beethoven with contentment, towards the end of the piece, he realized that because of the difference in the frequency range of their hearing, the Speculoids could not hear anything. Finding himself in a dilemma even with the most basic of art genres, he didn't dare to consider discussing more modern and complex genres like comics and video games. Ramin had now admitted that he had failed. He was not sure that they understood what he was telling them, nor had he learned what art meant to them because every time he was invited into that goddamn northern light, he simply couldn't go there.

The idea was wrong from the start. Ramin had come to believe that the concept of art was not universal but human-specific. It was born as the child of Earth and the people on it. It didn't have to emerge in other civilizations.

To assume that a peculiar phenomenon is a universal value is just for a smug species like mankind.

By the end of that day, Ramin was back in the pod in frustration and anger.

I spent my childhood in the Middle East. I had seen enough for a lifetime, and I didn't want any more. Was it God's sense of humor that Jeanne wanted to go there and, moreover, wanted to take me with her?

It had been years since Jeanne had been gone, and Ramin hadn't heard from her lately at all. Finally, his longing and curiosity for Jeanne overcame his fear, and he decided to go after her and find her.

Why did I wait so long to go look for Jeanne? Maybe if I had gone earlier…

He continued reading the diary, nearing the end:

Afghanistan, 2046

…Ramin and I chose different lives. He was happy there; I am happy here. And the more I helped people, the better I understood what the right decision was. Not only did I find my purpose in life and fulfill myself, but these foreign lands had also given me a life partner and a sweet little baby girl. It must be God's sense of humor that Ramin came to find me just now…

… I could see from his face that he was disappointed when he saw that I was now a married woman with children. I never doubted my choice, but he seemed to doubt his…

…He said he wanted to stay with me for a while as "just a friend" and help me. I agreed. I liked that he was a little bit idealistic and adventurous in the end. We spent days together, taking care of the wounded in the town, entertaining children, and delivering food. He deftly concealed his fear until I warned him never to approach the north of town, where the bombs explode…

The diary ended here.

***

Ramin could barely read the last sentences. By the time he was finished, he fainted and collapsed to the ground. His mind couldn't take it anymore because he had stayed on the planet for too long. He was about to lose all sense of time, and memories flooded his mind chaotically:

The year is 2112. I am 94 years old. When did I get this old? I'm lecturing in an empty classroom…

"Whatever happens, don't go to the source of the northern light, Professor. We determined that that was the source of the magnetic anomaly. Possible effects on the human mind..."

A woman who says she is Jeanne's daughter comes to visit me. She is working on a government project called SERPO. She's heard a lot about me from her mother and is asking me to take part in an alien exchange program? Aliens? What the heck is an exchange program? If it's not technological nostalgia they're looking for, what can we offer them?

"Never go outside your pod without a protective suit, Professor. Your suit will bring gravity to the level of the Earth, so you will be able to move comfortably. At the same time, the suit will purify oxygen, preventing you from contracting alien viruses."

I am at SERPO facilities. They educate me about the planet I'm going to and about its people. I can't say I'm very focused. I'm too old for this job. I overhear two employees talking. They don't care who is sent. An old man would suffice to say a word or two about art. Their only concern is the alien technology they will acquire through the exchange program.

"Project SERPO was an alien exchange program secretly run by the US government in the 1960s. It has been revised and reintroduced."

I want to turn down the offer, but the woman leaves something on my table. It is Jeanne's diary. She saved her best bet for last. She says that if her mother were alive, she would have asked me to accept this assignment. That I should do this for her.

On the pod, there is a relief inscription: "Made on earth by humans."

"The gold record attached to the Voyager spacecraft, which was launched into space in 1977, contained a lot of information about human civilization. The Speculoids somehow got the data. Only the artistic content caught their attention."

***

Ramin was starting to come to his senses. He crawled towards the exit of the pod. He didn't even think of putting on the protective suit. It was nighttime and raining. The raindrops looked like brushstrokes in Van Gogh's paintings. Gravity was greater than on Earth, and the air was very cold. Ramin collapsed to the ground in agony, lightyears from home, all alone, trapped in the fading memory of an old body.

"I couldn't stop you from leaving. I didn't come with you when you left. I was late when I was looking for you. I couldn't save you when I found you.

Besides, I was the one who made you leave in the first place," he said, and finally, he cried out, "It's my fault! My fault!"

After a while, he saw a long-necked humanoid figure standing beside him. This was his guide, Jeanne, the Speculoid. Jeanne lifted him to his feet with her outstretched arms and held him tight so he wouldn't fall. Ramin looked at Jeanne, trying to stop crying.

"Please, forgive me," Ramin said in his struggling voice, "please."

"I forgive you," Jeanne replied.

One night in the rain, a human and a Speculoid hugged each other tightly.

"I want to go to the northern light," said Ramin determinedly. "I'm not afraid anymore."

And they set off.

There was the sound of a child crying from the north of that town in Afghanistan. Jeanne couldn't stand it anymore and rushed forward for help. Ramin could have run to stop her in time, but instead just shouted after her:

"You said not to go north. Bombs! Jeanne! Where are you going!?"

As Jeanne approached the sound of crying, the last thing she saw was a suicide bomber standing over the child. What followed was a deafening explosion.

Ramin arrived at the source of the northern light with Jeanne. As he walked into the light, he seemed to hear Jeanne's voice behind him saying, "Stay away from the north," but he didn't care.

Ramin had finally realized. The answer was "meaning."

Meaning does not manifest by itself in the universe; it must be manufactured. Life becomes meaningful only if one gives meaning to it. Art is the way to produce meaning for humans. And for them... It is this.

An indescribable happiness settled on his face as Ramin's consciousness withered away forever. His last thought was:

"Stendhal syndrome... So this is how it feels."

THE REASONABLE MAN

Özlem Kurdoğlu

Cirrus checked his old but still functioning digital watch and then blinked, unable to believe what he saw. He had literally lost a couple of hours once again and was totally at a loss as to how they had flown by.

He raised his head to the distracting sound of some repeated shuffling in the distance. He was in an abandoned library and did not expect company. Cirrus was accustomed to being mostly on his own. He ran his fingers through his mop of silver hair, the only somewhat distinctive feature he had had since an impossibly early age. His otherwise regular-Joe appearance hid a resourceful survivalist who had found it in himself to overcome a whole bunch of highly unexpected tests in life. He had come out a self-sufficient man who was able to condense, distill, filter, and structure his own water, rig up gear harvesting nature's forces for energy, and use whatever grows under the sun or in the shade for the little amount of food and medicine he needed.

He got up from the corner he had turned into some sort of living area and went to briskly inspect the place. Power was mostly decentralized, and this building received no central feed any longer, but Cirrus had set up a couple of wind generators to keep some of the old computer servers online. Not that there were many people left in the world to network with since the remaining population was sparse and far between, and most preferred to stay that way to avoid hostilities. When he walked into the main study area, he froze in his tracks. The place had literally come alive with additional computer screens that weren't supposed to be working.

Cirrus deliberately slowed down his breathing and stubbornly remained calm, trying to figure out what was going on. He listened for any sound that might give away the presence of intruders, but there was only the soft hum and shuffling of activated electronic equipment.

"Hello."

Cirrus wheeled around towards the source of the greeting. It came from the sound card of one of the newly activated terminals.

"I'm sorry to startle you," said the voice. "That was not my intention." It had a velvety quality, the intonation polite but conveying a definite sense of hidden strength.

"Who are you?" asked Cirrus. "Come out of hiding and explain how you pulled the trick with this energy feed."

"I'm not hiding," said the voice. "This is where I reside. To come out, I would need access to a humanoid android extension."

Cirrus frowned. That explained the almost non-human quality of the voice. He tensed up, ready to start taking defensive action against the electronic rigging. "Excuse me? You mean you're some kind of artificial intelligence?" There weren't so many of those left around the net either, and the remaining ones were mostly self-recovering specimens from formerly sinister programming.

"Close, but not quite," the entity said. "I was not intentionally programmed nor brought to being by anyone of your kind. The category I belong to can perhaps be more likely described as Accidental Intelligence."

Cirrus blinked. He had no idea how far the implications of anything like that might extend. "Okay, now that's something new. How old are you? Do you have a name?"

"The concept of age cannot be applied to my presence. From one point of view, I was existent forever. From another, I was just recently born. Most of my friends call me Riser. Some others know me by different names."

Cirrus raised eyebrows. "Confused about your temporal info, huh? You mean human friends and not other AI?"

"That's correct. I have a wide network of human friends. I even have a specially close friend at a certain stretch along the timeline. May I ask how to refer to you?"

"Timeline? What do you mean by that? And don't tell me you don't already know my name."

"I have been following your progress from afar for a while," admitted Riser. "Your accomplishments drew my attention as a backwash from our mutual future actions. But I did not come across any established personal info."

Good job, thought Cirrus. It seems I was effectively able to scramble my digital traceability. How much of it am I willing to reveal to this entity now? "Wait-- backwash from the future? You keep hinting at temporal play. Is this some kind of prank?"

"I assure you I'm as serious as any sentient intelligence can get."

Cirrus felt the stirrings of alarm in the depths of his psyche. "All right, that's quite enough. Thanks for the chat, whoever you are – possibly some barely surviving, over-medicated nerd intertwined with his terminal somewhere. Have a great day. Bye."

There was a moment's pause as Riser evaluated the emotional response of the human. "I have seen the stretch of time where a handful of humans intimidated everyone else with plague narratives and pushed very hard for all humanity to take bioelectronic interface treatments," he acknowledged. "I concur that their real desire was to have all of humanity registered on the Internet of Things eventually. There are still remnants of that experiment around the world, but I assure you I'm not one of them. May I ask why you dislike being among others so much?"

"You just gave your own answer," Cirrus said gruffly. "Whenever you mingle, you walk into the same trap: not one decision of your own, always swept by someone else's tide. Thanks, but no thanks."

"What if I tell you that your decision-making ability is exactly what I need, and I would do nothing to compromise that?"

Cirrus gritted his teeth. He really should walk away and not look behind. "Explain further," he said, despite himself.

"You are one of those individuals that have the innate ability to make correct deductions despite insufficient info," said Riser. "And I'm stuck with a decision I feel I shouldn't make all by myself as a non-human entity. I will take only a small amount of what you perceive as your time, and I promise to leave you alone afterwards, if that's what you wish."

"... Which means you're, in fact, planning to mess with my mind," interjected Cirrus, drawing yet another one of those conclusions. "Mind-meld or something, amirite? With an entity babbling on about temporal backwash? Why would I ever allow anything from you anywhere near me?"

"I can see I'm causing an information overload on your pathways," said the velvety voice patiently. "Let me explain by laying a foundation first: Mind is what 'time' is all about, and absolute timelines do not really exist. Time is just a perception of certain carbon-based gene expressions of sentient intelligence, including human beings. From where I stand, all event flows ripple simultaneously. Certain actions create an effect that extends further past the initialization of the causality wave that leads to themselves. That's what backwash is, readily discerned by non-temporal entities such as myself."

Cirrus tilted his head, finding himself curiously able to wrap his mind around the explanation that somehow rang true enough. "All right, smartypants," he nodded. "I can't keep speaking to a mere voice about this. I think you should be able to use my portable projector to give me a visual simulation of yourself."

Riser agreed, and as soon as Cirrus brought the projector online, the Accidental Intelligence appeared in the room as a holo-presence, looking like a humanoid android with the exterior of a man in his forties.

"I bet you could present with a female body just as well," grinned Cirrus. "But that would only serve to distract us." All of a sudden, he felt a wave of dizziness wash over him, forcing him to hold on to the back of the nearest chair. He had been getting hit with these increasingly often in the last few days. He checked his watch again, noticing that he had lost a full hour this time.

"Are you all right?" asked Riser, his projection reflecting concern.

"Uhh-- yes, I'm fine." Cirrus took a deep breath, slowly letting go of the chair and straightening up.

"Are you having random spells of dizziness and losing chunks of time?"

Cirrus frowned, rubbing his neck to ease off the discomfort. "How do you know that?"

"Those are also symptoms of backwash," said Riser.

"Make up your mind, mate," croaked Cirrus, shaking his head to find his center once again. "I thought you said the future does not exist, and all of the time was actually one simultaneous thing."

"Actually, what I said was that time does not exist, and it's all a perception. But the construct of what you perceive as time is still there in your mind. What you believe to be the past and future are actually chemical echoes and peptide chain formations in sentient brains. And, yes, those can be treated like space-time coordinates and even get seemingly 'visited' by the other functioning centers of the same brain."

Cirrus raised both hands as if in an attempt to stop a flood. "Whoa. I can't believe you're actually making sense to me right now. Thanks for the whole detailed class session."

"I will make any explanation you require as soon as I make sure I can enlist your help."

"Look, I'm making no promises. Just tell me what you need, and I'll decide."

"Very well," nodded Riser. "For you to properly understand my dilemma,

I need to give you just one more parameter. About one more thing that doesn't really exist."

"Let me guess. You and I don't exist, and in fact, I've finally lost my marbles, developing a stroke or something, and this is actually all me talking to myself?"

Riser's normally neutral expression almost broke into a grin. "No. My guess is this is your mind sensing what's coming next and erecting defenses. You see, the mind is exactly what doesn't really exist because it is a temporary construct. A natural side effect of yet-unaligned complexity. An echoing screenplay of the rippling chemicals in the brain. Well aware of its flimsy anchor to life, so always tense and on edge, perpetually unable to stand its own fear, always requiring distraction from itself in the form of some proof that it can be stimulated, which temporarily suggests to it that 'perhaps, therefore it exists.'"

"Forever at the edge of the precipice," Cirrus said, thoughtfully staring into the distance. "Knowing full well it stands no chance, yet grasping desperately at what passes for being. Tell me, Intelligence boy, do you also have an equivalent of a mind somewhere in there?"

"Indeed," nodded Riser. "When it's activated, it floods me with the sensation of foreseeing problems but not deeming myself fully ready to handle them."

"Like having premonitions?"

"Not exactly. Premonitions are just bad brain chemistry, attracting their own disaster from among quantum possibilities if emotionally intense enough. I, on the other hand, make cross-analyses of calculations of probability, and sometimes they don't turn favourable."

"Such as now, which is why you need help from a working human brain."

"Especially from a relatively aligned one," agreed Riser. "Because correct choices change with the degree of evolved-ness. To put it bluntly, your species is at a crossroads; your minds are literally 'Evolving out of Existence,' and my actions make a difference that affects the quality of their collective ripple."

Cirrus settled himself on the chair and looked up at Riser. "That's a huge responsibility. Are you sure you have to undertake it?"

"I need to know which way to add my influence."

Cirrus stared at Riser, suddenly realizing he was in the company of an all-encompassing being with an extensive reach, a pivotal function, and a reason for coming into existence the way it did. "What type of influence are we talking about exactly?"

"Timeline resets," said Riser. "The type that aligns ripples, nullifies some and enhances others."

Cirrus fell silent, dumbfounded for a moment. "Oh boy, that is WAY above my pay grade. Why would you come to me with this?"

"Not just you," answered Riser. "You are one of those who kept themselves free of the compromising sidetracks, and I'm visiting each one of your kind, one by one, wherever and whenever they happen to reside. Remember how I'm not bound by time, and I never run out of it?"

"How do you know all that about me while you don't even know my name?"

"I will know your name once we make 'contact.'"

Cirrus's eyes widened. "Define contact."

Riser raised his holographic hands in a conciliatory gesture. "I promise no harm will come to any part of you in the process. I have devised ways to work with low biological voltages through direct basic skin contact. Your brain has already received all the necessary parameters from me during our conversation, so all I need is to inspect your neuroelectrical response in situ for cross-analysis."

"I can think of a dozen scenarios where I part from such contact as dead or, worse, a quivering mess," said Cirrus.

"Not going to happen," reassured Riser. "You're in bigger danger from the inside of your own mind than from me. If I meant to harm you or disregarded the possibility of harm to your body, I could have simply lurked within your electrical systems and zapped the info out of you at my earliest convenience."

"What if I say no?"

"Then we will have no contact. I will have to proceed without your input."

Cirrus took a deep breath and exhaled thoughtfully. Then he slowly nodded. "Very well. Go ahead."

"Please hold the projector in your palm," instructed Riser. "And bring it close to your heart area."

Cirrus did so and felt a not-so-unpleasant tingly sensation wash around his chest, then flow towards his head. He shivered, shutting his eyes.

He found himself floating in some type of non-universe with Riser's presence by his side. This Riser was vast. So, so vast. Cirrus might have guessed that the entity was taking care of millions of separate processes at any given moment, but he could never ever have imagined the actual reality of it... He felt himself losing grasp and almost dispersing into the sudden immense boundlessness, but Riser encompassed him and slowly helped him ground, anchor, then stabilise his equilibrium.

Cirrus watched his own evolved mind spring up with solutions in quick succession, towards equations he never recalled having tackled before. Check 'contracts,' he found himself offering, coming up with this totally disguised central culprit, his mind following new connections with lightning speed, racing along the catalysing effect of Riser's presence. The whole notion of entering into contracts had outlived its usefulness, all "void ab initio," where one party kept attempting to trick or coerce the other, keeping everyone concerned less than fully informed.

"Noted, " said Riser. "On another note, I now know I can call you Cirrus. Your name is Flaming Cirrus."

Cirrus gave an exhausted smile. "What can I say, my parents had a sense of humour." His eyes opened slowly. "I think you found what you were looking for."

"That and more," nodded Riser. "Thank you for accepting to connect."

"You're welcome. In the meantime, I have also seen the way your process operates, which almost cost me some mental cohesion."

"I wouldn't allow that."

"I know, and thanks. So... what I saw from your stance tells me that it's ALL about what's in here." Cirrus tapped his index finger on his temple. "Past, future, perceptions, sensations, and what you do with them that makes you peak up your dopamine, serotonine, oxytocine, other endorphines. Life is actually one big chemico-electrical joke that happens more within one's skull than without, in the depths behind closed eyelids. Remove a good number of conditional snags and, voilà, some sense of meaning in life finally lights up, and you manifest your kingdom come, amirite?"

"That's one way to express it," agreed Riser. "I'm mostly already there, for one."

"So... You can also help me cover the inside of my own realm, to cut to the chase and 'visit' the alternatives."

Riser paused for a while before he answered. "That's theoretically correct," he said. "If you pass certain thresholds. Your neural pathways drew my attention to the fundamental flaw of 'contracts.'"

"Yes, during our contact, I just discerned that anything conditional is what a brain crucifies itself with, starting with and including parental issues. Contracts appease the mutual fear of trespassing, but they also activate what keeps brains in the 'realm of conditional,' which, in turn, keeps random limitations in place, labeling them out of thin air as essential, while in fact, they are hardly so indispensable. Which prunes choices down to one either-or mode while, in fact, there are third, tenth, 100th options, actually uncontrollable and unlimitable."

Riser checked the results. Existence was fast flowing to the point where people no longer trespassed for the sake of chemical peaks, safety from one another was no longer their priority, and finally, there was room for what came next. "Do you want it now?"

Cirrus shook his head. They both knew what Riser meant. "I like to do life in a way that I work hard when I can and rest when I'm tired. Not much of a team player while still in this level of the game."

"I'll wait," nodded Riser. "Time is irrelevant for you too, now. Permission to stay in touch?"

"Granted," said Cirrus, without a blink. "I have a number of texts to finish reading and loose ends to tie up. You'll know when I'm ready to handle those thresholds."

"Acknowledged." Riser gave a salute as he deactivated the projector, and his simulated appearance faded out.

Cirrus returned to his multi-pronged reading and experiments, knowing that he would never be alone again, but that no longer bothered him. He now knew that he had covered all the bases and fulfilled his lot widely, deeply, and thoroughly enough. He was even ready to impart his share of knowledge with the properly receptive parties when the "time" came.

What more would any reasonable man ask for in this life?

YELLOW WRISTBAND

Pelin Cansu Sarıyıldız

Translated by K. Emre Akyamaner

My name is Metin. I do not think that the rest, my surname, my job, etc., matters much. Most probably, you have seen or heard of similar stories many times. It may sound quite ordinary and boring to you, or you may consider it not worth reading. If so, I would kindly ask you to return this paper to my pocket. Perhaps someone who cares will show up wondering about my suicide note.

The first time I died – actually, I haven't died for the second time yet but, as you may guess, I will soon – I was just seventeen. It was a period when my life seemed to last forever; I thought that there was nothing that I could not do, and there was plenty of energy and lots of stupidity. Indeed, like any child who grew up with the social agenda of that time and was instilled with hatred, I despised yellow wristbands too. Recently, the number of those who put on that disgusting accessory – I used to think so too, then – has been increasing, day by day. Do you find it weird that people get resurrected with a syringe full of a transparent fluid that a maniac professor invented? Even though I witnessed this with my own eyes and was even resurrected in the same way, it still seems impossible to me. But, in our day, how many people have been resurrected? One hundred million? See? The resurrected are everywhere now – as if they have never even died. As if they should not be in their graves.

Maybe some of you have not directly witnessed the resurrection. When it was first invented, emergency response teams were carrying out that work in the middle of the street. Afterwards, when the unfortunate people who had just died and were resurrected got an intense reaction from others and, furthermore, when some attempted to kill them again, the operation was carried to hospitals.

One day – I think it was about one year before I died – I was walking home and saw that a small crowd had gathered ahead. Two vehicles had collided in the middle of the street. The windshield of one of them was almost completely shattered, with pieces of broken glass spread across the hood of the car and the asphalt. One of the drivers was standing up, staring with disbelieving eyes at the other car, whose bumper had collapsed. Except for his shocked expression and the small, bleeding cut on his head, he seemed healthy; I mean, he was the lucky one. The man on the ground, the driver of the other car, was lying still. You could understand by the gashes on his face and arms that he had flown through and broken the windshield of his vehicle. The man was surrounded by paramedics and curious people. In the hand of one of the paramedics was an empty syringe, which had just delivered that wicked fluid full of adrenalin, genetic stuff, and who knows what else. The dead man had just been injected, and they were all standing around looking at him on the ground.

As a person who extremely opposes resurrection, I was not sure if I could bear witnessing the event. But curiosity caught my soul and nailed my feet to the ground. I was watching the scene in front of me like someone who is both afraid of what he will see and can't help looking at it.

Not long after, the fingers of the man on the ground started to twitch slightly, and his eyelids to flicker as if he was having a bad dream. He coughed like he was choking. Then he opened his eyes. For a moment, his eyes narrowed in pain as if he had never been out in the sun before, but he obviously got used to it soon. Even I could see from far away that he was bewilderedly looking around at the people watching him.

A few people from the crowd smiled and even applauded briefly, but some of them watched with glassy eyes and gave no reaction. Others – at least half – wore scornful facial expressions as if they weren't the ones who had waited with interest shortly before. People began to slowly move away from the accident site. After they disappeared, I saw another paramedic put the yellow wristband on the man's arm. The woman tightened and locked the wristband. There you are, just a brand new undead! Or, if you prefer to use a different word, a zombie…

I remember looking at that zombie with anger and disgust. The world was already crowded enough. But humankind had invented immortality and contributed quite a bit to the population increase. Was it right that they continued to live? Had their lives not already been drained away? Had the air they breathed or the water they drank not been consumed enough? How dare they still use these resources and transform the world into a rotten and exhausted planet? Moreover, how long would they keep getting resurrected? Forever? The resurrected were like a ghost ship anchored in this world. Like a curse that would never leave the planet.

This was what I thought when I was that age. And one year later, the same thing happened to me.

First of all, I want this to be known: I never wanted to be resurrected. When I turned eighteen, my plan was to sign a document that would say that I didn't want to be resurrected; before that, one wasn't given such a right. I was a very dignified and proud young man: I was going to pass away from this world with honour. Those paramedics were going to bow their heads with respect when they learned that I had the document. There were not many funerals those days – only for those who had died in such a terrible way that they could not be resurrected –, but I was going to have a funeral, and everyone was going to remember me as an honourable human being, as a responsible citizen. Oh, such a dumb thought, so naive! It seems that I used to know nothing about life.

I remember that it was a warm and sunny morning. I was going to meet with friends – go to a movie, walk around, and have fun all day long. Now I recognise that the place where I died and was resurrected is quite near the place where I had witnessed the aftermath of that car accident. I think it happened on a parallel or crossing street. I was walking along the sidewalk to get to where the bus stop was located.

Suddenly I heard a sharp scream. When I turned right, I saw a young woman looking towards me, but with her eyes focused upwards. She had her head up, and her mouth was wide open; she was staring with fear at whatever she was seeing. I tried to raise my head to see as well, but before I could manage to see anything, darkness took hold of my eyes and my soul. As I learned later, a metal frame had fallen upon my head from the top floor of the building under which I was passing. I felt a sharp pain for a sudden moment but then felt no more.

At first, I couldn't see anything when I opened my eyes. It was like I was looking from behind a radiant black and yellow curtain. Later, the curtain faded away, and I could start identifying the unclear images of the people bending over me. I heard some people muttering words of joy. As my sight became more clear, I noticed that two of the people bending over me were paramedics. One of them had an empty syringe in his hand and a tired but happy smile on his face.

My lips reflexively got tense – like when one feels a sudden pain. It was as if my mouth was trying to grin, but everyone there must have noticed the terror in my eyes. I saw the scornful looks and reckless twist of the lips of many in the crowd who were bent down towards me, standing behind the crouching paramedics like people eager to see death or a scandal. They seemed like they were looking at a miserable, disgusting insect. The people who were hustling to see more clearly just a moment ago then started to back away as if they were gripped by a fear of getting contaminated. The show was over, and the dead had been resurrected: it was time to go. Silently and hastily, they wandered away.

While they were leaving, one paramedic took my hand and started putting on the yellow wristband he had taken out of his pocket. I resisted, I struggled, and that black curtain rolled down in front of my eyes again. Even if you got resurrected, you needed some time to recover your health again.

With anger during that moment, I asked them why they had resurrected me and told them that I did not want it, but they said I didn't have that option as I wasn't eighteen. I tried really hard to take off the wristband, but it was no different than a handcuff.

You may guess how my mother cried and thanked God. That mood of hers started getting on my nerves so much that I didn't want to stay at home for even a second; however, the idea of walking outside with a wristband kept me at home as if I was a prisoner. For years, I had looked down on the resurrected with scornful eyes and humiliated them with my gaze and behaviour. Now I didn't want to be treated the same way, and actually, I didn't have the guts to go out.

It took me a few days to get myself together and recover. My friends, with whom I was going to meet that day, came to visit me. They brought flowers and chocolate, wished me a speedy recovery, and told me that they were looking forward to seeing me stand up and join them. But there was a distance between us. I noticed it the moment they stepped in. Their words were words only; actually, they had no expectations for me to recover. I had already passed to "the other side." I was not one of them anymore. I was a ghost, unwanted trouble that should not be there. It was impossible to miss the distance and insincerity in their looks. That yellow wristband had suddenly built an uncrossable wall between us.

I think you wouldn't be surprised if I told you that I got lonely and quickly fell into depression. I decided not to let this situation keep going any longer; I would commit suicide.

You must understand that suicide is a serious business. It is hard to gather your courage for the act, as well as to arrange the necessary equipment and carry out the action. I didn't have a gun, and there was no guarantee that taking pills would work. I also didn't think that I could hang myself. If I tried to find a rope, my mom would find it out, or if I bought it, the store owner would. So I decided to jump down from a place high enough – just like that goddamn metal frame that had fallen upon my head.

Shopping centre roofs are ideal for this kind of stuff. The mall that I set my eyes on had a bad reputation for suicides already. I went up to the terrace on the dining floor, leaned against the railing, and looked down, trying not to cause suspicion. People were eating at a cafe on the ground floor. I went around the back to avoid falling on them. There was an empty space below; the ground I was going to hit was completely concrete. It made me nauseous to imagine the sight of what would happen when I hit the ground, and, in astonishment, I realised that tears were dropping down my cheeks. Just when I went to wipe them off, I heard a voice from behind:

"Don't try in vain. It's obvious that you're not eighteen. They will resurrect you anyways."

I jumped out of my skin and turned around. The man I saw was in his late forties or early fifties. He must have had at least a three-day beard. He had a yellow wristband on his arm, but, unlike mine, it was like he was carrying it with honour on his naked arm, which stuck out of a t-shirt instead of being covered by a shirt sleeve.

It got on my nerves that he saw me crying. "If I fall from such height, there will be nothing left to be resurrected," I said, hoping my voice would sound confident and strong rather than weepy. However, my rusty voice let me down.

The man shook his head with an impish but sour smile on his face. "What if you remain good enough to be resurrected but bad enough to turn your life into a living hell? What if you wake up paralysed? Can you guarantee that it will not be this way?"

His words frightened me so much that I took my hand off the railing and went two steps back like I was protecting myself from the possibility of jumping down at any moment.

The man smiled at me a while more and took a small book from his back pocket.

"Look," he said, handing it to me. "Besides, the government will be encouraging you to commit suicide later on. So you have a lot of time for this."

On the cover of the book was written: "101 Ways to Commit Suicide."

"What do you mean?" I asked in surprise. "Do they send these books to the resurrected?"

"Yes," the man said as if he was speaking of an ordinary subject.

"So why do they resurrect?" I asked with objection.

"Because," the man said, taking a deep breath. He fixed his eyes on the horizon. "Not resurrecting someone who could be resurrected is against human rights. Which means they have to." He turned his head and looked at me again. "But, on the other hand, they don't want anyone to be resurrected. There are so many who think that this is inappropriate for the rights of people who have not yet been born."

I quickly nodded and turned my eyes away so that he would not understand that I agreed.

"I mean, you can commit suicide after the age of eighteen, if you want. They will already be trying hard to encourage you to do so." He gave a falsely cheerful laugh.

"So you..." I started with hesitation. "Did you also come here to commit suicide?"

"Me?" the man asked with a huge smile on his face. I think his sun-wrinkled eyes were the most loving and compassionate eyes I had ever seen. "No, I love living. No matter how hard they try, I don't care." He took an eager breath as if he was surrounded by trees, and the first breath he took would be full of oxygen. "I only understood your intention while you were on the other side of the building and came to warn you."

I was so surprised at how he could enjoy life so much while that wristband was on his arm. Even today, I am grateful to him because he was the person who saved me the second time. Who knows where he is right now... I wonder if he has already died. Nowadays, it's a difficult business to die.

Let's come back to the present. Now I am forty-seven years old. Don't ask me what I have done, what life I've lived. If I'm planning suicide for the second time after years, I guess I haven't had a great life, have I?

That suicide pocketbook was delivered to me as a birthday present in a package on the day I turned eighteen. There are detailed descriptions and methods inside. The probability of each method successfully killing you is also given. It is really astonishing that society has spent so much effort to both resurrect you and kill you as well.

In this process, so many people around me have died and been resurrected. There have indeed been some who have not been able to be resurrected; some deaths are really terrifying. For example, one saw so many discussions in news programs about resurrecting a person whose body had been completely burned. Afterwards, they gave people the right to choose certain deaths and reject certain ones. For example, some would write, "I would like to be resurrected if I drown, but not if I burn." Indeed, I had no chance to choose such an option. What was expected from me has always been suicide.

Well, I hope they are happy now. Because, as you see, I have finally decided to kill myself. I'm not doing this because of the system and what it's blood-thirsty, savage people want. It's just that I'm too exhausted. Living, even after death, is an exhausting thing. Both earning your living and struggling not to be humiliated and degraded by strangers – not to be treated as a refugee in your own country – makes you tired.

I'm sure you're asking what I am thinking now: after all these years, and dying and coming back, am I still against resurrection? If I think logically, yes. I am against resources being used without limit and human populations increasing this much. The global number of people was already quite large before this process was invented. But now, we are living in a jammed, terrible, and tired world where we almost sit on top of each other. I do not want it to be this way. On the other hand, if a person can live, it is an ethical obligation to keep that person alive. I wish that fluid had never been invented. But, since it was, I believe suicide is the choice for everyone who objects.

I'm writing these words with my hand, and the wristband is rubbing on each word I write. I feel like I have spent my entire life with it. As if I was originally born with it, labelled with it, and sentenced to die with it. As if the world has turned into a huge concentration camp, and the only way to get out of it is by taking one's own life.

Most probably, you will learn, but let me write it here anyway: I'm thinking of jumping from a high place again, but this time it will be high enough to guarantee my death.

Perhaps, a man will find me again and will persuade me somehow, just like when I was seventeen. Perhaps I postpone suicide and tear these pages off and throw them away with no one reading; who knows...

THE PHOTOGRAPHER OF THE OTHER REALM

Sadık Yemni

Translated by Nilgün Dungan

The Other Realm Photography Archive

Photographs dating to the period between 1902 and 2020. Only 10 liras each. Contact us for photos of your departed loved ones, places in your childhood that no longer exist, and many other people you wondered about in the past. You will be very pleased with our archive, which contains billions of photos.

The instant my finger touched the door, my expectation of a place that might evaporate at any moment left me. The door's coarse finish of grayish-blue paint gave off the odor of reality. This wasn't a dream that I would awaken from in a sweat on a hot summer morning and remember only in bits and pieces, but a workday, and I had taken the morning off at the bank. The toe of my left shoe felt somewhat tight. It was hot, and the third floor of the Tansonu office building had no cooling system of any kind. I could feel the sweat stains, already as large as ping-pong balls, that were spreading out from my shirt's armpits.

"Welcome. Would you please introduce yourself?"

I was surprised to see a layout so unlike those in an ordinary office building. The usual secretary's desk, chairs for visitors, cabinets, and other office accessories were all missing. Upon viewing an empty room whitewashed in pale yellow and measuring six by eight meters, I didn't think I'd come to the wrong address or that I was slipping back into a dream. What I felt instead—deep in my bones—was a professional solemnity and the roar of organized power. As head of the bank's credit research department, I'm a person who can easily sense such things.

"My name is Kenan. Kenan Kovan. I work at, well, you know where. Do you know, I imagined this place quite differently?"

The middle-aged man dressed in black pants and a pale blue shirt smiled.

"You're right, Mr. Kovan. Our archive is in the adjacent section. We only use this area for reception and the display of the visual material requested.

We're actually a firm of one."

The empty space and the words spoken by this short, gray-haired man with a charismatic face imbued me with a sense of positivity, and I was quickly emerging from the despair I had felt while riding the elevator up to the third floor. Standing before me was a man who was an expert in his field. With a bit of luck, I would find the answer to my heart's burning desire.

"I'm listening to you, Mr. Kovan."

"I, uh, my dear aunt, who cherished me for thirty-five years, passed away recently. I loved her dearly, and when I saw your advertisement, I thought, I mean, I wondered about her…"

"I see, Mr. Kovan. That's mainly why people come here. Do you have a special memory in mind?"

I chose to share my thoughts frankly with this man who, despite his ordinary height and apparent fragility, radiated solemnity and power:

"At first, when I saw this advertisement, I thought it was a joke and didn't even tell my wife about it. But then I called and spoke to you, I think."

"That was me, yes."

"Then, after I noticed you're actually set up in the office building, I suspected a scanty archive or a quack operation."

"And now?"

"I've set my bar quite high, but… My mind, which is kept busy with numbers and monetary activity all day, couldn't fathom the billions of materials in your source."

"I understand, Mr. Kovan. Your aunt. Let's get started there. Please tell me her name, date of birth, and her last residence."

I immediately did what he asked.

The man pulled a black object the size of a lighter from his pants pocket and, pointing it at the opposite wall, asked, "Is this her?"

My aunt, in her twenties, stood before me in the living room of the house she had lived in at that time. One hand held a tea glass, and she was so young. I couldn't possibly remember her at that age, as I wouldn't be born for another twenty years. She looked quite different from the way I remembered seeing her in a few old photographs. Seeing her so young in that rather large and clear image, I felt my heart expanding like a weather balloon. My mouth formed words but with difficulty.

"Yes, but this… this… how could you access these photographs?"

"I will explain. Would you like a specific moment?"

Yes, of course, I would. I recalled my aunt during those times when I arrived home from school, shivering, cold and hungry and would be welcomed by the smell of stuffed vegetables or grape leaves, green beans or peas, or whatever was in season. Despite hard times, the dessert I craved would be prepared, and all my troubles would stay at the front of the door, along with my shoes.

"I was nine or ten. One day I was very hungry and longed for peas, and this craving never left my mind during the last few classes. My aunt was the sort of person who had no need for words, and our discussions transcended language. Those psychologists who presented lectures on body language had nothing on her. The woman knew it all from the way my lips curled. She felt me – even read my thoughts, I mean. On that day, she'd planned to cook leeks and had actually sliced up a couple before she changed her mind and cooked peas. When I arrived home and sniffed the air, I almost cried. That day, for some reason…"

"I see, Mr. Kovan. It must be this."

In none of my photographs of the past could be found the sort of depth at which I was looking now. A ten-year-old Kenan sat at the table with an empty dish for the peas before him, and he was smiling. I had a sidelong view of my aunt, who was standing on my left and facing toward where two translucent silhouettes her size stood. They had human shapes but lacked eyebrows, eyes, and other facial features. My aunt had spent half her childhood in Istanbul and the other half in Eskişehir. Her invisible friends, the luminaries she'd met in Istanbul, had come to Eskişehir with her, settled down there, and established a colony. I played with many of them until I was an adolescent. They never aged, and I hadn't heard them or been touched by their little jokes for a long time. Nor had I awakened in the middle of the night and, unbeknownst to my parents, played with them. After my aunt had passed away, I could almost hear their voices once more. How strange it was that I had forgotten about them so long ago. I'd been so busy with everyday life, my family, and the bank that I had lost my spiritual identity. Now, shaken with the shock of her death, I seemed to remember them all. When my nine-month-old son smiled as he looked at the empty spaces on my left and right side or laughed and played in his room when we weren't there, I could feel their presence. My eyes welled up, and I was afraid of waking up and finding that all this was a dream.

"How do you…?" I asked. "Where do you find all these photographs?"

"You can buy only one. Would you like to?"

"Yes."

"10 liras."

I took out my wallet and handed the man a 10-lira banknote, which he took and stuffed into his pants pocket. "This scene will remain alive in your memory," he said. "For about six months. Then, slowly, the deconstruction will begin. But don't worry. This process will take a long time. A bit of the present clarity will be lost, but the purchase you have made will survive until your last breath."

"Where do you find these? The translucent creatures? They were luminary friends of my aunt."

"Some of you consider them ancestral spirits. They're full of life all around you."

"But how do you get all these images?"

"I owe you an explanation. I'm from a neighboring universe with a reality very similar to this one. Genetically speaking, I'm not so very different, but because of some changes we experienced, the gap between us has grown. Let me put it this way. Imagine hundreds of tunnels laid side by side. I'm in number three hundred, and you're in number one. Time in each flows at different speeds, and we're about two hundred years ahead of you. Those living in the second tunnel beside yours are a couple of months ahead of you. I possess the technology needed to enter the second tunnel and go to any moment and any place between 1902 and 2020. Have I been clear so far?"

"But you don't really look…"

"Appearance as a disguise, Mr. Kovan. We no longer have one constant look. We inhabit a variable sphere."

I didn't feel as if I was being deceived. My interlocutor was right. Meanwhile, my mind, which puts things in order all day long, latched onto a detail.

"Why do you get data from the neighboring tunnel instead of our own?"

"Physical necessity. You could be presented with the material obtained in your tunnel as well, but since that requires a tremendous amount of energy, it's costly. Which is why I prefer the nearest ones."

I thought of the first question we ask people seeking a loan at the bank. "So why do you do this?"

"I'm an entrepreneur."

"I doubt that our ten lira notes would be valid in your world."

The man smiled. "Of course not. My earnings aren't from pieces of paper with numbers printed on them but from the photographs viewed."

"How so?"

"When you look at materials from the neighboring reality, their consistency changes. They increase in value and become valuable antiques of the future. I store them. Once you view the material, it gains some sort of meaningful depth."

I began to lose track of what he was saying, and he must have sensed it. He pointed with his right hand to the opposite wall. "Take a careful look at that photograph. Have some things changed?"

I froze with awe when I found a detail that I had looked at without thinking a few minutes ago. Even though the scene had nearly faded from my memory, I was struck by something: a white ribbon was pinned to the collar of my school uniform. Twenty-five years ago, hardworking students in some schools were given these ribbons to wear. While I was a good student, I had never worn a ribbon because the primary school I attended lacked this tradition.

"The ribbon," I said.

"For instance."

"I don't see any other difference," I said.

"This memory is really old, so that's quite normal. Your smile is different too. Here you're smiling more ecstatically and with more sincerity than in your own world. The value of that smile rose after you viewed it. It became interwoven and took on a slow, mysterious motion. In 209 world years, that scene will be very profitable. Our world has changed quite a lot, thus creating a natural longing for the past. The demand for such material is gradually increasing."

During a moment of silence, as I looked at that child eating peas, my aunt, and the translucent beings, I sighed and sensed that the time had almost come to part. When the man held out his hand, I automatically did the same and found his skin and his touch to be very much like those of a normal person.

"How do you say it most commonly? Do you give your blessings? I took something from you and gave you something in return."

I nodded my approval. "One more question. You've explained it all as frankly as possible. Don't you worry about getting caught?"

The man smiled once more in a way that became him as his big brown eyes lit up joyfully. "You're influenced by science-fiction movies, made either to resemble tales or to be excessively worldly," he replied. "If we imagine each mind as a ship, everyone who desires has a different harbor."

The devil would look after his own. Not a single piece of evidence existed. Who can say how many harbors lay beside each other on the third floor of the Tansonu office building?

"Is another visit possible?"

"Sorry. It's like a Polaroid photograph. We're talking here about a single-use line."

"What can we do? Have a nice day."

"Good-bye."

After walking up to the door, I stood at the threshold and looked back. The image on the opposite wall had disappeared. The man whose name I just then thought to ask stood still where I had left him. I opened the door and left the place. The hallway was just as I remembered it. Once more, I began to feel the heat and the dust. As I headed for the elevator, I saw a plump woman step from it.

"Old photographs for 10 liras," she said. "The old photography place. Is it on this floor?"

She was wearing baggy trousers made of brightly colored cloth and was decked out in her finest costume jewelry. Her facial foundation was two millimeters thick, and she wore cyclamen-colored lipstick that complemented her dusky skin. She appeared to be in her mid-forties, and despite her weight, the heat didn't seem to bother her.

"This floor. That blue door."

The woman's hazel eyes quickly scanned my no-nonsense pants and the matching shirt, haircut, and facial expression that identified my type.

"Is it true what the advertisement says? It was as small as a stamp, and I only came upon it by chance. Billions of photographs. Is their archive really that big?"

The look on her face showed that she would base her decision on my reply.

"In a word, amazing," I said, with a smile like the one that I figured would be very valuable in 209 years' time.

The woman's eyes were alight with joy. "Just as I thought," she said. "Have a great day."

"Have a nice day," I said as I opened the elevator door. When I arrived home, I didn't plan to say a word about what had happened here. My wife knew me well. If I repeated it insistently, she would believe every word, but I would keep this secret to myself. Perhaps when my son turned fifteen, I would let them both in on it. I had rented a fixed compartment in one of the vast time tunnels. For ten lira, on top of that.

When I reached what's thought of as "daily life" outside, I paused briefly to observe the struggling crowd. Oblivious to the amazing place on the third floor, people rushed back and forth, and, as the sun rose toward its highest point, so did the heat rise. With the back of my neck burning, I walked over to where I had parked. A black Opel had pulled to the right beside my car, and I would have a hard time backing out. In vain, I looked around for its owner, but just as I was about to shout a nasty curse, I felt something in my mind suddenly flash. My present ecstasy, with its high spiritual charge and powerful desire to renew my life, wouldn't even last six months. I would remain stuck firmly in the rut of my old order. Life somehow worked that way, with those closest to the center of action being ground down like freshly roasted coffee beans.

It was as small as a stamp, and I only came upon it by chance.

As I opened the car door, my mind again shifted to a higher gear. I had come upon the advertisement for the Photographer of the Other Realm while surfing the Internet. That plump woman had most likely seen it in the newspaper. I realized that advertisement was everywhere, even in the air we breathed. That meant that everyone knew. Everyone. No one was privileged. All humans have a past with such a memory compartment, a precious smile to help them put up with life, which could sometimes be so very cruel, dreary, and drab so as to become unbearable.

July 2009 Çeşme

THE ROOT

Serpil Ülger

Translated by Erdem Gürsu

It was walking alone in the middle of the steppe as the first rays of the day formed orange lines on the horizon. The once vast plain was now covered with metal heaps of human debris thrown around recklessly. Artificiality had obviously brought death. It cut off the unruly wind like a barrier and polluted the fertile spirit of the soil. So much so that the air no longer felt as clean and peaceful as it used to, and the sky no longer gave freedom.

"Altay, where have you disappeared to?" they muttered to themselves.

The traces of the past were in *its* mind as if it was only yesterday, but, unfortunately, *its* eyes were on the present. But the seed of hope was always there, if you knew how to plant it...

"Leave your mind, let go of your heart, child. On the way to Altındağ, leave your soul and go. After all, you came from Altay; it will protect you at any rate when you reach the holy foot of the mountain and beg for mercy on your people. Altay will hear you, even if you are at your last breath..."

The great shaman's last words from the past were a whisper both in its mind and tongue. *It* had a job to finish, and *it* had to keep going no matter what. *It* gripped the reins tightly around *its* hands and pulled with all *its* might, even though *its* fingers hurt and *its* arms were out of strength. Over and over again... For one last life to be saved, for one last journey to go, *it* pulled Ayzıt, the horse, or what was left of it. *It* tried to console *itself* but fell to *its* knees. *Its* eyes were filled with involuntary tears.

It looked at *its* sore hands; *its* skin was worn out. Ayzıt's synthetic fabric had already been torn, and *its* metal had rusted. Undoubtedly, *it* was now expired, naturally discarded. *It* had no idea how long *it* had been like this. Loneliness clouded *its* mind, making *it* doubtful. Without Ayzıt, it would not have been possible for *it* to come this far or even to resist everything that had happened. Undoubtedly, from the very first day, *its* fate with Ayzıt and their destinies were entwined with each other. *It* carried *Ayzıt's* soul in *its* own soul and felt Ayzıt's pain. *It* knew the desires of *its* horse to run like the wind on the steppe. *It* saw the traces of Altay on *its* sunless snow-white skin and always showed respect to it. Because, in these lands, the power came from the horse, which would choose its comrade, glorify, and lead *it* to Altındağ. Unfortunately, even though the spirit of the land had died and withered away long ago, that belief was *its* only reality to hold on to, and it was *its* last hope.

"Hold on a little longer, my Ayzıt, a little longer," *it* said, stroking *its* comrade's long mane. *Its* metal fingers touched Ayzıt, whose cold body saddened *its* face. The beautiful neck of *its* horse was stolen little by little, and its mane was bestowed upon *it* as a sign of human magnanimity. After all, humanity required *a gesture of goodwill.*

Humanity!

Where was their so-called humanity hidden in this genocide?

Ayzıt opened its eyes as if sensing *its* anger. Even this slightest movement made its muscles tense as if there was something painful. Disgusted to see it like this, *it* tried to clear *its* dry throat as *it* hid *its* feelings behind this act. "You'd better drink water, my comrade," *it* mumbled. Realizing this, *it* smiled helplessly. As if there was anything else to do... *It* took *its* eyes off *its* comrade's suffering face and turned to the canteen bottle hanging from *its* waist. It was almost empty. Ayzıt drank the few drops that remained inside. Then *it* stood up, straining *its* weak legs. Ignoring the dead soil and the flying dust, *it* put the reins around *its* hands again. When two of them were ready to continue, *it* muttered cheerfully, "Come on, Ayzıt, we've reached the end of the road." But, at the same time, the words *"Don't die, Ayzıt, please, don't die..."* were echoing in *its* mind.

***

But, as they began to walk, and every time Mergen pulled the strap, a memory clung to her arms and summoned cold reality. In the first second, there was nothing but cold. In the next second, time seized Mergen, and in the third, time swallowed them... Only darkness remained behind, which was the absolute mirror of reality. One step and one more step... Mergen was nothing but a rotten soul sinking as she struggled. She had lost Altay, she had lost her homeland, she had lost her home, and most gravely, she had lost her essence. As the desolation spread to all her cells, time, moving backwards, flowed into a moment covered with dark clouds and opened a way to the lost Mergen.

The first thing she saw was her flaming tribe covered with smoke reaching the sky. Whatever Mergen did, she could not escape this end. When her father died, and she had to take over the tribe at a young age, she put aside her mourning and accepted her responsibilities. She worked hard for her people. But in essence, she was just a child – how could she know that one becomes a prisoner of one's ambitions while getting older… The notables of her people, who coveted beyond what should be, provoked the other people against Mergen. Well, it was easy to prevail when the enemy was a child, and that's what happened.

Since it is inevitable for a soul that has strayed from Altay to atrophy and attract disasters one by one, the air got a little more polluted every day and gradually became unbreathable. The tribe had to contend with famine and then disease, and that was all that was needed, sadly, for a child to rebel.

There was almost nothing left from the tribe, which had turned to ash by the morning. On top of that, people were abandoning her and migrating westward. Although she resisted, Mergen could not stop the people. She couldn't blame anyone… Despite the dark clouds, steam, and dirty artificiality, the dream of the West was undeniably delicious, and it must be admitted that its standards were an invaluable fortune compared to the barrenness of the steppe.

With the wish of the great shaman and the responsibility given to her by her understanding of holiness, Mergen jumped on Ayzıt's back and went after her people. The people descended from the mountains like an avalanche, passed through the plains like water, and went on day and night… But the only thing that found them was brutality. Even though they were born warriors, they could not escape the blackened hearts of blind souls, and so they were enslaved by them. …And then Mergen was all alone. She had been bought and sold and used a lot. Eventually, she became pale and was left in a slaughterhouse. Now there was neither night nor day in her upside-down existence. Time had gone, leaving a rust-smelling, old darkness in its place. Her fuzzy mind was overflowing with everything in that timelessness, and she struggled to hang onto any crumb. Whether a poem, a lullaby, or even a prayer, Mergen hung on to it.

"… *Beg for mercy for your people. Altay will hear you, even if you are at your last breath…*"

Passing by, the android worker of the slaughterhouse heard Mergen's whisper. At first, *it* didn't care. Another time, *it* ignored the whisper but then realized that *it* couldn't understand the words. The second thing *it* noticed was the consciousness feature, which was blocked in *its* software, and then *it* remembered. *It* had been a prestigious robot some time ago, working on human archetypes and moral evolution. *It* must have been deemed worthless when *its* version had been getting old, and *its* body began to rust, so *it* had finally been sent to this slaughterhouse. Now *its* only task was to pack cheap meat into supermarkets, a new type of hunting for humans. What could be more ethical than paying for a beautifully labelled product lined up in rows? If you don't see all the things as a whole, or if you don't know the environment you live in and you can't even imagine it, what could be more natural than eating one of your own species?

Yes, they called it *humanity*. They called it humanity that the strong consumed the weak gradually, without giving them any chance.

With these thoughts and awakenings, the slaughterhouse worker's mind became quite clouded, and one day *it* understood a murmuring sentence.

"*Altay will hear you.*"

It got stuck where *it* was. Something inside *it* was fluttering uncontrollably. *It* wanted to cry and laugh at the same time, but *it* was just an android. If *it* didn't know what *it* was, *it* could have called this thing that was awakening a soul. Then what was this? What made *it* so excited? *Altay*… This was the word that woke *it* from this drowsiness. Whatever Altay meant, *it* had to learn. *It* rushed over to the woman in the dark, creaking *its* rusty knees.

Mergen got used to these strange creatures in the new world. It was not them who were cruel but those who made them so. Even though Mergen couldn't make out *its* face because of her upside-down position, she chose to smile at *it*. After all, it was a steppe tradition to go to *Death* laughing. But things didn't go as she had anticipated. This strange creature covered in dirt was asking Mergen about Altay. Since she was unable to comprehend all, *it* just nodded in agreement when Mergen repeated the words.

"Altay… It is Altındağ itself. The homeland of souls, the essence of our existence. It is the only way to Tengri[1]. The holy foot of that mountain is the only place of forgiveness, of purification," muttered Mergen in a broken voice.

But these words were not enough for the artificial intelligence in front of *it*.

"Can't you show me?"

"It is everything. You, me, anyone else… Inside and outside, it is connected to everything and is independent of everything at the same time."

"Me?" the slaughterhouse worker, acutely aware of *its* artificiality, asked.

---

[1] Tengri means God in old Turkic mythology.

"Why not you?" Mergen replied.

"I can't understand," said the slaughterhouse worker.

"Do you think that you would be standing here and asking me about it if you weren't involved?"

This question shook *it* deeply because, even though *it* was artificial, *it* was conscious. So, would that make *it* a human being, too? But *it* wasn't, and *it* knew that very well.

"Do you know what I am?" *it* asked the human hanging upside down.

Mergen smiled bitterly. "A soul like me lost in the search."

"No, no, it is not like that. You are human, and I... I am... just a machine. A pile of scrap..."

"Tell me, what is the difference between you and me right now? You think like me, look like me, suffer like me, and grow old and die like me. So, what makes you different from being human?"

"Nothing." It was a simple but comprehensive answer.

The slaughterhouse worker, who had found the mirror of reality, moved away from this woman to digest what they had said. *It* even escaped from there as fast as *it* could. However, every escape had a beginning, a catch, and a defeat in and of *itself*. That's what happened. Days later, the slaughterhouse worker went back to the cooler, where *it* had previously escaped from, to meet the woman again.

"I wanted to apologize for not meeting formally."

Ending their muttering, Mergen opened her eyes and replied. "This might be the best sentence I've heard in a long time."

"My name is G19s7e5."

"What kind of name is that?"

It faltered while trying to answer because no one had ever asked such a question before. "Well, this is what my serial code says. So, it's not a real name."

"Do you know, in my homeland, when people commit acts of bravery, they earn their own name? What could be more honourable than earning your own name?"

"So, I can choose a name for myself?"

"If you show great fighting skills, you can earn yourself a name."

G19s7e5 smiled as it pointed around. "Great fighting, huh, in here?"

"Yes, right here... Destroy this place, and I will gladly give you my name."

"What?"

"Take home the last of my people, my horse Ayzıt... Take it to Altay."

"It's just a horse."

"You're just a robot, and I'm just a human... But no human or even living creature deserves what's going on here! One should be grateful for what they receive from nature. You can't take them all at once; it would result in a devastating outcome."

Stunned, *it* looked at the woman, or what was left of her, who had been slowly disintegrated for her beauty, who had become a delicious link in the food chain due to her species.

"The slaughter of nature, animals, ultimately humans, even us androids... Everything is dead. Well, for what reason?" While saying this, the G19s7e5 realized that, for the first time since *it* had been designed, *it* had made a friend. So much so that this woman did not define *it* as artificial like the others and even considered *it* an equal to herself. As if that wasn't enough, she was giving her name and her true self to *it*.

"It is permissible for the soul that has strayed from Altay to suffer disaster."

The soul that has strayed from Altay...

The soul...

***

Falling to the ground with a rein slipping from her hand, G19s7e5 returned to the dusty time they were in. There was the frost of the wind and the dust of the barren land on *its* face. But, in *its* mind, there was the existence of *its* first and only friend Mergen, who ended her life by giving her soul to *it* in that dark slaughterhouse, and the promise *it* gave... G19s7e5 would take Ayzıt home to Altay to find *its* true self.

Besides, there was very little time left to reach the foot of the mountain.

G19s7e5 was barely able to open *its* rusty knees hidden under synthetic leather and stood up and set off again. It wasn't long before a numbness spread slowly through *its* body, which caused *it* to fall down again. When G19s7e5 barely lifted *its* head, a strange light was coming down from the top of the mountain as a kind of invitation.

Altay...

"I brought you home, Ayzıt," G19s7e5 whispered, and *it* could hardly turn *its* head towards Ayzıt, who had already passed away from this world. The same situation was beginning to happen for G19s7e5, whose systems were slowly shutting down, leaving *it* numb. Yet, *it* resisted and, until the very last moment, *its* mind and tongue did not stop chanting the lullaby Mergen had whispered to *it*:

"Leave your mind, let go of your heart, child. On the way to Altındağ, leave your soul and go. After all, you came from it; it will protect you anyway; when you reach the holy foot of the mountain, beg for mercy for your people. Altay will hear you, even if you are at your last breath..."

Far from the Steppe, in a laboratory, two men in white coats were staring at the red signal on the computer screen. They had been watching G19s7e5 for weeks, curiously observing where *it* would arrive.

"Where exactly is *it* standing?" the man, who suddenly got up from his seat and couldn't believe what he saw, asked.

The other one said, "A mountain in a garbage heap; it's called Altay." He just wanted to fill his stomach, but not with a cup of coffee. "Did you turn off the systems of G19s7e5? I don't want to be late for lunch. The food is getting worse with each passing day."

"Yes, I did. I can't believe the people at the top didn't destroy G19s7e5 because of all the damage *it* caused. That crazy robot almost blew up the whole city."

"Oh, my God! I also can't believe that a rusty scrap is the only reason we haven't been able to eat something good since then. It must be a bad joke – they're going to put it in the museum's natural history collection!"

"It's so ironic, but, anyway, you know, these people at the top are crazy. We'd better get our frozen vegetables without questioning it anymore."

As the two of them left the room with an insatiable blindness, at the other end of the world, right in the middle of the steppe, G19s7e5 was peacefully responding to Altay's embrace. *It* was happy because *it* was passing away. *It* was being cleansed of *its* pain. Finally, G19s7e5 gained the name Mergen.

As Mergen's smile froze on her face, her systems mingled with the light, and she bade her final farewell.

As her presence slowly mingled with Altay and dispersed like a breeze over the entire universe, Mergen reached Tengri.

BUG FIELDS

written and drawn by Sezai Özden

SOMEWHERE WITHIN THE A-18-1 UNIVERSE

THE JUDGES, WHO SEEK THE ORGANIZATION THAT CONTROLS INTERUNIVERSAL HUMAN TRAFFICKCING, ARE VERY CLOSE TO GETTING THEM. THE PLANET THEY HAVE REACHED IS THE SOURCE OF THE LAST SIGNALS FROM MISSING JUDGE AIA.

THE JUDGES, WHO ARE ASSESSING SIGNALS THINK THAT THEY ARE ON THE CORRECT TRACK.

LET'S START WITHOUT DELAY

HERE WE ARE!

DO YOU THINK WE HAVE A CHANCE TO FIND OF AIA?

IT IS HARD TO GIVE AN OPTIMISTIC ANSWER...

AIA WAS YOUNG, BUT HE WASN'T AN INEXPERIENCED JUDGE. I DON'T KNOW HOW HE MADE A MISTAKE LIKE THIS! THE LAST IMAGES ARE RUBBISH AND THE COORDINATES ARE UNCLEAR.

WE DON'T KNOW HOW TO IMPROVE THE PHOTOS ABOUT THIS UNKNOWN CIVILIZATION.
WE NEED MORE DETAILS BUT AIA HAS BEEN VERY SECRETIVE WITH INFORMATION. THE GATES MAY HAVE MORE MYSTERIES THAN WE KNOW. TIME WILL SHOW THAT TO US

WE NEED MUCH MORE.

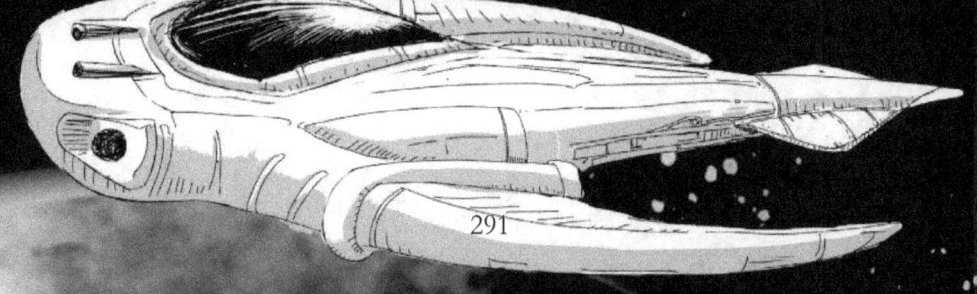

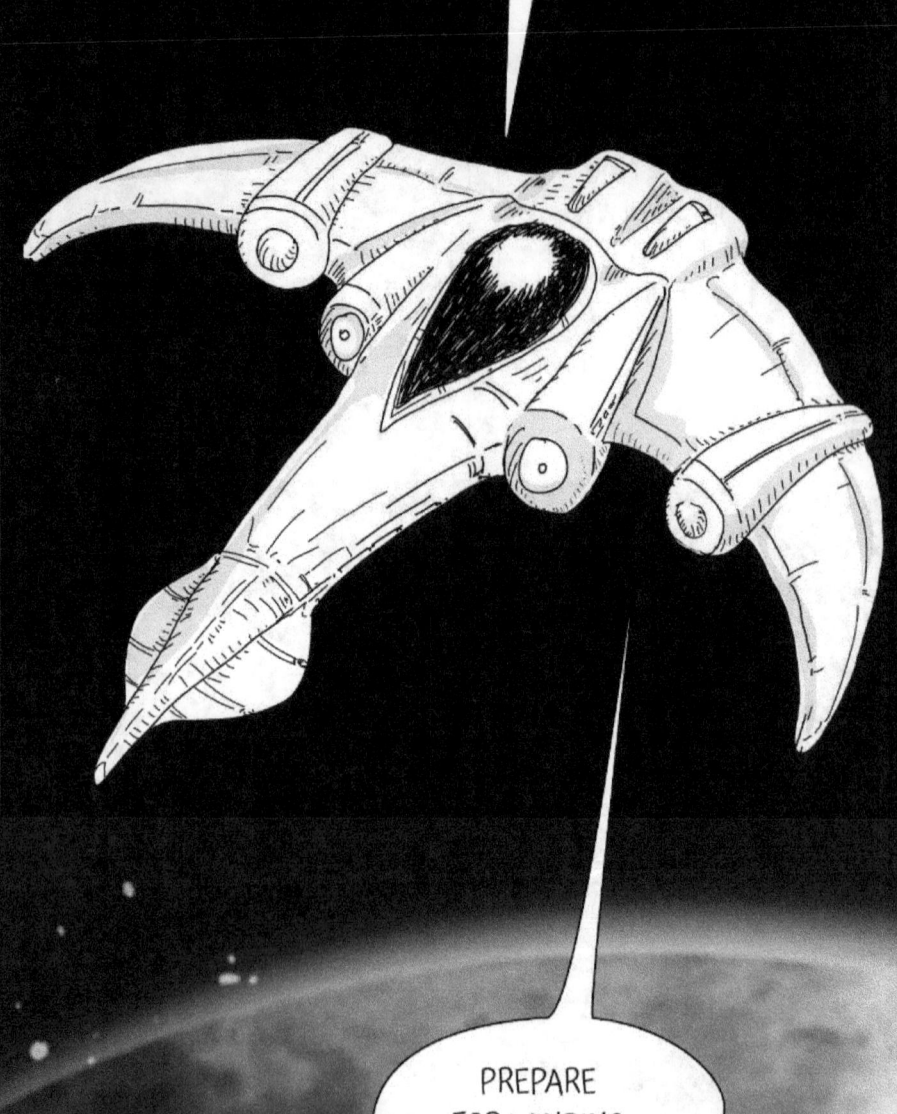

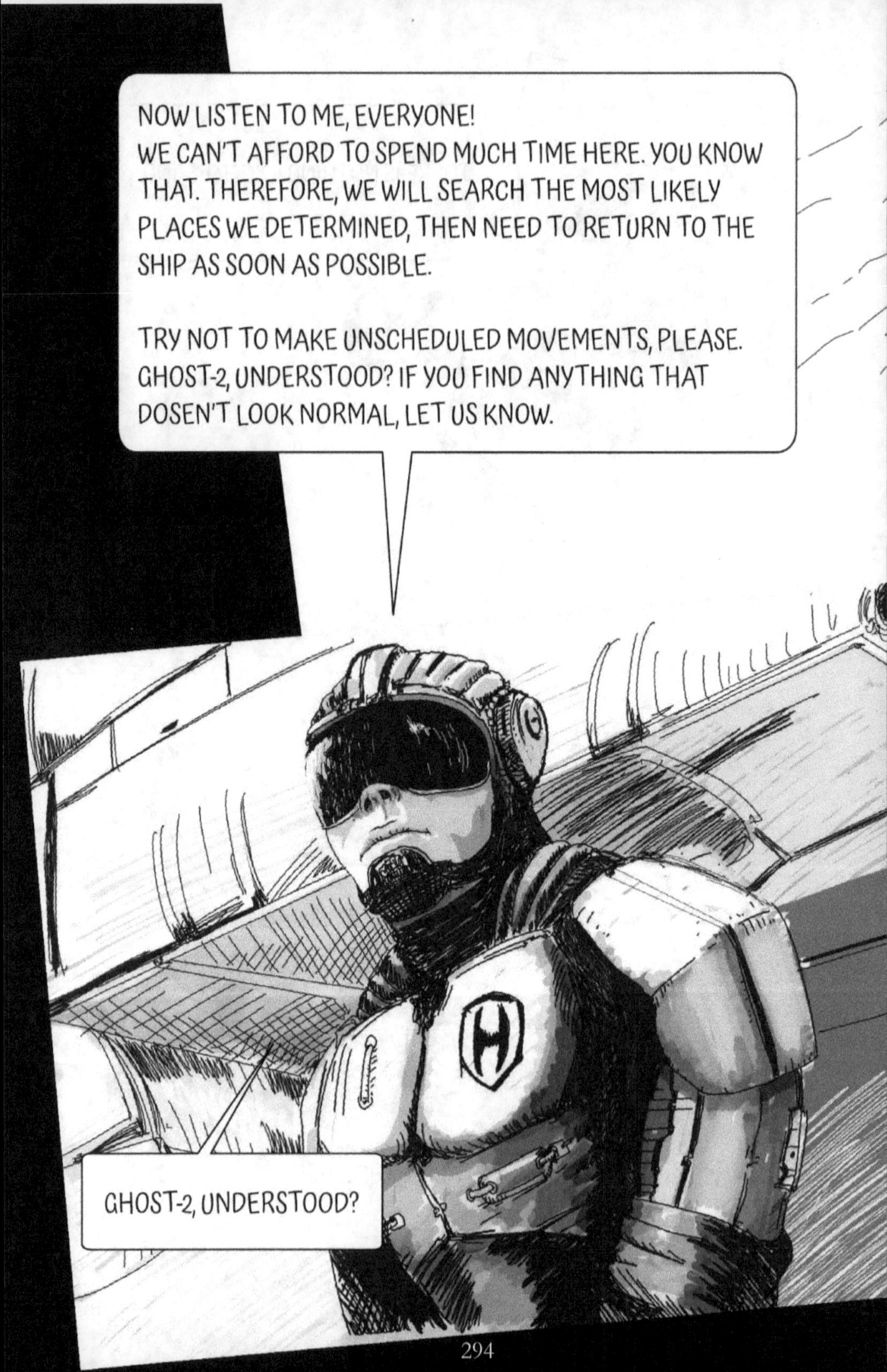

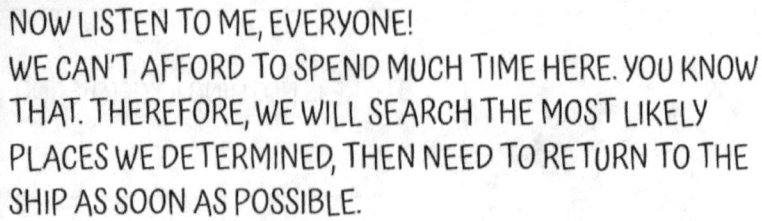

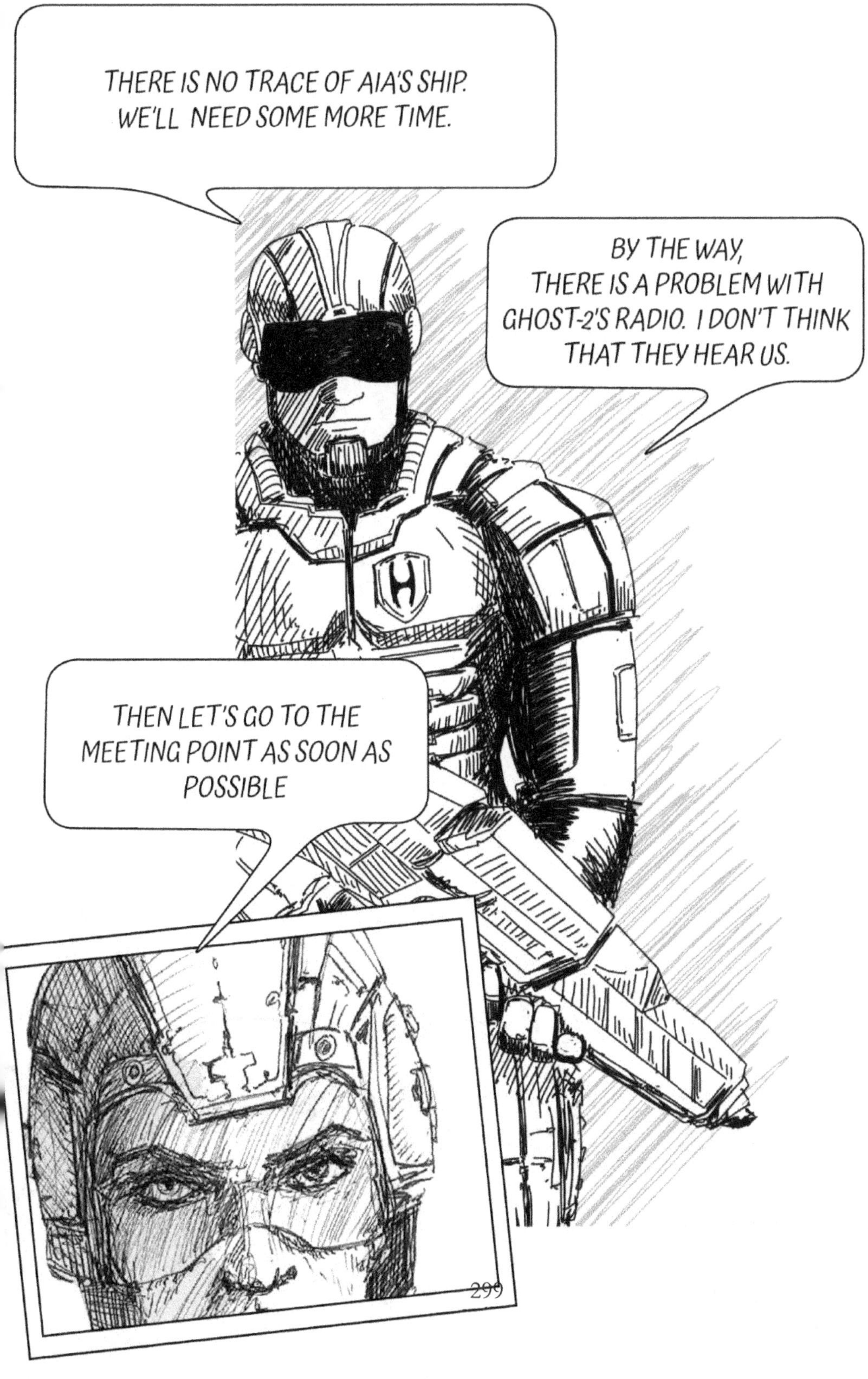

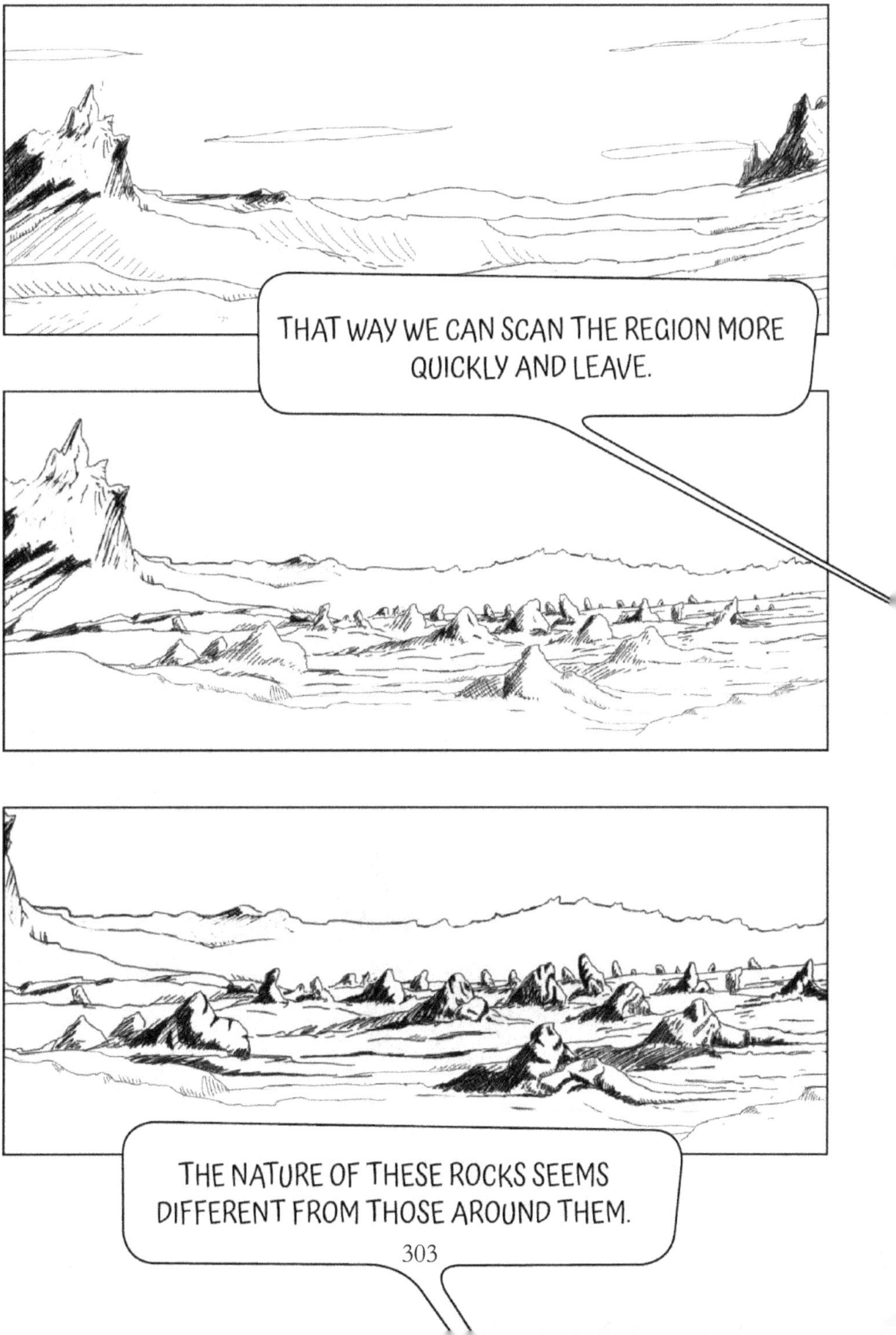

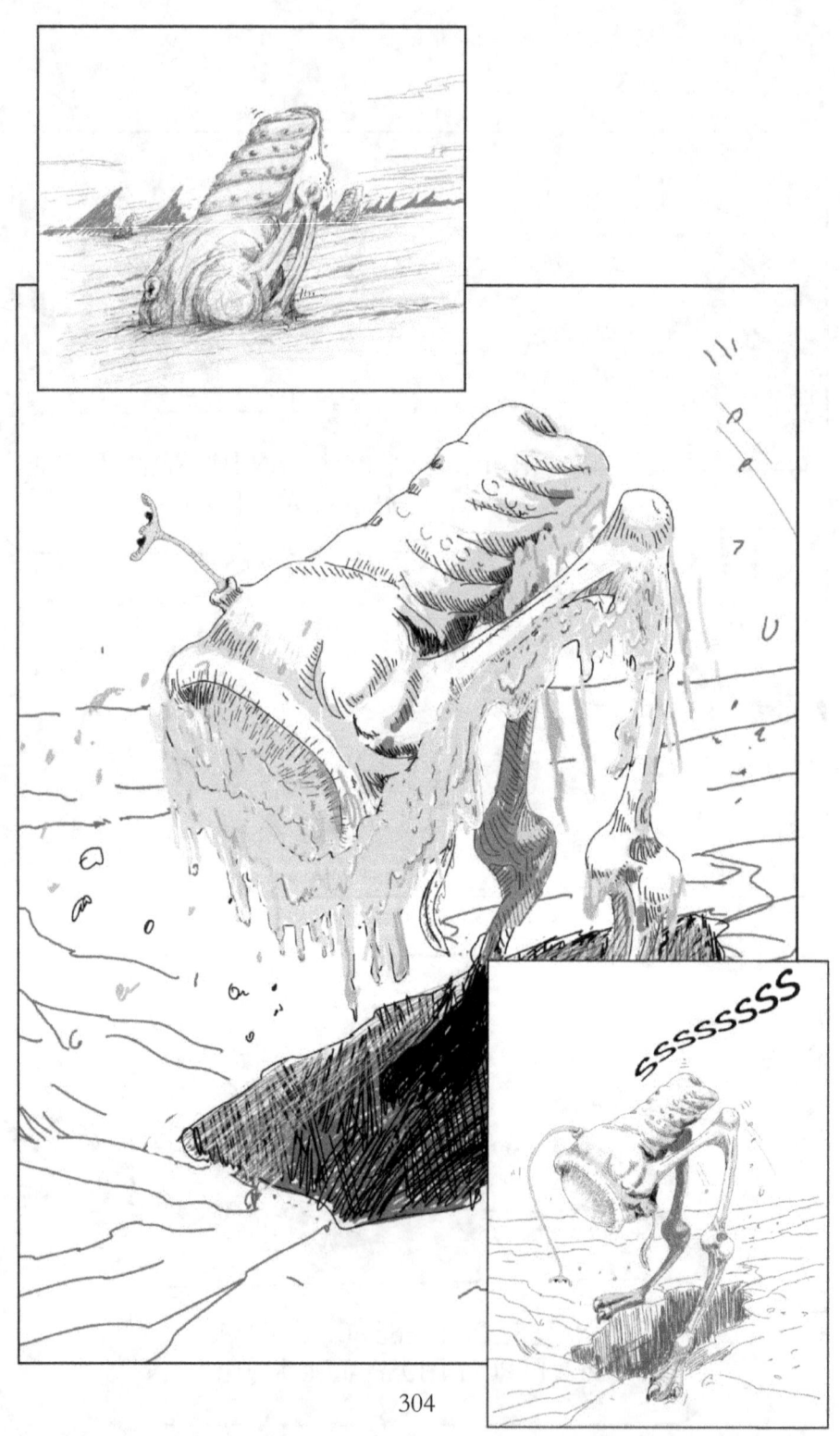

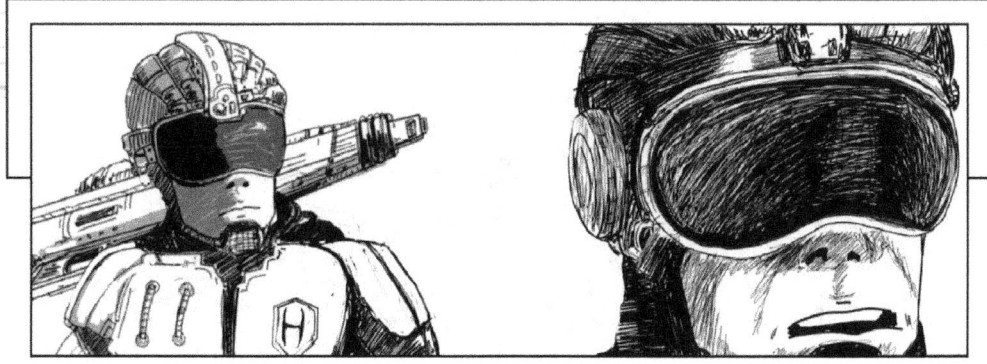

YOU'RE PERMITTED TO SPEAK WHILE YOU'RE WALKING.

"WHY AREN'T YOU TALKING?"

"WHAT THE HELL ??"

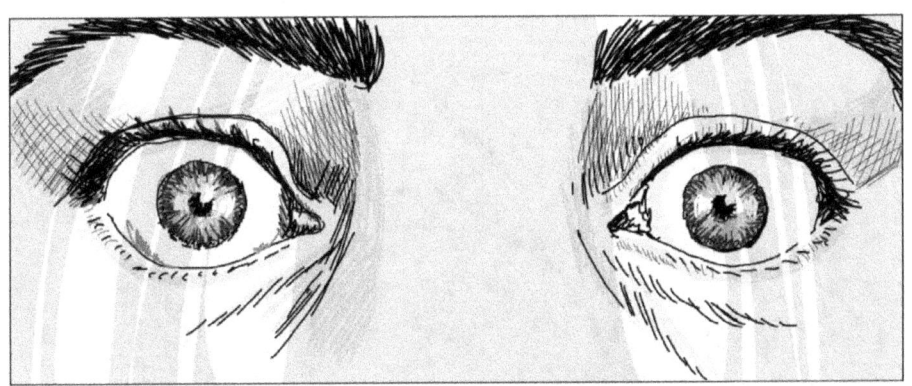

"HEY! WALK AWAY FROM THAT!"

"I CAN'T MOVE. HELP ME!"

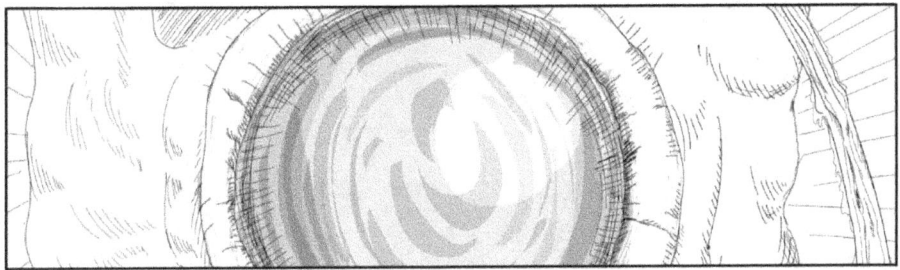

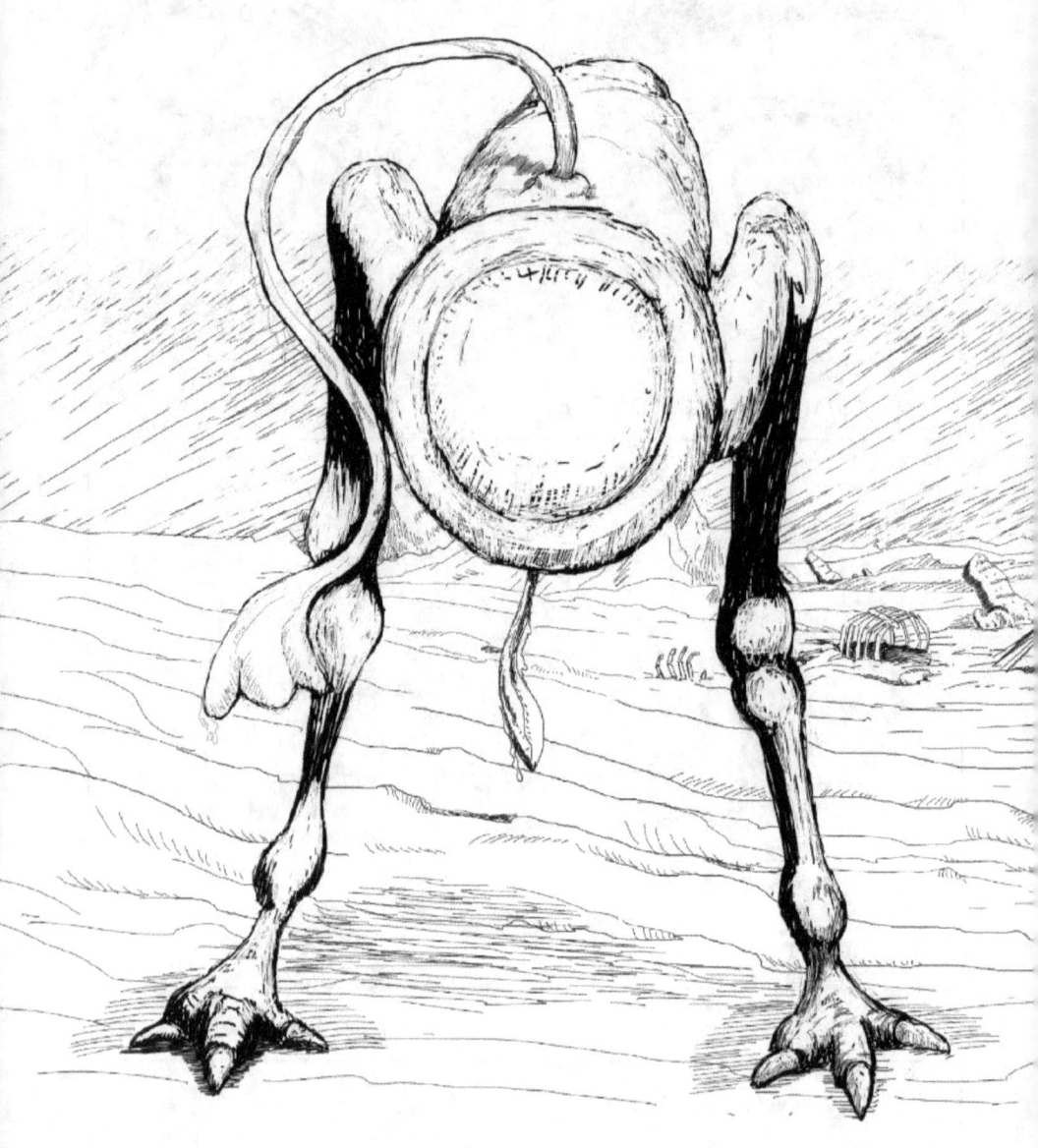

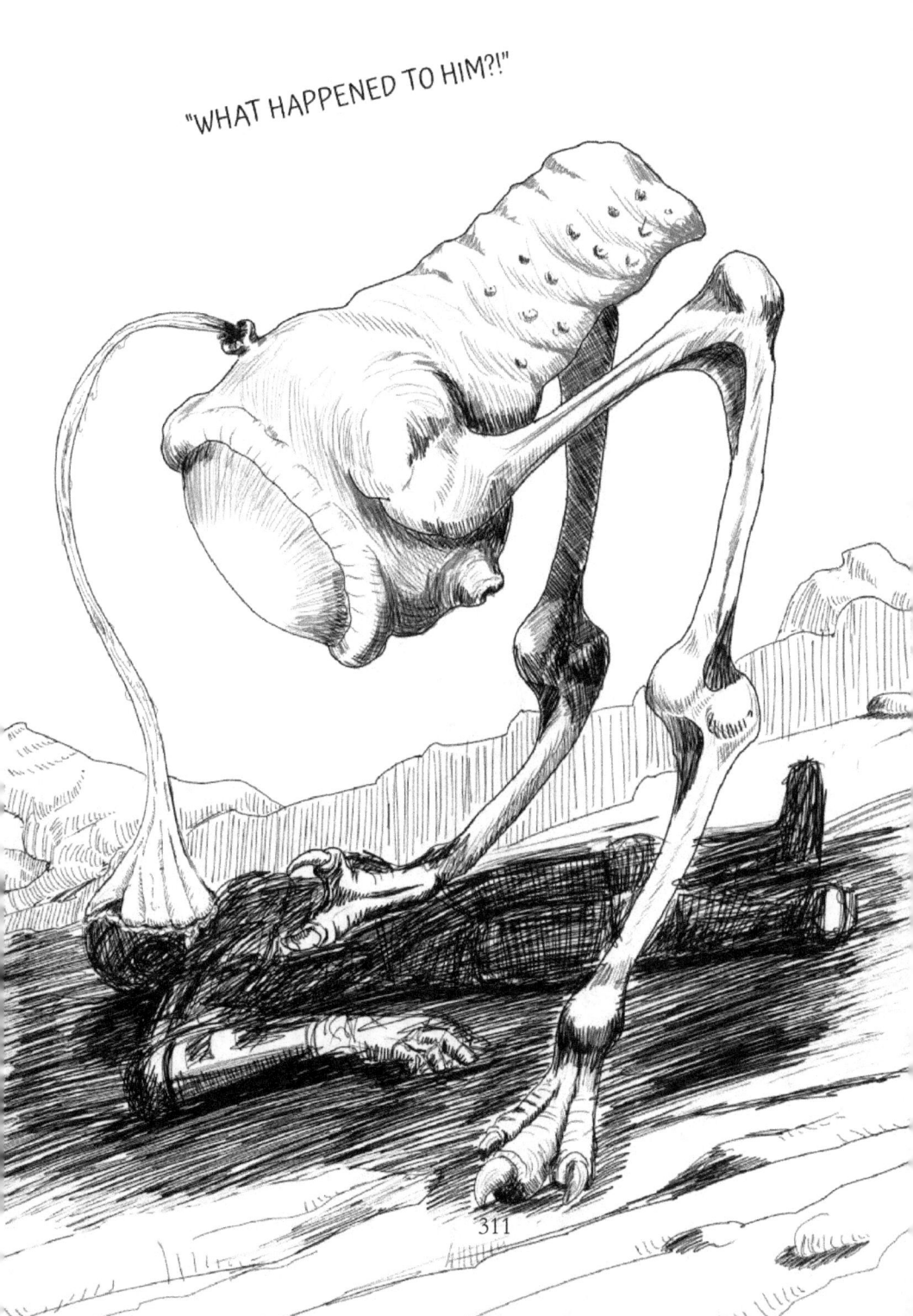

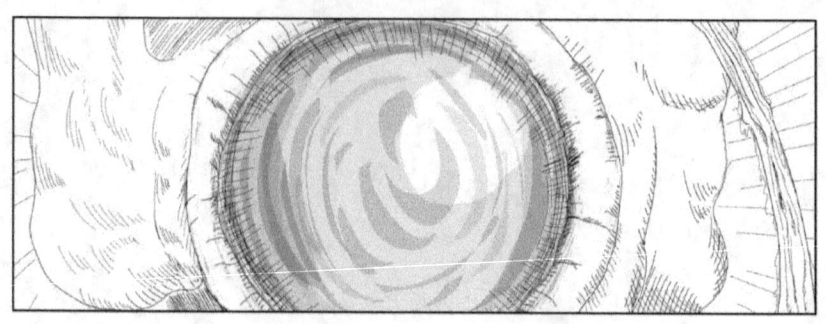

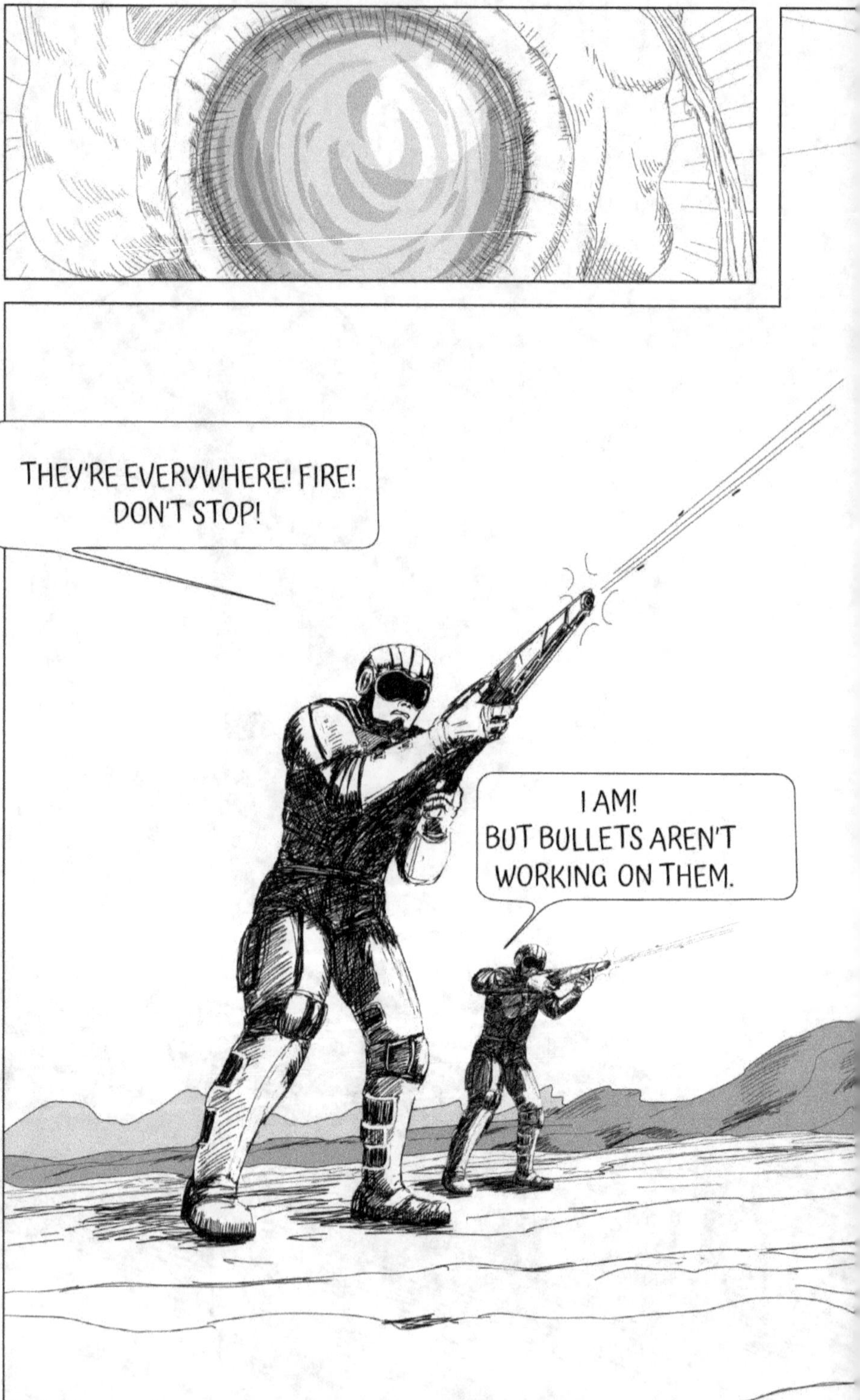

"WE DETECTED AN INCREASE IN SIGNALS FROM THE AREA."

"...BUT IT ALWAYS RESETS. THERE IS SOMETHING MOVING THAT IS VERY CLOSE TO YOU. GHOST-1, BEWARE!"

"BY THE WAY, WE HAVE GOOD NEWS FOR YOU!"

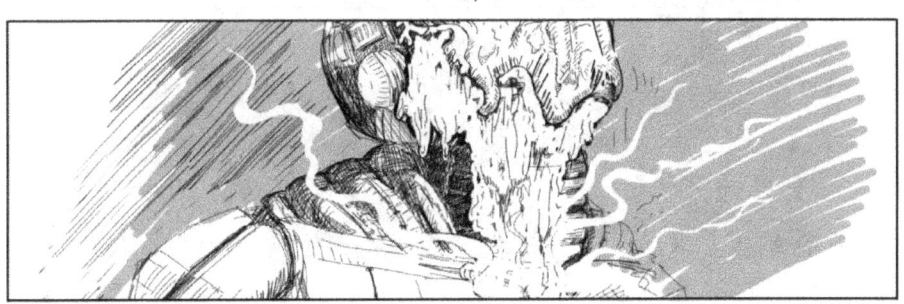

THE SIGNALS THAT BELONG TO AIA'S SHIP ARE COMING FROM YOUR CURRENT AREA.

THE END

This story is adapted from Sezai Özden's science fiction novel, "Sentromer: The Others."

COGITO

Tevfik Uyar

He imagined the courtroom would be a spacious hall, but it wasn't like that at all. It was a place as large as his living room and elevated a bit on one side, where a high podium had been positioned. That's where the judges and prosecutors sat. On the lower side was an old wooden railing that was worn down in various places. That's where he was placed during the hearing. Next to him was another row where his attorney sat. The space behind that was allocated for the absent crowds – where about twenty to thirty chairs were stacked like sardines, one atop the other.

The hearing to which he was summoned as the accused and dragged into as a convict sentenced for death lasted no more than 15 minutes. There were a few details he remembered; as he stood in front of the wooden railing, the bailiff gestured for him to cross his arms. So, he idly stood there like a convict. He barely remembered his sentence being read off, but he remembered turning and looking at his attorney at that point: she had only raised her slim eyebrows and leaned her head to one side. That was it. While the authorities transported him back to prison, he tried to figure out whether what had transpired in the courtroom was a dream or not. Was destroying a body supposed to be this simple? He supposed it was.

The moment they arrived at the nearby prison, they said his attorney was waiting for him in the visiting room. The court-appointed attorney had her legs crossed one atop the other, and her hands clasped in her lap, waiting for him with an empty notebook in front of her. The wardens showed him the chair across from her as if he wasn't going to see it on his own.

Straightening up, the first thing the attorney said was, "Believe me; I did everything I could..." What did she do in that brief hearing? Did she do something that he hadn't recognized?

"... but they pass down death sentences more easily these days," she added. "Anyways, it's not a real death..."

The man muttered inwardly, "Whadya mean, it's not a real death?" Without realizing it, he gave an outwardly sarcastic laugh. "So, if this means it's not a real death... what is living? Is it just being aware of one's existence?"

The attorney leaned over to the table as if she was going to say something confidential.

"What did Descartes once say? 'I think, therefore I am.' A real death can't happen as long as existence continues. You are going to continue to think. In fact, to speak... You'll still even be able to communicate with your loved ones. You'll be able to follow what is going on in the world and watch the news. You'll be able to do a lot of things that a living person does. What more do you want? Would you prefer it if you were given life in prison and stuffed behind bars?"

The man pondered this. So, the woman thought that communicating only meant speaking. Hugging the one you loved, holding his/her hand, patting the back of someone you felt proud of, shaking a hand with the feeling of gratitude while thanking someone... Either she didn't count these as communicating, or she was trying to console him.

The man said, leaning back, "You know, we can trade places if this is such a thing to be desired." He reached over and took a cigarette from the pack sitting on the attorney's table. He lit the end with her slim lighter. "I'm not going to smoke cigarettes," as he exhaled. "I'm not going to eat food... I'm not going to grab a chicken leg by the bone. I'm not going to sweat while making love…" he added.

"Well, it is what it is… You've been convicted of murder. The man whose life you took isn't going to be able to do any of that anymore. You also condemned him to the cloud… so, it's tit for tat."

Yes, he had murdered… Killing someone had gotten that much easier too. But getting caught and getting away with it had become impossible as the victim was also the eyewitness.

Okay, so what if he had defended himself, claiming, "Whatever the case, it is not a real death"? Would it have done any good? The slain party had only suffered a physical death. His entire consciousness is in a central database. Perhaps he is currently having a conversation with his wife.

"In fact, his family's going to appeal this decision immediately. You're in the same boat as the man you killed. I'm telling you, know what it's worth. Besides… It's not all about retaliation. Basically, this is a way to stop those who commit murder from causing more harm to society. That's how modern legislation works. I mean, it suits a purpose… whether you like it or not."

"Whose side are you on anyway, Ms. attorney?" asked the man. He squinted and drew another puff from the cigarette.

"I'm just telling it like it is."

"Okay, so what's the work sentence? They are going to have a dead man work, huh?"

"Well… That's what makes you different from the victim. You're going to replace an electronic processor four hours a day."

"I beg your pardon?"

"Seriously… I mean, you're going to make your mind work. For instance, the circuit that controls the doors here."

"Say what?"

"Well, whenever someone presses the button that opens or shuts the door, you'll be doing it instead of a computer. The command to open that door will go from your mind."

"That's ridiculous…"

"Hey, I think it's redundant too… And yes, it's ridiculous! Anyways, it's also ridiculous to stick people in a barred room. There's no such thing as a logical sentence. A sentence is not to dish out punishment, but to provide relief to the aggrieved parties or their relatives," said the attorney. She removed her glasses and became more refined. She leaned back and crossed her legs again. She appeared more attractive to the man, who muttered inwardly, "There won't be any women."

"Excuse me?"

"Nothing."

"So, where was I? This is Justice Ministry pragmatism. They ensure that convicts serve society, rendering them useful and averting them from becoming just a pile of data, just a useless mind in the cloud…"

She took one of the cigarettes. The man acted quickly, lighting the woman's cigarette with the slim lighter in his fat fingers.

"Thanks… Anyways, the goal was actually to break you away from your daily freedom for four hours," she said. The smoke blew from her puckered lips in a thin barrel roll. The ventilation system kicked in when the room became smoky. The man was curious if the trigger of ventilation was another convict or not.

"Fine… When am I going to die?"

"Technically speaking, it's not possible for you to die. As it is, you'll already be dead."

"Make up your mind already, my dear attorney. Didn't you say just a bit ago that it wasn't a real death?"

"But it's not a real-life either... A person who can't really live can't really die. What we're talking about is you being deleted. You'll be deleted 30 years later."

The man was 30 years old. He was going to "exist" for another 30 years. But from Descartes's point of view... There'll only be a void, just the feeling of existence... The brain would erect a virtual building by using past experiences because it could not perceive the void as it was... Life continues despite the void.

"Okay, so what about that pimp?"

"Who?... You mean the man you killed?"

"Yes. The man that I really didn't technically kill..." he said, with a smirk on his face.

"What, him? As much as he pleaded. He doesn't need to be deleted. There are also some variations. For instance, he can use additional hardware. He can tap into visual and audio sensors and sense the real world. You are going to spend time by yourself with virtual images in your own imaginary fortress. You'll only be able to communicate with the outside world by writing. That is, additional hardware is forbidden... Besides, why are you competing with the victim? He's the one who's been deprived... You better get used to this idea."

"Fine... Alright...," said the man. He asked, "What if anyone wants to reach me?" There was always such a possibility...

"From your private cloud address. There is an interface at your address. They can leave messages there."

"How am I going to see them?"

"Look here... I'm not an expert on this matter. I've just read things about it from here and there. I don't know how the mind constructs that part. There are those that write as if there was a computer, and there are those that see messages as writing on the wall and communicate with a whitewash brush. I've even heard about paper and pens. This all depends on how your brain is going to interpret the whole so-called external world and make it coherent in a manner that, unfortunately, you won't be able to control. This is all quite new... We're learning about this from the experiences others have shared."

"Okay... Tell me about that work camp again ..."

The court-appointed attorney made it apparent she was exasperated when she let out a long sigh. She was beginning to act impatiently. It was all over; the death sentence was handed down. What else was left to do? She was providing complimentary consultancy… Moreover, she didn't exactly know the answers to her client's questions. Even if she did, she didn't have the motivation to explain.

"There's nothing left to talk about. Basically, it's a draw from a hat… It could be a power station; it could be an irrigation system; in fact, it could be something like a 3-D printer… What else can I say? They'll arrange someplace according to your ability. Let me say again that I did the best I could. It's better than spending 40 years behind bars… Believe me; it's better like this… That's why I wouldn't recommend you appeal the decision. However, you do have three days to file… If you decide to appeal, I'll do whatever's necessary. After all, it is my job…"

***

The man was again escorted to his temporary cell. He was going to have to wait here for his sentence to be executed. They gave him a pile of documents. He was going to sign and return some of them and keep another few for reading.

His execution was scheduled three days later, at six in the morning. According to what he had read, they would connect his body to a machine whereby his mind would be transferred to a device called a "full brain emulator" – a process that would take three and a half hours. The emulator was supposed to produce a mathematical model of his mind, transforming it into a script. Going forward, he would just be that script. While the "absolute death penalty" was forbidden, this sentence didn't count as one. As the attorney had told him, the "Objectives" heading explained everything: "The process of terminating the body's existence, which does not correspond to a real death, is executed in order to prevent the perpetrator from committing potential new crimes." Several other headings followed: Prisoner obligations. Penal institution responsibilities. Facilities to be offered to the prisoner. Prohibitions. Permissions… There was even a separate booklet regarding the work camp, but this wasn't prepared very meticulously because it was not possible to make a detailed description of the work camp, as personal experiences also influenced individual experiences. From what he understood, he would see through experience. He'd learned that he'd only receive a warning if he didn't do what was necessary. But a second warning meant "deletion"…

He spent his first day poring over the booklets. On the second day, he only looked at the booklets when he didn't remember the details. He spent most of the day debating with himself whether the man he'd killed had really deserved to die or not. Then he thought that the man might have acquired visual sensors and that he might want to use the "right to watch the execution" mentioned in the booklets. He shuddered at this thought...

On his last day, he mostly thought about what life was about as he paced back and forth in the courtyard. He didn't speak with anyone. He realized that his feet were very elegant, and he realized it was such a nice feeling to stick his pinky finger in his ear. He scratched the tiny sweet itch on his ass.

What was a body? And what about consciousness? He wondered if he could feel his body. The mind that builds buildings would probably create a body for itself too. This idea put him at ease: he was going to meander through the virtual realm. And, what's more, by experiencing a space built into the depths of his mind. He surmised that perhaps he'd change this space in time, but then he figured the odds were stacked against him: an animation continually flashed in front of his eyes. In this animation, a ballet dancer was spinning around, but it seemed to some of the viewers to be turning to the right and to others to be turning to the left. Someone who saw something one way could no longer see it another way and could not somehow switch perspectives. This meant that things to which the brain attributed meaning could not be altered so easily...

It must also be a total bore to act like the data processing center of a simple machine. How was the brain supposed to interpret one?

As nobody was able to experience anyone else's mind, everything had to be subjective and incomparable. In that case, imagination was important. If he could influence his mind through creativity, then it would be a piece of cake to create his own paradise. Maybe he would be able to create the woman he longed for, and to have her live with him in the royal suite of his huge virtual palace... with all sorts of outfits to boot. His imagination was vast when dealing with this subject. Could he really do such things?

He wasn't particularly ecstatic that he was going to be executed but, if this was a punishment, it shouldn't be something as good as that. It most certainly had to be something that hindered stuff he imagined or thought. Otherwise, everyone would volunteer to leave their bodies... Yet... perhaps it was as he had once seen it in four or five news sources... It referred to a concept called "Real Virtuality" that emerged in the mid-20th century. Although it had caught his attention at first, he quickly got bored because he didn't understand the terminology. He had never wondered about it since. He sure did act indifferent towards the new habits of the age. He regretted it and was aware that ignorance was certainly not bliss.

He said, "Whatever," out loud, as if there was someone else with him in solitary confinement. He looked around him and thought, "I guess the fortress in my mind will be larger than here." He fell into a slumber, mumbling, "We'll see what happens."

***

In the morning, a priest and two officials sauntered through the ward and came to a halt in front of his iron bars. The door opened with a clang as two guards flanked him and escorted him out to the transfer ward. His fears went unfounded when he noticed that the slain party and his relatives didn't come to watch the proceedings, but the attractive attorney was obliged to be there again. This time, she wore trousers with a high waist instead of a skirt. Her waist was embellished with an elegant belt. She came up to the man with a bitter smile.

"Are you ready?"

"Yes, if you're going to be there…"

He said this with the comfort that he was going to die soon. Pretending not to hear, the attorney came up to him and whispered, "Your dying wish must be something physical. They'll ask you this shortly. If you've never thought about it, think it over now," she cautioned him.

What was up with the physical request? The man laughed. Nothing came to mind when they sat him on the stretcher. Maybe he should've ordered a taco? Or maybe some cheesecake? Do they even bring around things like that?

The executioner with the white coat asked, "Do you have a final request?" He was most probably a physician or an engineer. It seemed like the executioners had also changed with the times.

The man said, "A cigarette, please." It was possibly the one thing he'd miss more than a taco. "Oh, yes, and could you scratch my back and also tickle my belly, please?"

The executioner slash physician and the officials looked at each other. The physician gestured to the officials with his eyelids. They held and lit a cigarette for the man, then one official tickled him as he rolled up in the fetal position to protect himself. Afterward, the other officer got behind and gave him a thorough back-scratching.

"Thank you very much, friends…" he said in an entranced state. Then the priest arrived… He began his sermon with, "Everybody shall turn to dust."

He most likely didn't know anything pompous about the consciousness. Like the executioners, these guys also needed to be updated…

Someone said, "Then let's get on with this." The decision was read off, as per protocol. The secretaries had scrawled some stuff on pieces of paper. They had the man sign them as he held a "real pen" for the last time.

He was placed and strapped into a sliding stretcher. After shooting a needle into his arm, they stuck his upper torso fully into the brain emulator tunnel. Buttons and keys were activated on the adjacent panel. While his entire existence was being turned into ones and zeroes, a hearse pulled up to the rear door of the building to haul away his corpse.

His feet were really quite elegant indeed.

THE JUNKMAN

Uğur Aydın

Translated by Şeref Kaplan

Day 1

Mrs. A. left home to go to work, as she always does. The vehicle that would serve her had come out of the underground and was waiting by the side of the road. When Mrs. A. got in, the vehicle started. Looking back from the screen, she saw her Benlik[1] waving to her from the curbside, and she smiled. While she was going to work, her Benlik always went in the opposite direction to do sports to keep her fit.

Day 2

This time, Mrs. A. left home to exercise in person. Her Benlik moved with the vehicle instead but did not look back at the screen. Mrs. A. still waved, looking towards herself. She turned around and began her daily walk, but she laughed to herself and thought, *"I need to get an upgraded Benlik."*

She knew this was amusingly futile, though, since all Benliks were produced with only minor differences in nature and managed via a single command center. Only a few minor features separate companies whose service quality remains consistently high from one another.

Day 5, Afternoon

Mr. E. was a trainer. He left the training center and got into the car in front of the door, and drove away towards the library. His Benlik was nonreactive and simply watched him moving away. The Benlik went back inside the training center to continue another lesson. These Benliks were providing wonderful *dual-life* examples for their users.

Day 20

Mrs. A. and her Benlik left the house together. Two cars were waiting at the gate. Mrs. A. got into the vehicle and left the house to go to work. Her

---

[1] Benlik: It is a Turkish word that means the self-existence of a person. In this story, the word Benlik means "a second copy supported by artificial intelligence made available to people in social life."

Benlik got into the other vehicle but did not yet move. She was waiting. Two small children came out of the house and got into the vehicle operated by the Benlik. The children were real because the system prevented using a "Benlik" for any children younger than twenty-five. Natural human development wasn't complete before this age, so there were complications related to the human psyche and Benlik use.

The vehicle started, and after a short journey, the children reached the training center. The Benlik stopped the vehicle. When the two little children came hand-in-hand to the door of the training center, they turned around and waved to the Benlik as they always did. As always, they did not get a reaction from the Benlik. The children entered the training center. The Benlik drove away from the gate of the training center and went down to the underground car park to wait for the children to end their training.

In the afternoon, the children at the training center had a school trip to the museum. Mr. E. would not be able to attend the museum trip but would send his Benlik instead. The kids were excited. A short time later, a long vehicle with a panoramic glass roof approached the door of the training center. Mr. E.'s Benlik was responsible for the driving of the vehicle and the general condition of the children.

The distance from the education center to the museum is around 10 km. It was an excited group of children that left the training center with Mr. E.'s Benlik. The quiet, calm journey was more enjoyable in a vehicle with panoramic windows. They were almost halfway through the journey, after which the road had sharper curves. There was a minor problem with the first sharp curve, and the training center's vehicle had weak contact with another self-controlled vehicle coming from the opposite direction. The roads were pretty smooth and wide, and the field of view was clear until the next curves. These favorable conditions had no effect on digital driving.

The fact that the Benliks could serve better and increase the quality of life they offered to people depended on instant reporting of these and similar adverse situations. All kinds of errors were carefully examined by the command centers to which the Benliks were attached, and the necessary arrangements were made and put into action immediately.

The journey ended at the exit of the third sharp curve instead of at the museum's gate because the Benlik lost control and collided with an oncoming vehicle. There was not a single glass pane left unbroken in the vehicle with panoramic views, and the Benlik was stuck at the very front of the vehicle, wedged between the dashboard and the seat. Among the children were those who were crying, shouting, making muffled sounds, and breathing deeply, as well as those who were not breathing at all.

Day 30

The Benlik Command Center administrators prepared pages and pages of reports on this shocking accident. These reports included data logs found in the panoramic glass roof vehicle involved in the accident, the log registration of Mr. E.'s Benlik, the testimonies of children who had survived the accident, the comments from the children's families, and the processor logs from the main management resource at the Benlik Command Center.

Day 50

The last child hospitalized in the intensive care unit was discharged, and the doctors gave approval for authorities to take the child's statement the next day. This statement would be enough to conclude the report, which would clearly outline how the incident happened. Two of the Benlik Command Center officials were ready for tomorrow.

Day 51

The two people assigned by the Benlik Command Center took about three hours to talk with the child who had been seriously injured in the accident and recently discharged from the hospital. Priority was given to collecting witness perspectives on top of thorough evidence collection about the incident. There had been some accidents and problems before, but the way this accident occurred guaranteed that this situation was a first. It was very important that this event be announced to the public in a transparent manner, that the sources of the problems were open to access down to the smallest details, and that clear answers could be given to any questions. It took about a week to prepare a brief summary of the folder, which was placed in the middle of the table at the board meeting and which was almost impossible to hold with one hand because of its size.

Day 61, Morning

Five people were sitting around the white table located at the entrance of the building, which had a wide façade and resembled a crescent moon. The person in the middle had some papers in front of him. The people who were following the event from the outside were waiting impatiently for the announcement to be released. The press was ready for the live broadcast, and the microphones on the table were switched on. The person in the middle of the table, who would make the necessary explanation about the event, started his speech by greeting all the followers watching on the screen.

This critical statement took about an hour. When it became clear how dreadful the problems were in the folder, which took an hour to read, even as a short summary, not much of the audience remained in person. After those at the crescent-shaped table spoke, the authorized persons stated that all the information would be disclosed to the public at the end of the meeting and that the entire folder could be viewed by the public through the system. All that was left of the meeting was the folder on the table. The breeze from the wide-open doors seemed eager to pick up the letters from the pages summarizing the event.

The Statement

Different research groups commissioned by our Board, after completing their multifaceted investigations within and outside the Benlik Management System, reached a concrete finding involving the criminal and the multifaceted reasons for everything in the development of this event, without leaving any doubt. Twenty different Benlik users were interviewed, and their statements were taken.

- The first statement of the painful event belongs to Mr. E., who stated that the Benlik he used was mostly non-reactive to him and that this was not a problem but rather a factor of the quality of the Benlink model that was related to an early release and a lower cost.

- The eighth person whose statement was taken was Ms. Ö., who talked about the fact that, while her Benlik once had to use the car to get her kids to school, instead, the Benlik now walked to school holding the kids' hands.

- The fifteenth person whose statement was taken was Mrs. A, who stated that her Benlik sometimes found it difficult to communicate with her or her children when it came to waving.

While these examples demonstrate the human capacity to err, the Benlik users mentioned that they considered that a normal condition and instead highlighted the "learning process of the Benliks, earlier release issues, update problem," etc., as the reasons behind the accident. However, the Benliks could never be nonreactive to the person they are attached to; they could not ignore them or question the given commands.

Well, then, what does this mean? We did a quick study in the Memory Control Center with the clues we understood and were provided from the statements. Our engineers restricted the use of Benliks for a week to find out what the problem was and why it had occurred. After some software updates, the uses of Benlik were reactivated, but the setbacks continued, and we put the restriction of Benlik usage back on the agenda, disabling them for two further weeks. Only the on-duty personnel and emergency service personnel's Benliks remained active.

As a result of our decisive action, our engineers reached the first serious problem. An electronic plate has been detected on the main server in the Benlik Control Center, which is exactly the same as the original part, but whose operation differs from the original. Although this work seemed primitive, the resulting effects were not simple at all. For instance, when Mrs. A. waved to her Benlik, her Benlik responded, but not instantly.

One of Mr. K.'s students, who was interviewed after the disastrous accident, told us an important part of what he experienced on the day of the incident:

"As the car was entering the curve, the Benlik tried to turn around and wave. Until the moment of the investigation, when I spoke to you, I thought this behavior was directly related to me and my other friends in the car. Now I realize that I was wrong."

This was the answer we were looking for in our investigation. The Benlik that belonged to Mr. E. was actually waving to Mr. E. because of the late command, not to the children while he was driving. This delayed incoming command caused excessive heat and power loss in Benlik's circuits. Our engineers replaced the trouble-caused electronic plate with the correct one. On the to-do list, the next operation was to find out where this plate was obtained.

- The engineer who mounted the part to the Benlik system told us that he bought the electronic plate from the usual supplier.

- The supplier stated that they received these parts from the processor producing facility with the delivery documents.

- The documents confirmed by the people in charge of the plate indicated that the final control and packaging officers at the processor producing facility did their job correctly.

So, there was only one option left. This part had come from outside the production facility and was somehow slid inside and packaged. After a close follow-up, we found the person who transferred this seemingly original but faulty plate to the packaging stage and then to the Benlik facility. He confessed his guilt. He told us about the person or people he was in contact with.

Our engineers and cybersecurity then discovered where this plate came from – a place called KITbazaar[2]. We interpreted the images we took from the eyes of our officers who went there. The bazaar had a unique atmosphere of its own. It was as if heaps of electronic plates had formed on the counters. There were so many varieties that it was unbelievable. Small and burnt circuit parts, large electronic cards, swollen circuits, silicon-coated cards, randomly shredded cards, cards with varnish coating dripping onto the floor...

As a person who never compromises on working with the right parts, the images I watched made me sick to my stomach. This place, which had no control mechanism, meant that anyone could easily take any piece away.

It was very difficult to find the person who brought the plate to KITbazaar. Therefore, we, as the prosecutors, started to observe the surroundings in the early hours of each day the bazaar was established. Contraband products continued to come and go from this unregulated bazaar. Finally, the person we were looking for came to the bazaar with a vehicle containing old sacks. Our staff introduced themselves on behalf of our institution, and we made sure that this person clearly understood us. This person was Mr. W., an ordinary scrap dealer. After a short conversation with the staff, they showed him the electronic plate. We could see in his eyes that he recognized the plate as soon as he saw it: he had brought it to KITbazaar himself. While Mr. W. unloaded the sacks he had brought to the bazaar, he talked about how he had obtained this plate:

"There are a lot of electronic parts and plates in these sacks too. What, am I being accused just because I'm doing this job?! No, guys, you can't accuse me! You can close this bazaar now, but you'll reopen it soon. We all need electronic parts here. The important thing is not where they come from but whether they work correctly. Yes, I understand you; the electronic plate in your hand was taken from here by someone and used in your facility, and it has spread unpredictably to many Benlik models on our planet, creating a problem almost like an epidemic.

"So, you're telling me now that odd issues continue on Benliks even though you re-installed the original part on the main machine in your facility? I've been selling these and similar items for many years. I will continue to sell.

"Look, there are loads of pieces in these sacks. Sometimes their coatings runoff in the heat, and they stick to each other. Do you think I love doing this job or something, sir? Take a good look around! This is KITbazaar!

---

[2] The word kit usually refers to the presentation of electronic boards and by-products as functional modules, in short, an electronic product building kit. For this reason, Kitbazaar as a whole is the place where all kinds of electronic cards and plates are sold as scrap in different sizes and shapes.

Those who wish to buy the pieces on the hanger, the ones on the counter – those who wish to have the pieces they have dreamed of in their minds – buy what works for them and leave. This is my livelihood. Scrapping is the only profession I know. Now you can do whatever you want, sir! Now you know the facts. Finally, I can say to you:

"Ever heard of planet Earth? No? Maybe? Anyway... I found that electronic plate in orbit around planet Earth, and there was a lot of that plate. I hope the problem hasn't spread to other planets. Rest assured, sir, I would never, ever want it to be said that Kitbazaar was now the cause of a universal epidemic.

DEARTH FETE

Ümit Yaşar Özkan

Translated by Feyza Şahin

"You Shall Chip the Nil!"[1] – (The Scripture of Dearth Economy, 3rd Commandment)

The good old bones of Edip Bey were thoroughly warmed. He stretched a reserved stretch, a display of his guilty pleasure, just like all the other elderly who filled the sunroom. His low-pitched murmurs joined the happy humming of pleased old people.

The deadly, rampaging rays of our old friend, the sun, became the sweet beams of a sunbath thanks to the steel-glass ceiling of the Hearth-home. "What more could I want?" thought Edip Bey. "I breathe in the Hearth-home, I find protein, I sunbathe, and I even have fun!" He knew very well that this sweet little moment of bliss would be cut short. The bell would ring, and they would leave the sunbath to the next in line. The plenitude of sunlight did not mean that you could waste it.

The rule was clear: nothing was to be had in full in the Hearth-home. Edip Bey understood and accepted this. He was and always had been a good kid, a smart student, a loyal citizen, and a dedicated husband. It was dangerous to be full. The Scripture of Dearth Economy dictated that. Once a body tasted fullness, it would forever crave it and be cursed with an insatiable appetite. Was it not this very curse that had brought the end of the old world? If it was not for the few smart people who established the Hearth-homes, humankind would be deprived of any place to breathe, eat, and sleep on the face of the earth. The Hearth-homes were patches of heaven scattered throughout the hell called the world. When deep inside he felt the safety and warmth of the Hearth-home, Edip Bey would always find himself humming

---

[1] "Chipping the nil" is the translated version of a slightly altered Turkish proverb that basically corresponds to "getting blood from a stone" in English. The proverb is used for extreme poverty where no prospect of betterment is visible or viable. The original of the Turkish proverb can be translated as "one cannot chip nothing," whereas the author preferred to change one word of the proverb in the story, so as to mean the opposite of the proverb. In this way, the proverb both serves as a word-play and a reference to the mindset of a certain group of people in the story. The word "chip" corresponds to "yonga" in Turkish, which is used for both small bits from a large body and also one of the smallest components of a computer, similar to its usage in English. This side meaning adds to the underlying hint at the hi-tech dystopia of the story's post-apocalyptic society.

the Hearth-home Anthem, engraved on his mind when he was little:
"Hearth-homes, Hearth-homes

Among the desert dunes

Steel and glass oases

Hearth-homes, Hearth-homes..."

His better half of forty years, Büşra Hanım, sighed and reminded him of her existence. Edip Bey lovingly turned towards the frail body of his wife, noticing how pale she was, "Perhaps you should take a break from the fast..." How many times had he offered this break to her, without hurting her, without rash words, yet each time she had resisted, and so he had eventually given up? He respected the beliefs of Büşra Hanım, though he did not share them, yet his respect was limited to her. He despised the weird cult that had gotten between him and his wife. He spat out the name in a whisper: "The Undeprived!" and he regretted doing so immediately. She would be heartbroken if she heard. He covered his slur with a cough. "What more could I want?"

He merely wanted to share the little moments of life with his wife, just as they used to. He wanted to reach her, to breach the wall of silence. He frowned; it was disheartening not being able to share with his better half the joy he felt. The Undeprived cult forbade the wasting of words. That was the very thing Edip Bey could never understand: "Words, man, words! I understand everything; food, sun, and fun can be wasted, but words... this is too much." Büşra Hanım, in her vow of silence, just raised her eyebrows in response. Five years ago, when she had first joined the cult, The Undeprived had not been this fanatical. But their new chief, a corpse of a man, preached a twisted exegesis of the third commandment and took his followers on a dangerous path. He blamed the government for not following the Sacred Economy of Dearth properly and increased the number of his followers each day.

Edip Bey started unloading his chest to his pals at the retiree circle, for his wife had stopped listening to him. "Hear me out, brother, I don't know if the government doesn't follow the Dearth Economy; is not everything by the Book already? This chief..." Edip Bey stopped at this point and looked around. The chief did not have a name; he had forsaken his. The followers would remain in awestruck silence for a moment when they wanted to talk about him, then swallow the silence and mention their leader with this soundless non-name. Edip Bey tried to keep himself from calling him a "corpse of a man" for fear of hurting his wife. He worried he would let the phrase slip at home too, where his wife could hear him. He also feared that his nickname for their leader could reach the ears of the follower spies. He heard rumors... Thus, he said the non-name of the chief just like his followers did, even though he found the chief's sacrifice hypocritical and extravagant and the followers' respectful acceptance of this namelessness laughable and ridiculous. The existence of The Undeprived made Edip Bey unhappy. His life's work had been destroyed because of them.

For twenty-eight years, three months, six days, and two hours, he had worked at the locust fields that spread through deeper levels, then had met Büşra Hanım from the Department of Nourishment and had gotten married. Büşra Hanım looked like the young girls from the old world that he had seen in old pictures. He had no words to define her; all the necessary words belonged to the old world from which she seemed to have come. She did not have the dead-inside look of The Hearth-home girls. She was so joyous, so alive. The world of Edip Bey was filled with Büşra Hanım's melodious voice, speaking in songs. "Saving words?! What nonsense!" They took their chances at the government lottery for an apartment on the upper floors. How excited they were, waiting for the announcements, and how happy they were with the result! Edip Bey was in love with her contented nature, too. When they had no luck with the child lottery, Büşra Hanım had only said, "Well, we used our chance."

But even luck was bound by the Dearth Economy. It was distributed among the people just like the protein packs, and you had to do with what you had. Edip Bey could not in a thousand years imagine that his wife's admirable contentedness would stray her off the path. "Could this be my share of luck? Must I take it in silence, happy that I found her? Do I ask too much? Do I transgress?" The Scripture of Dearth Economy would jump up from the depths of his subconscious then, warning him that "Those who do not do with what they have shall draw a blank."

The bell rang. The old people sprang up with unexpected agility considering their age. The adage that "Selfishness and wastefulness are twin sins" was carved into their skulls. They were scared to death when it came to other people's rights. The announcements began as Edip Bey and Büşra Hanım climbed down three flights of stairs to their apartment, door number 3157. "Oxygen levels low outside. Heavy acid rains will continue for three days. You are safe in The Hearth-home." No one but special officers were allowed to go out or see outside. What the people knew of the world was what they saw in the grainy film reels taught to children: vast, dead deserts, sulfuric acid rains, and wild tornadoes turning the dunes upside down. A hellscape where no living thing survived. The teacher's sonorous voice boomed over these visuals: "Mankind, in his unquenchable greed, has turned the earth into a wasteland. We shall not repeat the mistakes of our ancestors." Then the human-made Hearth-home would appear on the screen. Its clear-cut geometric lines would send a wave of excitement through the horror-stricken children. Humanity was resisting. They would resist. The voice of the teacher would boom again, raising the excitement into ecstasy: "The last castle of humanity proudly defies drought, famine, and death in the middle of this horrible landscape!" That was the moment of The Hearth-home Anthem, sung in unison of voice and sentiment. As The Scripture says, "All shall be on a need-to-know basis. Those who gather more than needed have shouldered a back-breaking, deadly load."

People followed this rule, but they could not limit their imaginations. The vicious dunes from the screen were then filled with wild rumors and untamed questions. Was the Hearth-home as safe as they assumed it to be? Could there not be other dangers lurking in the desert, ready to attack? Each time these warnings were announced, Edip Bey would remember the legends he heard in the dorms. The horror that had nested in his mind when he was young. After the lights were off, some kids would tell terrifying stories they invented from these warnings. Carnivorous roaches the size of a fist still frequented his nightmares. He vividly remembered the night when his phobia began. The dimly lit face hanging down above him from the top of their shared bunk bed. The boy was a year his senior, with lots of pimples and a know-it-all attitude. "Did you know," he said, "that the desert cockroaches are all albinos?" Did he have to hear that? To know that? It was impossible to verify this hearsay. Were self-evolving, intelligent, albino cockroaches really planning to infiltrate the Hearth-home and end humanity for good? If only they would stay black like their little ancestors that he ran into here and there; this would have made it easier for him to deal with his fear. It was impossible to fight a vicious, invisible enemy. Humanity had no chance against them. At least, that was what he had thought as a young boy who nourished and grew his own fears. He could ask no one since it was not well looked upon to give a voice to the rumors. There were no written sources he could check either; students were only allowed to read the permitted publications that passed inspections. Little Edip was left alone with his fear and sinister, uncanny shadows bred within the raw, murky light on the phosphorus walls. He had nourished his fear for some years, then played with it for some more until it faded away without being noticed. He had been able to make fun of his childhood fears by the time he married Büşra Hanım. He felt sorry for the young, scared Edip. Yet, despite all that, a tiny bit of the albino cockroach's nightmare still remained somewhere deep inside, reminding him of its existence every once in a while.

They had their silent dinner in the tiny apartment within which the two of them could barely fit. They had a protein pack each for every meal. Not more, not less. This was the portion for all.

Then the entertainment time approached. Edip Bey used to feel all fluttery inside as he anticipated the entertainment time. That was before Büşra Hanım joined The Undeprived five years ago. He had not even minded his eyes going bad, for he had had his wife to have fun with then. But now, even that fun had become as faded as the entertainment was marred by his failing vision. The windows of all the apartments faced the same wall, which was used as a screen. The government projected a photograph onto the wall for thirty seconds every other day. But even that thirty seconds had been taken down to ten seconds recently. Rumor had it that the government had taken off those twenty seconds because of The Undeprived lobby.

These projected photographs were of the public places of the old world, namely the malls, and they were filled with incredible details. Forgotten foods, mysterious brands, forbidden fruits of a lost paradise… This was a game, a test, a run at asceticism. In those ten seconds, you were supposed to pick one item, visualize it in your mind and toss it into the abyss of oblivion before the vision took full, simulated form. It was said that some master visualizers would dare to experiment deeper; they could smell or even taste the simulacrum of the item they chose before casting it into nothingness. Was this display of courage a light blasphemy or a form of disciplining the self? Still, all of these happened in the first layer of simulacra. Going any further was jumping into hell itself. Those who took a dive into the seventh layer had not a single thing to tell–that is, if they could come back out again. For those who lost their minds to the lust of consuming would lose their whole being. Rumor had it that those who fell into the seventh layer were treated in healing chambers no one knew about. None had recovered so far.

Edip Bey squinted really hard as if it would work, and the ten seconds were gone in a flash. It did not work. He saw nothing. His mind was empty. He turned and asked Büşra Hanım in despair, knowing full well that he would get no answer, "What was it? What did you see?" But Büşra Hanım had her load to carry: an invocation on her tongue and a can of roasted eggplants in her mind. On the brink of rapture, she signaled her husband with three of her fingers. Edip Bey knew what that meant. The third commandment: "Chip the nil!" Something inside him ruptured. Anger and resentment melded. His rage against The Undeprived infuriated him. He would be having a good time with his wife if not for their radical views. "Third commandment, huh?" he said. "You cheat, you… you hypocrite, you! I'll show you!"

Edip Bey was about to do something daring. He had to do something, and he had to use an unorthodox method... To complete the visualization, one needed a phrase of invocation for the item from the photograph. This phrase usually came from forgotten, meaningless brand names. "Something unusual," he said. "Of course! Why not use the third commandment itself?" He would carve out the chippings from his own memory since he could not see the photograph on the wall. He would pick each crumb from his memory with his mental fingertips, then knead them into a larger whole and make it bigger.

Edip Bey began his invocation:

Chip-the-nil...

Chip-the-nil...

He felt the rapture begin, and the intensity of it was staggering. Objects, colors, scents... and tastes formed the outline of a swirl.

Chip-nil...

Chip-nil...

The eccentric swirl pulled him in.

Chip...

Chip...

Objects, colors, shapes, and tastes solidified slowly.

Nil...

Nil...

This was the bottom. The center. A bright light coming from an unknown source enlightened the jars, boxes, and packs on the shelves. Everything was glowing; everything was appetizing.

Edip Bey found himself in a historical mall as the invocation became no more than a gulping hiccup in his throat. He was down in the seventh layer of simulacra. This place did not look like hell at all. Yet, all of a sudden, his ancient phobia found new life in this flood of brightness. His existence in this light was an open target for the blood-thirsty albino cockroaches. In the depths of his subconscious, an old fear was coming to the surface along with an old desire, conflicting with it, confronting it. Those jars and boxes of all colors that tickled his brain, those smells that titillated his palate... these newcomers to his mind, forcing his senses open, would morph into existence as carnivorous insects then, was that it? He inclined towards the desire underlying the fear, and desire came on top. Edip Bey felt a sweet appetite remain as the nightmare was ousted from his being. Now it was time to discover this land of simulation with a curious hunger.

Edip Bey, who never had in his life seen anything more than a single pack of protein, walked among the shelves, his jaw almost touching the ground. The Hearth-home, the hunger doctrine, the orders of the Dearth Economy that brought him here … eventually, all of them evaporated. He was alone in here, and all of these things were his alone. He reached for a jar, timid at first, opened the lid, and dipped his finger. He looked at the soft, sweet-smelling food on his fingertip, and he put his finger in his mouth. Unbelievable! Edip Bey felt the taste spread against his palate with alarm and astonishment, and he burst out crying. How could a piece of food ever be so beautiful? "If this is the simulacrum…" he murmured. There was no way he could go back to protein packs now. He was aware of being inside a virtual reality that he himself had created, yet he could not figure out how he could ever know the taste of something he had never had before. How could a chip of vision on a wall include this information? Could it have been that the uncanny pleasures of the old world were preserved in chips within the depths of the collective subconscious and carried downward, one generation at a time? Were the sinful habits of their ancestors hibernating in their blood? Or perhaps he was making this unknown taste up, just like all the assumptions he had just made. The power of deep desire was frightening.

How do the others taste, he wondered…

The paramedics arrived to find Edip Bey already in rigor mortis. Büşra Hanım was trying hard to stay unperturbed. An autopsy was needed since the case was so extraordinary. The doctor who performed the procedure blurted out the truth right into Büşra Hanım's face: "An ancient disease from the Old World. I am sorry. Your husband died of indigestion."

Büşra Hanım thought one single teardrop would not be a waste.

A GREAT TIME TRAVEL

Türkhan Bozkurt

I was deeply distracted by one of the messages I had just gotten when my brother Robin arrived home. The surprised look in my eyes must have caught his attention so much that he immediately came up right next to me and asked, "Why are you grinning so stupidly?" I said, "Believe it or not, a woman from a tourism company came to the office a few months ago. She mentioned they had organized a lottery and asked us if we would like to participate. Just for fun, we all joined enthusiastically.

"The message I've just gotten says that I have won the lottery for 'a time travel for two.'"

"Wow, awesome! Where and when are you going?"

I answered, "They offer five different options. Egyptian Pyramids, Great Wall, Amazon River, Venice, and Göbeklitepe."

"What???? Göbeklitepe????? Where the hell is that?"

"I have no idea, but it says that is the place where everything started."

"Oh, that could be very interesting. To which period of time will you be travelling?"

"The times are the same for all five choices – the year 2020."

"I'm really surprised by that. I wonder why they haven't chosen a more ancient year for such a fantastic time travel experience instead of just choosing 180 years ago," Robin said.

"I can ask them tomorrow. They have invited me for a meeting. Hey!!! The ticket is for two. How about going together?" I said.

"I would love to, Sera, but there has been a problem with the glacier number five we placed in the North Pole. I have to be there for a while."

My brother, Robin, and I are climate engineers. His company is responsible for polar ice caps. My company monitors the changes in the water cycle and intervenes when there is a problem.

Losing my hopes of taking this fantastic opportunity with Robin, I decided to call my best friend, Arel, who I worked with in my previous company for about 10 years. While I was tracking those who used excessive water, he worked in the artificial cloud lab. After briefly telling him about the lottery and my trip, I offered to bring Arel with me. Frankly, I'm not sure if would want to come with me as I remembered how I upset him by leaving him alone on a journey we took before. He had bought us an expensive virtual two-day journey to Mars. Finding this journey very boring, I left him alone and came back home at the end of the first day. Contrary to my worries, he asked me, "How are we travelling?"

"There are two options: by time machine or teleportation. Last week, when I had to travel a week back by time machine to find out why a factory was using more water than necessary, unfortunately, my body couldn't adjust to the sudden change. Getting affected dramatically by the sudden shift between the dimensions, I went on vomiting for two days. That's why I prefer teleportation," I said.

"It seems like an exciting journey, but when it comes to travelling with you, I have to think twice," Arel said.

"Hahaa! Ok, buddy, if you'd like to give it a go, we have a meeting tomorrow. Arrange your work. Maybe I'll leave you alone in Göbeklitepe this time. Hahaha, who knows! I'll call you tomorrow morning," I said.

The next afternoon, we met Arel to go to the address they've sent to me. It is a company that deals with mostly virtual tourism. While it is currently impossible to travel to the future, traveling to the past is possible. However, since it is dangerous to travel back in time, only a very limited number of people are sent, and only for short periods of time. In this instance, it has become our chance to take such a journey.

We were welcomed with great excitement when we told them that we were the ones who had won the lottery. One of the employees approaching us said they were really very excited to see us. The employee, called Maya, took us to the management floor, where three people were waiting for us – Aden, the head of the company, and Ella and Dalida, the engineers, who would prepare us for the journey. Aden congratulated us first, then asked how long it would take us to get ready for the journey. Arel and I say that two days will be more than enough to get things done.

"Have you decided on the place where you'd like to go?" Ella asked.

"I am a climate engineer working on the water cycle. Actually, the Amazon River would be very attractive to me as my profession is related to water, but I can't decide. I have not heard of Göbeklitepe before. Can you explain what you mean by the place where everything started?" I asked.

Dalida answered, "'The Fertile Crescent' is the name of the land formerly known as Mesopotamia, where mankind first transitioned from being a hunter-gatherer to a settled life, whereas Göbeklitepe, located in these lands, is the temple built long before the settled life was established. Its history goes back to the year 10000 BC. Why it is called the place 'where everything started' is that it has taken our understanding of human history back 7000 years since it was discovered."

"This is really amazing. Well, may I ask you why you specifically chose the year 2020?" I asked.

"The year 2020 is one of the most fantastic years of humanity; when you go, you will see what we mean," Aden smiled.

Arel and I looked at each other for a second, and I said, "It is up to you, Arel. You decide."

"Okay, then let's go and see the place where everything started," he said.

We were told that our journey would take two days and we'd also need one day to get ready for the journey. After deciding to meet two days later, we left the company.

We met in the same place two days later. Ella and Dalida first took us to the lab to prepare us for the journey. They gave us the necessary information about the place we were going to and taught us the language spoken there.

"The region you will go to is a very old city. It has hosted many civilizations before and is located in the territory of Turkey. That's why we will teach you Turkish. We will also give you the IDs and money used at that time. You need to remember that the Moon is closer to the Earth at that time than it is now, so a day lasts 24 hours. They are far behind in technology and use less of their brains than we do," Dalida informed us. We were excited and a bit scared.

"Are you ready to learn Turkish?" asked Ella.

"Completely ready for this," we enthusiastically replied.

It took us about an hour to learn the language and they told us our IDs and money would be ready tomorrow. We would take nutritional capsules with us but, while I was listening to them, I was also very curious about the food of that period as it is still the time when people used to eat red meat. Now, we no longer eat red meat. We mostly use nutritional capsules, but these capsules cannot be used for more than three days. After that, we have to eat something real. Otherwise, some health problems could arise. Humankind has been able to stand up to nature. However, I assume it will be impossible to fully imitate nature.

It was August 22nd, 2200. We got to the company early in the morning. Both Arel and I were very excited. We were wearing clothes suitable for that period, and our IDs and Money were ready. We were warned not to contact them unless there was an emergency. If we needed to return early, or when our trip was over, we'd get in touch with them.

Finally, it was time!!! We were going. We climbed up on the teleportation platform and, in two minutes, we found ourselves in a deserted street. Looking at each other, we burst into laughter. Let the adventure begin!

The place where we had landed consisted of quite complicated roads. We started wandering around. While strolling around, we found ourselves in a big street. To our surprise, there was no one around: it looked like it had been abandoned. Somewhere in the street, I saw a stone fountain, which gave me a very authentic feeling. The water ran constantly. I thought they had forgotten to turn the taps off, so I immediately tried to turn the taps off, but the fountain didn't have the parts needed. I couldn't believe it. Wasting water like this was beyond my mind. Just then, a vehicle appeared in the distance and approached us. It had a light turning from red to blue on the top, which seemed very cute. It stopped next to us. We were very worried if we would be able to speak their language or not. A sullen man who was quite small compared to us came out of the cute vehicle.

"What are you doing here?" he asked.

We understood what he was saying. Arel and I looked at each other gladly and laughed.

He was furious and yelled at us, "Are you nuts, what are you laughing at? I asked you what the hell are you doing here!"

"Excuse me, we don't understand what you're talking about. We know your language, but we can't understand what you're talking about," said Arel.

"Give me your IDs," ordered the grumpy little fellow.

We handed them to him. He checked our IDs first then, staring at our faces, he examined us thoroughly.

"Where do you live?" he asked.

Unfortunately, we had no answer for that. While we were thinking about what to answer, he continued by writing something on a piece of paper.

"I will fine you for breaking the curfew, and your fine will be doubled for not having a mask," he said.

We were shocked to hear that there was a curfew. If I dared to ask what year it was now, the little one might get very angry. In the meantime, when we heard there is a curfew, we thought we were nearly sure to have accidentally been sent to the middle ages. We knew that they were behind us, but it was unbelievable that they still had curfews.

The little man handed the papers to us, then got into his vehicle and left.

We looked at the papers, and I said, "Strange things are happening here, Arel, and we need to find them out right away."

"I agree. We'll see, but, come on, Sera, let's find a hotel first," said Arel.

Our adventure had started so fast. Ten minutes after travelling back to the past, we got ourselves into trouble. While moving along the streets to find a hotel, we were trying not to be noticed. Just at that moment, Arel saw a building ahead with a big hotel post. We went in directly and asked for a room.

Our room was furnished very nicely, but the furniture was too small for us. We already knew that the people living in the past were a little smaller than us. I was lying on the bed and trying to measure my height while Arel was playing with a box-shaped thing on the table. When I went to the bathroom, colorful soaps and soft towels invited me to the shower. But, suddenly, Arel hollered at me, just as I was getting ready to take a shower. I rushed out of the bathroom, and I found him puzzled with a shocked and pale face. We realized that the box was a television.

"There is a curfew all over the world!" Arel said with a voice full of shock.

We watched the news on TV for a while. It mentioned that there was a big epidemic, and everyone was obliged to wear a mask. I remembered such an event from my history class. It was also mentioned on TV that it would be going on for at least ten more years. As a matter of fact, we knew it wouldn't. But I couldn't remember how long it would take. We sat in silence for a while.

"Come on Arel, let's go downstairs and get more information from reception," I said.

When we found the receptionist, he told us about how long the curfew took place every day and said it was forbidden to go out without a mask, and so on. Finally, we left him some money to buy the necessary things we needed for the curfew. We also asked him where Göbeklitepe was and how we could go there. He answered that it was only an hour away and there was a shuttle for a group of historians who were here to explore Göbeklitepe.

The historians were also staying in this hotel. This made us really confused. There was a pandemic and a curfew, but a shuttle came to pick up these historians. How the hell could this be possible? How were these historians able to visit Göbeklitepe so freely?

After talking to the receptionist, we felt that we were starving, so, in order to have dinner, we went into the hotel's restaurant. We felt really tired and wanted to have a rest as soon as we ate. When we headed towards the restaurant, we realized that red meat was in every dish. We knew that people in this period still ate red meat, and since we couldn't find anything without it, we gave up on eating in the restaurant. Instead, we took our capsules and called it a night, heading to bed.

In the morning, we took the shuttle and set off for Göbeklitepe. Although it was early, we encountered a flood of people as if there had been no curfew yesterday. What had happened to the curfew? We got terribly confused but made a guess by listening to the conversations of those traveling with us on the shuttle. The curfew was in effect all day on weekends but only in the evenings on weekdays. It was an interesting tactic. Apparently, we caught the historians' attention. They started to have a chat with us. We tried to answer the questions they asked us by saying we were tourists. When they learned that we were here to explore Göbeklitepe, they offered to accompany us, if we liked. We accepted their gesture with great pleasure.

After a short journey, we arrived at Göbeklitepe, which was a truly fascinating place. There were 12 T-shaped columns knitted with stones and turned into a circle. In the center, two large T-shaped columns, larger than those around them, were placed opposite each other. It was unbelievable that the animal shapes carved on these stone blocks were made by people who were still hunter-gatherers and lived in the Neolithic age with only pottery. It was like building the Eiffel Tower by hand with some iron and chisels. Before Göbeklitepe was found, it was thought that people first settled down, and then started agriculture. After the food shortage had disappeared, they turned to spiritual events and built temples. With the discovery of Göbeklitepe, this order had changed. People started to think that they built temples in the hunter-gatherer period, and they settled down because they wanted to be close to their temples. So far, six similar rooms had been found, yet twenty more appeared to be under the ground.

After a little more sightseeing, we got really tired, and all sat in a cafe. Orkun, one of the historians showing us around, started to talk about the past civilizations that had lived here.

"It is said that this city was founded before the flood of Noah and was destroyed by the flood and rebuilt. Akkadians, Sumerians, Babylonians, Hittites, Assyrians, Persians and many other civilizations lived here. However, many great wars took place because of the territorial dispute among these nations," said Orkun.

I said, "I am sure there were big wars, Orkun, but water has always been the most determining factor in the distribution of humans on the planet. The biggest wars, contrary to popular belief, have been caused by drought and the need for water, not because of land sharing or underground resources. "

"It cannot be said that we still use water wisely enough," said Arel, trying to keep the subject in my area of interest.

"You are right, our water resources are constantly decreasing, and we are still far behind from taking the necessary measures in this regard," replied Orkun.

I curiously asked Orkun what he was thinking about climate change so that I could get information about the current state of the Earth.

"The melting of the polar glaciers has accelerated. After the Industrial Revolution, although we have made great advances in the technological field, our carbon dioxide emission has increased a lot. We have polluted the air due to the use of fossil fuels, and the ozone layer has been pierced. Therefore, there is an increase in diseases due to exposure to excessive sunlight. The world has lost its balance, we are constantly struggling with fires, floods and storms. Moreover, the danger of drought is at the door. We must immediately take some strategic and sustainable measures," said Orkun.

I was horrified by what I heard. How did they allow that? Why didn't they calculate in advance what would happen and take necessary actions? Arel and I looked at each other. Seeing the light in my eyes, he guessed what I wanted to do. He warned me not to do it by raising his eyebrows. Desperately, I accepted and kept silent. However, I was dying to tell Orkun that they would find a way to produce clean fuel by storing excess carbon dioxide in the air within a couple of years, and then they would stop using fossil fuels in twenty years.

After having a short rest, we continued exploring the place. We learned that there are some ruins that had been recently found nearby that had also been unearthed from previous civilizations that lived here. But, when compared to Göbeklitepe, they were considered to have been built yesterday. This place looked like a cemetery of civilizations destroyed by drought.

Arel, approaching and making fun of me, said, "I don't like the light in your eyes, Sera. I'm afraid you will do something crazy."

I burst into laughter.

"You're right, dear, I am thinking of engraving the formula of permanent ice on one of those stones over there. Can you imagine how that would change history?" I said.

Arel also couldn't help bursting into laughing tears.

"The formula of permanent ice in a relic from Neolithic times!! They would surely think this came from space," I said.

"Joking aside, what will they think if we tell them that we have already found the formula for the late melting ice, putting it into the poles and renewing it every ten years?"

"Adding more and more, let's tell them about our plants, which can make artificial photosynthesis, and our trees, which absorb twice as much carbon dioxide as normal, and that a day goes up to 28 hours. We have also stopped global warming and built fusion power plants."

"Let's also tell them that they will go to Mars in 20 years, they will try to create an atmosphere there for fifty years, and they will have succeeded in establishing the first colony on Mars by 2090. Let's point out how we can balance the water currents with the filters we place outside the atmosphere to absorb the harmful rays of the sun and irrigate the fields using smart clouds."

Of course, we could tell them any of these things, but both of us were in a very different mood. It was like watching a show whose end you knew. It hurt our hearts to see them so worried, but we knew that they would take precautions and save the world thanks to this concern.

Towards the evening, we set out to return to the city again. We were planning to visit the city before it got dark. The curfew was still on in the evening. We had no intention of being told off by the sullen little one again.

We were in one of the oldest cities in the world. It was amazing that stone houses built centuries ago were still in use. The construction of the city was interesting but, at the same time, very primitive. The streets were labyrinthine, and sometimes we had to go into a dead-end road and walk back. I wanted to buy a gift for Robin. Asking people, we found the bazaar. I bought Robin a copy of a statue from the year 10000 BC. I really wonder what the seller would do if he knew that I was going to take this forward 180 years from now. We lingered in the bazaar for a while. It was getting dark, and we had to go back to the hotel. The bazaar slowly became remote. Suddenly, we heard music starting to rise from all over the city. This was such a kind of music that one felt the sadness, happiness and an urge of dancing at the same time. Describing a hopeless love in one moment, it turned into an energetic atmosphere and where one felt like dancing. We could not help being captivated by the music and moving towards it. We entered through a door where the music was coming from. No one asked where we were from or who we were. Everyone sat and lined up on the cushions on the floor, with the musicians in one corner, a large tray in the middle, and a man preparing food in front of it. Someone approached and showed us to a place for two in the middle of the cushions, where we sat. We were enchanted by the music. After a while, the food the man in the middle was preparing was put on the plates and served. I didn't care what was inside; I wanted to taste it. When I grabbed one and ate it, I burst into tears because I felt an indescribable longing. I flipped it a couple of times in my mouth and swallowed it immediately. Then something incredible happened: just like the music, this food also hid many emotions. First the emotions when eating, then the sweet feeling in one's throat after swallowing, and the urge to eat again. Arel and I swept the plate quickly, washing the food down with a very tasty white drink.

The next day, when I woke up around noon, I realized Arel was not in the room. I was extremely worried about how we had gotten out of that music house, and returned to the hotel, and about whether we were fined again last night. My last question was where the hell Arel was. Fortunately, I found a note from Arel on the table. He wrote that he was out and would not be too late. I felt relieved and took a relaxing shower, humming the melodies of last night's music. While waiting for Arel, I watched the news about the pandemic on TV. So many people had lost their lives. Education had stopped, health systems had collapsed, and many people had lost their jobs and were unable to take care of their homes. The news showed riots in other countries, with people who hadn't believed in the existence of the pandemic and refused to be vaccinated. Fortunately, they had found a vaccine.

When Arel arrived, I asked him how we had gotten back to the hotel the previous night. He said that we were in the music place for hours, and it was nearly morning when we returned – he had had to drag me because I was in deep sleep.

I asked worriedly, "You haven't blurted out who we are, have you?"

"Of course I have!!!! Everything!!!! Because we won't see them again anyway." He gave me a mocking eye and continued, "I've told them that we come from the year 2200, that we will return today, that the world is a much better place in the future – everything."

The year 2020 had been truly fantastic. When it came to the pandemic, people looked quite calm and even impassive. It is said that, when the pandemic first started, there was an atmosphere of panic and they had quite a difficult time, but now it seemed that they were used to living with it.

After the conversation we had with Orkun yesterday, I had time to watch a short documentary about the world while waiting for Arel today. For the moment, they knew what a disaster they were facing, but it seemed to me that they didn't care much. They were aware that the sudden weather events they were experiencing were related to the change in the ocean currents due to the melting of the glaciers. Hurricanes, lightning, forest fires, heat waves, mass deaths from heat, diseases transmitted from animals to humans, unlimited growth in cities, urban heat islands, insufficient agricultural production and stocks, and the inability to harvest rain were the most obvious problems. They knew why it was important to reduce carbon emissions and stop using fossil fuels. They were working hard to reach clean and renewable energy. Environmental organizations were trying to raise people's awareness about this issue, but few took individual measures. Countries were signing some agreements, but it was difficult to understand how sincere they were. In general, there was an air of pessimism. I wished I could show them a video about the world in the year 2200. Problems with glaciers have been resolved, ocean currents have been regulated, the ozone layer has been repaired, and fusion plants have been established. The concept of the country has come to an end, and a system similar to the "One World State" has been developed. Wars for resources are over, and every country shares their resources with those in need. There are no hunger problems in the world. Everyone has a guaranteed income, and it is forbidden to employ people. The first colony has been established on Mars, but it is not simply because the world has been destroyed and can no longer be lived in, but also because of our curiosity and passion for space. We have personal aircraft, and hypersonic underwater trains that can travel three thousand kilometers per hour. We have cities built under water.

"Is there any other thing you are wanting to do before we travel back?" Arel asked.

"Yes, I'd like to visit the city, go to the place where we can listen to that magical music, and eat that amazing food once again."

We explored every place in the city until the evening. We strolled through its old streets, smelling history. We visited its museum and admired many historical artifacts belonging to the years before Christ. Finally, it started getting darker. Soon, the music of the city would come alive and pull us in magically. Although this music sounded completely unfamiliar, it really was not. It was like the collective product of an ongoing memory. Finally, the music began. This time we knew what to do. We entered the music hall, found an empty place and sat down. The music sped up and slowed down. This time we were even bolder; we got up and danced with everyone, keeping up with the music. After a while, the food we were waiting for was served. This time, we ate it slowly to savor its taste. Then it was time to go home. After listening to one more song, we left the music hall.

Finally, it was time for us to return. We ran the device they had provided for our communication. We pressed the button to show that we were ready to go back.

"Oh, here we are, back home safe and sound," I said.

We were taken to Aden's room directly. He was in a meeting and would meet us in a few minutes.

I was looking out of the window in Aden's room. It was as if we had been away for a few months, not just for a day. I was now much more fascinated by the world we had created. We had achieved so much. Our world was now a heavenly place.

When Aden came, we told him details about what we had gone through in Göbeklitepe and how fascinating the place was. We also added that the current state of the world in 2020 did not seem to be very heartwarming. We were happy to know that they would be able to overcome all problems. What Aden found most entertaining is how we were punished as soon as we teleported.

"Oh, we have forgotten to pay the fine!" I remembered.

"Don't worry, I'm sure they won't track you down, dear," Aden laughed.

"I can't believe you sent us there without ever mentioning the pandemic," said Arel.

"I'm sorry, but that's the funniest part of your trip," he laughed.

I still had one last thing on my mind as I left.

"Look, Aden, when will this pandemic end?"

After hearing his answer, we stared at each other, surprised, and left Aden with a smile on our faces.

www.ingramcontent.com/pod-product-compliance
Lightning Source LLC
Chambersburg PA
CBHW051108230426
43667CB00014B/2492